ARCHITECTURE AND THE UNCONSCIOUS

Architecture and the Unconscious

Edited by

John Shannon Hendrix
University of Lincoln, UK

and

Lorens Eyan Holm
University of Dundee, UK

Routledge
Taylor & Francis Group
LONDON AND NEW YORK

First published 2016 by Ashgate Publishing

Published 2016 by Routledge
2 Park Square, Milton Park, Abingdon, Oxon OX14 4RN
711 Third Avenue, New York, NY 10017, USA

First issued in paperback 2017

Routledge is an imprint of the Taylor & Francis Group, an informa business

British Library Cataloguing in Publication Data
A catalogue record for this book is available from the British Library.

Library of Congress Cataloging-in-Publication Data
Architecture and the unconscious / [edited] by John Shannon Hendrix and Lorens Eyan Holm.

pages cm
Includes bibliographical references and index.
ISBN 978-1-4724-5647-2 (hbk)
1. Architecture--Psychological aspects. 2. Subconsciousness.
I. Hendrix, John, editor. II. Holm, Lorens, editor.
NA2540.A6123 2016
720--dc23

ISBN 13: 978-1-138-50692-3 (pbk)
ISBN 13: 978-1-4724-5647-2 (hbk)

Contents

List of Illustrations

and buildings are not. Words vanish with their utterance, and buildings are fixed, but the significance of words and buildings to the subject are enduring and mutable. Imagine that this diagram is a plan of Rome or a section of Plug-in City.

5.3 Aldo Rossi, '*Il Teatrino Scientifico* with the hand of a saint (1978)'. © Eredi Aldo Rossi / Courtesy: Fondazione Aldo Rossi, Milano + FFMAAM | Collezione Francesco Moschini e Gabriel Vaduva A.A.M. Architettura Arte Moderna. An inventory of architectural elements overshadowed by the hand of the Other; instead of Adam Smith's invisible hand driving the economy, or Halbwachs's subject of economic memory.

5.4 The origin of architecture, in the Cesariano edition of Vitruvius, *On Architecture* (1521). Public domain. Or, the birth of the multitude, in which architecture and language, called together by fire, constitute the field of the Other. The multitude is born in the collective processes of construction and speech, and will remain a multitude so long as construction and speech do not terminate in objects of conscious self-reflection.

6 Seducing God(s): Renaissance Ideal Cities as Mirror-images of Western Subjectivity

6.1 Leonardo da Vinci (c. 1500), *The Virgin and Child with St Anne and St John the Baptist* ('The Burlington House Cartoon'). © The National Gallery, London.

6.2 Lorens Eyan Holm, visual pattern of the perverse as gazing at the perspective window. Courtesy of Lorens Eyan Holm.

7 Unconscious Places – Thomas Struth and the Architecture of the City

7.1 Thomas Struth, Sommerstrasse, Düsseldorf, 1980.

7.2 Thomas Struth, West Broadway, New York, Tribeca, 1978.

7.3 Thomas Struth, West 44th Street (Mummenschanz), New York, Theater D, 1978.

7.4 Thomas Struth, Dallas Parking Lot, Dallas, 2001.

7.5 Thomas Struth, Shinju-ku (die Hochhäuser), Tokyo, 1986.

7.6 Thomas Struth, The Shimada Family, Yamaguchi, Japan, 1986.

8 X Marks the Spot that Will Have Been

8.1 Mark Wallinger, *Labyrinth*, 2013 (Kennington Station). Commissioned by Art on the Underground / LUL, 2013. The work © the artist, courtesy of Hauser & Wirth. Photograph © Thierry Bal.

9 Psychoanalytic Diagnosis in Architecture and Urban Design

9.1 The Bingham Copper Mine, Utah. Public domain.

9.2 Bernard Tschumi, Parc de la Villette, 1982–98. Photo by Tim Martin.

9.3 Robert Smithson, *Partially Buried Woodshed*, Kent State University, Ohio, 1970. © Estate of Robert Smithson / DACS, London / VAGA, New York, 2015.

10 Architecture and the Unconscious: Fantasy, Construction, and the Dual Spatiality

10.1 Man's Encounter with History. Courtesy of Nikos Sideris.

10.2 Architecture = The Architect's Fantasy (Re)Formulated (Elevated) in the Language of Construction. Courtesy of Nikos Sideris.

10.3 The Architect and the Other. Courtesy of Nikos Sideris.

10.4 Casa Batlló. © Casa Batlló S.L.U.

10.5 Casa Batlló. © Casa Batlló S.L.U.

About the Editors

John Shannon Hendrix is a Professor at the University of Lincoln, UK, and Roger Williams University, US. He has authored and edited several books on architecture, philosophy and psychoanalysis, including *Unconscious Thought in Philosophy and Psychoanalysis*; *The Contradiction between Form and Function in Architecture*; *The Cultural Role of Architecture*; *Architecture as Cosmology*; *Architecture and Psychoanalysis*; and *Architectural Forms and Philosophical Structures*.

Lorens Eyan Holm is Reader in Architecture and Director of the Geddes Institute for Urban Research at the University of Dundee. He has taught at the Architectural Association, the Bartlett, the Mackintosh, and Washington University in St. Louis. His teaching/research focusses on the thought threads that link architecture, philosophy and psychoanalysis, in so far they concern cities, space and machines. Publications include *Brunelleschi, Lacan, Le Corbusier: Architecture, Space and the Construction of Subjectivity* (Routledge 2010). His papers have appeared in *The Journal of Architecture*, *Perspecta*, *Critical Quarterly*, *Architecture Theory Review*, and *Assemblage*.

About the Contributors

Andrew Ballantyne is Professor of Architecture at Newcastle University, UK. He has a longstanding interest in philosophy and architectural history, and his engagement with psychoanalysis is most apparent in his books *Deleuze and Guattari for Architects* and *Architecture Theory*. His other books include *Architecture: A Very Short Introduction*; *Key Buildings from Prehistory to the Present*; *What is Architecture?*; *Tudoresque*; *Architecture, Landscape and Liberty*; *Architectures: Modernism and After*; *Architecture as Experience*; *Rural and Urban: Architecture Between Two Cultures*; and *John Ruskin: A Critical Life*. His work has been translated into many languages, including Chinese, Portuguese and Turkish.

Kati Blom studied architecture and philosophy in Helsinki, Finland. She has practised, taught and commented on contemporary architecture in Finland, Canada, Ireland, and the UK. She is currently a Lecturer at Newcastle University, UK. She is interested in the origins of spatial imagining in architectural experience, especially in unsettling, provocative, or sensuously excessive or deprived instances. She is the organiser of the Architecture's Unconscious Network at Newcastle University.

Hugh Campbell is Professor of Architecture at UCD School of Architecture Dublin. He is co-editor of *Architecture 1600–2000* and Volume 4 of *Art and Architecture of Ireland* (Yale, 2014). He curated, with Natalie Weadick, Ireland's pavilion at the 2008 Venice Biennale, 'The Lives of Spaces'. His current research focusses on the relationship between photography and spatial identity as manifested in architecture and cities.

Emma Cheatle is Post-doctoral Research Fellow at Newcastle University Humanities Research Institute (NUHRI), where she is undertaking a new research project, '"The dark and airless room": Architecture and the rise of gynaecology, 1750–1880'. She is also NUHRI's 'ambassador' for humanities research across the University and further afield. An architectural historian and designer, Emma's research explores works of architecture and art as material and spatial sites of cultural and social history. In order to 'reconstruct' the past lives of buildings in the present, she practices a critical-creative writing which employs different forms of text, drawing, and audio. Her PhD thesis, 'Part-architecture: The *Maison de Verre* through the *Large Glass*' (Bartlett School of Architecture, UCL), received a 2014 RIBA President's Award for Outstanding PhD Thesis, and is a forthcoming publication: Emma Cheatle, *Part-architecture: The Maison de Verre, Duchamp, Domesticity and Desire in 1930s Paris* (Farnham: Ashgate, 2016).

Gordana Korolija Fontana-Giusti, MArch, PhD, is an architect, urban designer, architectural historian and theorist, and Professor of Regeneration, Director of the PhD programme, and of the MA in Architecture and Urban Design at Kent School of Architecture. She was the Assistant Director of Histories and Theories at the AA Graduate School (1990–2000), was involved in setting up and teaching at the London Consortium Doctoral Programme (1994–2000), and was the Director of Urban Design at Central Saint Martins College of Art and Design, London (2003–7). She has published scholarly papers in *The Journal of Architecture*, *ARQ* and the *AA-Files*; and is the author of *Foucault for Architects* (Routledge, 2013), co-editor and author of *Scale: Imagination, Perception and Practice in Architecture* (Routledge, 2012), and co-editor and author of *The Complete Works of Zaha Hadid* (with Patrick Schumacher, Thames and Hudson, 2004).

Stephen Kite is a Professor at the Welsh School of Architecture, Cardiff University, UK. His research explores the history and theory of architecture and its wider connections to literary and visual culture. Publications include: *Adrian Stokes: An Architectonic Eye* (MHRA, Legenda, 2009); *Building Ruskin's Italy: Watching Architecture* (Ashgate, 2012); and *Shadow-Makers: A Critical History of Shadows in Architecture* (Bloomsbury Academic, 2016–17, forthcoming).

Dr Christina Malathouni is Lecturer in Architecture at the School of Architecture, University of Liverpool, UK. She is a qualified architect and holds a PhD in Architectural History from the Bartlett, UCL, UK. Her research focusses on the early history and multi-disciplinary origins of the notion of 'architectural space'. Publications include: articles in *The Journal of Architecture* (2013); *Claude Bragdon and The Beautiful Necessity* (edited by E.V. Ellis and A.G. Reithmayr, 2010); and *From Models to Drawings* (edited by Marco Frascari et al., 2007). Dr Malathouni also has extensive experience in the heritage sector, specialising in twentieth century architectural heritage. She is a full member of the Institute of Historic Building Conservation (IHBC, UK), and associate member of ICOMOS's International Scientific Committee on twentieth century heritage (ICOMOS-ISC20C).

Dr Timothy D. Martin was Reader in Architecture and Cultural Theory at the Leicester School of Architecture. He has trained in psychoanalysis at the Champ Freudien, Paris, and is an affiliate member of the New Lacanian School. His publications include *Essential Surrealists* (1999), 'From Cabinet to Couch: Freud's

Clinical Use of Sculpture' (2008), 'Donald Judd: Architecture and Φ Space' (2008), and 'Psychosis and the Sublime in American Art: Smithson with Rothko' (2010). He is currently working on a monograph on Robert Smithson.

Francesco Proto is a Senior Lecturer in Architecture, Visual Culture and Critical Theory at the University of Lincoln, UK. A practising architect and a theorist, he is currently investigating the 'inhuman strategies of the subject'. He is the editor of *Mass Identity Architecture: Architectural Writings of Jean Baudrillard* (John Wiley & Sons, 2006), and author of the forthcoming *Baudrillard for Architects* (Routledge, 2016).

Jane Rendell is an academic and writer, with a training in architectural design and history. She has developed concepts of 'critical spatial practice' (2002–6) and 'site-writing' (2007–10) through such authored books as *Transitional Spaces: The Architecture of Psychoanalysis* (2016, forthcoming), *Site-Writing* (2010), *Art and Architecture* (2006), and *The Pursuit of Pleasure* (2002), and co-edited collections like *Pattern* (2007), *Critical Architecture* (2007), *Spatial Imagination* (2005), *The Unknown City* (2001), *Intersections* (2000), *Gender, Space, Architecture* (1999) and *Strangely Familiar* (1995). Recent texts have been commissioned by Jasmina Cibic, Apollonia Susteric and transparadiso, FRAC Centre, Orléans, and Hamburger Bahnhof, Berlin. She is Professor of Architecture and Art at the Bartlett, UCL. For more information see http://www.janerendell.co.uk

Nikos Sideris was born in Athens (1952) and studied Medicine at the University of Athens. He then settled in Paris for his postgraduate studies (Psychiatry, Neuropsychology-Neurolinguistics and History). He has a PhD from Panteion University Psychology Department, Athens, is a teaching psychoanalyst, and member of the Strasbourg School of Psychoanalysis (E.P.S.) and the European Psychoanalysis Federation (FEDEPSY). He works as a psychiatrist, psychoanalyst and family therapist in Athens. He is teaching a course on 'Architecture and Psychoanalysis' at the Postgraduate Program of the School of Architecture of the National Technical University of Athens. For more information see http://www.siderman.gr

Alla G. Vronskaya is a postdoctoral fellow at the Institute for the History and Theory of Architecture (gta) at the Swiss Federal Institute of Technology (ETH Zürich). She holds a PhD from the Massachusetts Institute of Technology and a candidate of science degree from the State Institute for Art Studies in Moscow. She has published her research in peer-reviewed journals and edited volumes, and has been a recipient of research fellowships from Dumbarton Oaks, Washington, DC; the Getty Research Institute, Los Angeles; and the Canadian Center for Architecture, Montreal.

Introduction

John Shannon Hendrix and Lorens Eyan Holm

THREE ANECDOTES BY WAY OF INTRODUCTION

There are a number of recent texts that draw on psychoanalytic theory as an interpretative approach for understanding architecture or that use the formal and social logics of architecture for understanding the psyche.[1] But there remains work to be done in bringing what largely amounts to a series of independent voices, into a discourse that is greater than the sum of its parts, in the way that, say, the architect Peter Eisenman was able to do with the architecture of deconstruction or that the historian Manfredo Tafuri was able to do with the Marxist critique of architecture. The present volume focusses for the first time on the subject of the unconscious in relation to the design, perception, and understanding of architecture. The hope is that the volume will make a major contribution to architectural theory, expanding it to an unexplored area, and enriching architecture in relation to the humanities.

The aim of this collection on architecture and the unconscious – as was the aim of the paper session of the same title at the SAH conference that forms the heart of this collection – is to bring a group of people into discourse.[2] A collection of chapters focussed on this subject area represents a return to earlier times. If we glance sideways at modernism, texts like Sigfried Giedion's *The Eternal Present* and Lewis Mumford's *Technics and Civilization*, simply assumed that their readers had a working knowledge of psychoanalytic concepts. Giedion has no trouble sliding from inside/outside the house to inside/outside the psyche. Jumping from the 1950s to the 1970s, a postmodern avant-garde congregating around Eisenman's Institute for Architecture and Urban Studies in NYC – the likes of the architects Aldo Rossi, Rem Koolhaas, and Bernard Tschumi – were able to draw on the texts of Sigmund Freud and Jacques Lacan as instruments of radical critique. The 'discovery' of the unconscious by Freud and its instrumentalisation at the centre of the twentieth century discourse of the individual, is one of the hallmarks of modernism; and we would be within our rights to expect that an architecture that stakes its claim in modernism or its legacy, would address it. We would like to bind Le Corbusier's free plan (*le plan libre*) and free façade with Freud's free association and free floating attention which constitute the discourse of patient and analyst.

Most people today, including most architects, who are not part of this project, in other words, part of the self-selected audience for this book, will wonder about the plausibility of putting such a public and material practice as architecture together with such an inaccessible and symbolic entity as the unconscious. Every time we touch a doorknob, we touch architecture; and we can all touch it together, even in the case of a private house. The only person who has access to an unconscious is the person whose unconscious it is – perhaps also his/her analyst – and it is touched with words, if it is touched at all. Let's begin therefore with three anecdotes that draw architecture and the unconscious together.

> *The best image to sum up the unconscious is Baltimore in the early morning.*[3]

Jacques Lacan once remarked that the unconscious was rather like Baltimore very early in the morning. It's in a paper on the unconscious that Lacan presented at a conference at Johns Hopkins University in Baltimore. Imagine the situation. You've just pitched up at your hotel in a strange city. It's either too early in the morning or too late at night. You are jet lagged and not a little nervous about delivering your paper the next day. The only thing going on are traffic lights and neon advertising signs and electric clocks. All these messages flashing on and off, only no one is watching. It's like that expression 'Light's on, nobody home'. The language goes on working, whether anyone is paying any attention or not, and that is the unconscious.

Lacan was not without a sense of humour. Baltimore and the unconscious can be dreary and pedestrian places, a far cry from the exotic unconscious celebrated by the surrealists. Lacan has mapped the unconscious onto the city. What we assume to be the most intimate and internalised processes of the psyche, have been externalised and made machinic and impersonal. In his major texts he maps the unconscious onto language. This is a strange thing to do – rather counterintuitive – and he calls it *the field of the Other*. Both the city and language are external to us. If one of the main aims of Lacan's text is to articulate what we might call a linguistic unconscious, Lacan is here offering the tantalising possibility of an urban unconscious, an environmental one. Lacan is alluding to the material aspect of the unconscious and to its Otherness. The unconscious is about the spoken word, the words of others, and what words do when they are left alone and without the constant interference of our attention. When you slip your tongue and you disown it (*I didn't mean that!*) and your analyst responds with silence. It is in this sense outside us, in others, a collective entity like the architecture of the city.

> *In order to be significant, architecture must be forgotten, or must present only an image for reference which subsequently becomes confounded with memories.*[4]

In *A Scientific Autobiography* (1981), Aldo Rossi wrote that architecture must be forgotten, it has to slip under the taught surface of consciousness, in order to be significant. It has, in other words, to be symbolised, so that – like language – it becomes a field of signs. It is not the real Parthenon that haunts me or haunts modern architectural discourse – that is just a pile of rocks – but the symbolic one. Remembering is the flip side of forgetting. In *The Architecture of the City* (1982), Rossi rethinks the city as the repository or reserve of collective memory. The city is always under construction. The theory of architectural types, which he develops in this context, is such a project of symbolisation. The type is a logical principle, not a form. The typological project is arguably about understanding Architecture as a signifying field, in which one symbol replaces another, according to a history and rules of engagement, which – like Lacan's *field of the Other* – is the exteriorised impersonalised locus of the unconscious.

> *Now let us ... suppose that Rome is not a human habitation but a psychical entity with a similarly long and copious past – an entity, that is to say, in which nothing that has once come into existence will have passed away and all the earlier phases of development continue to exist alongside the latest one .... In the place occupied by the Palazzo Caffarelli would once more stand – without the Palazzo having to be removed – the Temple of Jupiter Capitolinus ...*[5]

From a dreary night in Baltimore to Freud's Rome. In the opening chapter of *Civilization and its Discontents* (1930), Freud uses the Eternal City as an analogue for the unconscious. Freud is arguing that 'everything is preserved' and nothing that is forgotten is lost to the unconscious. The unconscious is the inexhaustible reserve that makes memory possible. In Freud's Rome, buildings from antiquity to the present coexist as if they interpenetrate. Freud writes that one would only have to shift the angle of one's view to see a building from a different period. Freud describes a city in which each building marks a site of continual exchange and replacement (Caffarelli-Capitolinus). It is not hard to read Rossi's project in this passage by Freud. Although he is using Rome as an analogy to explain the unconscious, Freud could be using the unconscious as an analogy to explain Rome.

This passage is tainted by an inexplicable ambivalence. Firstly, Rome is invoked to explain the so-called 'oceanic feeling', a phenomenon with which Freud has no sympathy whatsoever. Secondly, to his readers' discomfort, Freud concludes that Rome is *not* analogous to the unconscious: the simultaneity that is a condition of the unconscious is spatially impossible, 'only in the mind is such a preservation of all the earlier stages alongside of the final form possible, and ... we are not in a position to represent this phenomenon in pictorial terms' (pp. 7–8). Elsewhere Freud will write that although the unconscious has a spatial and temporal logic, it is not the logic of conscious life and representation. And when Eisenman quotes this passage about Rome in his introduction to *The Architecture of the City*, he intends it to say something about the equivocal position of modernism for Rossi and the post-moderns, but – again – it is not clear what. This ambivalence seems to mask a lingering anxiety about putting the unconscious in relation to space, putting the unconscious in space, putting space in the unconscious. If it is an anxiety about the project of modernism, then it is an anxiety that a generation of avant-garde responses to modernism have done nothing to dispel. If there is a problem with placing architecture and the unconscious together, it is probably because the unconscious is not a possible object of representation. It can only ever be alluded to. It seems to point to the failure of representation itself upon which architecture depends. Something haunts representation, representation lacks something and the unconscious seems to underscore it.

The unconscious seems to have three conditions: it is inaccessible, purposive, and in Lacan's reading of Freud, externalised. We are driven by we know not what, and we know not where. Psychoanalysis focusses on the unconscious as the key driver of the subject's psychic life and interaction with others, but the unconscious remains an internal horizon to the subject that no sail can reach.[6] Exploring the unconscious takes the form of retrospection and remembering; it is known only through its effects. Freud argued that the dream is the 'royal road to a knowledge of the unconscious activities of the mind',[7] and that the meaning of the dream is an unconscious wish. The path from wish to action is labyrinthine. The dream expresses a wish, but it is not the sort of wish that can be enunciated so directly by the *I wish* or *I want* of consciousness. Instead, it is enunciated in the dream whose displaced image fragments the subject remembers upon waking. These remembered fragments become the object of free association in the analytic situation.

Lacan's key contribution to psychoanalytic research is his close attention to the speech of the subject. In a rigorous analysis, all that is admitted as evidence in the analytic setting is what the subject says. It is not the remembered elements of the dream that constitutes the royal road to the unconscious, but what the subject associates with them. The unconscious remains inaccessible to the subject, because all that are known of it are its signifiers, the significance of which the subject is largely unaware. Lacan insists that the aim of analysis is not to explain the dream, to arrive at an interpretation of it that makes sense (it will never make sense), but rather to put into play the subject's signifiers, so that the subject can reposition him/herself within them and they can be instrumentalised in new ways. The unconscious is as externalised and inter-subjective as the language of which it is a function. In this sense it is like architecture, at least an architecture that can be formalised as a system of signs so that it can communicate.

Here we need to pursue our assault on popular notions of subjectivity. The subject is positioned and formed by the signifying system within which s/he finds him/herself and does not exist outside of it. The paradigm is language. Grammar positions subject-verb-object. A subject is a signifier within a signifying system and is subject to its grammar or rules of engagement. '[A] signifier … represents a subject for another signifier'.[8] It is not possible to articulate the concept of the subject without reference to a form of grammar and language. The subject of the king has a particular position with respect to royalty that is articulated through the rules for engagement with kings – tithes, genuflection, obeisance – which define the significance of our kingly actions and from which our subjectivity to the king derives. In his essay 'From Structure to Subject', Mario Gandelsonas argued that only once architecture has been worked through as a sign system, in other words, as a series of elements with a grammar or rules for their combination, can we speak of a subject of architecture.

> *At the point when this object [i.e., architecture] becomes clearly, and almost autonomously, defined in its systematic internal, formal relations then does*

> *the subject take on a clear configuration. In linguistic terms the definition of an organisation as a normative system, which in architecture would be the constitutive rules of the object, implies at the same time its subject.*[9]

He references the project of Peter Eisenman to develop a formal geometric syntax for architecture as the clearest attempt to produce a subject of architecture since the formulation of the classical language of architecture, but he could as well have mentioned Rossi's typological project for the city. Architecture is not a language. We do not speak architecture, nor do we communicate with it so directly because it does not mean the way words mean, but it may be possible that it is structured like a language.[10] There is thus a conscious subject and an unconscious one. We can speak of a subject of consciousness and a subject of the unconscious; they are not the same, and there is no clear link between them. The subject has a position, but it is a position within a signifying system and not space; it is at once a great interference to the psyche and a keystone of sanity, that this subject position is always conflated with another position, the position of the subject's body.

In these anecdotes, there is the recognition that architecture constitutes a form of a cultural unconscious, even as the relation to the unconscious remains problematic. The unconscious is the most speculative of entities. It is contested territory even within psychoanalysis. People tend to disown it; and when confronted by it, tend to get angry. It has a bastard logic that infuriates people and muddles their arguments. Yet the unconscious is one of the few places where alternative narratives are still possible. And where could be a more strategic place to insert the unconscious than in a practice as dominated by rational thought as architecture? Sometimes by understanding something in a new way, you change it for yourself and for others.

Architecture continues to be seen to be a reflection of clients' demands as opposed to an intervention in the field of their unconscious wishes or desire. Architecture is dominated by rational discourse and conscious thought. Psychoanalysis has established that human experience is not limited to consciousness. Important aspects of human experience also include dreams, desires, imagination, memory, emotion – aspects affected by unconscious processes. We are sceptical of the possibility that the present project will lead directly to alleviating unhappiness by an architectural procurement process that taps into the client's unconscious. We do not think that discipline building can be so instrumental, although it would be interesting for an architect and an analyst to co-analyse the client/patient of architecture/psychoanalysis. We can still ask the questions: How do architecture and the unconscious engage each other? How does architecture speak to the unconscious? How can unconscious processes be incorporated into architectural design? How can architecture appeal to the broader scope of human experience?

This book seeks to build a task force for building the unconscious into architectural design and theory. Architectural metaphors and theories of perception, imagination and space, in Freud, Lacan and other psychoanalysts, and theories of the structure of the psyche, are a rich source of understanding for architects to create architecture that responds to the field of unconscious desire. Chapters explore the intersections of architecture and psychoanalysis – historical or current, theoretic or practical – for the purpose of broadening the approach to architectural design and theory based on the unconscious.

What follows is a brief history of the unconscious in Western philosophy and psychoanalysis. The certainties of history may help us situate the relation between architecture and the unconscious even if we cannot fix it permanently. We will see that the unconscious is a conceptual fact about the world, not a material one; a consequence of this status is that it has undergone review and revision throughout its history.

A BRIEF HISTORY OF THE UNCONSCIOUS IN WESTERN THOUGHT

The possibility of the unconscious was suggested in the writings of Plato, Aristotle, Plotinus, Leibniz, Kant, Schelling, Hegel, and Schopenhauer. Theories of the unconscious were established in the writings of Christian Wolff, Ernst Platner, Carl Gustav Carus, Eduard von Hartmann, Theodor Lipps, and Gustav Fechner. The science of the unconscious was established by Sigmund Freud and Jacques Lacan. Freud's early 'topographical metapsychology' gave way to a later 'structural metapsychology', paving the way for Lacan's science of the letter. The study of the unconscious grew beyond the romantic idealist response to the reign of reason in the Enlightenment, into a science itself. A goal of this book is to establish the science of the unconscious as a theoretical basis of the study of the design and perception of architecture.

The chapters reference the theories of a variety of writers, including Immanuel Kant, Arthur Schopenhauer, Hermann von Helmholtz, Eduard von Hartmann, William James, Sigmund Freud, Martin Heidegger, Wolfgang Köhler, Walter Benjamin, Melanie Klein, Adrian Stokes, Jacques Lacan, Gaston Bachelard, Maurice Merleau-Ponty, Jean-Paul Sartre, Roland Barthes, and Gilles Deleuze and Félix Guattari. A variety of concepts are explored, including transcendental idealism, a priori intuition, apperception, theories of the unconscious, mysticism, unconscious fantasy, libidinal transformations, subjectivity, diagnosis, symbolic substitution, dream work, hysteria, transference, projection, therapeutic practice, eros and thanatos, historical materialism, psychoanalytical method, subjectivism, reactology, psychodynamics, empiriocriticism, the Other, collective memory, neurosis and psychosis, narcissism, topographies and topologies, projection, part-objects and part-architecture.[11] The concepts are applied to a variety of architects, architectural practices, and architectural conditions.

This summary considers the phenomenon of the unconscious. Various writers have attempted to describe how it works, especially in relation to conscious thought. It is clear that the concept of the unconscious, as it has been established, contributes a great deal to human identity, thus it would stand to reason that it would contribute a great deal to architecture. Conscious thought is influenced by unconscious thought. The unconscious plays a role in sense experience, perception, vision, intellection, the formation of ideas, abstract thought, language, creativity, judgement, imagination, dreams, and artistic production, all involved in the experience and production of architecture. There is currently much interest in unconscious thought in cognitive science. For example, Unconscious Thought Theory examines the role that unconscious thought plays in everyday thought activities and events. It is necessary to look to philosophy and psychoanalysis to understand the possible roles that unconscious thought plays in more advanced creative activities, thus in architecture. How is unconscious thought known, conceived, and apprehended by conscious thought? Is conscious thought possible without unconscious thought? In order to answer these questions, it is necessary to consider, not just pathologies, as introduced by Freud, but the history of philosophy, and the ways in which an unconscious element of thought has been conceived, prior to the coining of the term 'unconscious', and after.[12]

Various modern thinkers, including Leibniz, Kant, Schelling, Hegel, Carus, Platner, Hartmann, and Freud, have been given credit for inventing the unconscious. The truth is that the concept of the unconscious, that part of our mind that functions without our awareness in conscious thought, has been around since the beginning of philosophy, even if the word 'unconscious' was not used. Many terms throughout the history of Western philosophy suggest the concept of the unconscious, terms such as active intellect, *noesis*, *nous poietikos*, intelligible, and productive intellect in classical philosophy; and a priori intuition, apperception, subjectivity, inner experience, the real, the absolute, the noumenal, and being-in-self in eighteenth and nineteenth century philosophies. Classical and medieval conceptions of the unconscious were very different from Enlightenment and psychoanalytic conceptions, which is not surprising given the different epistemological frameworks. The classical and medieval conceptions focus on a higher form of thinking in our minds that comes from an external source, of which we are not aware, an immaterial agent or divine intellect that deals in intelligibles not connected to sense perception or sensory awareness. This concept persists through the writings of Kant and Hartmann, but with Schelling and Hegel the source of unconscious thought is located in the organic real, the noumenal being of the material world. Elements of metaphysical philosophies persist in psychoanalysis, but the focus of psychoanalysis is empirical and materialist, grounding conceptions of the unconscious in experience, in particular dreams and language.

Christian Wolff (1679–1754), in *Rational Thoughts on God, the Soul of Man, and also all things in General*, defined conscious thought as the representation of external objects of thought and sense perception. Conscious thought is the ability to differentiate particulars, and to differentiate external objects from the self. There are many objects that we are capable of perceiving that we do not perceive. Awareness is the basis of conscious thought, and it is possible to infer unconscious thought through conscious thought, to identify ideas in conscious thought that are caused by unconscious thought, through different levels of awareness and differentiated particulars, and the distinction between clear thoughts and obscure thoughts. Alexander Gottlieb Baumgarten (1714–62), in *Metaphysica*, saw obscure perceptions as being the foundation for the soul. In his *Aesthetica*, obscure thoughts and perceptions are connected to the particulars of sensuous cognition, while distinct thoughts are connected to higher forms of intellect, such as *nous poietikos*, or poetic intuition, in the classical tradition. Johann Georg Sulzer (1720–79), in the *Brief Definition of All Sciences and Other Parts of Learning*, saw unconscious ideas as underlying and causing conscious ideas. Unconscious ideas are dark and unclear, but have considerable effect. Dreams prove the existence of unconscious thought. Conscious thought is connected to apperception, the conceptual gathering together of perceptions, and the differentiation between self and the perceived world. Abstract thoughts, the product of forms of intellect not connected to sense perception, have no connection to the perceived world. Conscious thought is dependent on representation (*Vorstellung*) in the imagination. Conscious thought is itself a representation. The most fundamental activity of the mind is seen as the production of representations.

Ernst Platner (1744–1818), in *Philosophical Aphorisms*, is credited with being the first to use the term 'unconscious' (*Unbewusstsein*).[13] Unconscious ideas play a role in conscious ideas. Conscious ideas are connected to apperception, the cognitive combining of perceptions into totalities, while unconscious ideas are connected to perception. Unconscious ideas are obscure images or representations. Conscious and unconscious, apperception and perception, are in constant oscillation. Johann Friedrich Herbart (1776–1841) wrote textbooks on psychology: *Textbook in Psychology*, and *Psychology as a Science Newly Founded on Experience, Metaphysics and Mathematics*. He developed theories on apperception, representation, and conscious and unconscious thought. Apperception is associated with conscious thought. Ideas are products of representations, as for Sulzer, which are seen as dynamic forces, both conscious and unconscious. Obscure ideas are unconscious and distinct ideas are conscious. Unconscious ideas may become conscious ideas as they pass a threshold or limen in the 'law of the threshold' (*Schwellengesetz*), as Herbart explained in his *Textbook in Psychology* (*Lehrbuch zur Psychologie*, 1816). Herbart's law of the threshold was developed by Gustav Theodor Fechner (1801–87) in his *Elements of Psychophysics*. For Fechner, unconscious ideas are dynamic forces that are lost in conscious thought. The psychological threshold is an important basis for the concept of the unconscious in psychoanalysis. Fechner's adherence to empirical science had an influence on Freud. He was a pioneer in experimental psychology and the founder of psychophysics, the study of the relation between physical stimuli and sensations and perceptions. Freud followed Fechner in differentiating dream processes from conscious thought.

Carl Gustav Carus (1789–1869), with the publication of *Psyche: On the Developmental History of the Soul*, is considered to be the first to develop a systematic theory of the unconscious with the unconscious as the focus of a theory of mind. *Psyche* begins: 'The key to an understanding of the nature of the conscious life of the soul lies in the sphere of the unconscious'.[14] Conscious thought can only be understood through unconscious thought. It is possible to be aware of unconscious thought in conscious thought; while it might seem impossible, it is the task of science to discover how unconscious thought can be accessed by conscious thought. The majority of the psyche is unknown to us in a present moment, lying in 'the night of the unconscious'. If the evolution of an idea is traced, its unconscious components can be discovered. Thoughts travel between conscious and unconscious realms in a dynamic cycle. The external world cannot be the source of conscious thought, as the external world is the subject of sense perception and sense-based reason, necessitating the existence of unconscious thought. Conscious thoughts are based on images that have been formed in the imagination, but have then sunk into the unconscious. Ideas that have travelled from conscious to unconscious thought continue to develop in unconscious thought. We do not stop thinking while we are sleeping, for example. Unconscious thought is instinctual, the necessary organic real of nature, following Friedrich Wilhelm Joseph von Schelling. The oscillations between conscious and unconscious thought are seen as a dynamic flux in an organic system. The passage from conscious to unconscious thought is the highest form of human fulfilment, and is connected to pleasure and desire.

In *Lectures on Psychology*, Carus outlined the development of the unconscious on a biological model. The development of the psyche, the ontogeny, is a microcosm of the evolutionary development of a species, the phylogeny. This theory would influence both Freud and Carl Jung. The conscious psyche is divided into consciousness of the world and consciousness of the self. The unconscious psyche is divided into the relative unconscious, predicting the preconscious of Freud, and the absolute unconscious. The absolute unconscious is the most basic biological aspect of mind, and can involve both sentient and non-sentient activity. The absolute unconscious is the basis of organic growth, and is in constant activity. The sentient absolute unconscious is created by the nervous system of the biological organism. Mental activity takes place in the relative unconscious, which is connected to conscious thought. The relative unconscious is the permanent repository for conscious ideas, the storehouse for memories. In summary, Carus articulated a psychical field that includes conscious and unconscious memory, and conscious and unconscious imagination. This reflects Kant's distinction between reproductive and productive imagination.

In the thought of Immanuel Kant (1724–1804), many of our ideas and representations are too obscure for us to be aware of them, as he explained in the *Attempt to Introduce the Concept of Negative Magnitudes into Philosophy* (1763), and *Anthropology from a Pragmatic Point of View* (1798). The higher levels of imagination, productive imagination, are not connected to sense perception or empirical experience, as explained in *Reflections on Anthropology* (1776–8) and *Critique of Pure Reason* (1781, 1787). The forms in sense perception are determined by intelligibles, called categories of a priori intuition. Conscious thought depends on the transcendental synthesis of the imagination, which is inaccessible to conscious thought. The principal categories of a priori intuition are space and time. An exploration of the suggestion of the unconscious in the writings of Kant can be found in the second chapter of this volume.

The relative unconscious of Carus is also where dreams are produced. Dreams are combinations of biological forces from the absolute unconscious and traces or residues of images that are formed in the imagination and that enter the relative unconscious from conscious thought. The relative unconscious is a threshold, as in the *Schwellengesetz* of Herbart, between the absolute unconscious and conscious thought, what can be revealed to conscious thought of the unconscious. Ideas flow back and forth as dynamic forces, as in the psychophysiological energy of Fechner. The psychophysiological energy of the nervous system causes unconscious sensations and causes them to emerge in conscious thought. In conscious thought, consciousness of world is given by the faculties of sense, connected to the dynamic energy of the nervous system, and continuously affected by the relative unconscious. Consciousness of world depends on 'the condition of one's own organization',[15] and is also dependent on memory and representations (*Vorstellungen*) in imagination. While unconscious mind is an undifferentiated universal shared by all organisms, the individual is differentiated and made particular in conscious thought.

Karl Robert Eduard von Hartmann (1842–1906) is known as the 'philosopher of the unconscious' because of his most influential work, *Philosophy of the Unconscious*. Hartmann saw Kant as the inventor of the unconscious. In contrast to Kant, for Hartmann not every conscious idea is a clear idea, and not every obscure idea is an unconscious idea. A conscious idea is only clear when it can be distinguished from other ideas, in a 'consciousness of the discrimination'.[16] The unconscious idea is distinguished from the conscious idea in the form of representation: the *repraesentatio* that is the genus of the unconscious idea, which is differentiated from the *perceptio* in the conscious idea. In *The Interpretation of Dreams* of Sigmund Freud, Hartmann is quoted as asserting that the unconscious underlies combinations of sensuous representations in the imagination, and that all unconscious ideas are purposive. Hartmann sees intellectual intuition as 'divine understanding' that produces intelligible objects and creates the 'world of noumena', while conscious thought is a 'derived and dependent human understanding'.[17] Hartmann sees the unconscious as a metaphysical principle, in a system of 'transcendental realism' involving the induction of what lies beyond experience, by first considering all possible experience. The unconscious is pure potentiality, the noumenal or thing-in-itself, which is created by intellectual intuition, as in *nous poietikos*. It is the ground of existence, combining reason and will. The redemption of the human condition is a return to the unconscious, as it is seen as the absolute in transcendental idealist terms.

Theodor Lipps (1851–1914) was a leading figure in academic psychology and an influence on Sigmund Freud. In *The Interpretation of Dreams*, Freud cites Lipps as establishing the unconscious as the key issue of psychology, and establishing the study of the unconscious as a science. It was thus Lipps who began the focus on the unconscious in psychoanalysis, broadening psychological studies from studies of sensations and empirical experience. Despite Freud's claim that his goal was to move beyond the 'metaphysical' conception of the unconscious, the classical metaphysical conceptions of unconscious thought play a core role in Freud's definition of the psyche. In classical philosophy, for example, the thinking subject as potential intellect or conscious thought is defined as 'I' (*to egô*). According to Lipps, in his lecture on 'The Concept of the Unconscious in Psychology', delivered at the Third International Congress for Psychology, all psychical phenomena exist unconsciously; 'the unconscious must be assumed to be the general basis of psychical life', as quoted by Freud in *The Interpretation of Dreams* (p. 651). Freud also cites Lipps's most influential work, *Fundamental Facts of the Inner Life*, as refuting the theory of somatic stimulation, arguing that dreams are not determined by external stimuli. Lipps is also well known for his aesthetic theory, in particular his theory of empathy (*Einfühlung*), the act of projecting oneself into the object of a perception. Although empathy theory does not directly invoke the unconscious, it was one of the key places where psychology extended into aesthetic – and hence architectural – discourse.[18]

Sigmund Freud (1856–1939) is seen as the founder of psychoanalysis, a discipline that he regarded as a science. In *The Interpretation of Dreams*, dreams are the 'royal road to a knowledge of the unconscious activities of the mind' (p. 647). According to Freud, the dream is not unconscious thought, although it reveals the structures of the unconscious, and only the memory of the dream can be analysed. Unconscious thoughts are revealed by images in the dream. The memory of the dream is the manifest content, and the object of the analysis of the dream is the latent content, or dream thought, unconscious thought. The analysis itself is a product of conscious thought. Dream work transforms the latent content of the dream into the manifest content, the dream images, in the process by which the dream is generated from the unconscious. The mechanisms of representation in the dream, as they are developed between the dream thought (unconscious) and the dream image (conscious), are different from conscious mechanisms of representation, although conscious and unconscious thought share particular linguistic constructions. Unconscious mechanisms are seen as a variation of conscious mechanisms not under the control of conscious thought. The ego, conscious thought and perception, is always present in the dream. The mechanism of the transposition from dream thoughts to dream images is labeled 'imagination' by Freud in *The Interpretation of Dreams* (p. 116), which is liberated from the control of reason. The linguistic structure of the dream image is missing the organisation of conscious thought, while its forms are mimetic of it. Dreams have no ability to represent logical relations between dream thoughts or conscious thoughts. Dreams have no intention of communicating anything, although they express an unconscious wish.

According to Freud, unconscious thoughts are represented in the dream as fragmented images that are recombined, by processes of displacement (*Verschiebung*) and condensation (*Verdichtung*). Dream interpretation involves the restoration of the connections between dream thoughts that the dream work has destroyed. Thinking does not occur in dreams themselves. A thought process in a dream is a representation of a thought process in the dream thought, which is a representation of a conscious thought process. The thought process in the dream is thus a *Vorstellungsrepräsentanz*, a representation of a representation. This theory can be traced to the classical definition of *eidos* and the formation of images in *phantasia* or imagination. The logic of the dream is independent of conscious logic. The network of logical relations between dream images is too complex to be unravelled in dream analysis. 'The most complicated achievements of thought are possible without the assistance of consciousness' (p. 632), according to Freud. Traces of perception (*Wahrnehmungszeichen*) become mnemic residues of perception and consciousness, the representations of which are the dream images. Unconscious thought can also be made known in conscious thought as the absence in the gaps in conscious thought. The goal of psychoanalysis is to fill in those gaps in order to have access to unconscious processes. It is impossible for conscious thought to fully understand itself or unconscious thought.

In later writings (*Beyond the Pleasure Principle, The Ego and the Id, An Outline of Psycho-Analysis*), Freud expanded his concept of the unconscious to include the elements of *eros* and *thanatos*, life and death instincts (the death drive), and dynamic relationships between the ego, id and superego. In *An Outline of Psycho-Analysis*, the dream consists of visual residue (*Sachvorstellung*) and auditory residue (*Wortvorstellung*). In Lacan's reading of Freud, these are combined in a 'double inscription' (*Niederschrift*) involving displacement and condensation.[19] The later writings also mark a shift in Freud's thought on the organisation of the psyche from the so-called 'first topography', in which the psyche is divided into conscious, preconscious and unconscious processes or *systems*, to the 'second topography', in which the psyche is divided into three *agencies*, the ego, the id, and the superego. Between psychical processes and psychical agencies there is but an approximate correspondence. When Freud diagrams the ego-id topography, it is clear that he is thinking of bodily organs or containers (it looks like a brain or a liver). Indeed, the shift in topographies seems to be largely a shift in metaphors, from metaphors of space and the physical sciences that describe the first topography of systems, to the biological metaphors of the second.[20]

The id is the locus of libidinal and destructive impulses, what in *The Interpretation of Dreams* Freud called the unconscious wish, and in Lacan's text becomes *desire*. The ego is a modification of the id in the development of the subject. The ego is the agency of repression of the id. It is the threshold between the id and reality. It appears in Freud's thought as a glittering reflective outer surface screening a seething cauldron of desire. The ego involves both conscious and unconscious thought. The superego projects the ego into the macrocosm of culture and universal ideas, what Lacan would call *the Other*. In *The Ego and the Id*, 'conscious' and 'unconscious' become descriptive terms that qualify processes rather than topoi or processes themselves. The essence of the psychical cannot be found in conscious thought. States of being conscious are transitory, in relation to the more permanent condition of the unconscious. The ego, conscious thought, is 'that part of the id which has been modified by the direct influence of the external world',[21] through the medium of the perception-consciousness system. In *An Outline of Psycho-Analysis*, the inaccessible unconscious, 'cut off from the external world',[22] is dynamically repressed, though there is also a preconscious (*Vorbewusste*), which is that which is accessible to conscious thought in the unconscious, and that which is capable of becoming conscious. What passes from preconscious to conscious thought is not sustained in consciousness. The ego is defined as the organisation of mental processes, and is the ground for conscious thought. The preconscious thought becomes a conscious thought when it is connected with word presentations or language.

Jacques Lacan (1901–81) introduced important new concepts of the unconscious, many of which have a strong application to architecture. The following is a summary of Lacan's concepts of the unconscious. Lacan regarded himself as Freud's closest reader and most important student. He is largely responsible for rewriting Freudian psychoanalysis in the terms of structural linguistics, thereby lifting Freud's thought out of its nineteenth century preoccupation with biologism and rebooting it for the twentieth century. This linguistic model has several consequences for psychoanalysis, most notably ontological. His theoretical work has made it possible to banish the quasi-non-material entities that have haunted prior treatments of the psyche. There is no ghost in the machine, no breath, no spirit, because the psyche is a language machine. The etymology of topography combines place and writing: a writing place, a place of writing, a place for writing, a place made by writing. Topography has a history that goes back to antiquity, in the recognition that thought is organised into places. We can assume that Lacan, the psychoanalyst influenced by the structural linguistics of Saussure and the structural anthropology of Claude Lévi-Strauss, was predisposed to Freud's first topography (writing place and place writing) and the aesthetics of surface. In most of his texts, he crosses Freud's two topographies, using ego-unconscious to describe the form of the psyche. This implies psychical agency, largely a function of images, within a field or surface of signifiers.

Lacan's concept of the unconscious combines an analysis of Freudian dream work with an analysis of the structural linguistics of Ferdinand de Saussure. He calls analysis the science of the letter. In the structural linguistics of Saussure, the word is divided into the signifier, the phonetic sound, and the signified, the idea to which the phonetic sound corresponds. Saussure, in the *Course in General Linguistics*, suggests that any relationship between the two is arbitrary. In 'The instance of the letter in the unconscious or reason since Freud' (1957),[23] Lacan, following Saussure, places a bar between the two, suggesting the inaccessibility of the signifier to the signified, or the inaccessibility of conscious speech to unconscious thought. The signifier, according to Lacan, represents the speaking subject to another signifier; it represents the insertion of the speaking subject into language. The sliding (*glissement*) of the signifier along the bar of signification constitutes a system of relations between signifiers, and a deferral of meaning. Jacques Derrida identified the same phenomenon of the differing, deferring and temporising of meaning in his essay '*Différance*' (1982).[24] Meaning can only be present as an absence, as unconscious thought can only be present as an absence in conscious thought.[25] The bar between the signifier and signified reifies the presence of the subject in signification, as that absence which is present in every signifier. Language produces the subject, rather than the subject producing language.

Metaphor and metonymy are the principal operational rules that determine language. A metaphor is a condensation of signifiers ('the world is a stage'); a metonym is a displacement of one signifier for another ('fifty sails' for 'fifty ships'), in the terms of Freudian dream work. The bar between signifier and signified is maintained in the displacement of the metonym, but it is crossed in the condensation of the metaphor, in the elision of a second signified, which creates an absence in the signifying chain. The bar is only crossed because one signifier is substituted for another. The absence in the signifying chain is what constitutes the speaking subject, which is other to itself, as conscious thought is other to unconscious thought. Signification only occurs retroactively, in retroactive anticipation, in the play of signifiers, at the 'anchoring point' (*point de capiton*), which is the point at which the subject inserts itself into language as absence. I can only communicate an idea to someone when they anticipate what I am going to say, when a connection is made in the *glissement* between signifier and signified, as at a 'button-hole' (*point de capiton*), which cancels me as a communicator of an idea. Language is a self-enclosed system with gaps or absences that reveal a connection to what is other to it, the unconscious. In structural linguistics, language is divided into *parole* and *langue*. While *parole* is individual enunciation, *langue* is the collective system of relationships. *Parole* is the conscious use in speech of unconsciously determined structures, or *langue*.

Lacan divides the Freudian psyche into the Imaginary, Symbolic, and Real. The Real is that which is inaccessible to the Imaginary or Symbolic orders. The Imaginary, the identity of the perceiving subject in the image, precedes the Symbolic, the speaking subject in language. The Imaginary ego is formed in the 'mirror stage', when an infant first identifies itself as image in a mirror. The Imaginary other is then interwoven into the Symbolic, in the matrix of language which is the Other, which Lacan defines as the unconscious. The Imaginary, image-based thinking or immediate experience of perceived objects, is absorbed into the Symbolic when the subject begins to speak; immediate experience becomes symbol in language, as in the *Fort! Da!* Game described by Freud in *Beyond the Pleasure Principle*, where the infant compensates for the temporary loss of its mother by exclaiming 'Gone! Here!'. As Lacan says in *Seminar I*:

> *If we must define that moment in which man becomes human, we would say that it is at that instant when, as minimally as you like, he enters into a symbolic relationship.*[26]

The Imaginary and Symbolic are interwoven in conscious and unconscious thought, as in a Borromean knot. The Imaginary is primarily conscious in primordial image identification, while the Symbolic is primarily unconscious in language, as the matrix of language is the unconscious. The subject becomes divided between the Imaginary and Symbolic, causing a gap in the subject, between image and word. This is the fundamental problem in Lacanian psychoanalysis. The Other is the network of identifications that determine the subject in interpersonal relations. Perception is a dialectic of the Imaginary and Symbolic; as the Imaginary is absorbed into the Symbolic, immediate perception of sense objects is impossible. As in classical philosophy, perceived objects are given by intelligible concepts in unconscious thought. As in Kantian philosophy, experience is determined by the categories of a priori intuition in unconscious thought. The thinking subject is formed when it enters into a symbolic relationship in language. When the subject enters into language, it is represented by a signifier, a pronoun, and the subject is always excluded from the signifying chain, becomes an absence, at the point that it is represented in it. Language defines the subject and assures its non-being. The ego is formed as a replacement for the elided subject in language.

The subject is composed of the ego, the unconscious, the Other and the other (perceived object identification), what Lacan calls the 'quadrature' of the subject.

Conscious thought in the ego is determined by unconscious thought as the Other. The resistance of the conscious ego to the unconscious is the resistance of the signifier to the signified, the inaccessible source of conscious ideas. The unconscious speaks though the subject, but conscious thought cannot know the unconscious, or itself. Conscious thought is constituted by *méconnaissance*, misknowing or misrecognition. The reality beyond language in the unconscious is revealed in the absences in language, the gaps and scotomata. Freud drew attention to those gaps in the form of jokes, puns, slips of the tongue, etc., but he failed to recognise the significance of them, according to Lacan. The unconscious is found in the gaps between signifiers, where the ego is revealed as representation. Absence and presence oscillate in the *glissement* of signifiers.

In *The Four Fundamental Concepts of Psycho-Analysis*, the unconscious is 'manifested as that which vacillates in a split in the subject'[27] between the Imaginary and Symbolic, according to Lacan. The unconscious is a primordial cut in thought, manifested in a temporal pulsation in language, as the subject is elided and then re-emerges. The oscillation is also present in the dream, which contains the dialectic of the Imaginary and Symbolic. Unconscious thought perpetually opens and closes with conscious thought. It is only present as an absence in the gap between the Imaginary and Symbolic, in which the subject is 'born divided' (p. 199). The subject becomes the network of signifiers in language, and in the layers of images in dreams. That which passes in the gap between perception and consciousness, Imaginary and Symbolic, other and Other, and in the *glissement* in the signifying chain in language, is what Lacan calls the 'gaze'. The gaze is the absence in conscious thought. The result of the split between Imaginary and Symbolic in the subject is desire, caused by the impossibility of fulfilment, and the absence in conscious thought, the inability to know the unconscious. The object of desire is the Other, which is a substitute for the absence of the subject (the *objet a*). Lacan's concepts of the unconscious, as summarised here, have been the most influential of any as applied to theory in the last 50 years, including architectural theory. Lacan's unconscious is an architectonic one, and easily given to spatial relations that are played out in architecture (concepts such as the mirror stage, for example).

Art, architecture and philosophy define the relation between ourselves and the world around us; they reveal ourselves to ourselves, and they reveal the presence of the unconscious in conscious thought. Architecture has as much capacity as any form of expression to represent human identity; the application of psychoanalysis to architecture can only enhance that capacity. For Schelling, art is the highest form of philosophy, or the only true document of philosophy. The making of art and architecture is a form of philosophising, of defining and expressing the human condition. Friedrich Nietzsche wrote, 'I philosophize with a hammer'.[28]

A SUMMARY OF CHAPTERS

This volume contains 14 chapters organised into four thematic sections. The first section of the volume explores historical paradigms for architecture and the unconscious and examines the unconscious at work in their protagonists (Dürer) or in their stated interests (Bragdon, Ladovskii). In 'The Unconscious and Space: Venice and the Work of Albrecht Dürer', Gordana Korolija Fontana-Giusti offers a revisionist interpretation of the spatiality in Dürer's work involving an unconscious engagement of the mind with the city of Venice. Fontana-Giusti argues that the Renaissance brought about a different understanding of spatiality based on unconscious projections, libidinal transformations, and painterly imagination, constituting a new freedom of expression. In 'Architecture and the Kantian Unconscious', John Shannon Hendrix argues that architecture can be seen in Kantian terms as the a priori categories of space and time applied to the phenomenal world. The totality of architecture is given by unconscious apperception and the categories of a priori intuition; thus the totality of architecture is given unconsciously.

Christina Malathouni, in 'Gradations of Consciousness and Claude Bragdon's "Space-Conquest"', examines the theoretical importance of the work of American architect Claude Bragdon in relation to psychology and psychoanalysis. Bragdon was primarily influenced by the philosophical writings of Arthur Schopenhauer, and was also influenced by the psychoanalytic theories of Hermann von Helmholtz, Eduard von Hartmann, William James, and Sigmund Freud. By merging these with novel mathematical ideas, the result was a discussion of new concepts of space in relation to architecture. In 'Composing Form, Constructing the Unconscious: Emperiocriticism and Nikolai Ladovskii's "Psychoanalytical Method" of Architecture at VKhUTEMAS', Alla G. Vronskaya explores the influence of German philosophy and aesthetics on the introductory architecture course at the Moscow Institute of Higher Art and Technical Studies during the 1920s. She focusses on empiriocriticism, a theory which presented the world as a sum of subjective sensations, and demonstrates how it was employed as the foundation for a theory of architecture based on an analysis of spatial perception.

The four chapters in the second section use the unconscious as a critical frame and conceptual category for interpreting architecture and the city. In 'Aldo Rossi and the Field of the Other', Lorens Eyan Holm draws on Lacan's account of the unconscious as *the field of the Other* to elaborate and extend Aldo Rossi's account of the architecture of the city (construction, typology, collective memory). Forgetting is simply the flip side of memory. Accordingly the city can be understood as the unconscious reserve of collective memory, which addresses the multitude. If we refrain from dismissing Rossi's project for collective memory as metaphor, and instead recognise it for what it is (he is attempting to rethink the city as a symbolic construct; this is the import of the analogical city), we might realise the implications of his project for the concept of class consciousness (*where does it reside?*) and for urban renew (*who is being demolished?*).

In 'Seducing God(s): Renaissance Ideal Cities as Mirror-images of Western Subjectivity', Francesco Proto sees the built environment as a reflection of subjectivity, manifest according to the Lacanian orders of Imaginary, Symbolic, and Real. Proto traces the genealogy of the city from the Renaissance to the present as reflecting the narcissism of religion and science, culminating in the postmodern capitalist megalopolis. The genealogy of the city is a mirror-image of subjectivity and the unconscious. In 'Unconscious Places – Thomas Struth and the Architecture of the City', Hugh Campbell argues that Struth's photographs reveal the fabric of the city and episodes in the urban landscape which would normally remain unconscious. Campbell explores the psychology of the viewer and the psychologising of the built fabric, applying theories of Jacques Lacan, Wolfgang Köhler, Fritz Perls, Walter Benjamin, and Aldo Rossi. The chapter addresses the question 'What is an unconscious place?', and demonstrates the importance of the concept in the conscious shaping of the city. Jane Rendell, in 'X Marks the Spot that Will Have Been', focusses on the site-specific artwork *Labyrinth* by Mark Wallinger for the London Underground, to explore the relation between psychical space and urban space, applying the topographies of Freud and the topologies of Lacan. Psychoanalytic accounts of the unconscious spaces of the psyche are interwoven with an urban narrative based on her own experience.

The chapters in the third section explore specific psychoanalytic themes relating to the unconscious and apply them to architecture, including transference, desire, fantasy, and diagnosis. Timothy D. Martin, in 'Psychoanalytic Diagnosis in Architecture and Urban Design', argues that the process of diagnosis is the key element of psychoanalysis as a curative practice, and hence the starting point for bridging architecture and urban design, and the unconscious. In 'Architecture and the Unconscious: Fantasy, Construction, and the Dual Spatiality', Nikos Sideris, a practising analyst, describes architecture as a double spatiality, combining conscious and unconscious thought and experience. Unconscious fantasy as defined by Lacan mediates between the subject of the unconscious and the manifestations of the subject's desire. The fantasy of the architect is reformulated in the language of construction, and the signifying building is an outcome of the encounter with the Other – that is, with multiple alterities, personal or impersonal, functioning in the dimensions of the Lacanian Symbolic, Imaginary and Real. In 'Shadows of Venice: Adrian Stokes, Aldo Rossi and "Interior Darkness"', Stephen Kite describes the shadows of Venice as metaphors of the unconscious, applying the interpretive framework of the aesthetics of Melanie Klein, the readings of Venice of Adrian Stokes, and the memory theatres of Aldo Rossi in Venice. The analysis is broadened to Stokes's definition of unconscious fantasising in the creation of art.

The three chapters in the final section use the Maison de Verre in Paris by Pierre Chareau as a case study to explore ways in which the unconscious is evoked or manifest in architecture. The chapters are contributions from the Architecture's Unconscious research symposium at the University of Newcastle. Each chapter applies a different model or criterion to the building. In 'Projection: On Approaching the Maison de Verre', Andrew Ballantyne applies the theories of Freud, Klein, Deleuze and Guattari, and the film-maker Robert Bresson, to describe how architecture can enact unconscious projection, which influences how the architecture is experienced. In 'Imaginative Enclave in the Maison de Verre', Kati Blom explores how architecture can evoke the experience of unconscious and preconscious imagination. The Maison de Verre is seen in relation to Philp Johnson's Glass House, as Blom applies the theories of Freud, Lacan, Christopher Bollas, Maurice Merleau-Ponty, Gaston Bachelard, and Gernot Böhme, exploring issues of the partial object, subjectivity, phenomenology, latent imagery, and negation. In 'Part-architecture: The Manifest and the Hidden in the Maison de Verre and the *Large Glass* (or Towards an Architectural Unconscious)', Emma Cheatle introduces the term part-architecture in order to put architecture in relation to Lacan's concept of the part object. Cheatle relates the part object to the construction of space and the unconscious, revealing the unconscious content of objects and space in architecture.

CONCLUSION

Today, a project on architecture and psychoanalysis has to address not only the slipping interest in psychoanalysis in an age when empiricism is equated with what can be measured (to the contrary, the psychoanalytic method is rigorously empirical, accepting into its discourse only what the patient says about him/herself), but also address a more general problem about how to make theory in an architectural world that is no longer interested in theory or that no longer sees that it is capable of solving the problems confronting us.[29] This may be a reaction against the postmodern avant-garde rejection of modernism which drew for its critique so heavily from philosophy.

By addressing the unconscious we may open up new ways of thinking about architecture. An interdisciplinary discourse between architecture and psychoanalysis may be able to address the link between individuals, cities and communities. Psychoanalysis is the talking cure: it is a model for a certain kind of problem solving, which involves solving seemingly intractable problems in the real world by untying the internal knots that prevent thinking creatively about solutions (in this case, not internal to the individual but internal to the institution, the policy, the task force, the social group).

The project on architecture and psychoanalysis also raises the question of how writing in a theoretical register constitutes research. These texts constitute a form of pure research in architecture, to be distinguished from practical research in architecture, or pure or practical research in psychoanalysis. Pure research in architecture tends to be a conceptual and interpretative practice. Architecture draws on the theoretical discourses in other disciplines as an act of self-reflection and to situate itself within the cultural matrix. In this way, architecture builds its edifice. This was true of the first extant architectural treatise, Vitruvius' *Ten Books on Architecture*, which includes a section on the areas of knowledge that an architect has to master in order to be an architect (philosophy, literature, mathematics, material science).

With one exception, the contributors to this project have been architects or theorists of architecture. We are treating an interdisciplinary topic (architecture, urbanism, psychoanalysis, philosophy) from within a single discipline. Our aim is to focus on how architects construct the meaning of their discipline by drawing on psychoanalytic and philosophical thought, and not to explore the full extent of the crossover between architecture and psychoanalysis, to which analysts would undoubtedly make valuable contributions. How and to what extent do architects assimilate (introject, internalise) the concept of the unconscious in their practice? Architecture is a praxis that takes our collectively held ideas, and puts them concretely into the world. The architect must reflect upon social formations and project them as material form into the environment. Our aim is to focus on how architects interpret their practice, which, like interpretation of the unconscious in psychoanalysis, is never complete.

PREVIOUS BOOKS

A word should be said about previously published books that have laid the foundation, as it were, for this book. These books, all published in the last ten years, have established the foundation for the study of architecture in relation to psychoanalysis, and for the use of psychoanalysis as a basis for architectural theory. The present volume, *Architecture and the Unconscious*, brings together leaders in this field to address specifically the role of the unconscious in the design and perception of architecture, building on the foundation of the books by John Shannon Hendrix and Lorens Eyan Holm. A few recently published books, such as *The Political Unconscious of Architecture* (2011), *Uncovering the Unconscious Dimensions of Planning* (2012), and *The Geographical Unconscious* (2014), all published by Ashgate, use the word 'unconscious' in the title as a metaphor for some underlying reality in the practice of architecture, without ever addressing the subject of the unconscious, or the concept of the unconscious in philosophy and psychoanalysis. The same can be said for Fredric Jameson's *The Political Unconscious* and Rosalind Krauss's *The Optical Unconscious*. The purpose of the present book is to address the concept and phenomenon of the unconscious, in scientific detail, in relation to architecture.

Psychoanalysis and Architecture (Catskill, NY: Mental Health Resources, 2005), edited by James William Anderson, Elizabeth A. Danze, and Jerome A. Winer, presents essays by architectural historians and psychoanalysts exploring the relation between psychoanalysis and architecture. Topics include D.W. Winicott, Sigmund Freud, Adrian Stokes, Frank Lloyd Wright, Adolf Loos, the Bauhaus, the Vietnam Veterans Memorial and the Jewish Museum in Berlin. Issues discussed include the inner monologue, dream formation, nurturing, spatial orientation, aesthetic judgment, boundaries, and creativity. *Space and Psyche, Center 17* (Austin, TX: Center for American Architecture and Design, 2012), edited by Elizabeth Danze and Stephen Sonnenberg, presents essays by architectural historians and psychoanalysts exploring the relations between space and psyche. The collection discusses emotional space, childhood play and fantasies, the relation between the psyche and the body, the id and superego of the city, the collective psyche of the urban environment, responses to traumatic experiences, dream construction, psychosocial development, imagining and daydreaming, and haptic experience. An essay by Juhani Pallasmaa, 'In Praise of Vagueness', addresses the subject of the unconscious.

K. Michael Hays's *Architecture's Desire: Reading the Late Avant-garde* (Cambridge, MA: The MIT Press, 2010), discusses desire, cultural representation, semiotics, typology, interiority, absence, performativity, repetition compulsion, Lacan's symbolic order and gaze, excess and *joussaince. Architecture and Psychoanalysis: Peter Eisenman and Jacques Lacan* (New York: Peter Lang, 2006), by John Shannon Hendrix, focusses on the psychoanalytic theories of Sigmund Freud and Jacques Lacan, and the architecture and theories of Peter Eisenman. The book discusses linguistics, signification, the Imaginary and Symbolic orders of Lacan, Freudian dream work, dream images, the ego, desire, the Real and the Gaze of Lacan. The subject of the unconscious is addressed throughout the book. *Brunelleschi, Lacan, Le Corbusier: Architecture, Space and the Construction of Subjectivity* (London and New York: Routledge, 2010), by Lorens Eyan Holm, discusses Renaissance perspective in relation to contemporary theories of desire and power, and the career of Le Corbusier in relation to the death drive. The book explores the unconscious subject of space and time.

Stephen Kite, in *Adrian Stokes: An Architectonic Eye* (Oxford: Legenda, 2009), examines the theories of Adrian Stokes on architecture in relation to art and psychoanalysis. The book discusses empathy theory, craft, space, material, otherness, envelopment and the organic. *Surrealism and Architecture* (New York and London: Routledge, 2005), edited by Thomas Mical, explores the relation between architecture and surrealism. The book discusses desire, transgression, surrealist space and interiors, the uncanny, automatism, language, petrification, metaphysics, potlatch, projection, imago, and alienation. Nikos Sideris, in *Architecture and Psychoanalysis: Fantasy and Construction* (Athens: Futura, 2006/ Kindle edition, 2013), focusses on the role of fantasy in architectural design. The book discusses desire, creativity, imagination, psyche, and language, conceptualising architecture as the fantasy of the architect reformulated in the language of construction. This book, *Architecture and the Unconscious*, focussing specifically on the phenomenon of the unconscious in architecture, should be of interest to architects, architecture students at the graduate and undergraduate level, and anyone interested in psychoanalysis and the unconscious (philosophers, psychologists, psychoanalysts, and students of those subjects). The book should have broad appeal to disciplines in the humanities.

NOTES

1 For which, see the literature review at the end of this Introduction and in the Bibliography.

2 This collection began as a paper session called 'Architecture and the Unconscious' at the annual Society of Architectural Historians conference in Austin, Texas in April 2014, which was co-chaired by the two editors. There is also an architecture research group at the University of Newcastle that runs a symposium called 'Architecture's Unconscious'. Members of this group are contributors to this collection.

3 Jacques Lacan, 'Of structure as an in-mixing of an Otherness prerequisite to any subject whatever (1966)', in R. Macksey and E. Donato (eds), *The Structuralist Controversy: The Languages of Criticism and the Sciences of Man* (London and Baltimore, MD: The Johns Hopkins University Press, 1972), pp. 186–95, p. 189.

4 Aldo Rossi, *A Scientific Autobiography*, trans. Lawrence Venuti (Cambridge, MA: The MIT Press, 1981), p. 45.

5 Sigmund Freud, *Civilization and its Discontents, Standard Edition vol. 21*, trans. Joan Riviere, ed. James Strachey (London: Hogarth Press, 1975), p. 7. First published 1930. Cf. Chapter 1 and in particular pp. 6–8. Freud's thesis is that discontent is the condition of civilisation, because civilisation depends upon repressing unconscious desire and instinct which, if unchecked, would tear civilisation apart.

6 Psychoanalysis is quite unlike most disciplines. Freud's 'discovery' (so-called by Lacan) was to place the concept of the unconscious at the centre of the new and emerging praxis of psychoanalysis. Most disciplines are built upon a foundation of knowledge upon which they depend, but Freudian psychoanalysis is built upon an object that remains central and unknown. If an architect were to diagram psychoanalysis, s/he might draw a series of complementary interpretative practices as trajectories converging on an absent centre.

7 Sigmund Freud, *The Interpretation of Dreams: The Standard Edition*, trans. James Strachey (New York: Avon Books, 1965 [1900]), p. 647.

8 Jacques Lacan, *The Four Fundamental Concepts of Psycho-Analysis (Seminar XI)*, trans. Alan Sheridan (New York: W.W. Norton Press, 1981), p. 207.

9 Mario Gandelsonas, 'From Structure to Subject: The Formation of an Architectural Language', in *Oppositions* 17 (New York: Institute for Architecture and Urban Studies, 1979), pp. 6–29, p. 19.

10 'Structured like a language' is borrowed from Lacan, who writes that the unconscious is not a language, but it 'is structured like a language'. Cf. for instance *Seminar III*, p. 167. Jacques Lacan, *The Seminar of Jacques Lacan, Book III, The Psychoses, 1955–1956*, trans. R. Grigg, ed. Jacques-Alain Miller (New York: W.W. Norton, 1993).

11 'Part-architecture' is a term coined by Emma Cheatle in 2008. Her chapter in this volume and her forthcoming book *Part-Architecture: The Maison de Verre, Duchamp, Domesticity and Desire in 1930s Paris*, to be published by Ashgate, define part-architecture as a new form of architectural critical history writing.

12 The following summary is taken from John Shannon Hendrix, *Unconscious Thought in Philosophy and Psychoanalysis* (Basingstoke: Palgrave Macmillan, 2015), revised by the present editors.

13 Angus Nicholls and Martin Liebscher (eds), *Thinking the Unconscious: Nineteenth-Century German Thought* (Cambridge: Cambridge University Press, 2012), p. 9.

14 Carl Gustav Carus, *Psyche: On the Development of the Soul, Part One: The Unconscious* (1846), trans. R. Welch (New York: Spring Publications, 1970), p. 1.

15 Carl Gustav Carus, *Lectures on Psychology* (*Vorlesungen über Psychologie, gehalten im Winter 1829–30 zu Dresden*, 1831) (Leipzig: Verlag von Gerhard Fleischer), p. 111.

16 Eduard von Hartmann, *Philosophy of the Unconscious* (1868), trans. W.C. Coupland (London: Routledge & Kegan Paul, 1931), p. 21.

17 Ibid., p. 23.

18 The terms 'space' and 'form' enter aesthetic discourse for the first time in the texts of Lipps, Heinrich Wölfflin, August Schmarsow and other late nineteenth century German psychologists and art historians. One of the key problems they addressed was how space and form become accessible to and have an effect upon pleasure and emotion. They shift the aesthetic content of form from the forms themselves to the relation between form and the subject that receives them. Essentially empathy theory

is a theory of projection. Wölfflin wrote that we experience the column as heavy because we experience our own body as heavy: 'Physical forms possess a character only because we possess a body'. 'We read our own image into all phenomena'. 'They [forms] can communicate to us only what we ourselves use their qualities to express'. The definitive publication on empathy theory is Harry Francis Mallgrave and Eleftherios Ikonomou (eds), *Empathy, Form, and Space: Problems in German Aesthetics 1873–1893* (Santa Monica, CA: Getty Center for the History of Art and the Humanities, 2000 [1994]). This publication includes translations of key texts by Robert Vischer, *On the Optical Sense of Form: A Contribution to Aesthetics* (1873); Heinrich Wölfflin, *Prolegomena to a Psychology of Architecture* (1886) from whence the above quotes come, pp. 151 and 152; and Adolf Hildebrand, *The Problem of Form in the Fine Arts* (1893). The introduction by the editors is an important and scholarly survey.

19 Jacques Lacan, *Écrits: A Selection*, trans. Alan Sheridan (New York: W.W. Norton, 1977), p. 160.

20 Jean Laplanche and Jean-Bertrand Pontalis make a similar comment in *The Language of Psychoanalysis*. Cf. the entry on 'Topography', pp. 449–53, and in particular 'the model here ... is instead shot through with anthropomorphism ... autonomous persons-within-the-person', p. 452, in Jean Laplanche and Jean-Bertrand Pontalis, *The Language of Psychoanalysis*, trans. Donald Nicholson-Smith (New York: W.W. Norton, 1974). Freud diagrams the ego/id/superego twice: in 'The Ego and the Id' (1923), and in *New Introductory Lectures on Psychoanalysis* (1933). There are key differences between the diagrams. The former looks like it was drawn by a calligrapher; the latter by a technical draftsman.

21 Sigmund Freud, *The Ego and the Id: The Standard Edition*, trans. J. Riviere, ed. James Strachey (New York: W.W. Norton, 1960), pp. 18–19.

22 Sigmund Freud, *An Outline of Psycho-Analysis: The Standard Edition*, trans. and ed. James Strachey (New York: W.W. Norton, 1949), p. 85.

23 Jacques Lacan, 'The instance of the letter in the unconscious or reason since Freud' (1957) in *Écrits: The First Complete Edition in English*, trans. Bruce Fink (New York: W.W. Norton, 2006), pp. 412–41. Lacan discusses the 'algorithm' S/s, signifier over signified, which he attributes to Saussure, in the beginning of this essay, pp. 414–16.

24 Jacques Derrida, '*Différance*', in *Margins of Philosophy*, trans. Alan Bass (Chicago, IL: The University of Chicago Press, 1982), pp. 1–27.

25 There is a world of difference between meaning and signification which is beyond the scope of this introduction to untangle. We regard meaning as largely a matter of the dictionary definition, and signification about the message. If a parent says to a child 'it's time to brush your teeth', the meaning of this sentence will have something to do with teeth and oral hygiene; but it may *signify* that it is past bedtime, or that the TV is starting to become intrusive, or that the child's breath smells. Georges Bataille said that if you want to understand the meaning of words, don't go to a dictionary, look at how they are used. In Lacan, meaning is imaginary, in a dyadic reflective relation to the subject, it is what only you mean; whereas signification is symbolic, or involving a triadic relation to the subject that goes through other speakers, though the system of signification, through the field of the Other. In *Poetry and Repression*, Harold Bloom argues that there is a confusion between meaning and signification, 'a confusion still evident even in the most advanced models of post-Structuralist thought' (Harold Bloom, *Poetry and Repression: Revisionism from Blake to Stevens* [New Haven, CT: Yale University Press, 1976], p. 240). In *A Map of Misreading* (1975), he argues 'that poetry ... continues to be a discursive mode, whose structures evade the language that would confine them' (Harold Bloom, *A Map of Misreading* [Oxford: Oxford University Press,

1975], p. 77). He is writing about the Romantic poets; he is arguing that the meaning of the poem erupts from the system of signification, transcending it.

26 Quoted in Fredric Jameson, 'Imaginary and Symbolic in Lacan', in *The Ideology of Theory, Essays 1971–1986, Volume I: Situations of Theory* (Minneapolis, MN: University of Minnesota Press, 1988), p. 90.

27 Jacques Lacan, *The Four Fundamental Concepts of Psycho-Analysis*, p. 28.

28 Friedrich Nietzsche, *Twilight of the Idols, or, How to Philosophize with a Hammer* (1889). Translation of *Götzen-Dämmerung, oder, Wie man mit dem Hammer philosophirt*. The German word for idols, *Gotzen*, also means false gods. The book is a critique of different forms of idealism that reject the world of sensory experience and nature for the world of thought, from Plato's ideal forms to the false promise of heaven. By contrast, Nietzsche's thought is a constructed material philosophy. From the Preface, 'Finally to pose questions with a hammer, and sometimes to hear as a reply that famous hollow sound that can only come from bloated entrails'. He is critiquing the '… eternal idols [Christianity, idealism], which are here touched with a hammer as with a tuning fork: there are no idols that are older, more assured, more puffed-up – and none more hollow'. The reference in the context of this introduction is ambivalent for Nietzsche does not spare psychology either. This very good translation by Walter Kaufmann and R.J. Hollingdale was published online. Available at: http://www.handprint.com/SC/NIE/GotDamer.html#sect2 [accessed 21 April 2015]. It will also be published in hard copy in the Top 100 Classics Book series (Createspace 2014).

29 Rem Koolhaas says in 'Junkspace' that 'God is dead, the author is dead, history is dead, only the architect is left standing … an insulting evolutionary joke …' (his ellipses). Rem Koolhaas, 'Junkspace', in *October* 100, 'Obsolescence' (Cambridge, MA: The MIT Press, spring 2002), pp. 175–90, p. 184.

PART I
Historical Paradigms for Architecture and the Unconscious

1

The Unconscious and Space: Venice and the Work of Albrecht Dürer

Gordana Korolija Fontana-Giusti

This chapter focusses on the unconscious and space in the work of Albrecht Dürer (1471–1528). By unearthing the layers of history and mapping the dynamics of Dürer's spatial unconscious, it proposes a multifaceted argument of his work that considers Dürer not solely as a painter and engraver, but as a theorist of perspective, mathematics and human proportions, as evident in his treatises and commissions. The proposed analysis of Dürer's opus examines the nature of his understanding of space and spatiality in the context of the late fifteenth and early sixteenth centuries. It considers relevant works by Dürer in relation to his place of birth and subsequent travels. The attention is directed to the nature of Dürer's stay in Venice and the ways in which the city affected him on various levels including the unconscious. The argument concludes by discussing how Dürer's spatially innovative work was constituted in relation to *melancholia imaginativa*.

INTRODUCTION: DÜRER AND THE UNCONSCIOUS

Dürer's spatial unconscious can be reconstructed through the analysis of his work and the events of his life. By focussing on the spatial experience of his travels, this chapter sheds light on what might be thought of as his unconscious libidinal economy in relation to spaces, places and cities.

Let us begin by asking: how was the 'unconscious' defined in Dürer's time? The concept of the unconscious in the contemporary sense did not exist as such; at the same time, people must have been profoundly aware of the realm of the unknown within themselves and how it can determine their lives in a compelling manner, allowing them to fight personal battles, suppress desires and test their anxieties, acts and morals.

In the late fifteenth and early sixteenth centuries the 'unknown within oneself' was contemplated and controlled by different sets of practices that included education, reading and contemplation of the stories from the Bible and the New

Testament. As the practice of reading gained momentum with printed books replacing manuscripts, the boundary between the realm of reading and that of contemplation about one's life became blurry.[1] The dynamics concerning meditation and the realm of life/action were mutually dependent and triggered by recognisable signs. Such signs could be unusual celestial occurrences, rare animals, plants or any other striking phenomena. Signs were discussed, written about and painted. Significantly for our considerations, they appear in Dürer's prints and paintings. Signs are often strategically placed in Dürer's self-portraits giving them a particular meaning.

Other secular practices that arose in search of the unknown within oneself included apprenticeships and travels (*Wanderjahre*) often to other places, corresponding to what Michel Foucault called *heterotopia* – the places where individuals, in development or crisis, learn something about themselves that was not possible in their usual environment.[2] The aspects of the unconscious were thus dispersed over the spaces and events in one's life. They were recognised, referred to and interpreted according to the understanding of the world-view at the time and a person's role in this setting.

Various scholars largely agree that despite his fame and certain vanity about his looks, Dürer was a pious person, devoted to his family. He attended a religious school, before joining his father's practice. Albrecht Dürer the Elder was trained in the Netherlands 'with the great masters' and had thus served as an early intermediary between his son and 'the very fathers of modern European painting'.[3] According to the self-portrait now kept in Vienna, at the age of 13 young Albrecht was already a skilled draftsman. Many other self-portraits followed, as Dürer became the first painter to represent his own likeness in a systematic manner on important occasions, most famously in the paintings of 1493, 1498 and 1500.[4]

In 1494 after four years of travel in search of painterly knowledge and experiences, Dürer headed back to Nuremberg to marry. He was probably disappointed that he had not visited Italy – the major destination for aspiring artists, as Italian cities were leading in the revival of the arts. For my argument it is significant to recognise this moment in what I call 'the libidinal economy' of Dürer's life. It is here understood as the distribution of the unconscious sexual energy (*libido*) on the level of the individual as they go through life and make different choices that are seen as libidinal investments. Freud argues:

> *Libido is an expression taken from the theory of the emotions. We call by that name the energy ... of those instincts which have to do with all that may be comprised under the word 'love'. The nucleus of what we mean by love naturally consists ... in sexual love with sexual union as its aim.*

Importantly for this chapter Freud balances this statement by saying:

> *But we do not separate from this – what in any case has a share in the name 'love' – on the one hand, self-love, and on the other, love for parents and children, friendship and love for humanity in general, and also devotion to concrete objects and to abstract ideas.*[5]

Although Dürer submitted to the will of his parents and married his bride, it is noticeable that his libidinal investments remained in his work and in the abstract idea of explorations. The family-imposed interruption to his unconscious libidinal desire to continue travelling and exploring life and arts, returned with force. It fuelled Dürer's subsequent travels to Italy and his interest in art, sublimating in the life-long dedication to the art that must be based on scientific knowledge.[6] This quest for 'scientific explanations' became obsessive and, I argue, could be recognised as his symptom.

THE ART OF SUBLIMATION: THE FIRST TRIP TO VENICE, 1494–5

On his return to Nuremberg in 1494, and before setting out for Venice, Dürer married Agnes Frey in July of the same year. Dürer's 1493 self-portrait with the thistle makes a reference to his future marriage in the inscription 'My affairs will go as ordained on high'.[7] It supports the hypothesis about Dürer's compliant attitude to his marriage as it turned into a socially acceptable model that would allow him to explore the life of an artist as he desired it. This model that included a license to travel accommodated the healthy and vigorous libidinal drives of Dürer's curious and complex personality.

Interpreters have agonised about the question of Dürer's wife as they agreed that the wedlock was not a particularly happy one. Yet, Dürer remained attached to Agnes, and defended her from his friends' criticism. It is important to think of Agnes's role as a wife of a blossoming artist who had numerous responsibilities in supporting her husband's career. Apart from being responsible for the household and providing food for family members, the apprentices, maids and various guests, Agnes was involved in selling and promoting her husband's work. Dürer's letters express confidence in Agnes and her professionalism.[8] She was responsible for Dürer's legacy, and posthumously initiated the translation of his *Art of Measurement* into Latin (1538).

This kind of complementary marriage is consistent with Dürer's acceptance of the 'orders from above' and the related process that we can call the sublimation of libidinal energies towards an agreeable purpose. Sublimation is here understood in the Freudian sense of being a defence mechanism where socially unacceptable impulses are transformed into socially acceptable actions or behaviour. As such sublimation has always been recognised as 'an especially conspicuous feature of cultural development that makes it possible for higher psychical activities, scientific, artistic or ideological, to play an important part in civilised life'.[9] We can recognise this process in Dürer's case. I emphasise this condition by naming it a libidinal transformation. By this I mean a transfer of personal energies where the individual assumes a different attitude to life and where this dynamism can be traced to his/her primary libidinal energy.

This libidinal condition that sublimates the drives and consoles Dürer's desires into continuous studies of art in far-away places, was in the heart of his marriage. Before the end of 1494 Dürer was on his way to Venice via Augsburg, Tyrol and Trento. The trip was a fulfilment of his desire to experience the Mediterranean world and the arts of classical antiquity. Given that Durer's libidinal energies have been sublimated into total dedication to his art, we can see how this trip took priority over any other duties.

Other factors that played a part in Dürer's choice of Venice could be mentioned as he must have known about the city from various artists such as the Housebook Master and/or Erhard Reuwich. Dürer was familiar with the related woodcuts of the city views that were available in Martin Wolgemut's studio where he worked; the five-foot-wide representation of Venice by Reuwich was impressive and technically advanced enough that it alone could have been the reason why Dürer hurried to Italy.[10] Within the scholarship, there is some controversy about Dürer's travels to Venice and whether there were one or two trips, as there is no firm textual documentation of the trip other than two brief references.[11]

Given the profound transformation of Dürer's opus since 1495, I tend to agree with Panofsky et al. who believe that there were two trips. The fact that the first trip is poorly documented supports my thesis about the unconscious nature of the city's impact. It indicates that Dürer's relationship with Venice was compelling and decisive as it fuelled the obsessive life-long quest for scientific explanations about arts, which meant conceptualisation of the Northern practices of art previously based mostly on intuition and craftsmanship.

From the point of view of the scholarship, there is evidence that Dürer made copies of Mantegna's engraved 'Bacchanal' and 'Battle of the Sea Gods' dated 1494, and that he was received by Giovanni Bellini,[12] who had welcomed Dürer into his circle of friends. They were reportedly close enough to share models as Bellini let Dürer paint the 'Three Orientals' that also appear on Bellini's 'Procession'.[13] Dürer learned from Bellini about light and shadows, most evident in his paintings for altarpieces.[14] He probably met Jacopo de' Barbari, from whom he learned about the mathematical studies of Luca Pacioli and their importance for the theory of beauty and harmony in art.

The scholarship is unanimous in stating that the Italian stimulus is most evident in Dürer's representation of human figures.[15] The bodies became less static and more expressive of movement in space. Panofsky argued that the studies of the nudes that were developed in Venice served to render a series of female bodies

1.1 *Nuremberg Chronicle*, public domain.

back in Nuremberg for years. This is evident in 'Ladies in Venetian Costumes', 'Nude Woman Seen from the Back', 'Young Woman in Oriental Dress', 'The Rape of Europa', 'Apollo', 'Alchemist', 'Three Lion's Heads', and 'Rape of the Sabine Women', all dated 1495. Because the drawings appear more intense and vivid in comparison to Dürer's previous drawings, we can speculate that these studies embody the effects of the encounters with Venetian men and women.

RETURN TO NUREMBERG: A PERIOD OF GREAT PRODUCTIVITY, 1495–1505

Dürer returned to Nuremberg in 1495. The years that followed were productive with works of both secular and religious nature. The typical art pieces from this post-Venetian period are the prints of secular subjects with nudes such as 'Women Bathing', 'Bathhouse', 'Four Witches', the 'Fall of Man', the 'Dream of the Doctor' and the 'Sea Monster'. They show the impact of studies elicited in Venice as noted by Panofsky et al. Featuring either water or voluptuous female bodies or both, the series stands out in the way in which human figures emerge in space, in their postures and proportions, containing subjects of sexual temptation and mysticism. Similarly enticing are Venetian dresses that appear in the representations of female bodies in 'Martyrdom of St Catherine' and the 'Babylonian Whore'. Dürer's newly-acquired skills of *contrapposto* and other classical positions that emphasised liveliness, sexuality, physical energy and movement evidently came from his encounters in Venice.

Dürer made several compositions based on classical narratives copying from Pollaiuolo's 'The Ten Nudes', Mantegna's 'Battle of the Sea Gods' and the 'Death of Orpheus' among others.[16] 'Hercules' (1488–9) completes this series of secular prints summing up the Italian experiences. By employing one of the maenads from 'Death of Orpheus' for Virtue and the voluptuous woman from 'Battle of the Sea Gods' for Pleasure, Dürer crystallises the idea of moral choice. He deployed 'Mantegna's pagan pathos' for the revitalisation of 'Psychomachia' illustrations where Vices and Virtues are shown in combat.[17] Although these themes are classically inspired, Dürer adds his own layer of interpretation, conveying the idea of the undisciplined, raw libido, what Panofsky calls 'unregenerated sensuality'.[18]

In 1498 Dürer published a book entitled *Book of Revelation*, known as *The Apocalypse* by John the Apostle, with a cycle of 15 woodcuts that provided him with fame and income that were able to sustain him in doing the things which he craved for, such as the investigation into classical studies of proportions. When addressing various themes from the scriptures, Dürer always marks a slight departure from the canonic representations and moves into the world of the human psyche, studying the turmoil of the soul, moods and their bodily expressions, demonstrating a profound interest in the essences of men and women. This art inspired by humans led Dürer to what he called the 'inner imagination'.

Having heard about the prominence Leonardo da Vinci gave to mathematics meant that Dürer intensified his studies on proportions. His art from 1500 onwards exhibited the influence of these studies as evident in the 1500 self-portrait taken

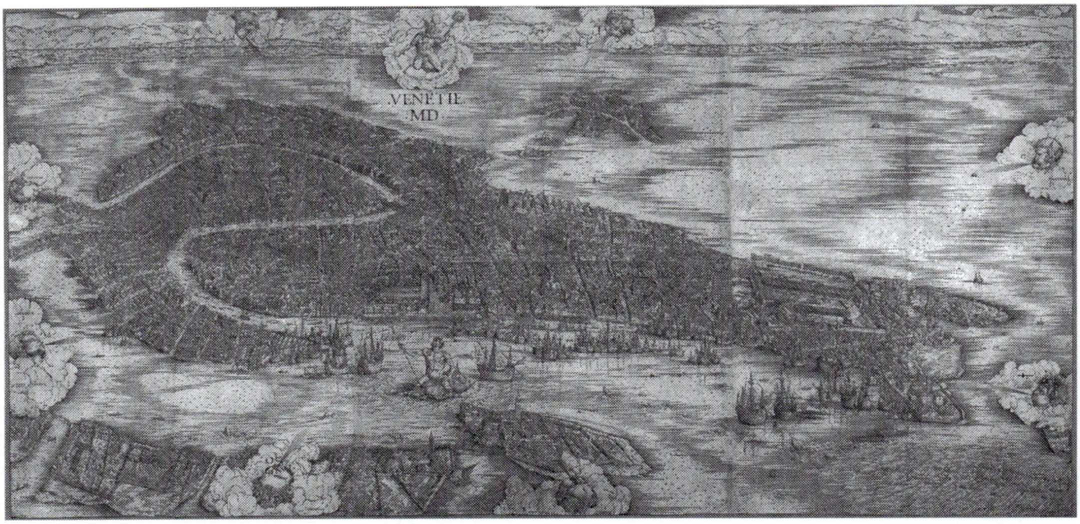

1.2 Jacopo de' Barbari, 'View of Venice', Minneapolis Institute of Arts.

frontally and implying the presence of Christ. Dürer's figures become more constructed according to the rules of measurements.[19] He read about the works on proportions following the advice of Jacopo de' Barbari.[20]

It is significant to highlight that Dürer probably met Jacopo (de' Barbari) in Venice and later in Nuremberg, where the author of the masterly 'View of Venice' (1500–1) was a portrait painter and illuminator in the service of Emperor Maximilian from 1500 to 1503. The two artists met and exchanged experiences and certain similarity can be observed between their two engravings of *Apollo and Diana*. That the Italian artist remained a puzzle and a constant reference for Dürer who must have admired his innovative view of Venice is evident in his writing:

> *If I cannot find someone else who has described how to make human proportions, then there is always Jacopo (de' Barbari), a lovely painter, born in Venice. He showed me (figures of) man and woman which he had made from measurements; and at that time I would have preferred to have had his judgment than a new kingdom, and if I had it, I would have put it into print in his honour for the general good. But at that time I was still young, and had not heard of such things. … I realized that Jacopo would not clearly explain his principles. So I set to work on my own and read Vitruvius, who writes a little about a man's limbs. Thus I took my start from or out of (the work of) these two men, and since then have continued my search from day to day according to my own notions.*[21]

Permanent improvement in respect to the proportional representation of the human figure is evident in Dürer's powerful engraving 'Nemesis' (1502). Set above the Alps, the goddess of retribution holds in one hand the goblet of rewards and in the other the bridle of restraint. She stands precariously on the sphere hovering over the Alpine landscape and the town Dürer had visited on his way to Venice in 1494. This dramatic figure has the features of Durer's wife suggesting that the work had an intricate, more profound meaning for the artist concerning his wife and the libidinal nature of his transalpine travels.[22]

1.3 Albrecht Dürer, 'Nemesis', Minneapolis Institute of Arts.

The results of Dürer's continued and symptomatic studies of the art of classical models feature prominently in the 'Fall of Man' engraving of 1504, where the ideal forms of the ancient 'Apollo Belvedere' and 'Venus Pudica' can be observed in the figures of Adam and Eve elaborately constructed by compass and ruler.[23] Mastery of perspectival space and knowledge of geometry are stated prominently in Dürer's celebrated woodcuts such as the 'Life of the Virgin' series of 1502–5, where the 'Annunciation' for example features a perfectly constructed central perspective of the internal space of the house as a background for the Virgin and the angel.[24]

In all these examples (1495–1505) we can observe how Dürer deployed the heightened perception of human figures and lived-through experiences of art that he gained in Venice. They are also indicative of how the work bears the traces of Dürer's exuberant quest for the inclusion of the scientific approach to bodies, and space. His mission is a research into space and spatiality, resulting in human figures that are captured moving through space. In analytic terms we may identify that these works contain at least three layers of narratives: personal, literary and scientific. Indeed Dürer's symptom opens up and suggests these layers of interpretation as his libido gathers momentum and regroups to each of them. These layers also seem to correspond to the layers of interpretation identified by Panofsky in his studies of iconology.[25]

SECOND TRIP TO VENICE, 1505–7: THE EFFECTS OF THE CITY

In addition to seeing different artists and styles of painting, the libidinal pleasure of the visit to Venice was in the overall urban experience. Its climate, its air, its rich scenery, the lavished decorum, voluptuous textures, variety of exotic spices, scents, foods and wines were all felt consciously and unconsciously. Geographically, from the point of view of a traveller from Nuremberg, Venice appears as the place where Europe's most sublime mountains slope into the floodplain, giving way to the Adriatic. Winding roads take the voyager down the Alps meditating about the descent during which the climate becomes milder, light more luminous, vegetation diverse, odours more fragrant, sounds of nature increasingly sonorous.

The city appears in the nexus of the continent meeting the sea. For the late-fifteenth and early-sixteenth century traveller the arrival to this place must have been unforgettable. The immensity of the sea and its promises of distant shores must have mesmerised the travellers from landlocked places. This port has always been an open city: on the one hand, to other cultures with which the city used to trade, and on the other, it was open towards the inner exploration, soul-searching and humanist knowledge. Venice seduced and teased Dürer's curiosity nurturing his imagination. He is comforted by Venetian appreciation of the arts and enchanted by its novelties: from people of distant cultures, via the colourful street life and costumes, to the previously unseen sea creatures.

During Dürer's lifetime, the city experienced a boom in the publishing business; despite the German invention of the printing press in the 1450s, more than half of all printed books in Europe at the time were published in Venice.[26] As the mercantile and cultural capital of the world, Venice was the centre for the first printers, publishing houses and bookstores mostly due to its freedom, wealth and high literacy level of its cosmopolitan population, many of whom were coming from the East following the advances of the Ottoman Turks across the countries such as Greece, Serbia and Croatia among others. These peoples were bringing their books and artefacts best exemplified in the St Mark's library *Bibliotheca Marciana* whose nucleus stock comes from Cardinal Bessarion of Constantinople, who donated his 482 Greek and 264 Latin manuscripts to the Senate of Venice in 1468.

These conditions provided for the revival of classical knowledge that underpinned the arts and excited Dürer, his friend Pirckheimer and other humanists. Ancient treatises previously known as manuscripts and circulated for limited audiences became available in print. Dürer acquired some including a copy of Vitruvius. He bought artefacts, painterly materials, rare pigments, textiles, etc. Above all he appropriated the experiences of the new world in its making (*theatrum mundi*).[27] The cosmopolitan make-up of the 'world stage' unleashed creativity that came from the exchange with the communities of the numerous diaspora residing in Venice. Conscious of his growing reputation Dürer became more involved in promoting his work[28] and constructing his own place. Many art historians have traced the Venetian influences in Dürer's opus, agreeing that Venice gave him both pleasure and a well-disposed attitude.

Dürer felt unencumbered as he relaxed in the Fondaco dei Tedeschi, branded for its clientele of German-speaking fraternity of businessmen who offered him commissions such as the altar-painting of the local San Bartolomeo church. This commission resulted in the colourful and versatile masterpiece, the 'Feast of the Rose Garland' now kept in Prague. While these effects of Venice have been acknowledged, how are we to account for them within the context of the questions raised about Dürer's unconscious spatiality and his libidinal economy? What was the nature of the overall impact of this city space? How did the city's unusual configuration affect this artist?

The hypothesis is that there is an impact of the city on the level of the spatial unconscious – something that traditional scholarship does not account for. This impact of Venice seems to have affected Dürer as he was reportedly 'full of images'. The city and the artist interacted in the ways that were dynamic, ground-breaking and soul-searching. Given that the urban fabric is formed of numerous layers that cannot be simply inventoried, this experience needs to be carefully reconstructed. For that purpose an operative statement will now follow with the aim to facilitate the analysis of the unconscious effects of the city.

ON THE UNCONSCIOUS EFFECTS OF THE CITY: OVERALL LEVEL, LEGIBILITY, *LOCI*, MENTAL MAPPING, DEEP IMAGES AND WATERCOURSES

Overall Level

Each city produces its own discourse; by means of its position, general configuration, streets, watercourses and landmarks, it communicates to its inhabitants and the inhabitants respond by living in it, watching it, traversing it, by gathering in specific places, orienting gardens or directing water in particular ways. We speak to the city through our behaviour and through the manner in which we relate to each other. We also unconsciously adjust our behaviour as we move from one city to another.

In order to conduct this analysis of the urban unconscious, it is important to extract the language we need to use from any metaphorical usage. This needs to be done in the manner in which Freud had managed to extract the expression 'language of dreams' from its metaphorical meaning in order to give it its actual meaning in psychoanalysis. The same process of extraction is required in relation to the unconscious and the city. We ought to excerpt and undo the metaphors in order to be able to fully participate in creating and using the language of urban effects. We need to be able to differentiate various effects, as certain elements of the city are strong while others are not even marked. The effects of the city space are often the outcome of the relationship between the two: marks and voids, presences and absences, solids and liquids as they always read in relation to each other.

Legibility, *Loci* and Mental Mapping

The legibility of the city is of great importance to any person experiencing it. More precisely, I am referring to a kind of reading that is concerned with the setups of memory and the importance of what Frances Yates, quoting Cicero, called the 'backgrounds' (*loci*). The subject is able to recall the object by its background, as the subject unconsciously (and involuntarily) remembers the set-ups (*loci*) that become instrumental for the recollection of objects.[29] Hereby I wish to extend Yates's argument in relation to the city, and in doing so I am bringing it closer to the idea of mental mapping as argued in cognitive psychology and as expressed in Kevin Lynch's image of the city.[30] In this interpretation the legibility of the city (*imago urbis*) is understood as a similar process of the unconscious recognition of the form within its background – the city space. The city plan is not made completely transparent, because this would undermine the (involuntary) memory and imagination that are part of an enjoyable urban experience. Based on fragments, the mental mapping of the city is reconstructed whenever we take a walk, while the recognition of the variety and the richness of fragments and layers harmonising into a whole is what gives us a libidinal pleasure whenever we engage with an intriguing city.

The awareness and knowledge of the space are determined by our primary perception, but also by our dreams, our unconscious desires and passions.[31] The space within which we grew up determines and holds within itself many intrinsic qualities: it could be light, ethereal, transparent, or dark, uneven and cluttered. There is space of peaks, heights, lights and towers as well as of depths, mud, wells and dungeons. This space is an inner space, a part of the configuration of our unconscious. Wherever we travel it is with us and in a corresponding relation to the outside space that keeps on adjusting. Roland Barthes argues that in the same way as phenomenology and semiology do not posit the existence of the definite signified, in relation to the city we find ourselves confronted with the infinite chain of metaphors whose signified is always essentially recessive – the structure that was explored in Jacques Lacan's psychoanalysis and in Jacques Derrida's study on writing, the structure that has an erotic dimension.[32] Eroticism is here understood in a general sense whereby the city is comprehended as the site of our encounter with the other in which certain subversive forces appear and we may encounter rupture and various ludic forces. We could see how this description echoes aspects of Dürer's experience of Venice.

Deep Images: Watercourses and the Phenomenon of Disorientation

Amongst the myriad of urban elements that we experience there are some that stand out. Barthes identifies these as 'deep images' and thinks of them in psychoanalytic terms.[33] It is at this point that he argues about the relevance of the imaginary function of the watercourses, stating that rivers, canals and waterways generally impress deep marks in the minds of people.[34] Barthes argues that there is a relation between the road and the watercourse, as they both excite strong (memorable) impressions, stating that all cities that lack watercourses have difficulties with their legibility. The cities with good watercourses offer clear legibility of their space, and as a consequence they have a strong sense of identity.[35] This legibility and related sense of identity are therefore primarily unconscious.

Because it has an unusual balance between land and water, Venice has always been a specific case. The abundance of watercourses and relatively few roads give visitors a saturation of deep images. This predominance of waterways subverts our usual mental map by turning it into its negative. The process of orientation, which now depends on the negative of the customary mental mapping, cannot work as previously. We cannot as it were orient ourselves as usual in relation to a (single) river as the main watercourse and the chief reference for orientation. Venice simply has too many watercourses, and solid roads can't be clearly mapped on this unstable ground saturated by the unconscious deep images of water. This explains the disorientation visitors often experience in this city that constantly mirrors itself in more ways than one.

Evidence suggests that this mirroring and the configuration of Venice, including the general effects of its morphology, the disposition of its roads, watercourses and landmarks, could have affected Dürer. Coupled with the exotic experiences of carnival dresses and masques, the phenomenon could be seen as an urban device for creating dis-ordination of various kinds and for amplifying the city's erotic dimension. These urban effects subvert the usual social relations, by means of licensing and encouraging pleasures that appealed to many visitors including Dürer. That he was carried away by unusual treats such as attending costly dancing lessons appears in his letters.[36] Further effects of Venetian adventures could be found in Dürer's confession about his fears concerning his sexual health, which could be interpreted as a consequence of unusual sexual behaviour.[37]

Overall Dürer enjoyed Venice but strangely did not paint it. He produced only the plans and elevations of one Venetian house. The lack of cityscape drawings or views such as those by Erhard Reuwich or Jacopo de' Barbari is unusual, and further supports the argument about the effects of water impressing and perplexing the visitor. The important effect of this phenomenon is that in the process the multitude of deep images exaggerates and augments one's own inner spatiality. Dürer experienced these exaggerations: he reports about great pleasure with some of his Venetian friends, and exaggerated fear with others. The vivid result of amplified pleasure slips into his numerous drawings of Venetian women and in the magnificently coloured painting the 'Feast of the Rose Garlands' (1506) where we find the unrestrained depth of Dürer's expression affected by heightened sensuality and libido.[38]

In addition to his art that flourished, Dürer's symptomatic libidinal drive to learn about the science of art had come to play when he went to Bologna, where he had learned about the science of perspective as formulated by Leon Battista Alberti and Piero della Francesca. Here his unknown teacher was probably Luca Pacioli, who was believed to be in possession of the mathematical secrets of art and of editions of Marsilio Ficino's work that became of interest to the German artist. Inspired by his encounters, Dürer returned to Nuremberg determined to pour his libidinal energies into writing his own treatise on mathematics and its application for the visual arts.

Water as Screen

The final effect of water as screen needs to be addressed. It comes into play as a result of the city's detachment from the continent that provides Venice with a horizon of almost 360 degrees. Uninterrupted brightness, enhanced by the reflection of the sea, allows the viewer to clearly perceive the city and the outline of its silhouette against the blue of the sky and the water. The surrounding sea makes the citizens and visitors aware of its enormous horizontal surface upon which they are enticed to project their gaze, and through the depth of this gaze – the unconscious. This long and deep projection of one's sightlines relaxes and, importantly, lures the unconscious, allowing the phenomenon of anamorphosis to play itself out by constructing the imaginary shapes and figures on the surface of the marine screen. On a different scale, the same projections occur on the top planes of the canal water allowing for further aspects to emerge.[39]

The phenomenon of anamorphosis that enables us to construct and see the images works with libido and contributes to explaining Dürer's experiences of Venice that are 'full of images', making him both outgoing and introspective. He interacted with people and contemplated about the city in the context of life and the world around him. On a general level, we can conclude that this is the reason why the urban sites of Venice mark such a significant exteriorised field of the unconscious. This is also the reason why the city has for centuries continued to attract visitors and tourists. In the words of Dürer's admirer and compatriot Friedrich Nietzsche, 'A hundred deep solitudes taken together form the city of Venice – that is her charm. An image for the men of the future'.[40]

INNER SPATIALITY AND THE LANDSCAPE OF THE SOUL: 'MELENCOLIA I'

In Venice the image of *theatrum mundi* stood out more glaringly than in other cities and Dürer felt part of it. The participation of *imago urbis* within *theatrum mundi* fascinated him. Propelled by the unconscious libidinal force, Dürer's desire is also highly rational. It seeks for and is determined by the laws of the sciences and arts as they were changing and coming to new prominence. The first decade of the sixteenth century was increasingly showing signs of emerging new practices and attitudes. Dürer's search for mathematical knowledge grew steadily and continually until the end of his life. Indeed his book on proportions would never be finished, suggesting that in the heart of it was a constant lack that always needed to be filled in.

1.4 Albrecht Dürer, 'Melencolia I', Minneapolis Institute of Arts.

Significantly for our argument (and symptomatically) overall, Dürer's drawings addressing his perpetual quest for mathematical knowledge date from the same period (1510–15) as his most celebrated 'Melencolia I' (1514). This magnificent engraving which embodies his technical achievement, spatial knowledge and higher learning at their best, is Dürer's masterpiece of outstanding beauty and of highest esteem. It is also a representation, not of the disease but of a problem that was part of the artist's experience. The depiction of this enigmatic lady reveals Dürer's symptom and his complex state of mind.

'Melencolia I' depicts a moment when Dürer's personal quest for knowledge becomes a cause of melancholy. The engraving shows a winged angel looking like a young woman, who sits in apparent sadness, surrounded by unused objects of mathematics, science, craft and art, holding a pair of dividers. Her face is masked by darkness, while her eyes glare with intensity, revealing the sharp mind in distinction to her tired bodily pose.

Interpreters are divided as to whether 'Melencolia I' was intended to be the first in a series, or whether the 'I' in 'Melencolia I' stands for *melancholia imaginativa*. This notion is derived from Heinrich Cornelius Agrippa of Nettesheim (1486–1535), a German alchemist and theologian, a contemporary of Dürer and astrologer who describes *melancholia imaginativa* as a state in which the person is subject to 'imagination', that predominates over 'mind' or 'reason'.[41] We can see how this description could have appealed to Dürer.

The condition of *melancholia* is rooted in medieval medicine: according to the theory of the 'humours', melancholy was caused by an increase of black bile that shows in the darkened face of the muse-like angel. At the same time, Dürer portrays something new: a sense of a soul burdened by its own intellect. The fact that this is Dürer's only engraving with a title inscribed within the plate, testifies to its conceptual importance as a statement of a condition that Dürer deliberately wished to publicise and disperse to a broad audience.

'Melencolia I' contains the first magic square to be seen in Europe, including the date 1514 as two entries in the middle of the bottom row. Of spatial interest is Dürer's inclusion of the polyhedron, the faces of which appear to consist of two equilateral triangles and six pentagons. This could be a reference to Luca Pacioli and the painting usually attributed to Jacopo de' Barbari showing Pacioli with the same geometrical body. The engraving contains several references to time symbolizing Saturn; it also shows a blazing comet that appears on the sky. In contrast to the main figure of the angel-muse we have a small busy-looking putto taking notes and a skinny dog sleeping uncomfortably.

It is impossible not to recognise this aggravated figure sitting amidst the disorderly scientific instruments as embodiment of Dürer's spirit of intellectual research. The quality of detail presented is so refined that it must be based on the knowledge of the work of philosophers such as Marsilio Ficino,[42] whose work was incorporated by Pacioli in *De divina proportione*.[43] Writing about melancholy, the fifteenth century Florentine philosopher claimed that intellectuals, humanists and artists, talented and introspective souls, were predisposed to melancholy. In this way Dürer translates Ficino's ideas into a mysterious heroic figure.

From all this we can conclude that the artist was personally affected by melancholy. He could have heard from Pacioli that this was the condition of another great artist whom he admired: Leonardo da Vinci, who notoriously suffered from a strange affliction that stopped him finishing his paintings. Dürer recognised the infliction of *melancholia* and through relentless introspection he was able to represent it. By means of this introspection Dürer's interest in science was not only the one of a painter/engraver, but of a person who by means of observation, detection and painting aimed at reaching explanations in scientific knowledge including medicine. This aspect of Dürer's work (which resembles the work of Leonardo) was the reason why the humanists such as Pirckheimer, Erasmus, Philip Melanchthon and Celtes Conrad spoke highly of Dürer and why they wanted to interact with him.

After returning to Nuremberg in 1425 from his final trip to the Netherlands, where amongst other things Dürer hoped to find Jacopo de' Barbari's book on proportions, Dürer's health deteriorated. His major effort went unabatedly into his treatise on proportions, and although it was not completed in 1523, Dürer realised that it implied a high-level of mathematical knowledge, so he decided to write a more approachable text. He published this more elementary treatise *Unterweisung der Messung mit dem Zirkel und Richtscheit* in 1525. It is the first book on mathematics published in German, making Dürer one of the key Renaissance mathematicians. Dürer's sources for this work are threefold: the practical recipes of craftsmen; classical mathematics from printed works and manuscripts such as Vitruvius's; and the manuals of Italian artists.[44] And yet this contribution to mathematics is mainly due to Dürer's personal strife driven by his symptom that was sublimating his libido and making him obsessive about both art and mathematics.

Dürer's last masterpiece, his treatise on proportion, was at the final stage at the time of his death. In this treatise Dürer set the foundations of Descriptive Geometry as he developed one of the methods of overcoming the problems of projection and describing the movement of bodies in space.[45] Dürer's remarkable achievement was that by applying mathematics to art, he developed a fundamentally new and important knowledge within mathematics itself.

Dürer's opus therefore emerges in the interplay between, on the one hand, the conscious exploration of the arts by applying mathematics, and, on the other, the pursuit of unconscious passions in search for mathematical postulates. This tumultuous interplay produced qualitatively new results for spatial studies taking knowledge into novel directions and paving the way for René Descartes and Gaspard Monges.

This chapter has therefore demonstrated how Dürer's opus developed in relation to his unconscious and his libidinal drives. It was argued how the dynamics of his personality drove him to explorations. In particular it was my aim to show how the effects of Venice on Dürer were complex and multiple due to the city's specific disposition, its urban morphology and the presence of the surrounding water that resulted in the intensification of perception, deep mental images, and the increased quantity of images.

Crucially by means of these intertwining experiences that were 'full of visual images' Dürer brought together the discourses that were previously separate. He did not give up on these images, but sought how to make them communicable with a belief that they can disseminate ideas and knowledge. Propelled by his symptom and its libidinal force, Dürer explored Venice learning about its arts of representing that both excited and troubled him. By being dedicated to present these internal struggles in full, Dürer produced a significant elaboration on these inner contentions, their constant questioning, mirroring and self-examination. By putting his own life in the line of questioning and erosion, this cycle of experiences made Dürer the artist as we know him.

NOTES

1 Michel Foucault, *The Order of Things: An Archaeology of Human Sciences* (London: Routledge, 1991), pp. 17–42.

2 Michel Foucault, 'Of the Other Spaces: Utopias and Heterotopias', in Joan Ockman (ed.), *Architecture Culture 1943–1968* (New York: Rizzoli, 1996), pp. 421–2.

3 Erwin Panofsky, *The Life and Art of Albrecht Dürer* (Princeton, NJ: Princeton University Press, 1971 [1943]), p. 4.

4 These are: the self-portrait with the thistle on the occasion of his engagement (1493), Louvre, the self-portrait in new clothes with black and white hat (1498), Prado, and the frontal self-portrait for the occasion of the jubilee of 1500 (1499–1500), Munich.

5 Sigmund Freud, *Group Psychology and the Analysis of the Ego*, trans. James Strachey (London and Vienna: The International Psycho-Analytical Press, 1922), p. 33.

6 Max Steck, 'Dürer', in Charles Coulston Gillispie (ed.), *Dictionary of Scientific Biography* (New York: Scribner, 1970–1990).

7 'Myn sach dy gat als es oben schtat' (Erwin Panofsky, *The Life and Art of Albrecht Dürer*, p. 6). The plant on this self-portrait, identified as the thistle, was considered to be the sign of marital fidelity.

8 Jeffrey Chipps Smith, *Dürer* (London: Phaidon, 2012), pp. 52–5.

9 Sigmund Freud, 'Civilisation and Its Discontents', in *The Complete Psychological Works of Sigmund Freud: The Future of an Illusion, Civilization and its Discontents, and Other Works, The Standard Edition*, vol. XXI, trans. James Strachey (Hogarth Press: London, 1961), pp. 79–80.

10 Although Panofsky refers extensively to the Housebook Master, he does not mention this woodcut or Reuwich himself. See note 7, p. 8.

11 Katherine Crawford Luber, *Albrecht Dürer and the Venetian Renaissance* (Cambridge: Cambridge University Press, 2005), pp. 40–77.

12 Mark Evans, 'Dürer in Italy Revisited: The German Connections' (2003), paper delivered at the 2003 Albrecht Dürer and his Legacy Conference, organised by Giulia Bartrum. British Museum Online. Available at: https://www.britishmuseum.org/pdf/1%20Durer%20and%20Italy%20Revisited.pdf [accessed 25 August 2015].

13 Ibid.

14 Katherine Crawford Luber, *Albrecht Dürer and the Venetian Renaissance*, pp. 77–126.

15 Erwin Panofsky, *The Life and Art of Albrecht Dürer*, pp. 39–80.

16 Mark Evans, 'Dürer in Italy Revisited: The German Connections', p. 3; and Erwin Panofsky, *The Life and Art of Albrecht Dürer*, p. 74.

17 Erwin Panofsky, *The Life and Art of Albrecht Dürer*, p. 74.

18 Ibid., p. 73.

19 Ibid., pp. 80–107.

20 Ibid., p. 80.

21 Mark Evans, 'Dürer in Italy Revisited: The German Connections', p. 3 (n. 55).

22 In his 18 August 1506 letter from Venice Dürer expresses his worry about his sexual health in regards to a large number of men being infected with the French sickness (syphilis). Albrecht Dürer, *The Writings of Albrecht Dürer*, trans. and ed. W.M. Conway (London: Peter Owen, 1958), p. 54.

23 The process of their construction, which is displayed in many sketches and different stages of prints, is well documented by the scholarship. See Mark Evans, 'Dürer in Italy Revisited: The German Connections', p. 3; and Erwin Panofsky, *The Life and Art of Albrecht Dürer*, pp. 291–3.

24 There are other painterly aspects that are mentioned by both Aby Warburg and Panofsky which concern the question of pathos and affect and how they came to be construed in Dürer's work, best shown in the 'Death of Orpheus', 'Bacchanal with Silenus', and 'Venetian Women', showing different ways of portraying the female nude. The scope of this chapter does not allow for this expansion.

25 Erwin Panofsky, *Studies in Iconology: Humanistic Themes in the Art of the Renaissance* (Oxford: Icon Editions, Perseus, 1972 [1939]).

26 Alessandro Marzo Magno, *Bound in Venice: The Serene Republic and the Dawn of the Book*, trans. G. Conti (Rome: Europa Editions, 2013), pp. 1–5.

27 Here I reflect on Dürer's contribution to the establishment of the concept of *theatrum mundi* – the world stage where all beings play a part, consciously or unconsciously. See more in Michel Foucault, *The Order of Things*, pp. xv–xxiv.

28 Albrecht Dürer, *The Writings of Albrecht Dürer*, p. 51.

29 Yates talked about memorising places in the house and how certain well-acknowledged backgrounds work for memory. See Frances A. Yates, *The Art of Memory* (London: ARK Paperbacks, 1984 [1966]), pp. 12–13.

30 Kevin Lynch, *The Image of the City* (Cambridge, MA: The MIT Press, 1960).

31 Gaston Bachelard, *Poetics of Space* (Boston, MA: Beacon Press, 1969).

32 Roland Barthes, *Semiology and Urbanism*, Colloquium Op. 10 (Naples: University of Naples Institute of Architectural History, 1967), quoted in Joan Ockman (ed.), *Architecture Culture 1943–1968*, p. 417.

33 Ibid., p. 418.

34 Ibid.

35 Gordana Korolija Fontana-Giusti, 'Water, Cities and Signification', in *Book of Proceedings, 1st Symposium on Waterfronts in the Danube Region* (Novi Sad: University of Novi Sad, 2006).

36 Albrecht Dürer, *The Writings of Albrecht Dürer*, pp. 58–9.

37 See note 22 above.

38 Katherine Crawford Luber, *Albrecht Dürer and the Venetian Renaissance*, pp. 77–126.

39 Jacques Lacan, *The Four Fundamental Concepts of Psycho-Analysis*, trans. Alan Sheridan (New York: W.W. Norton, 1981), pp. 9, 79–119. I here refer to several concepts of Lacan addressed in this book such as the gaze, the screen and anamorphosis.

40 Friedrich Nietzsche, *Aurora e scelta di frammenti postumi* (1879–81), fragment from spring 1880, in *Opere*, ed. Giorgio Colli and Mazzino Montinari, trans. F. Masini and Mazzino Montinari, vol. 5, tome 1 (Milan: Adelphi, 1964), p. 296. Quoted in Manfredo Tafuri, *Venice and the Renaissance*, trans. Jessica Levine (Cambridge, MA and London: The MIT Press, 1989), p. xi.

41 Heinrich Cornelius Agrippa, *De occulta philosophia libri tres*, ed. Perrone Campagni (Leiden: Brill, 1992).

42 Erwin Panofsky and Fritz Saxl, *Durer's 'Melencolia I': Eine quellen-und typengeschichtliche Untersuchung* (Leipzig: B.G. Teubner, 1923); Raymond Klibansky, Erwin Panofsky, and Fritz Saxl, *Saturn and Melancholy: Studies in the History of Natural Philosophy, Religion and Art* (London: Nelson, 1964). See also on this subject Lurinda S. Dixon, *The Dark Side of Genius: The Melancholic Persona in Art, c. 1500–1700* (University Park, PA: The Pennsylvania State University Press, 2013).

43 Luca Pacioli, *De divina proportione* (Venice: Paganini, 1509).

44 Albrecht Dürer, *Underweysung der Messung mit dem Zirckel und Richtscheyt* (*Instructions for Measuring with Compass and Ruler*) (Nuremberg: Albrecht Dürer, 1525).

45 The first book was mainly completed in 1523, showing five differently constructed types of both male and female figures. Dürer based these constructions on both Vitruvius and empirical observations of 200 to 300 persons as he estimated. The second book includes eight further types, loosely based on Alberti, probably learned from Francesco di Giorgio's *De harmonica mundi totius* of 1525. In the third book, Dürer shows how the proportions of the figures can be modified addressing also human physiognomy. The fourth book is devoted to the theory of movement. Albrecht Dürer, *Vier Bücher von Menschlicher Proportion* (*Four Books on Human Proportion*) (Nuremberg: Hieronymus Formschneyder, 1528).

2

Architecture and the Kantian Unconscious

John Shannon Hendrix

In the transcendental aesthetic of Immanuel Kant (1724–1804) in the *Critique of Pure Reason* (*Kritik der reinen Vernunft*, A version 1781, B version 1787), what we perceive to be space and time do not actually exist outside of our thought. Geometry and mathematics are abstract representations of space and time which have no basis in the sensory world. As architecture is lineament, geometry and mathematics, it can be inferred that it only exists in thought as a representation of space and time. It can be concluded that architecture itself is an a priori category, projected onto the material or the real, as are space and time. Categories in a priori intuition can be seen to be functions of unconscious thought, thus architecture can be seen to be a function of unconscious thought, in that when we perceive architecture we are not conscious of the mechanisms behind our perception of it.

In the *Critique of Pure Reason*, knowledge can only relate to sensible objects by means of intuition. 'In whatever manner and by whatever means a mode of knowledge may relate to objects, intuition is that through which it is in immediate relation to them, and to which all thought as a means is directed' (A19).[1] The object, or phenomenon, is the 'undetermined object of an empirical intuition' (A20). The phenomenon consists of matter and form; the matter is that part of the phenomenon which corresponds to sensation, while the form is that part of the phenomenon which can be arranged under certain relations. The matter of the phenomenon corresponds to the sensible form as opposed to the intelligible form, which corresponds to the form of the phenomenon for Kant. Both the matter and the form of the phenomenon are determined a priori; the a priori conception of the sensible form results in the perception of the form, while the a priori conception of the intelligible form results in the understanding of the phenomenon as part of a synthetic whole in the ordering of the phenomenal world. The vocabulary forms of architecture, geometry and mathematics, are intelligibles, concepts not connected to sense perception. The intelligibles form a totality or manifold that organises the sensible world, in unconscious thought. The particulars of the sensible world, like the particulars of architecture, are perceived in such a way that they conform to a totality, through the process of apperception, a function of unconscious thought. Unconscious apperception organises the differentiated particulars of sense perception into a totality given only by the categories of a priori intuition. The totality of architecture as it is perceived is given by the categories of geometry and mathematics, derived from space and time, in a priori intuition in unconscious thought.

Sensibility, the capacity for receiving representations, is the source of intuition, which allows sensible objects to be thought in understanding, from which arise conceptions, according to Kant. Objects, and intuitions, are given by sensibility; they are thought in the 'understanding', from which arise conceptions. Thought is related to intuition, and to sensibility, by signs or symbols. Sensible objects can only be thought as representations. All material forms in architecture are representations, as are all words in a language. Sensations cannot arrange themselves or assume certain forms; forms must exist a priori in the mind, and be seen as separate from sensation. In the pure forms of sensuous intuition which exist in the mind a priori, 'all the manifold of intuition is intuited in certain relations'. Architecture already involves the ordering of the phenomenal world by a priori sensuous intuition.

Kant distinguishes between the sensation and the intelligible, as the intelligible entails an arrangement of sensations, and the sensation assuming a form. The matter of phenomena is given a posteriori, following the form of phenomena in the mind; the a priori form must thus be seen as separate from sensation, and juxtaposed to it, in a contradiction. What is a priori in the mind is the transcendental, pure form of sensuous intuition, which arranges the manifold and varied content of the phenomenal world. The manifold content of the phenomenal world is arranged and viewed under a certain set of arrangements, which are determined by intuition, and concept in understanding. Objects can only exist in perception in so far as they are in a certain relation to other objects; objects cannot exist in perception without a relation to other objects. In the transcendental concepts of time and space, a moment in time cannot exist without a relation to other moments in time, and a point in space cannot exist without a relation to other points in space. Time, space, and the manifold of phenomenal objects in perception thus can only exist in a conceptual continuity, a reality manufactured by human reason. Architecture, as the sequential organisation of space, only exists as a manifold continuity manufactured by human reason. Architectural forms only exist in relation to other architectural forms. Architecture is a projection of an a priori intuition, a manufactured totality, in unconscious thought, onto the phenomenal world. It entails the coexistence of the ideal and the real, the intuitive and the sensible, which constitute a contradiction in understandings.

Kant defines the 'Transcendental Aesthetic' as the 'science of all principles of *a priori* sensibility ...' (A21). There are two pure forms of sensuous intuition, which are principles of a priori knowledge: space and time. Space and time are not 'real existences', but rather 'merely determinations or relations of things ...' (A23). Space and time are not concepts which have been developed from outward or empirical experience in their entirety, but rather entail a dialectic between empirical experience and concept in understanding, manifest as intuition. Pure empirical experience does not exist. External or empirical experience is itself only possible as a result of a priori intuition, as sense experience is conditioned by what is understood in the mind, in unconscious thought. The perception of a sensible form is determined by an understanding of the corresponding intelligible form in the mind. A phenomenal object can only be perceived once it is understood in its relation to the totality or manifold of reality, as constructed in the mind. A form in architecture can only be perceived as it is understood a priori in relation to other forms in architecture, which constitute the totality or manifold of architecture. It is impossible to think of architecture without space, or time, thus space cannot be said to exist as a physical phenomenon. As a manifold totality constructed a priori in intuition, architecture cannot be said to exist as a physical phenomenon, but rather only as a concept.

The structural and functional requirements of architecture exist in the phenomenal world as products of the a priori concepts of space and time, in the relation of a posteriori perceived matter in relation to a priori conceptualised relations. The visual forms of architecture, when they are in direct relationship to the structural and functional requirements, are as the visual forms of matter, in relation to the manifold concepts of matter in a cause and effect relationship, as given by reason. If the visual forms of architecture contradict the structural and functional requirements, then the mechanisms by which architecture, and sensible reality, are understood in reason and perception, are revealed; the contradiction between the sensible object as perceived matter and a priori transcendental intuition is revealed. Architecture thus functions as philosophy, to examine and reveal the mechanisms of reason and perception, in order to describe the relationship between the human mind and the phenomenal world, and unconscious and conscious thought.

Space is a necessary a priori representation, and it is the condition for the possibility of all phenomena. It is impossible to conceive of the nonexistence of space; for that reason alone space cannot be seen as a phenomenal reality. It is also impossible to conceive of the nonexistence of time, and all relationships are perceived in space and time. Modern physics tells us that the universe had a definite beginning and will have a definite end in both spatial and temporal terms, but it is impossible to conceive of anything prior to or posterior to space and time, just like it is impossible to conceive of experience after death, except as a mythology. Architecture is also a necessary a priori representation; it is impossible to conceive of the nonexistence of architecture, thus architecture cannot be seen as a phenomenal reality. While space and time, and architecture, are manifest in discursive reason as containing relationships within a manifold totality, they themselves cannot be concepts of relationships, but rather pure intuitions, a priori concepts which are formed prior to sensory experience, much like the archetype or intelligible in classical philosophy, in the active intellect or intellectual principle (*nous*), which is manifest in intelligible form in relation to sensible form, or the unconscious in psychoanalysis. Following the intuitions of space and time, geometry and mathematics are also products of a priori intuition, thus architecture is a product of a priori intuition.

According to Kant, space is not a concept which is derived from outward experience, nor from relations between external phenomena. External experience is on the contrary only possible through the antecedent representation of space. Space is a necessary a priori representation; all conceptions of space are based on a priori intuition, as are the principles of geometry. Space is not a discursive concept, as it cannot be divided or multiplied. Architecture thus depends on a priori intuition in perception, rather than on sensory perception or discursive reason. It is impossible to think of architecture without space, thus space does not exist as a physical phenomenon, and it is reasonable to conclude that architecture does not exist as a physical phenomenon; architecture only exists as it is understood in the mind, as in the *lineamenti*, or lines in the mind of the architect, of Leon Battista Alberti.

Geometrical principles are apodictic, necessary truths. Rather than being based in the fragmented variability and malleability of the phenomenal world, they are a priori intuitions applied to reality. They cannot be varied to conform to sensible phenomena; rather, sensible phenomena must conform to them. The organisation of a building must conform to a priori, universal rules of mathematics and geometry; the building is thus taken out of its phenomenal existence, and through architecture it enters into a transcendental existence. Mathematics and geometry, time and space, are not properties inherent to sensible objects which have an existence in so far as they are in conformance with a manifold set of rules and principles. Space is not a quality of an object, nor is it a quality of relations between objects; it has no relation to sensible objects other than as providing a field in which sensible objects can be perceived and understood. The mathematics and geometry in architecture which organise a building in time and space have no relation to the material forms of the architecture, other than as providing a field in which elements of a building can be organised as architecture. An element of a building is transformed into an architectural form when it is understood in relation to mathematics and geometry, that is when it is transformed from a phenomenal object to a transcendental object of intuition (unconscious thought) and perception, from the real to the ideal, or the sensible to the intelligible, from any existence 'in itself' to an existence determined a priori in intuition.

The experience of a building as architecture depends on the a priori intuition of time, as temporal succession and coexistence do not exist in the phenomenal world. A part of time cannot be understood outside of the manifold of time, as a part of space cannot be understood outside the manifold of space. Time and space are, rather than qualities of the phenomenal world, qualities of the intuition of the perceiving subject. Time and space determine the 'relation of representations in our inner state' (B50), the representations of perceived phenomena. Time and space function as a syntax for the language of internal representation; they are the mechanism by which perceptions are organised and understood. Meaning is created in language through a relationship between signifiers, so time is a necessary a priori intuition for meaning in language, and the communication of meaning in the visual language of architecture, which also requires a syntax, an underlying matrix of rules of representation, which include mathematics and geometry, in order for meaning in representation to be communicated in so far as it participates in a manifold.

All communication in language requires a shared acceptance of a manifold, composed of syntactical rules based in the a priori intuitions of space and time. Space and time are constructed, artificial mechanisms through which all thought, language, communication, meaning and architecture are generated. If space and time do not exist other than as transcendental intuitions in the mind, in unconscious thought, then their grounding for all communication and meaning reveals a void within all communication and meaning, and within human identity. Meaning and communication have a metaphysical basis which is not to be found in phenomenal reality. Any meaning or communication which is achieved in a syntax in language, including the language of architectural forms, cannot be related to the phenomenal existence of the signifiers in the language, or the matter of the architectural elements.

Space and time, as internal a priori intuitions, can provide no form themselves, but can only be represented in forms, in formal analogies, such as cyclical or linear progression. The perception of a sensible object requires a dialectic between the sensible form of the object and the intelligible understanding of the object, as a relation in a manifold, which is given a sensible form in representation. Space and time can only be represented through figural language, in linguistic tropes; they cannot be represented in literal language, because they do not exist in the phenomenal world. Architecture represents space and time though the tropic language of mathematics and geometry. Architecture can only be understood as existing within and determined by the manifold framework of space and time which it represents through the figural tropes of mathematics and geometry in its execution and experience. Architecture, and human reason, are thus defined by a metaphysical foundation which does not actually exist, but is represented by analogies in its nonexistence.

It is impossible to perceive space or time; only relations within space and time can be perceived, as they have been determined in a priori intuition. It is thus impossible to perceive the epistemological basis of architecture; its basis is taken for granted as an unconscious, transcendental a priori intuition, which is not a quality of the architecture or reality themselves. The immediate condition of all internal, subjective phenomena, in perception and intellection, mediates all external phenomena in perception and intellection. Space and time are the modes of representation of the perceiving and thinking subject as object. Reason becomes aware of itself in consciousness, and objectifies itself, through the representations of space and time. Space and time are the conditions of the sensibility of the subject, the conditions of the subjective experience of reality, which is the necessary basis of reality. Space and time are the representations from which 'bodies of *a priori* synthetic knowledge can be derived' (B55), which include geometry and mathematics in discursive thought or cognition, and thus the concept of architecture. Architecture is an expression of the human condition in so far as the human condition is a subjective representation, of unconscious thought, and not an external reality.

Empirical experience is necessary in the development of concepts from intuition, according to Kant, for example the concept of change based in the intuition of time, as the succession of the determinations of an object. Empirical intuition is also a subjective experience, as relations between objects in space and time do not exist without the subjective constitution of the senses, or the perception of the subject. Objects are transformed into relations given by representations in intuition. It is impossible to know phenomenal objects outside of the subjective sensation of them, outside the subjective mode of perceiving them, which is a universal representation of a manifold. It is also impossible to know the mechanisms by which objects are represented in intuition in the framework of space and time; it is thus impossible to have complete knowledge of either the object or the subject in human perception, or to have access to unconscious thought. The human being is caught in a play of mirrors as it were, having access only to the subjective condition of human experience, with no accessible basis in either the phenomenal world of sense perception or the cognitive world of the unconscious. Architecture is a product of the play of mirrors; it is a conceptual mediation between intuition and phenomena, neither of which are entirely accessible. Architecture is a labyrinth, the originary architectural form that represents the lack of differentiation between life and death, the temporal and eternal, and the confining and expansive in the human understanding of the human condition. It is impossible to know a building architecturally outside the intuition of architecture, which is inaccessible, and it is impossible to know a building outside the concept of architecture.

Cognition only consists of relations in discursive reason, as given by a priori intuitions. It is impossible to know a thing in itself in phenomena through its relations, to either other things or the perceiving subject. The relations of a thing are determined in the manifold of intuition; particular relations cannot be known or perceived outside the transcendental matrix of relations as given by intuition in unconscious thought. All relations between phenomenal objects are representations of a priori relations in intuition; the reality of phenomena plays itself out only as it has been drawn up in the imagination. A building functions as architecture only to the extent that the architectural relations of the building, within the framework of space and time, geometry and mathematics, have been drawn up in the imagination, or in intuition. Phenomenal forms in reality are representations of forms in the imagination or intuition as they interact with the discursive functions of cognition. The higher imagination, or 'productive imagination' of Kant, depends on intuition or unconscious thought.

Knowledge consists of the power of receiving representations and the power of cognising by means of these representations, according to Kant. Sensible objects are received as representations by a priori intuition, as forms. The forms of architecture are perceived as representations in intuition. Sensible objects are cognised as forms of thought, transformed into signs and symbols, understood as abstracted universals, a posteriori. A priori cognition, in so far as it is dependent on understanding, is made possible by a synthesis or conjunction of a manifold of conceptions in relation to the 'unity of apperception' (B150), the synthesis of multiple singular perceptions of sensible objects. The synthesis is 'at once transcendental and also purely intellectual', and the 'synthesis of the manifold of sensuous intuition, which is possible and necessary *a priori*, may be entitled *figurative* synthesis (*synthesis speciosa*)' (B151), as opposed to 'combination through the understanding (*synthesis intellectualis*)', in cogitation, which is also a priori. The mechanisms of intuition are known by analogy, in tropic language, of the imagination. The architecture of a building, as it entails a synthesis of the manifold material parts of the building, can be seen as a priori cognition or intuition, as a model or catechism of the processes of perception and intellection, in an expression of the human condition. As Kant says, human reason 'is by nature architectonic' (A474), requiring an a priori unity, and accepting only principles which are part of a possible system.

Figurative synthesis is distinguished from intellectual synthesis: the intellectual synthesis occurs in discursive reason, in cogitation, while the figurative synthesis is related to the original synthetic unity of apperception and the transcendental unity which is the object of cogitation. Figurative synthesis is thus labelled 'the transcendental synthesis of imagination' (B151), imagination being 'the faculty of representing in intuition an object that is not itself present', belonging to sensibility. Architecture exists in the imagination, as a transcendental synthesis, and that transcendental synthesis is projected onto the material form of a building. Intuition cannot be separated from sensibility, but at the same time intuition can only be known figuratively, through representations, as a product of language. Architecture, thus, is a product of language, figural or tropic language in particular. Architecture is a product of the productive imagination. As Kant writes:

> *When, for instance, by apprehension of the manifold of a house I make the empirical intuition of it into a perception, the necessary unity of space and of outer sensible intuition in general lies at the basis of my apprehension ... (B162).*

Without the a priori intuition, apperception, cognition and discursive reason would not be possible. The form of the house is drawn according to the synthetic unity of the manifold in space, which does not exist in phenomena, but rather only in the mind. Sensual perception and apprehension must conform to the synthesis of apperception, which is intellectual and a priori, unconscious, and which is also spontaneous in productive imagination and apprehension. It is impossible to perceive or understand a form in architecture or phenomena without an understanding of the synthetic unity or manifold, just as it is impossible to understand the meaning of a word outside a syntax. It is necessary to understand the mechanisms of thought and perception in order to understand architecture; the mechanisms of thought and perception are not completely accessible to conscious thought itself, and must in part be ascribed to a priori intuition, or the mechanisms of unconscious thought. Architecture, as an accurate representation of human thought and perception, contains a metaphysical element that is not immediately accessible to sensory perception or discursive reason, but which can be understood through higher forms of intellection, in advanced forms of conceptual representation that involve an apprehension of unconscious processes.

Thought is the condition for the possibility of architecture, as it is the condition for the possibility of experience. The subject draws 'as it were, the outline of the house in conformity with this synthetic unity of the manifold in space', in geometrical representation. The synthetic unity is taken as a category of the a priori synthesis in intuition; the category exists in abstraction, in the visual representation of space in geometry, processed in discursive reason as a quantity, in a sequence of relationships, which conform to the manifold synthesis, as the manifold synthesis conforms to the categories. Human reason is 'architectonic' in that all thoughts or cognitions conform to a possible system, in the same way that all phenomenal objects exist in sequences of relationships. A building, as a collection of phenomenal objects in sequences of relationships, can never be adequate to an architectural idea, the transcendental idea in intuition, because the pure idea can never be completely represented in the phenomenal world.

Architecture, like all forms of human expression, is propelled by the fact that it can never be complete, as the human being can never be complete, because the relation between the transcendental idea and concrete phenomena can never be resolved. The continuous quest for completion by the incomplete human subject, in its reason and poetic expression (as in architecture), results in desire, wholeness being the inaccessible object of desire. Thus is the desire of architecture, the impossibility of the representation of sensible reality, which is beyond access, or unconscious thought in inner sense, which is beyond access. The architectonic, and architecture, are concepts which are necessary to experience what does not exist, which is a connection between mind and matter, thought and the phenomenal world, through intuition. Architecture, like the phenomenal world, is only possible because of thought, and the alienation of thought from itself in consciousness. When we build a house to shelter ourselves from the world, we also build an edifice that prevents us from being connected to the world, both literally and metaphorically.

According to Kant, the 'schematism of our understanding, in its application to appearances', forms and representations, 'is an art concealed in the depths of the human soul, whose real modes of activity nature is hardly ever likely to allow us to discover, and to have open to our gaze' (A141/B181). Productive imagination and intellectual synthesis are unconscious processes, while reproductive imagination and figurative synthesis are conscious processes. In the words of Theodor Lipps, in *Psychological Studies*, 'the pure concepts of the understanding (categories) seem to belong to the unconscious ideas, so far as they lie beyond cognition ...'[2] The source of cognition is left unexplained, except in so far as unconscious thought is the foundation for conscious thought.

The thinking subject is made possible by the synthetic unity of apperception and the representations that are presented by it in the process of thought. The thinking subject is split between the condition of its possibility in the inner sense and its activity in discursive or conscious reason; the subject is thus self-alienated, having no access to the necessity of its existence in intuition. The thinking subject is unable to think itself as inner sense or the manifold of intuition, the basis of its possibility. Cartesian self-consciousness is an illusion. Knowledge of the self is dark and obscure; it is given by the indirect, mediated (*mittelbar*), partially unconscious perceptions involving indirect representations that are dark and obscure (*dunkel*). In an early treatise, *Attempt to Introduce the Concept of Negative Magnitudes into*

Philosophy (*Versuch, den Begriff der negative Grössen in die Weltweisheit einzuführen*, 1763), Kant developed a theory about thoughts that are negated or cancelled, obscured or darkened, all suggesting unconscious thoughts. Thoughts come to be and pass away because certain thoughts are cancelled out by thoughts with greater force which oppose them. As certain thoughts become clearer, the other thoughts become less clear and more obscured (*Verdunkelt*). Kant's concept was influenced by the *petites perceptions* of Gottfried Wilhelm Leibniz. He invoked Leibniz in reiterating that only a small portion of the representations which occur in the soul, as the result of sense perception, are clear and enduring.[3]

Kant's *Anthropology from a Pragmatic Point of View* (*Anthropologie in pragmatischer Hinsicht*, 1798), although a late work, addressed subjects that went back to Kant's lectures at the Albertus University of Königsberg beginning in 1772.[4] In the *Anthropology*, Kant identified unconscious thought with the *petites perceptions* of Leibniz. 'Sense perceptions and sensations of which we are not aware but whose existence we can undoubtedly infer, that is, obscure ideas …', according to Kant, 'constitute an immeasurable field' (p. 19).[5] Clear ideas are only a minute portion of all ideas, most of which are obscure, Kant explained in Section 5 of the *Anthropology*, 'On the Ideas We Have Without Being Aware of Them'. He posited two levels of consciousness. The first is direct or unmediated (*unmittelbar*), full consciousness in perception. The second is indirect or mediated (*mittelbar*), partially unconscious perception involving indirect representations that are dark and obscure (*dunkel*): 'we can be indirectly conscious of having an idea, although we are not directly conscious of it' (p. 18). We draw conclusions about what we perceive without being conscious of perceiving every detail. The vast majority of our perceptions are of the details which we do not consciously perceive, but which contribute to the conclusions and judgements we make in the act of perceiving.

In the *Critique of Pure Reason*, self-knowledge on the part of the thinking subject, bound by the limitation of succession in time, is only possible in the activity of discursive reason connected to empirical experience. Self-knowledge is only possible as an other to self that is defined by temporal experience but made possible by the self (unconscious thought) that is inaccessible to temporal, empirical experience and the thought that is connected to it. The thinking subject within the representation of time, from the category in a priori intuition or the manifold of inner sense, would be the 'ego', according to Gilles Deleuze in *Kant's Critical Philosophy*, as opposed to the 'I' that is the inaccessible self in the inner sense. The inaccessible I in the interiority of unconscious thought affects and makes possible the cognitive activity of the ego in the exteriority of temporal discursiveness, creating a self-alienated and split subject. In the words of Deleuze, 'our interiority constantly divides us from ourselves, splits us in two: a splitting in two which never runs its course, since time has no end … an oscillation which constitutes time'.[6] The human subject is thus caught between the play of mirror reflections, having no access to the interiority of intuition or unconscious thought, or the exteriority of the objects of sense perception, both of which can only be known as representations in appearance, given by the imagination through language. The subject is defined as split, and in constant oscillation, circling around a void, an inaccessible object of desire created by the function of language that has no access to its source.

In the *Critique of Pure Reason*, time can only exist in the representation of it to the discursive ego by the inner sense. Time is represented a priori 'through the synthesis of the manifold which sensibility presents in its original receptivity' (A99–100). In the apprehension of the intuition, time is generated or manufactured, in the productive intellect and the productive imagination, in unconscious thought. Time is then the framework of the inner sense in which the faculties of the reproductive imagination can operate, combining the particulars of sense perception into the manifold of subjective experience. In the framework of time, imagination reproduces past representations, and anticipates future representations, in order to incorporate them into present representations, in a temporal succession. The associations of the different representations in time is based on a priori principles or the categories of intuition, communicated to the imagination by the schemata, or the logos, as it were, the *logos endiathetos* or unuttered word in classical philosophy.

The schemata, in the words of Rudolf Makkreel, in *Imagination and Interpretation in Kant*, are 'a priori products of the imagination that mediate between concepts and empirical appearances',[7] as the *logos endiathetos* mediates between the intelligible and the sensible. The schema has no empirical content, but must be both intellectual and sensible. The schemata apply the categories to imagination in order to form the groundwork of the subjective empirical experience of the objects of sense perception. Imagination mediates between the categories as universal concepts and sensible intuition as composed of empirical particulars. The framework for the mediation is time, within which the categories are unfolded as particulars, from the subjective intuition of inner sense to the objective cogitation of discursive reason. The framework of time allows for the temporal associations of representations to be combined in such a way as the manifold can be translated into sense experience. The most important function of the productive, transcendental imagination is to produce the temporal schemata, through representation in language, so that the sensible can be experienced as a manifold in intuition.

There are schemata of both sensible concepts in discursive reason and pure concepts of the understanding in intuition. As the framework for the function of imagination, which is both sensible and intelligible, reproductive and productive, schemata are both sensible and intelligible. The schemata of the pure concepts are independent of any sensible form and thus cannot be translated into an image, while the schemata of the sensible concepts are that through which images are possible in imagination. The schema is not a property of a sensible concept, but is a necessary basis for any sensible concept. The schema is an archetype, the universal concept or intelligible to which all particular forms must conform, but in relation to which all are imperfect or incomplete realisations. A building is always an incomplete realisation of the architectural idea of it. The source of the apprehension of architecture in unconscious thought is inaccessible to the experience of architecture in conscious thought and perception.

NOTES

1 Immanuel Kant, *Critique of Pure Reason*, trans. Norman Kemp Smith (London: Macmillan / New York: St Martin's Press, 1968).

2 Theodor Lipps, *Psychological Studies*, trans. Herbert C. Sanborn (Baltimore, MD: The Williams & Wilkins Company, 1926), p. 21.

3 Immanuel Kant, *Theoretical Philosophy 1755–1770*, trans. and ed. David Walford, *The Cambridge Edition of the Works of Immanuel Kant* (Cambridge: Cambridge University Press, 1992), p. 237. See Angus Nicholls and Martin Liebscher, 'Introduction: Thinking the Unconscious', in Angus Nicholls and Martin Liebscher (eds), *Thinking the Unconscious: Nineteenth-Century German Thought* (Cambridge: Cambridge University Press, 2010), p. 10.

4 Joel Faflak, *Romantic Psychoanalysis: The Burden of the Mystery* (Albany, NY: State University of New York Press, 2008), p. 48.

5 Immanuel Kant, *Anthropology From a Pragmatic Point of View*, trans. Victor Lyle Dowdell (Carbondale, IL: Southern Illinois University Press, 1978).

6 Gilles Deleuze, *Kant's Critical Philosophy: The Doctrine of the Faculties* [*La Philosophie Critique de Kant*], trans. Hugh Tomlinson and Barbara Habberjam (Minneapolis, MN: University of Minnesota Press, 1984 [1963]), p. ix.

7 Rudolf A. Makkreel, *Imagination and Interpretation in Kant: The Hermeneutical Import of the* Critique of Judgment (London and Chicago, IL: The University of Chicago Press, 1990), p. 1.

3

Gradations of Consciousness and Claude Bragdon's 'Space-Conquest'

Christina Malathouni

INTRODUCTION

The concept of 'space' has held a key role throughout twentieth century architectural theory and practice and continues to evolve and contribute to contemporary architectural discourse in the early decades of the twenty-first century. The earliest explicit introduction of the term as a principal architectural category has been dated to the early 1890s and attributed to a small group of German aesthetic philosophers.[1] Associated with Kant's naming of 'space' and 'time' as our two *a priori* intuitions, this use of the term space embraced its dual meaning both as a mental property and as a physical extension or dimension. It therefore associated architectural creation and architectural aesthetics with the human subject and was directly linked with the development of psychological aesthetics and a 'scientific' approach to art history.[2]

Overlooked in studies of these German origins of the association between space and architecture, the American architect, mystic and theorist Claude Fayette Bragdon (1866–1946) was equally a pioneer in this new tradition.[3] Bragdon lived and practised in the northeast of the United States of America – mainly within New York State and around the axis outlined by Rochester and New York City – with the exception of his *Wanderjahr* in 1893. He led a prolific and multifarious career. In addition to practising architecture from the 1890s to the early 1920s, Bragdon was interested, and actively involved, in graphic design, 'colour music' and theatrical design. He was also committed to the theoretical exploration of all such design activities and his multifarious interests included lecturing and writing on an equally varied range of subjects that exceeded the areas of art and design.

Bragdon's curious mind combined his mystically-inclined worldview with a profound interest in scientific developments. Both Modern Theosophy, that took on the role of the overarching expression of his mystical ideas, and his parallel interest in mathematics, which equally carried a mystical basis via the Pythagorean philosophy of 'number', supported his interest in a systematic, 'scientific' approach to knowledge and also lent his mystical ideas to what he repeatedly described as a 'modern' approach. His adoption and strong advocacy of the then particularly popular notion of the spatial 'Fourth Dimension' was also rooted in his interest in mathematics and further linked to both mystical and 'scientific' ideas. Through his articles in architectural and other magazines, his series of books, and his delivery of numerous lectures, his ideas were communicated to a wide audience.

Inherent in Bragdon's special interest in the 'Fourth Dimension' was his broader interest in the generic notion of 'space' and its adoption as a central feature of his architectural aesthetics. What is of special interest for the discussion here, both these central features in Bragdon's own theories – the generic notion of 'space' and its fourth-dimensional version – are directly linked to his interest in 'consciousness' and its various states and gradations, including the notion of the 'unconscious'. As a result, although Bragdon's work developed independently from those late nineteenth century art historians hitherto attributed with the earliest association of space and architecture, there are remarkable parallels. Although geographically and linguistically distinct, his thought was nonetheless influenced by the same leading philosophers, physiologists and psychologists that had influenced his German contemporaries. These parallels can serve as the particular lens through which we can start discerning the role that an 'architectural unconscious' could play in our readings of historic and contemporary architectural theory and practice. At the same time, though, Bragdon's engagement with new types of space and his various propositions for their representation carry the potential to serve as a link between the inner reality of subjects of architecture and the physical reality of objects of architecture, including such a concept of an 'architectural unconscious'.

This chapter starts with a discussion of Bragdon's association of space and architecture in relation to his architectural aesthetics, and also the impact that his interest in new types of space, with their complex relation to human subjectivity, had on his understanding of various states of consciousness. The discussion then traces various connections between Bragdon's ideas and nineteenth century developments in Idealist philosophy and in physiological psychology. The last two parts of the chapter present a brief summary of Bragdon's applications of these ideas into his design work and argue that his use of representations of higher-dimensional figures can help introduce the concept of an 'architectural unconscious'. By putting forward a speculative proposition for an 'architectural unconscious', the chapter aims to demonstrate how the concept of the 'unconscious' can serve as a reminder of the full scope of our subjective association with architecture as well as a reminder of the vast potential of architectural representations – beyond misleadingly utilitarian conventions or limiting connections to materiality and sensory perception, and thus also embracing ongoing digital innovations.

STATES OF CONSCIOUSNESS AND THE 'CONQUEST OF SPACE'

Bragdon introduced his adoption of a direct association of space and architecture in his principal treatise on architectural aesthetics, *The Beautiful Necessity: Seven*

Essays on Theosophy and Architecture.[4] In the opening pages of his treatise, he stated that various art forms are distinct, yet they merge into one another. In such a series of art forms:

> *music, which is in time alone, without any relation to space; and architecture, which is in space alone, without any relation to time, are ... seen to stand at opposite ends of the art spectrum.*[5]

This position can be traced directly back to Arthur Schopenhauer's principal treatise, *Die Welt als Wille und Vorstellung* (1818; 1844; 1859; first English translation, 1883)[6] and as such it bears the Kantian (and Schopenhauerian) position regarding space and time as our two *a priori* intuitions. What is more, Bragdon clearly underlined the direct association between space and consciousness in his own text as he named the twin notions of space and time 'what philosophers call the two "modes of consciousness"'.[7]

Following this adoption of the notion of 'space' as a principal category of architecture, crucial for the subsequent development of Bragdon's position was his interest in new ideas about types of space that did not follow the principles of Euclidean geometry. Although not exclusive, most important for Bragdon was his involvement in the 'Fourth Dimension' tradition which originated in the establishment of *n*-dimensional geometry as a valid geometrical system during the second quarter of the nineteenth century. As a novel geometrical system established for the very first time after almost two millennia, in the course of which Euclidean geometry had been thought to be the only possible geometry, *n*-dimensional geometry – together with non-Euclidean geometry[8] – caused no small intellectual turmoil. Both New Geometries[9] raised crucial questions concerning the nature of geometrical axioms – which was linked to the possibility of attaining true knowledge – and the nature of space. Subsequently associated with mystical ideas, both New Geometries had a widespread effect on the public imagination and early twentieth century artistic production.[10]

Bragdon first became acquainted with the novel notion of the 'Fourth Dimension' sometime by August 1900[11] and was so captivated by it that he came to be considered the key advocate of the 'Fourth Dimension' in the USA, known not only for his writings on the subject but also for his various graphic representations. As Bragdon's involvement in the 'Fourth Dimension' tradition developed, the direct continuity from his early interest in the notion of 'space' is strongly underlined by the number of alternative terms used to denote the 'Fourth Dimension': for instance, 'Higher Space', 'hyperspace', and '4 space'. This continuity is crucial as regards the transcendental connections of the notion of 'space' as this was derived from Schopenhauer's treatise and also has key implications as regards the principal discussion here about Bragdon's special interest in gradations of consciousness.

In his 1913 *Primer of Higher Space*, Bragdon introduced the idea that the revision of our perceived 'dimensionality' of space could address any seeming limitations of our 'consciousness'. In order to demonstrate this, Bragdon adopted the notion of a 'threshold of consciousness', as put forward by the German philosopher and spiritualist Carl du Prel (1839–99) in his 1889 book entitled *The Philosophy of*

Mysticism.[12] This 'threshold' was used to denote the line at which the distinction between the 'real' and the 'transcendental' is drawn, and Du Prel argues that this line was 'movable'. Bragdon explained how Du Prel links the organic evolution to the evolution of consciousness: 'From the standpoint of every animal organism we can divide external nature into two parts'. One of these two halves escapes perception, Du Prel argues, and this is therefore designated as 'transcendental' for the organism in question. As Bragdon adopted Du Prel's position, he quoted from *The Philosophy of Mysticism*:

> *The biological rise and the rise of consciousness thus signify a constant removal of the boundary between representation and reality at the cost of the transcendental part of the world, and in favour of the perceived part.*[13]

Although it is not clear how Bragdon became acquainted with Du Prel's 1885 text, this had been published in English by 1889 and his personal correspondence confirms that Bragdon read the book by 1912.[14] The Translator's Note in the English edition points out Du Prel's debt to the philosophies of Kant and Schopenhauer and this, as well as the principal title of the book, would have clearly caught Bragdon's attention. Not revealed in its title, but of special interest here, was Du Prel's principal discussion: 'Somnambulism'; with large sections devoted to 'dreams'. What is more, the translator C.C. (Charles Carleton) Massey positions the book within the early tradition of 'the Unconscious', and specifically points out Du Prel's debt to German metaphysical philosopher Eduard von Hartmann (1842–1906).

As Bragdon drew from theories on how to develop a new 'space sense' via education – as put forward by Charles Howard Hinton (1853–1907),[15] a key proponent of the 'Fourth Dimension' whose writings had a strong influence on Bragdon – he linked Du Prel's theory to the notion of 'space'. On this basis, he further argued that the evolution of consciousness is identical with the 'conquest of space':

> *if this shifting psycho-physical threshold is simply the dividing line between lower and higher spaces, then the whole evolutionary process consists in the conquest, dimension by dimension, of successive space-worlds.*[16]

To make this position clearer Bragdon presented examples of such successive levels of organic and spatial evolution and, eventually, also used these to pronounce our further potential:

> *everything which is to us transcendental exists nevertheless in some space. It is therefore possible that by an intention of consciousness we may be able first to apprehend, then to perceive as real, that which is now considered transcendental.*[17]

These aspects of Du Prel's work are not further developed in the *Primer*, but Bragdon addressed the matter of this 'conquest of space' in his book *Four-dimensional Vistas*, published ten years later.[18] Bragdon continued to use here mathematics and science as the foundation of his ideas. In his Introduction, he listed novel types of space and time which he saw as contributing to equally variable types and grades of consciousness: the idea of 'higher space', which he related here to the concept of the curvature of space, and the concept of 'curved time' (p. 9). Bragdon saw both these ideas as opening vistas, which 'offer "glimpses that may make us less forlorn"' (p. 9). Following from this tenet, Bragdon put forward the principal line of argument of his book: 'the need for an enlarged space-concept' (pp. 11–12).

Bragdon first elaborated on physical phenomena that can be informed by what he calls 'the dimensional ladder', and then moved on to a series of subjective experiences in which the notions of space and time take on qualities beyond their everyday understanding: 'transcendental physics' as well as sleep and dreams and the 'night side of consciousness'. Returning to discussions from the early tradition of the New Geometries that related the type of space accepted as real to the particular abilities of its 'inhabitants' (a point that we will see again in the discussion of Hermann von Helmholtz and Gustav Theodor Fechner below), Bragdon argued for the 'subjectivity of space' and also specifically referred to mathematician and philosopher Henri Poincaré (1854–1912) and his position that the assumed three-dimensionality of our space is only *'a property residing … in human intelligence'* (emphasis in the original) (p. 11).

THE 'NINETEENTH CENTURY UNCONSCIOUS'

The variations in states of consciousness to which Bragdon repeatedly referred do not always reflect a specifically psychological or psychoanalytical approach. Despite his frequent use of the term 'unconscious/ly', most of the times this appears commonplace,[19] rather than directly related to psychological or psychoanalytical theories of the 'unconscious'. Nonetheless, there is also ample evidence that his involvement in such ideas was committed and long-lasting and there are numerous, strong connections to the 'nineteenth century unconscious'.[20] In fact, Bragdon's approach reflected both key – and often competing – nineteenth century trends: firstly, a philosophical (metaphysical and Idealist) approach and, secondly, one based on the experimental methods of the emerging field of physiological psychology that was to lead to a formalist approach in late nineteenth and early twentieth century art history. In addition to the notions of 'unconscious' and 'subconscious', worth noting here is Bragdon's use of other variations of the notion of 'consciousness'. In 1924 he added the notion of 'super-conscious, or cosmic self'[21] to his list of degrees of consciousness, whereas there are also references to the possibility of collective states of existence: either referring to the possibility of a 'community of consciousness',[22] or arguing that we could 'conceive of each individual as a "slice" or cross-section of a higher being', subsequently pointing to the notion of 'humanity'.[23]

The primary link to the philosophical unconscious is of course Arthur Schopenhauer's principal treatise, *Die Welt als Wille und Vorstellung*, in which Bragdon's key association of space and architecture was directly rooted. A number of scholars have identified Schopenhauer's use of the notion of the 'will' as containing the foundations of the psychoanalytical 'unconscious'.[24] Consequently,

Schopenhauer has been named 'the true philosophical father of psychoanalysis'[25] and holds a prominent position in the history of the 'unconscious'. In his typically eclectic manner, despite the various direct influences from Schopenhauer's philosophy, Bragdon positioned the notion of the 'will' – that is, Schopenhauer's version of the 'unconscious' – among a number of other names used for 'the thing in itself': 'which has been variously called the Will, the Word, the One Life, the World Soul'.[26]

Besides this metaphysical approach to the unconscious, there are numerous elements in Bragdon's writings that reveal his exposure to key developments in experimental psychology which was to play an instrumental role in the subsequent association between sensory perception and formalist and physiological aesthetics. For instance, in his *Four-dimensional Vistas* Bragdon specifically referred to findings of the 'modern experimental science in the domain of physiology and psychology' (p. 71) and it is in the same publication that he related his discussion of special states of consciousness, such as sleep and dreams, to sensory perception and external stimuli. Bragdon stressed here that:

> *Sleep states are not abnormal, but part and parcel of the life experience of the individual. When a person is asleep he has only become unresponsive to the mass of stimuli of the external world which constitutes his environment (p. 77).*

To further support the position that 'dream experiences are [...] as real as any other' (p. 78), Bragdon linked his position to his earlier discussion of a 'movable threshold of consciousness':

> *Du Prel and others have shown that the difference between ordinary dreaming, somnambulance, trance and ecstasy, is only a matter of redistribution of thresholds – that they are all related states and merge into one another (p. 79).*

Other points in the same text also recall nineteenth century versions of the unconscious, as Bragdon related the role of the 'subconscious' to the 'stream of conscious experience' and stressed the importance of feelings and emotions as causes rather than effects:

> *Ideas, emerging from the subconscious, approach, intersect, recede from, and re-approach the stream of conscious experience; taking the forms of aversions and desires, they register themselves in action (pp. 72–3).*

Bragdon linked this position to the:

> *modern psychology [that] has demonstrated the existence of a great undercurrent of mental and emotional life, transcending the individual's conscious experience, in which the most complex processes are carried on without the individual's conscious participation (p. 92).*

Such connections between Bragdon's writings and psychological and psychoanalytical developments are not limited to anonymous references to key notions.

Instead, there are numerous references to key figures in these two areas in several of his writings. Very limited, but most notable, is Bragdon's reference to 'Freud'. In a 1920 article entitled 'Ouspensky on Love', Bragdon discussed the *Tertium Organum* by the Russian Peter Demianovich Ouspensky (1878–1947).[27] Bragdon mentioned here 'Freud' on the subject of 'love', but did not elaborate on his understanding of Freud's positions. Instead, he rather dismissed Freud's position (and, in fact, Schopenhauer's too) in favour of Ouspensky's.[28]

References to earlier proponents of experimental psychology appear more frequently in Bragdon's manuscripts and published writings. Specifically, references to two of the fathers of experimental psychology appear repeatedly in his writings: the eminent German scientist Hermann Ludwig Ferdinand von Helmholtz (1821–94) and the American psychologist and philosopher William James (1842–1910). Both James and Helmholtz serve as good examples of those particular aspects of scientific progress during the course of the nineteenth century that focussed on human nature and informed the way in which metaphysical inquiries were to be tackled in new ways that promised to manifest scientific rigour.[29]

Bragdon was familiar with James's work from an early age. Several clippings relating to James found their way into Bragdon's scrapbooks[30] and there is also a reference to James's article 'The Hidden Self',[31] including a discussion of 'M. Janet's experiments in hypnotism', in one of Bragdon's early 1890s manuscripts.[32] He also read James's *Varieties of Religious Experience* and in his 1904 article 'Maeterlinck' affirmed his perception of diverse expressions of 'mysticism' as equivalent in their essence by quoting James's book.[33]

Bragdon's mentions of Helmholtz reveal a more direct connection to experimental psychology and its relation to sensory perception and aesthetics. As Bragdon started publishing his architectural aesthetics, his writings included several recurring mentions of the role of the senses in relation to aesthetic judgment. In the very first presentation of his 'philosophy of architecture' to the public in 1901, Bragdon revealed the complex ways in which this interweaving of 'modern' mystical ideas and 'scientific' developments were to inform his aesthetics:

> *What aspects our architecture will assume, under the impulse of the mystical spirit, whether existing forms will be re-animated, or new ones evolved, it is impossible to predict, but the laws of beauty to which that architecture must inevitably conform may be known perfectly, for these are inherent in the nature of human intelligence, the same in all styles and at all periods.*[34]

Although not named in the above excerpt, Helmholtz is quoted as the source of this position in subsequent versions of Bragdon's treatise, as he wrote that:

> *Helmholtz says, 'No doubt it is now entertained that beauty is subject to laws and rules dependent on the nature of human intelligence'.*[35]

Neither James nor Helmholtz appears to have had a direct input as regards Bragdon's interest in special states of consciousness, however, it is particularly important to include them both in the discussion here. Not only did they both play a central role in the nineteenth century developments as regards experimental psychology,[36] but they were also familiar with the New Geometries: James was in personal correspondence with Hinton,[37] and took a particular interest in his fourth-dimensional ideas; whereas Helmholtz himself played a key role in the early popularisation of the New Geometries and is known for one of the earliest examples of imaginary two-dimensional worlds for the explanation of ideas of new types of space, first employed in the discussion of curved space.[38]

On this same line, there is another leading figure in the establishment of experimental psychology who must be discussed here in relation to Bragdon: Gustav Theodor Fechner (1801–87). Just like Helmholtz, Fechner's work serves as an introduction to the strong connections between the emphasis on the human, the development of modern psychology, the New Geometries, an interest in new understandings of the notion of 'space' in the course of the nineteenth century, and the possibilities that new types of space opened up as regards subjectivity.[39]

> *[Fechner] writing under the pseudonym of 'Dr. Mises' in Vier Paradoxa of 1846, may have published the first discussion of two-dimensional beings unaware of the third dimension that surrounds them, thus relating the type of space accepted as real to the particular abilities of its 'inhabitants' and suggesting an analogy of our three-dimensional existence in a four-dimensional world.*[40]

What is more, although Bragdon could not have read Fechner's foundational *Elemente der Psychophysik* (*Elements of Psychophysics*) (1860),[41] and he referred to Du Prel as the source for his use of the notion of a 'threshold of evolution', there are interesting parallels between Bragdon's and Fechner's employment of the notion of 'threshold' in relation to the 'unconscious'.

Fechner used the concept of the threshold in his *Elements of Psychophysics*, where, as the title suggests, he looked into the relations of the physical and the psychological worlds.[42] His interest in the relation between body and mind was typical of his time. It came as a response to René Descartes's division of the world of experience 'into matter (extended substance) and mind (unextended substance)'[43] and had a long past in mental philosophy. What was novel at this point in time was that the new approach drew extensively from developments in physics and physiology that fed into the study of perception, and from there on to modern psychology.[44]

Fechner stated that his work aimed to '[consider] the empirical relationship between these two sides of existence [body and mind] as a functional one, which itself excludes this one-sidedness [of materialism or idealism]'.[45] In this context, the concept of the threshold became primarily applied to sensations (*Sinnesempfindungen*)[46] and denoted 'the point at which a stimulus or a stimulus difference becomes noticeable or disappears'.[47] Fechner differentiated between outer and inner psychophysics and suggested that, as regards 'inner psychophysics', 'stimulus thresholds, differential thresholds, and relative thresholds' needed to be considered in relation to 'the underlying psychophysical processes', and perhaps assume 'a threshold value' for these processes.[48] As a result, Fechner went from his initial application of the notion of the threshold to sensations, i.e. relating to outer psychophysics, to the implications of such thresholds for inner psychophysics. His 'psychophysical parallelism' therefore formed the premise for Fechner's conception of the unconscious,[49] as he 'quite unintentionally discovered that':[50]

> *the relations between the conscious and unconscious life of representations, sleeping and waking, general and particular phenomena of consciousness, in short the most general relations of the life of the soul, allow a very simple and satisfying psychophysical representation [i.e. modeling] owing to the premise that the threshold concept is transferable onto the psychophysical movement.*[51]

Through such links to 'sleep', Fechner also directly related the concepts of threshold, unconscious and sensations by attributing to these positive and negative mathematical values. He wrote:

> *As long as the stimulus or stimulus difference remains below threshold its perception is, as one says, unconscious. As stimulus and stimulus difference fall deeper and deeper below threshold, the level of stimuli in the atmosphere stay below threshold and the corresponding unconsciousness becomes lower. Thus distant sounds or the olfactory sensations remain unconscious until their intensity exceeds a given magnitude, their threshold. We are naturally led to the use of negative values to designate these unconscious sensations, if we call the threshold zero and the conscious sensations positive.*[52]

'SUPERSENSUOUS LIFE' AND THE 'NEW AESTHETIC'

Although Bragdon referred to Du Prel for his use of the notion of a 'threshold', a comparison between Fechner's and Bragdon's use of this concept, and consequently their use of the unconscious too, is of special interest. It highlights the particular position that Bragdon adopted as regards the role of sensory perception and various states of consciousness in his architectural aesthetics. On the one hand, although Fechner's conception of the unconscious 'played a role in both scientific psychophysics and in his speculative philosophy',[53] 'when it came to the foundations of his science (i.e. that of psychophysics), [he] was even more critical of metaphysics than were his contemporaries'.[54] His 'point of departure was scientifically serious, or at least far less metaphysically suspicious and compromising than those of von Hartmann and Schopenhauer'.[55] On the other hand, Bragdon's work came about half a century later than Fechner's, yet his active engagement with mystical systems of belief constitutes the principal foundation of his theories and is clearly underlined by his references to mysticism and Theosophy in the titles of his principal texts on architectural aesthetics.[56] His approach retained elements of early metaphysical systems, with a clear adherence to Idealism. In addition to Schopenhauer, his interest in Idealism often took him back to the relation between phenomenal reality and 'shadows', as exemplified by Plato's allegory of the cave. In one of his last books Bragdon directly related the unconscious to such an Idealist viewpoint, as he wrote about:

> *forces [that may be] only the shadow-play of a conscious intelligence which for a lack of a better name we call the Unconscious – not because it is unconscious, but because for the most part we are unconscious of it (emphasis in the original).*[57]

Bragdon's engagement with mathematics and some limited understanding of scientific developments were added to his theories as a new, 'modern' approach to mystical beliefs, but he had never trained in, or practised, any scientific discipline. As regards psychology in particular, Bragdon specifically related his particular preoccupation with 'mysticism' to the 'modern' world and 'psychology' in three articles published in 1903 and 1904.[58] At the same time, though, his principal Idealist source – namely, Schopenhauer – also related to the scientific developments in the field of psychology, since he embraced contemporary developments in physiological experiments and is noted for his early contribution in the newly developed 'psychological aesthetics'.[59]

Bragdon's embracing of the key role attributed to 'perception' by Schopenhauer was further supported by several of his other sources too. Several of his reading notes in his 1890s journals reveal that Bragdon had found extensive discussions of the role of the 'senses' in his Eastern philosophical readings. What is more, in the same passage in *The Beautiful Necessity* where Bragdon associated space and architecture and named the twin notions of space and time 'what philosophers call the two "modes of consciousness"', he also introduced 'Art' as 'an expression of the Self in terms of sense' (p. 9). At the same time, though, adopting a position attributed to Honoré de Balzac, Bragdon also repeatedly wrote – in *The Beautiful Necessity* and elsewhere – that 'art is idealized creation: nature carried to a higher power by reason of its passage through human consciousness' (pp. 22–3).

It is these parallel 'vehicles' – of sensory perception and consciousness – that support Bragdon's dual understanding of 'beauty' as both aesthetic and 'significant':[60] aesthetic beauty is largely based on the role of the senses and the 'laws of beauty' that are linked to human intelligence; whereas 'significant' beauty is linked to mystical ideas and to human consciousness in its various states. What is of particular interest for the discussion here is the possibility of 'evolution' both of 'perception' and of 'consciousness'. Indeed, Bragdon embraced the idea of 'evolution of consciousness' from Du Prel's 'threshold' and, in two of his subsequent books, he also turned to Ralph Waldo Emerson's writings for further elaboration on 'perception', its link to 'consciousness' and its potential for 'evolution'. Bragdon quoted from Emerson the phrase 'Perception has a destiny' in his 1915 *Projective Ornament* and his 1916 *Four-dimensional Vistas*. In the latter, Bragdon simply included Emerson's phrase as an epigram ('"Perception has a destiny". Emerson'); yet, in the former he directly associated 'perception' with 'consciousness' and argued that the possibility of their 'evolution' was what provided hope for 'new beauty' and a 'new art'.[61]

In this same book, the *Projective Ornament*, Bragdon applied his ideas of new types of space to his own design theory. He linked both his choice of 'ornament' and his choice of fourth-dimensional geometry to the above discussion regarding the role of consciousness and its potential for evolution. He repeatedly stated that ornament is that element of design most directly related to psychology,[62] called this association a 'riddle' and argued that it 'may be solved by recourse to the fourth dimension of space'.[63] What is more, Bragdon stressed the role of evolving 'consciousness' and also the gradual distancing from materiality and sensory perception. He explained that he saw consciousness at that time changing direction and moving 'away from the contemplation of the facts of materiality towards the mysteries of the supersensuous life'. As he read in the phrase 'The Fourth Dimension of Space' the most comprehensive expression of this change in consciousness, he concluded that fourth-dimensional geometry was the most appropriate basis for the 'decorative motifs of the new aesthetic'.[64]

To achieve this, Bragdon adopted, or devised, various techniques that allowed him to represent 'higher dimensional' figures in three-dimensional space, or in the two-dimensional space of graphic representations, such as double parallel perspective, axonometrics, and 'folding down'.[65] Although these higher-dimensional figures cannot be realised in our physical space, and Bragdon's higher-dimensional theories could not be directly translated into architectural design, this hardly limits their value. Bragdon used these representations to mediate between 'sensory perception' and 'consciousness' and, similarly to Du Prel, to push back the boundaries of the 'real', away from the limitations of materiality and 'towards the mysteries of the supersensuous life'.

'ARCHITECTURAL UNCONSCIOUS'

Both the unconscious, as a special state of consciousness, and the 'Fourth Dimension', as a special type of space, offer us a new, extended reality in relation to our psychical and physical worlds respectively. Therefore Bragdon's engagement with both ideas invites a proposition for an 'architectural unconscious' that can be defined as the engagement of the full scope of human subjectivity with the full potential of space variations. Such space variations need not have an immediate application in our everyday physical environment, but can be communicated by means of architectural representations – either hand-drawn or digital.

Du Prel's argument for the role of the 'representation in terms of form' supports the 'reality' of Bragdon's representations of higher-dimensional figures for the generation of his Projective Ornament, as they push our 'threshold of consciousness' beyond our material world. When seen as architectural representations, the value of Bragdon's representations further supports the position here as regards an 'architectural unconscious': as Marco Frascari points out in his Introduction to the book *From Models to Drawings: Imagination and Representation in Architecture*, architectural drawings serve a role that is far wider than a mere operational convention within the profession and can be considered to be 'the most sophisticated expressions of architectural theory'.[66] 'The drawing process is a cosmospoiesis that can help to invent better futures and make potential worlds' (p. 4) and also the drawing 'teaches the gaze to proceed beyond the visible image into an infinity whereby something new of the invisible is encountered' (p. 7). Architectural drawings should be seen as 'a "shower of gifts", and this complex showering is the reality of architecture, understood graphically. Architectural drawings are psychophysical expressions of architecture' (p. 6).

By following the evolution of Bragdon's association of various states of consciousness with various types of space, before these found a graphic representation in his 'Projective Ornament', this proposition of 'architectural unconscious' can become clearer. The history of Bragdon's association of various states of consciousness with various types of space, or dimensional progressions, has been particularly long. First of all, the association between evolutionary hierarchy and dimensional progressions appeared in Bragdon's writings at a very early stage, long before his involvement with the 'Fourth Dimension' or Du Prel's text. On 10 February 1891, just one day before he quoted from Schopenhauer that 'architecture is in space alone',[67] Bragdon added to his notebook:

> *Everywhere is progression, that is evolution, the development of manifestation in space and time of that which is inherent. Points generate lines, lines surfaces and surfaces solids. The seed is a point, the stem is a line, the leaf is a surface, the fruit is a solid. In the mineral kingdom lines predominate, in the vegetable, surfaces, in the animal, solids.*[68]

Notably, this early discussion was limited to the first three dimensions (point-line-surface-solid); yet, suggestions of the potential for an expansion to a higher level were already present. References to Theosophical books over this same period included particular mentions of Theosophical ideas such as the 'higher plane' of existence, or 'higher life'.[69]

As his involvement in the 'Fourth Dimension' developed, Bragdon used the tenet on the 'conquest of space' in his *Four-dimensional Vistas* to cover a wide range of manifestations of life: the birth and growth of organisms; the fight of nations over land; or as measure of individual success by means of the amount of space each commands as part of his property (pp. 31–2). He also linked this discussion to the development of the skyscraper which he related to man's endeavour to augment 'his *space-potency*' (emphasis in the original) by expanding in a vertical direction. Notably, though, here again, in all architectural examples mentioned, Bragdon did not go further than the third dimension. As in all his discussion about dimensional sequence in humankind's creations, he justified this limitation to three dimensions as due to the difference between organisms and artefacts, that is, machines. He argued that it is the 'life principle', namely, the power of growth and renewal, that distinguishes the 'most perfect machine' from the 'humblest flower'; and, in an analogous way, 'the highest product of the vegetable kingdom' is inferior to man, since man 'can reflect upon his own and the world's becoming, while the plant can only become' (pp. 35–6).

Bragdon explained how 'the Higher Space Hypothesis' elucidates 'these differences of power and function' as dependent on 'varying potencies of movement in the secret causeways and corridors of space' and it is in this connection that he re-asserted the connection between 'evolution' and the 'conquest of space':

> *The higher functions of consciousness – volition, emotion, intellection – may be correlated in some way with the higher powers of number, and with the*

> *corresponding higher developments of space. Thus the difference between physics and metaphysics would become a difference of degree and not of kind. Evolution is to be conceived of as a continuous pushing back of the boundary between representation and reality, or as a conquest of space (p. 36).*

The 'negative' mathematical values that Fechner associated with 'unconscious sensations', as well as the negation implied by the prefix 'un-' in the word 'unconscious' (or the subtraction suggested by the prefix 'sub-' in the word 'subconscious'), may appear to be contradictory to Bragdon's designation of such functions of consciousness as 'higher'. If, however, the notion 'conscious' is seen as restrictive and limited, one can understand the 'elevation', or 'enhancement', suggested by the term 'higher'. It is in this sense that the notion of an 'architectural unconscious' is considered here in relation to Bragdon's use of fourth-dimensional geometry in design applications and their association to 'higher functions of consciousness', as the potential for architecture to expand beyond practical needs, physical presence or sensory perception and to relate to the full scope of human subjectivity.

To conclude this discussion, it is worth looking at the widely acknowledged origins of the use of the term 'space' in the modern architectural vocabulary and Bragdon's special role in this. As pointed out in the Introduction, Bragdon's adoption of the notion of 'space' as a central concept in his architectural aesthetics appeared exceptionally early but was not unique. The role of the notion of 'space' in modern architectural aesthetics has been discussed in several early studies of nineteenth century German aesthetics[70] and, more recently, has been further supported by Harry Francis Mallgrave and Eleftherios Ikonomou's 1993 publication of English translations of essays in German aesthetics of the late nineteenth century. The transition from metaphysical systems to physiological and experimental psychological approaches noted in the comparison between Fechner and Bragdon is also reflected in this early history of 'architectural space': Mallgrave and Ikonomou focus on the emergence of the 'science' of art history and the ways in which these essays were instrumental in the transition:

> *from the metaphysically based systems of Kant, Herbart,[71] and Friedrich Theodor Vischer to the more exciting formal analyses of physiological and psychological aesthetics, to the magisterial starts of Wölfflin, Riegl, Schmarsow, Frankl, and others (p. 66).*

Although Bragdon's work appears to have developed independently of his German contemporaries,[72] his manuscripts and published writings referred to some of the most important protagonists of these developments. For instance, Helmholtz and Fechner were two of the four scientists credited with 'the initial applications of the experimental method to the mind, the subject matter of the new psychology',[73] and both men are also specifically mentioned by Mallgrave and Ikonomou as having been a key influence on the development of 'psychological aesthetics'. Bragdon clearly picked on Helmholtz's point regarding the association of 'laws of beauty' and 'human intelligence'. What is more, Schopenhauer's emphasis on the perceptual act is also included in this discussion as having made an early contribution to this new approach to aesthetics.[74]

However, the particular novelty in Bragdon's work – his engagement with new types of space – allowed him to use particular symbolic representations to denote 'higher' qualities of human nature, including the 'unconscious' and various special states of consciousness. Bragdon therefore appears to adopt the 'recast[ing of] the foundations of architectural knowledge from objective nature to the subjective mind' that virtually a century later Mitchell Schwarzer was to identify in Schopenhauer's *The World as Will and Representation*, which he summed up as the transition from 'the classical to modern paradigms of architectural knowledge'.[75] At the same time, his in-depth involvement in the 'fourth dimension' tradition offered him a new design tool that served as a continuation of the 'spatial' appreciation of architecture that he adopted from Schopenhauer's philosophy and enabled him to extend the range of human subjectivity that is associated with architecture by encompassing various 'gradations' of consciousness.

CONCLUSION

By discussing the use of various gradations of the notion of 'consciousness' in Bragdon's work, this chapter highlights a significant transition as regards human subjectivity: from belief systems and metaphysics to an approach that aspired to take on the perceived epistemological rigour of mathematics and science. Nascent psychological and psychoanalytical explorations permeated Bragdon's work, which, in its turn, provides us with insights into their emerging relationship with architecture and the notion of 'architectural space' in particular.

The way in which Bragdon brought together all those various influences of his time was quite idiosyncratic and, to date, no direct following of his ideas has been established. Nonetheless, his work has been recognised as of historic significance for its early adoption of the direct association of 'space' and 'architecture' in the English language – albeit primarily from a German source, Schopenhauer's principal treatise. Although he was not alone in these endeavours, Bragdon went on to also adopt other crucial advancements in nineteenth century intellectual history, namely, the revolutionary establishment of new geometrical systems. A 'trademark' feature of Bragdon's theories – the 'Fourth Dimension' – lies at the centre of his particular contribution. Although this may appear as rather eccentric, this assessment is far from the truth if Bragdon's work is seen within its contemporary context.

The 'Fourth Dimension', and more generally the New Geometries, were widely popular and had a strong and widespread influence on early-twentieth century modern art, as Linda Dalrymple Henderson's seminal work demonstrated in 1983, with a second revised edition notably published as recently as 2013. Bragdon's engagement with new types of 'space', seen through the lens of innovative mathematical and scientific developments in the course of the nineteenth century, opened up new possibilities for our understanding of human subjectivity and the various degrees and states of consciousness, ranging from the unconscious and subconscious to the super-conscious. It allowed him to develop an innovative method by which to produce graphic representations that put forward a direct association between various special states of consciousness and manifestations of space that cannot be perceived by our bodily senses. In this way Bragdon's engagement with the 'unconscious' and other 'gradations' of consciousness invites the introduction and exploration of an 'architectural unconscious' that can enhance our readings of historic and contemporary architectural theory and practice and supports an appreciation of the full potential of architectural representations.

Considering that Henderson's work offers limited coverage of architecture, further research on the impact that special types of space had on architectural theory and practice is invited. Further research is also invited as regards the new possibilities offered by electronic media for architectural representations that allow the exploratory dynamic of Bragdon's 'space-conquest' – especially if we consider Bragdon's own very positive predisposition towards new technologies and the fact that digital technologies have been adopted in the investigation of new types of space, including the 'Fourth Dimension'.[76]

NOTES

1 Peter Collins, *Changing Ideals in Modern Architecture* (Montreal and Kingston, London, Ithaca, McGill: Queen's University Press, 1965; 2nd edn, 1998); Cornelis van de Ven, *Space in Architecture: The Evolution of a New Idea in the Theory and History of the Modern Movements* (Assen/Maastricht and Wolfeboro, NH: Van Gorcum, 1977; 3rd revised edn, 1987); Harry Francis Mallgrave and Eleftherios Ikonomou (eds), *Empathy, Form, and Space: Problems in German Aesthetics, 1873–1893* (Santa Monica, CA: Getty Center for the History of Art and the Humanities; Chicago, IL: University of Chicago Press, 1993); Adrian Forty, 'Space', in *Words and Buildings: A Vocabulary of Modern Architecture* (London: Thames and Hudson, 2000), pp. 256–75.

2 Harry Francis Mallgrave and Eleftherios Ikonomou (eds), *Empathy, Form, and Space*, p. 66.

3 See Christina Malathouni, 'In Search of the Beauty of Conscious Life: Claude Bragdon's "Spatial" "Philosophy of Architecture" and the "Fourth Dimension" Tradition' (PhD dissertation, University College London, 2010); 'Claude Bragdon Reads Arthur Schopenhauer: "Architecture is in Space Alone"', in Eugenia Victoria Ellis and Andrea G. Reithmayr (eds), *Claude Bragdon and The Beautiful Necessity* (Rochester, NY: RIT Cary Graphic Arts Press, 2010), pp. 3–8; and 'Architecture is the Pattern of Human Mind in Space: Claude F. Bragdon and the Spatial Concept of Architecture', in *The Journal of Architecture*, 18 (London: Routledge, 2013), pp. 553–69. See also: Jonathan Rider Massey, *Crystal and Arabesque: Claude Bragdon, Ornament, and Modern Architecture* (Pittsburgh, PA: University of Pittsburgh Press, 2009) and Eugenia Victoria Ellis and Andrea G. Reithmayr (eds), *Claude Bragdon and The Beautiful Necessity* (Rochester, NY: RIT Cary Graphic Arts Press, 2010).

4 First published in book form in 1910, but previously published as a series of articles: Claude Bragdon, 'The Beautiful Necessity: Being Essays upon Aesthetics', in *House and Garden* (New York: Condé Nast, January–June 1902); 'The Art of Architecture from the Standpoint of Theosophy', in *Theosophic Messenger* (San Francisco, CA: American Theosophic Society, May 1909); 'The Theosophy of Architecture', in *Theosophic Messenger* (San Francisco, CA: American Theosophic Society, June–November 1909); *The Beautiful Necessity: Seven Essays on Theosophy and Architecture* (Rochester, NY: The Manas Press, 1910).

5 Claude Bragdon, *The Beautiful Necessity*, p. 10.

6 'Architecture is in space alone, without any connection with time; and music is in time alone, without any connection with space. Schopenhauer'. Bragdon Family Papers [BFP], Department of Rare Books, Special Collections and Preservation, Rush Rhees Library, University of Rochester, NY, USA, A.B81 36:1, 11 February 1891. Also, Arthur Schopenhauer, *The World as Will and Idea*, trans. R.B. Haldane and J. Kemp, 3 vols (London: Routledge & Kegan Paul, 1964 [c. 1883]), vol. III, p. 239.

7 Claude Bragdon, *The Beautiful Necessity*, p. 10.

8 Various types of non-Euclidean geometry put forward the possibility of curved space and were first formulated in the 1820s.

9 'New geometry' is used as a relative term (Linda Dalrymple Henderson, *The Fourth Dimension and Non-Euclidean Geometry in Modern Art* [Princeton, NJ: Princeton University Press, 1983], p. xx, n. 3).

10 For a systematic study see Linda Dalrymple Henderson, *The Fourth Dimension and Non-Euclidean Geometry in Modern Art*. This publication remains, to date, the definitive study on the subject and a second revised edition by The MIT Press was published in March 2013.

11 BFP A.B81 1:6, Frank Gelett Burgess to Claude Bragdon, San Francisco, 1 August 1900.

12 Carl Du Prel, *The Philosophy of Mysticism*, trans. C.C. Massey, 2 vols (London: George Redway, 1889).

13 Claude Bragdon, *A Primer of Higher Space: The Fourth Dimension* (to which is added *Man the Square: A Higher Space Parable*) (London: Andrew Dakers Limited, 1939 [1913]), pp. 22–3.

14 BFP A.B81 27:9, letter from Claude Bragdon to Eugenie (Julier) Macaulay Bragdon, 16 August 1912.

15 Charles Howard Hinton, *A New Era of Thought*, completed by Alicia Boole and H.J. Falk (London: Swan Sonnenschein & Co., 1900 [1888]); *The Fourth Dimension* (London: Swan Sonnenschein & Co., 1906 [1904]).

16 Claude Bragdon, *A Primer of Higher Space*, pp. 22–3.

17 Ibid.

18 Claude Bragdon, *Four-dimensional Vistas*, 2nd edn (London: G. Routledge & Sons, 1923 [1916]).

19 See, for instance: Claude Bragdon, *The Beautiful Necessity*, pp. 63–5, 81–2; *A Primer of Higher Space*, pp. 27, 65, 71; *Architecture and Democracy* (New York: Alfred A. Knopf, 1918), pp. 4–5, 66–7; 'Experiments in a Language of Form', in *The New Image* (New York: Alfred A. Knopf, 1928), p. 124; *The Secret Springs: An Autobiography* (London: Andrew Dakers, 1938), p. 235; *The Arch Lectures (Eighteen discourses on a great variety of subjects delivered in New York, during the winter of 1940)* (Great Neck, NY: Core Collection Books, Inc., 1942), pp. 127–43.

20 See the discussion of Henri Ellenberger's *The Discovery of the Unconscious: The History and Evolution of Dynamic Psychiatry* (New York: Basic Books, 1970) in Matt Ffytche, 'Unconscious: Introduction'. Available at: http://www.bbk.ac.uk/deviance/unconscious1/intro.htm [accessed 25 January 2014].

21 Claude Bragdon, 'A Dissertation on Dynamic Symmetry', in *Architectural Record*, 56 (New York: McGraw-Hill, October 1924), p. 307.

22 Claude Bragdon, *A Primer of Higher Space*, pp. 73–4.

23 Claude Bragdon, *Four-dimensional Vistas*, p. 131.

24 Christopher Young and Andrew Brook, 'Schopenhauer and Freud', in *International Journal of Psychoanalysis*, 75(Part 1) (London: Institute of Psychoanalysis, February 1994), pp. 101–18. Available at: http://http-server.carleton.ca/~abrook/SCHOPENY.htm [accessed 25 January 2014]; Matt Ffytche, 'Unconscious: Introduction'; Christopher Janaway, 'The Real Essence of Human Beings: Schopenhauer on the Unconscious Will', in Angus Nicholls and Martin Liebscher (eds), *Thinking the Unconscious: Nineteenth-Century German Thought* (Cambridge: Cambridge University Press, 2010), pp. 140–43.

25 Sebastian Gardner, 'Schopenhauer, Will, and the Unconscious', in Christopher Janaway (ed.), *The Cambridge Companion to Schopenhauer* (Cambridge: Cambridge University Press, 1999), p. 370; as quoted in Christopher Janaway, 'The Real Essence of Human Beings'.

26 BFP A.B81 36:129 March 1891. See also BFP A.B81 41:3 January 10, 1892 (by mistake Bragdon writes '1891'), p. 4.

27 Claude Bragdon, 'A Voice Out of Russia', in *Theosophic Messenger* 7 (San Francisco, CA: American Theosophic Society, December 1919), pp. 198–201.

28 Claude Bragdon, 'Ouspensky on Love', in *Theosophic Messenger* 7 (San Francisco, CA: American Theosophic Society, March 1920), p. 289.

29 Duane P. Schulz and Sydney Ellen Schulz, *History of Modern Psychology*, 7th edn (Orlando, FL: Harcourt College Publishers, 2000 [1969]); Michael Wertheimer, *A Brief History of Psychology*, 3rd edn (New York: Holt, Rinehart and Winston, 1987 [1970]).

30 BFP A.B81 Box 33, vol. 5, March 1890; and Box 62, vol. 13, J: 'Did the Words Come from Beyond the Grave? Students of the Supernatural Are Interested in the So-Called Communications from the Spirit of Professor William James', in *New York Herald*, Sunday 20 November 1910, Magazine Section, p. 7; and 'Spirit of James Unhappy, It Says' (newspaper unknown), 20 February 1911. See also Claude Bragdon, 'Maeterlinck', in *Critic*, 45 (New Rochelle: G.P. Putnam's Sons, August 1901).

31 William James, 'The Hidden Self', in *Scribner's Magazine* (New York: Charles Scribner's Sons, March 1890).

32 BFP A.B81 Box 33, March and April 1890.

33 Claude Bragdon, 'Maeterlinck', p. 158.

34 Claude Bragdon, 'Mysticism and Architecture', in *Interstate Architect and Builder* (Cleveland, OH: Builder's Exchange of Cleveland, 13 and 20 July 1901), p. 10.

35 Claude Bragdon, 'The Beautiful Necessity' (March 1902), p. 91; 'The Theosophy of Architecture', p. 383.

36 Duane P. Schultz and Sydney Ellen Schultz, *History of Modern Psychology*, pp. 61–3; and Michael Wertheimer, *A Brief History of Psychology*, pp. 13–14.

37 Houghton Library, Harvard College Library, Harvard University, bMS Am 1092.

38 Linda Dalrymple Henderson, *The Fourth Dimension and Non-Euclidean Geometry in Modern Art*, p. 12. Regarding Gauss's two-dimensional analogy see Ibid., pp. 18–19.

39 Duane P. Schultz and Sydney Ellen Schultz, *History of Modern Psychology*; and Michael Wertheimer, *A Brief History of Psychology*.

40 See Gustav Theodor Fechner (Dr Mises), 'Der Raum hat vier Dimensionen', in *Vier Paradoxa* (Leipzig: Leopold Voss, 1846), pp. 15–40; as mentioned in Linda Dalrymple

Henderson, *The Fourth Dimension and Non-Euclidean Geometry in Modern Art*, p. 18. For other examples, see pp. 12, 18–21, 38–9 and 42.

41 Bragdon could have been aware of aspects of Fechner's work though secondary sources but he could not read German and Fechner's work was not translated into English before the centenary anniversary of its publication.

42 Daniel N. Robinson, 'Fechner, Gustav Theodor', in E. Craig (ed.), *Routledge Encyclopedia of Philosophy* (London: Routledge, 1998). Available at: http://www.rep.routledge.com/article/DC025 [accessed 13 January 2015].

43 Edwin G. Boring, 'Editor's Introduction' to Gustav Theodor Fechner, *Elements of Psychophysics*, p. ix.

44 Ibid., pp. ix–x.

45 Gustav Fechner, 'Author's Preface' to Fechner, *Elements of Psychophysics*, p. xxx.

46 Martin Heidelberger, 'Gustav Theodor Fechner and the Unconscious', trans. Simon Thomas, in Angus Nicholls and Martin Liebscher (eds), *Thinking the Unconscious* (Cambridge: Cambridge University Press, 2010), p. 225.

47 Gustav Fechner, *Elements of Psychophysics*, p. 199.

48 Ibid., pp. 199–200.

49 Martin Heidelberger, 'Gustav Theodor Fechner', p. 205.

50 Ibid., p. 222.

51 Gustav Fechner, *Elemente der Psychophysik*, vol. II, p. 435; as quoted in Martin Heidelberger, 'Gustav Theodor Fechner', p. 222.

52 Gustav Fechner, *Elements of Psychophysics*, pp. 205–6.

53 Martin Heidelberger, 'Gustav Theodor Fechner', pp. 203–4.

54 Ibid., p. 203.

55 Ibid.

56 Claude Bragdon, 'Mysticism and Architecture' and *The Beautiful Necessity*.

57 Claude Bragdon, *The Arch Lectures*, p. 42.

58 Claude Bragdon, 'The Modern Note', in *Reader Magazine*, 3 (Indianapolis, IN: Bobbs-Merrill Co., December 1903), p. 38; 'The New Mysticism', in *Reader Magazine*, 4 (July 1904), p. 189; 'Maeterlinck', p. 158.

59 Harry Francis Mallgrave and Eleftherios Ikonomou (eds), *Empathy, Form, and Space*, p. 9.

60 Claude Bragdon, 'Mysticism and Architecture'.

61 Claude Bragdon, *Projective Ornament* (Seattle, WA: Unicorn Bookshop, 1972 [1915]), pp. 77–8.

62 Claude Bragdon, 'The Language of Form', in Ralph Adams Cram, Tomas Hastings, and Claude Bragdon, *Six Lectures on Architecture: The Scammon Lectures at The Art Institute of Chicago* (Chicago, IL: University of Chicago Press, 1917), p. 162.

63 Ibid., pp. 162–5.

64 Claude Bragdon, *Projective Ornament*, pp. 9–11.

65 See Claude Bragdon, *Primer and Projective Ornament*.

66 Marco Frascari, 'Introduction: Models and Drawings – The Invisible Nature of Architecture', in Marco Frascari, Jonathan Hale, and Bradley Starkey (eds), *From Models to Drawings: Imagination and Representation in Architecture* (Abingdon: Routledge, 2007), p. 3.

67 BFP A.B81 36:1, 11 February 1891; Arthur Schopenhauer, *The World as Will and Idea*, vol. III, p. 239.

68 BFP A.B81 36:1, 10 February 1891.

69 BFP A.B18, Box 33, 20 and 21 March 1890.

70 See Harry Francis Mallgrave and Eleftherios Ikonomou (eds), *Empathy, Form, and Space*, p. 66, n. 1.

71 Johann Friedrich Herbart (1776–1841).

72 Christina Malathouni, 'Architecture is the Pattern of Human Mind in Space'.

73 The other two were Ernst Weber (1795–1878) and Wilhelm Wundt (1832–1920) (Duane P. Schultz and Sydney Ellen Schultz, *History of Modern Psychology*).

74 Harry Francis Mallgrave and Eleftherios Ikonomou (eds), *Empathy, Form, and Space*, pp. 9–10.

75 Mitchell Schwarzer, 'Schopenhauer's Philosophy of Architecture', in Dale Jacquette (ed.), *Schopenhauer, Philosophy, and the Arts* (Cambridge: Cambridge University Press, 1996), p. 277.

76 Christina Malathouni, '"Higher" Being and "Higher" Drawing: Claude Bragdon's "Fourth Dimension" and the Use of Computer Technology in Design', in Marco Frascari, Jonathan Hale, and Bradley Starkey (eds), *From Models to Drawings: Imagination and Representation in Architecture*.

4

Composing Form, Constructing the Unconscious: Empiriocriticism and Nikolai Ladovskii's 'Psychoanalytical Method' of Architecture at VKhUTEMAS

Alla G. Vronskaya

Nikolai Ladovskii's (1881–1941) so-called 'psychoanalytical' method of architectural pedagogy has attracted and puzzled architectural historians. The first 'left', radically modernist approach to architecture at the Moscow VKhUTEMAS (Higher Art and Technical Studios) in the early 1920s, it shaped the students' understanding of the discipline due to Ladovskii's control over introductory courses.[1] Not a prolific writer, Ladovskii preferred to disseminate his ideas through immediate contact and conversation. Alongside publications by his associates (most notably, Nikolai Dokuchaev, 1891–1944), documents related to Ladovskii's pedagogical activity offer the best insight into the theory of Rationalism, a movement centered around the Association of New Architects (ASNOVA). What was the theoretical premise and the goal of Ladovskii's teaching? And how, if at all, was it connected to Freudian psychoanalysis? At first sight it might seem that, defined as 'a discrete and consecutive (according to complexity) study of formal regularities of artistic forms, their elements and qualities on the basis of the physiology of perception', Ladovskii's psychoanalytical (sometimes called simply analytical) method had little to do with Freudianism.[2] However, although the architect indeed could hardly be described as a follower of Freud, I would argue that the similarity in the names of the two theories was more than a coincidence: Ladovskii's method drew upon a rich discourse of the unconscious that had been pertinent to modern European culture. In what follows, I will scrutinise the origins of Ladovskii's method in order to assess how in his theory – exemplary of the whole of modernist architectural thought – unconscious visual perception was subjected to the principle of economy. As a result, it was estranged from the subject and incorporated into the totalising social system predicated upon the relationships of production. Exploring the interplay between the conscious and the unconscious, Ladovskii and his followers created an ideological instrument that operated not through overtly expressed messages or directives, but though constructing that part of reality which usually remained beyond ideology's reach: the bodily, unconscious perception of physical properties of architecture.

As Jacques Rancière has noted, born as Alexander Baumgarten's discourse of sensation and later reinvented as the science of the beautiful in art, aesthetics transmitted into art its genetic connection with the unconscious: it was aesthetics that during the nineteenth century laid ground for Freud's later appropriation of the notion of the unconscious for psychoanalysis.[3] This connection between the aesthetic and the Freudian unconscious – which, one might suggest, was mediated by the biological (affective and physiological) one – was more self-evident at the beginning of the twentieth century than it is today, when the expulsion of beauty from mainstream artistic discourse led to a marginalisation of aesthetics in general. Reflecting upon and developing diverse interpretations of the unconscious, most notably those of Freud, sculptor and aesthetic thinker Adolf von Hildebrand, philosopher Eduard von Hartmann, literary critic and revolutionary Anatolii Lunacharskii, and the so-called empriocritical philosophers Ernst Mach and Richard Avenarius, Soviet architectural Rationalists elucidated a notion of the spatial unconscious produced by discreet optical and kinetic sensations. Their architecture became a material, if not always spatial (in the case of unrealised projects and student assignments), representation of this unconscious, an attempt at re-materialising psychological knowledge that emerged as a result of laboratory experiments and clinical observations.

Freud's name and ideas would have been well known to Rationalist architects.[4] Multiple translations of Freud were printed (and reprinted) in Russian both before and after the revolution of 1917. Books on Freud and discussions of Freud's work also followed. Psychoanalysis became particularly influential among fin-de-siècle literati and critics of literature and the arts, who eagerly applied it to biographical studies.[5] So eagerly, in fact, that in 1925 prominent Marxist critic Vladimir Friche's talk on 'Freudianism and the Arts' was met with an angry remark from the audience:

> *... In our country the interest in Freud has developed into a real psychosis. [...] Freudianism and Freudianism, again and again, for or against Freudianism, and with each new day more and more are contaminated, and with each new day we have fewer and fewer healthy Marxists.*[6]

The relationship between Freudianism and Marxism, indeed, quickly became the focus of the Soviet discussion of psychoanalysis. In the 1920s, a whole series of publications in academic and party journals undertook the task of reconciling the two schools. It started with a 1923 article by Bernard Bykhovskii, 'On the Methodological Foundations of Freud's Psychoanalytic Theory', published in *Pod Znamenem Marksizma* (*Under the Banner of Marxism*), the journal of the Communist Academy, the major intellectual centre of Soviet power. According to Bykhovskii, the core of Freud's teaching lay in his concept of the unconscious, which was fully compatible with both Marxism and materialist psychology.

> *When you learn psychoanalysis better, you not only become convinced of its compatibility with reactology, but also start doubting its subjectivism. Subjectivism seems to be a shell that obscures the essence. Indeed, psychoanalysis [is] a study of the unconscious, of something that happens*

> *beyond the subjective 'I'. The unconscious really impacts human reactions, frequently orchestrating them. The unconscious cannot be studied through cognition, subjectively. This is the reason why Freud studies objective manifestations of the unconscious (symptom, mistake, etc.), seeking the conditions of minimal participation of reason (dream, childhood). All this is undoubtedly admissible for reactology.*[7]

By displacing the unconscious away from the domain of subjectivity, which was tied to rationality and cognition, Bykhovskii connected it to the collective and the trans-individual, which he understood as the instinctive, that is, in an evolutionist biological sense as belonging to species. This unconscious was not opposed to consciousness, but rather presented consciousness's super-individual form, which enabled the coordination of individuals' efforts in the interest of the group. Leaving the correctness of such an interpretation aside, it is important to notice that the sexual component of psychoanalysis was consistently downplayed by its Soviet adepts, who identified it with a scientific study of the unconscious. Summarising this understanding of psychoanalysis, Valentin Voloshinov (often identified as Mikhail Bakhtin writing under his colleague's guise) defined its essence in a tripartite statement: consciousness does not always have access to true motives of human actions; actions can be defined by unconscious psychological forces; these psychological forces can be elevated to the level of consciousness with the help of special techniques.[8]

Instead of identifying it with repressed sexual desires, Russian interpreters of Freud followed an understanding of the unconscious that stemmed from the work of Eduard von Hartmann (1842–1906), who in his *Philosophy of the Unconscious* (*Philosophie des Unbewussten*, 1869, translated into Russian in 1873–5) made it responsible for performing many of the functions that had traditionally been ascribed to consciousness. Hartmann's unconscious acted as an agent of evolution – as a purely biological force peculiar to people and animals alike. The philosopher argued against Darwin's vision of natural selection, supporting, instead, a neo-Lamarckian theory of adaptation. If Darwinism, for him, professed a mindless causality, effectively denying the possibility of adaptation, Hartmann's unconscious provided evolution with a teleological, guiding channel, through which a species could move towards its biological goal.[9] Not chance but logic, even if unconscious, directed evolution.

The success of adaptation depended on a rational – economical and efficient – spending of resources available to individuals and species. The most important of those was energy – a meta-resource accumulated through the rational use of the others. The question of energy became a prominent part of scientific and general discourse after the discoveries made in physics in the mid-nineteenth century: the first law of thermodynamics, which declared that the amount of energy possessed by a system always remained a constant (energy could thus be transformed, but not created); and its second law, which, even more pessimistically, postulated an increase of entropy (and with it, the exhaustion of energy) in any enclosed system. A student of physicist and physiologist Ernst Brücke, who was credited with the invention of 'psychodynamics', Freud saw the unconscious as a repository of energy, making the notion of libido – sexual energy – the basis of psychoanalysis. Libido resided in the unconscious and always strove for release, often finding the way out in self-destructive neuroses and hysterias, or in sublimation, which enabled art and other forms of creative and productive work; it could also be artificially released in the course of psychoanalytic sessions. This aspect of psychoanalysis became especially important in Soviet Russia. Defending Freud in the course of the above-mentioned discussion of Friche's talk, a commentator noted:

> *What is so scary about someone telling you that a man is a machine, running on some ionic-chemical energy which is also called sexual when directed to securing progeny? This energy creates all social values because society is also a kind of progeny. Creation of all social values is called sublimation, or distillation.*[10]

The relationship between sexuality and energy was bilateral: as Jonathan Crary has observed, since the late nineteenth century sexual response became a model that described various kinds of nervous activity in the entire organism. It turned into an 'instrumental and reductive way to conceptualise and control the potential disorder of a body, whose different regions were traversed by varying intensities of energy'.[11]

Energy fed not only sexual, but all other types of human activity, such as perception or intellectual work. Possessing no destructive potential, it contributed to adaptation by enabling creativity, resourcefulness and dexterity. Rather than being simply released, it had to be used in the most efficient and economical way. In his *Philosophy as Thinking about the World According to the Principle of the Smallest Measure of Force* (*Philosophie als Denken der Welt gemäß dem Prinzip des kleinsten Kraftmaßes* of 1876, translated into Russian in 1913), German-Swiss philosopher Richard Avenarius (1843–96) argued that even the most theoretical of all disciplines – philosophy – served to facilitate biological adaptation by creating more logical and efficient (economical) thinking by summarising particular ideas into general notions and determining relationships between the latter. Avenarius believed that habit (*Gewohnheit*) displaced perception into the domain of the unconscious: for the latter, this displacement possessed an important evolutionary function, allowing perceptual energy to be economised. The philosophy of Avenarius, the so-called empiriocriticism, was so popular in Russia, that in 1895 the future first Soviet 'commissar of enlightenment' (the minister of education and culture) Anatolii Lunacharskii (1875–1933), then a young Kiev gymnasium graduate, went to Zurich to become the philosopher's student. And even though Lenin's major philosophical work *Materialism and Empiriocriticism: Critical Comments on a Reactionary Philosophy* (*Materializm i empiriokrititsizm: Kriticheskie zametki ob odnoi reaktsionnoi filosofii*, 1908) intended to combat the theory that he considered dangerous for orthodox Marxism, empiriocriticism's influence upon Soviet pre- and post-revolutionary thought remained immense.

According to Avenarius, while an increase of energy was supported, on a biological level, by an accompanying sensation of pleasure, the loss of energy provoked a feeling of discomfort. Such a connection related Avenarius's theory of the economy of perceptual energy to psychophysiological aesthetics, an emerging discipline that explained aesthetic experience through physiological reactions stimulated by works of art. Rapidly spreading across Europe and the United States in the late nineteenth century, it became particularly popular in Russia, with its strong tradition of physiological research. It was developed by such authors as Apollon Smirnov and Leonid Obolenskii, who aspired to get rid of aesthetic subjectivism and find an objective foundation for aesthetic judgment. An incorporation of Avenarius's program of the economy of energy into this aesthetics became the goal of Lunacharskii's *Foundations of Positive Aesthetics* (1903) – a declared attempt at the creation of an aesthetic system based on the philosophy of empiriocriticism (hence 'positive', that is, positivist, a term that was often used as synonymous to empiriocriticist).[12]

Lunacharskii's endeavor was not without precedent in the Russian empire: the concept of the economy of attention was explored by the powerful Khar'kov linguistic school, which instilled psychology into literary analysis. Its founder, Aleksandr Potebnia (1835–91), saw the clue to understanding poetic language in the study of unconscious human cogitative processes.[13] Potebnia's follower, Dmitrii Ovsianiko-Kulikovskii (1853–1920) identified the waste of psychic energy with attention, or the employment of intellect. Automatism, or the unconscious, for him, was its opposite, allowing one to achieve results without spending energy.[14] Ovsianiko-Kulikovskii argued that human mental life was defined by a constant dialogue between consciousness and the unconscious, so that memory, for instance, was presented as the storage of cognitive acquisitions in the unconscious sphere. Moreover, it was within the unconscious that the vast majority of cognitive acts took place as automatic activities, which consciousness noticed only in their latest stages. Ovsianniko-Kulikovskii saw a great potential for a rationalisation of thinking in this ability of the unconscious to undertake the work of cognition: 'This means that all the work was gratuitous [*darom*] for us, and a great economising of intellectual power [*umstvennoi sily*] is obvious'.[15]

Due to his position as the minister of culture and education between 1919 and 1929, and to a reprint, without any revisions, of his *Foundations of Positive Aesthetics* in 1923, Lunacharskii became successful in his propaganda of empiriocriticism among artists, architects and writers. By the early 1920s, it became a frequent point of reference for Russian theoreticians of art and architecture, among them Kazimir Malevich, the rector of VKhUTEMAS Pavel Novitskii, and aesthetic thinker Pavel Florenskii.[16] Alongside these artists and thinkers, Ladovskii defined the essence of (architectural) creativity as the economy of psychic energy. Explaining his method in 1926, he argued:

> *Like technical rationality, architectural rationality is based on the principle of economy. The difference lies in the fact that technical rationality is the economy of labour and material expended in the creation of an expedient building, whereas architectural rationality is the economy of psychic energy expended in the perception of spatial and functional qualities of a building. Rationalist architecture is the synthesis of these two rationalities.*[17]

This psychologisation of the principle of economy explained the disagreement between Ladovskii (accompanied by his associate Vladimir Krinskii) and the other

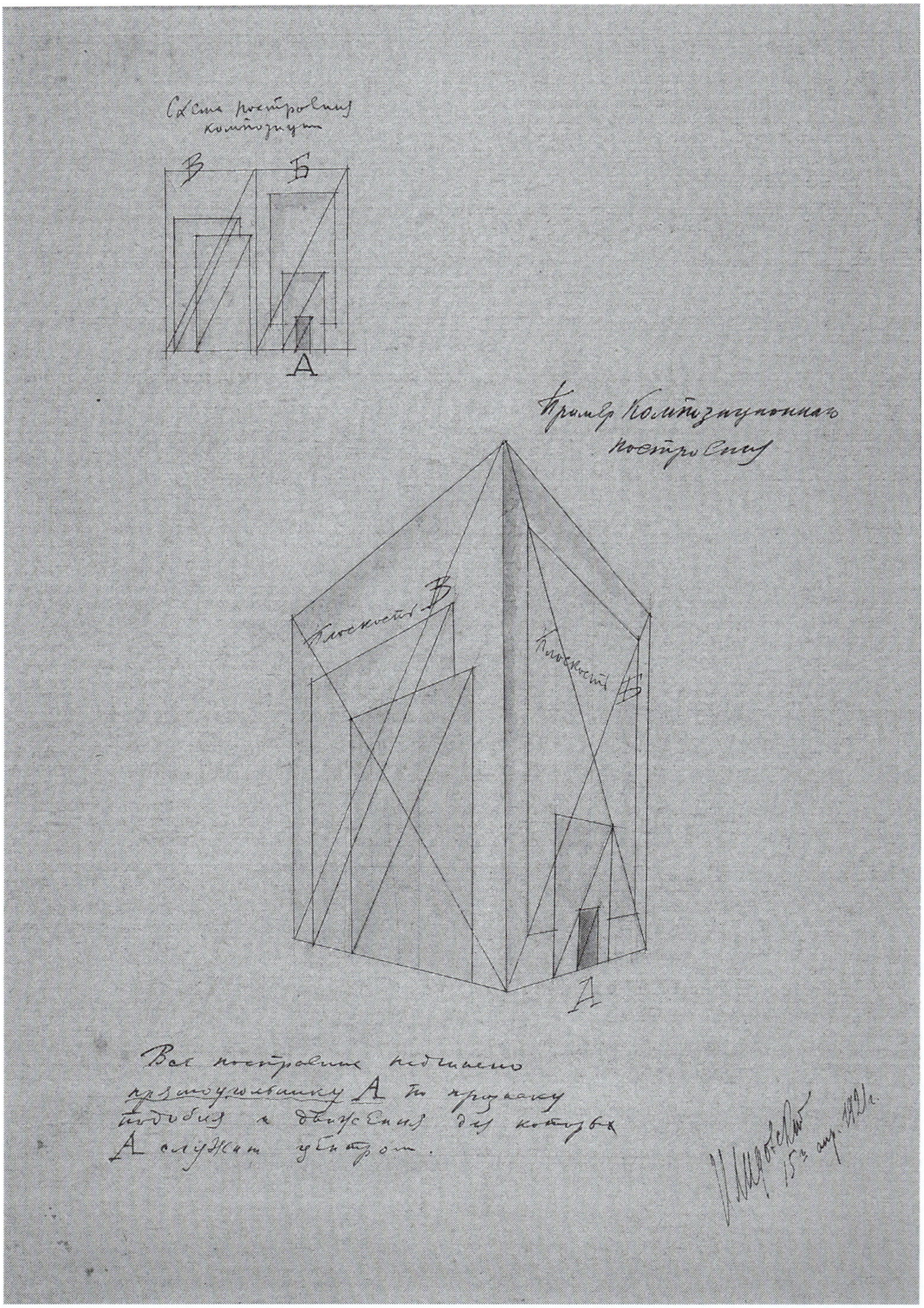

4.1 Left: Nikolai Aleksandrovich Ladovskii, Example of a Composed Structure, 1921, ink, ink wash and pencil on cardboard, 38 × 27.5 cm – State Museum of Contemporary Art – Costakis collection, Thessaloniki.

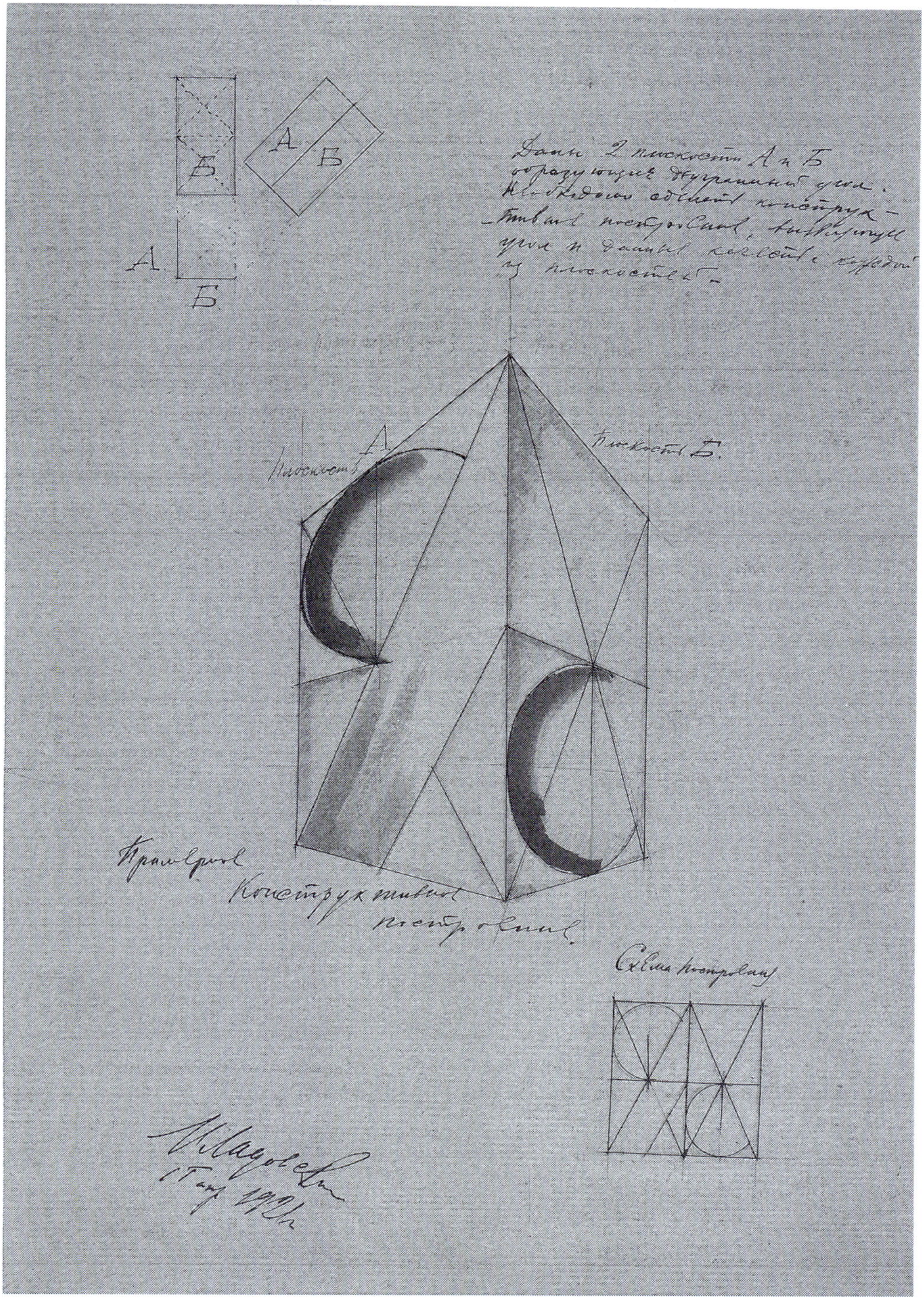

Right: Nikolai Aleksandrovich Ladovskii, Example of a Constructive Structure, 1921, ink, ink wash and pencil on cardboard, 38 × 27.3 cm – State Museum of Contemporary Art – Costakis collection, Thessaloniki.

discussants in the course of the seminal debate on the relationship between construction and composition at the Institute of Artistic Culture (INKhUK) in Moscow in spring of 1921. Alongside the architects, the conversation attracted radical artists, among them: Varvara Stepanova, Aleksandr Rodchenko, and Liubov' Popova. Opposing other participants, most of whom would soon become known as the Constructivists, Ladovskii and Krinskii identified themselves as 'the architects', emphasizing that their standpoint expressed the specificity of the discipline. It was, indeed, quite different from that of the rest of the group: rather than juxtaposing construction and composition to praise the former's engineering aspect while identifying the latter with artistic arbitrariness and personal taste, they presented the two as related, albeit different, architectural operations (Figure 4.1). Ladovskii defined construction as an absence of superfluous materials and elements. He illustrated it with a cube the surfaces of which were articulated in such a way that their proportions became easily apprehendable. Composition, on the other hand, was characterised by hierarchy and subordination; it exposed not the properties of form, but its inner logics. It was represented as a cube on whose surfaces Ladovskii inscribed several squares that accentuated a small dark opening at the bottom of one side ('the door') as the centre to which the entire composition was subordinated 'according to the principle of similarity and movement'.[18]

The economy of perceptive energy, which the Rationalists strove to achieve, served to facilitate the individual's orientation within the environment as a strategy of biological adaptation. In his overview of the course 'Foundations of the Art of Architecture' (note the emphasis on the status of architecture as art, which situated the discipline within the domain of aesthetic theory and distinguished it from the Constructivists' fascination with engineering), which the Rationalists developed for professional art schools, Dokuchaev defined the goal of the course as 'a study of (compositional and constructive) means of organisation of architectural form into a system, which gives the maximum of expressivity [*vyrazitel'nost'*] to form and provides the viewer with an opportunity to orientate in space'.[19] A building whose formal and structural properties remained inaccessible for analysis evoked in the beholder a feeling of confusion and disorientation, reducing the reserve of energy; likewise, energy balance decreased if the building's understanding required too much intellectual effort. Instead, a well-designed building, according to Dokuchaev, had to be understood immediately, without employing energy-expensive cognition. Like Freud's psychoanalytic sessions, Rationalist architectural analysis aimed at entering the unconscious in order to extract information and convey it to the subject. However, unlike Freud, the architects believed that in order to economise perceptual energy, this information had to remain within the domain of the unconscious. In the spirit of Avenarius, the Rationalists argued that a designer had to embed in architecture a code that would be recognised by the viewers' unconscious, provoking certain sensations or affections and allowing them to viscerally experience the buildings' formal and structural properties while freeing them from a necessity of discerning these properties logically.

This rationalisation of perception became Ladovskii's major preoccupation, which encompassed his other concerns: the development of a new visual language for architecture, establishing relationships between physiological sensation and visual form, and developing new pedagogical methods. The ambition of rationalising perception as a valuable state property, of making it more efficient and economical, was reflected in the expression 'rational architecture' (*ratsional'naia arkhitektura, ratsio-arkhitektura*) which the group used to describe its methodology, and which subsequently led to the emergence of the term 'Rationalism'.[20] The expression 'rational architecture' referred to 'rationalisation' (*ratsionalizatorstvo*), a movement in Soviet post-revolutionary industrial management, which encouraged workers to suggest new, more rational and economical, techniques and methods of their work. Similarly, Ladovskii's Rationalism instrumentalised the unconscious as a deposit of human energy, which had to be redirected to the creation of the Soviet economic miracle.

Within the modernisation project, rationalisation operated alongside science and technology, and Ladovskii's psychoanalytical method as a study of 'formal regularities of artistic forms, their elements and qualities', likewise, referred not only to the theory of the unconscious, but also to 'the method of science – the method of analysis', which dissected reality in order to expose its hidden mechanisms.[21] Juxtaposed to 'synthesis' in the artistic discourse of the time, the word 'analysis' was associated with a new, scientific approach to art – think, for instance, of Picasso's analytical Cubism – which undermined an old vision of artistic talent as both a technical skill and a divine gift. This analytical method was illustrated by the genre that Ladovskii foresaw for his textbook of architectural theory – an 'illustrated dictionary, which meticulously establishes the terminology and definitions of architecture as a form of art, architecture's separate properties, qualities, and so forth, and the relationships between architecture and other arts'.[22]

Ladovskii borrowed this representation of architecture as a system of separate properties and qualities from the work of Avenarius's co-thinker, another leader of empiriocriticism, Austrian physicist and philosopher of science Ernst Mach (1838–1916), who suggested that the material world should be reduced to colours, sounds, temperatures, times, spaces, and other subjective sensations of physical properties. Since every physical quality (or element, in Mach's terminology) existed in mind as a sensation, the old dualism of spirit and matter was overcome, explained away as a mere linguistic misunderstanding. The mosaic of elements/sensations that the world presented was not chaotic, but rather organised into complexes, which, although never absolutely stable, demonstrated a certain permanency. For the sake of ease in our orientation in the world, these relatively stable complexes of sensations, connected in time and space, were called bodies. As a result, concluded Mach, it was not bodies that produced sensations but, on the contrary, complexes of sensations (or elements) that made up bodies.[23] No single body was absolutely stable in Mach's worldview: 'My friend may put on a different coat. His countenance may assume a serious or a cheerful expression'. Nevertheless, 'It is the same friend with whom I take my daily walk' – we recognise a complex of sensations as our friend on the basis of permanent qualities, which outnumber transitory ones.[24] In other words, Mach saw a body as a combination of stable nucleus qualities and unstable, 'annexed', accidental ones.[25] The 'I', for Mach, was also only a relatively permanent 'complex of memories, moods, and feelings, joined to a particular body (the human body)'.[26] This postulation of the ultimate instability of the ego allowed Mach to argue for a principal inseparability between the 'I' and the world. This idea was most vividly illustrated by Mach's drawing that showed how closing one eye transformed the perceived image of the world, forcefully merging the body with it (Figure 4.2). The external world seen by Mach was framed with his own moustache, his nose and his eyebrow, while legs and hands became seamless parts of the environment.

The absence of a 'thing' and of a boundary between a thing and the 'I', was, for Ladovskii, the key lesson of Mach's epistemology, a lesson that subverted the familiar distinction between the object and the subject. This, Ladovskii believed, was a blow against both the Constructivists' absolutisation of matter and the idealism of the Kantians. Meanwhile, dissolved in the world of psychological sensations and merged with an object, the subject was not only demystified – it became analysable and therefore constructable. In 1921, during a discussion of the

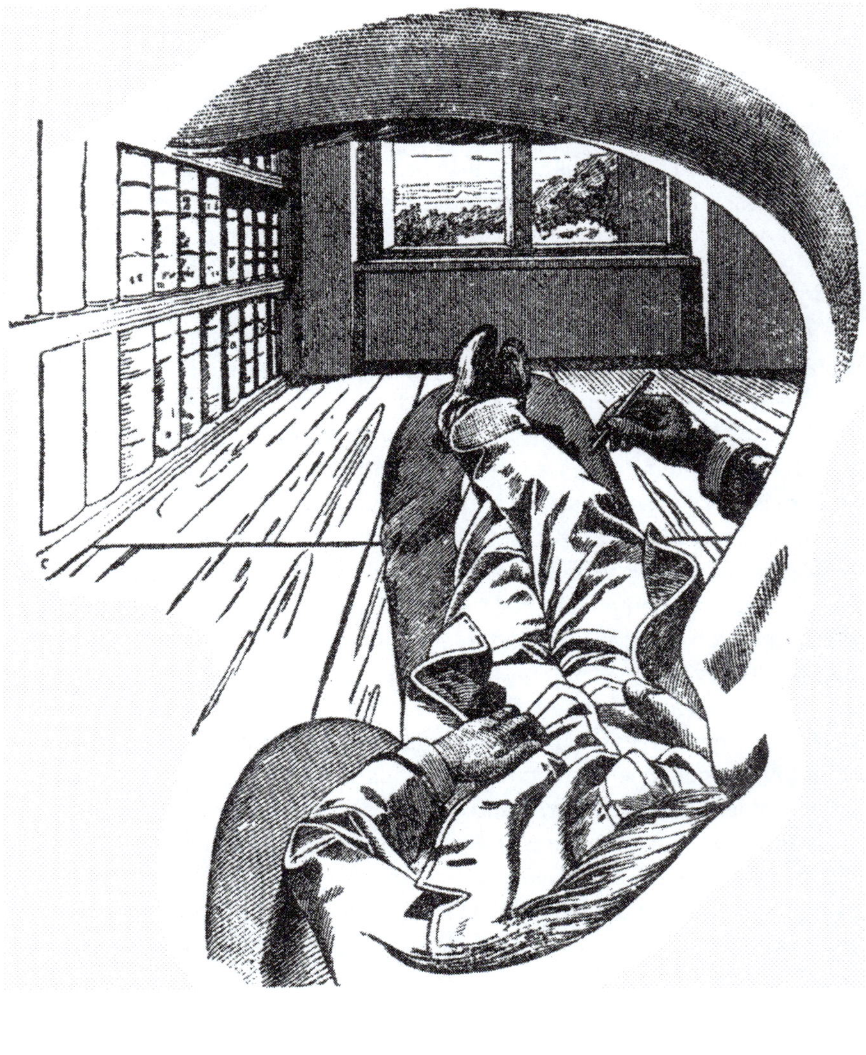

4.2 Illustration from Ernst Mach, *Beiträge Zur Analyse Der Empfindungen* (Jena: G. Fischer, 1886), p. 14, public domain.

laws of mechanics in architecture within the Working Group of Architects at INKhUK, Ladovskii presented empiriocriticism to his colleagues, effectively reducing it to a rejection of the notion of an object and its replacement with a vision of more or less loosely connected complexes of elements:

> *I will introduce you to the opinion of Mach, to his argumentation. You have drawn a construction and you argue that this is architecture. Let us take a clock: it too has a construction, but this does not make it architecture. We have, therefore, to start with establishing scientific terms.*
>
> *Mach says: 'Objects do not exist in the world'. Earlier, some theoreticians and philosophers told us that an object exists, while others claimed that only our perceptions are real. Both arguments, as it seemed, were correct, and no one could recognize a mistake in the assumptions. There is no difference between you and a thing … 'I' can be infinitely extended. Existent are your body, mind, clock. A body is connected to a thing – through the eye and the brain. I say about the eye 'this is me'. But I can also say 'the clock is also me'. There is no boundary between myself and the external world. I can connect myself to the globe. There is no boundary, but there is a link that is convenient to confine oneself to.*
>
> *What is an object? Earlier [people] thought about the object itself and its properties as an object. This led philosophers to mistakes. Think only of Kant's useless attempts to give corresponding notions. Mach is attempting to remove this strange error. He determines that 'only complexes of elements exist'. They are changeable, but connected in time. And those whose connection is more stable – these are the ones we talk about. Here is a dress. We could have said now that it is a complex of certain forces. But this would be inconvenient, because there are more stable and more temporal values; the latter do not give it a definite character. Thus Mach says: only changeable complexes of qualities temporally exist, while there are no things in themselves.*[27]

Whereas traditional, 'synthetic', courses at the VKhUTEMAS offered a practical approach to the development of artistic skill (painting, sculpting or designing under the guidance of a master), the modernist, or 'analytic', cycle gave students a theoretical knowledge of the psychology of visual perception. These so-called propaedeutic (introductory) courses were based on connecting each artistic discipline with a formal property dominant for that art: 'Colour' (taught by Liubov' Popova and Aleksandr Vesnin) served as an introduction to painting; 'Volume' (taught by Cubist sculptor Boris Korolev) – to sculpture; 'Drawing' (that is, line, taught by Aleksandr Rodchenko) – to graphic design; and 'Space', taught by Ladovskii – to architecture. The title of Ladovskii's course reflected his vision of architecture's new medium: 'Space, not stone, is the material of architecture'.[28] A psychological rather than an ontological phenomenon, a subjective representation of a three-dimensional environment, space was defined as a function of the physical movement of the viewer and as a result of the changing conditions of perception.

In the absence of objects that previously served as basic structural units of architectural language ('… a wall, a roof, a column, a beam, a plinth, a pediment, etc.' – Ladovskii described a list of such elements), the new architectural theory, for the architect, was to be comprised of perceivable spatial qualities in the same way that Mach's epistemology imagined the internalised universe as a set of elements of perception.[29] Just as Mach suggested going from sensations to bodies rather than from bodies to sensations, Ladovskii insisted on defining architectural elements first and only then, based on these definitions, developing a new notion of architecture: 'from a study of separate properties and qualities of a phenomenon – to building on these foundations conclusions and definitions of the phenomenon itself'.[30] These qualities – formal, subjective properties of spatial perception – in turn, comprised the essence of architecture and the object of architectural creativity.

Instead of starting with architectural details and gradually moving towards larger forms as was common within the academic tradition, Ladovskii proposed to begin with a study of the elements of perception and subsequently progress towards their combinations, finishing the course by mastering space as the integral psychological representation of three-dimensional reality. Spatial perceptual qualities were classified into geometrical and physical, which were to be analysed separately; the third part of the course was comprised of an analysis of their organisation into complexes. Thus, the structure of student assignments suggested by Viktor Balikhin, Ladovskii's former student who developed his pedagogical method, asserted and analytically described the categories of surface, volume, mass, weight, and construction:

A. Geometric qualities of form in space.
   1. Types of surfaces: a) plane; b) curved surfaces (cylindrical, conical etc., convex and concave); c) angles formed by polyline surfaces or by the intersection of planes – internal and external.
   2. Volume as a form, comprised of a closed system of surface. Typical volumetric forms: cylinder, parallelepiped, cone, sphere, etc., and their combinations. [...]

B. Physical-mechanical properties of form.
   1. Mass (of volume) – enclosed space infilled with matter. Systems of elements, which expose mass, have to evoke a visual penetration inside the volume and the sensation of the degree of density of its infill with mass.
   2. Weight (of volume) – the movement of mass downwards under the force of gravitation.
   3. Construction – a balancing system of couplings of interacting forms under the effect of the gravitation force.[31]

The very first assignment given by Ladovskii at his newly organised course at the VKhUTEMAS in October 1920 took the simplest three-dimensional figure, a parallelepiped (a figure formed by six parallelograms), to illustrate the Rationalist vision of architecture as an instrument of the organisation of optical perception. It asked to make the geometrical form of an object obvious even in a situation unfavourable for observation (or, as Mach could have put it, to emphasise nucleus qualities when they were obscured by accidental ones). 'What does it mean to *reveal a geometrical image*?' wondered Ladovskii explaining the assignment, stressing the word 'reveal'.

> *Would we see in a mathematically-correctly built parallelepiped some other form – a sphere, a cone, a cylinder, etc.? No, we will see neither a sphere nor a cylinder, but neither will we see a parallelepiped of the geometrical qualities specified in the assignment.*[32]

'Revealing' played a central role in his architectural and pedagogical theory. While Freud's psychoanalysis attempted to reveal suppressed memories and desires to cure neuroses, Ladovskii's psychoanalytic method revealed forms hidden behind phenomena to economise the viewer's analytical work. Ladovskii used a theory elaborated by German sculptor and aesthetic thinker Adolf von Hildebrand, whose major theoretical treatise, the essay *Das Problem der Form in der bildenden Kunst* (*The Problem of Form in the Fine Arts*, 1893) was translated into French, English and Russian, remaining popular well into the 1930s.[33] Hildebrand was convinced of the unhealthiness of dispersing attention as a waste of perceptive energy; a good work of art, for him, allowed assessing its formal idea at a glance.[34] The job of an artist, thus, consisted in separating the essential from the accidental and emphasising the former: 'When children draw a face as a circle with two dots for eyes, a vertical line for a nose, and a horizontal line for a mouth, they present just this necessary effect, as a wholly adequate image of our natural idea of effective form'.[35] 'Effective form' (*Wirkungsform*) was the phenomenal representation of an object, and was 'always a joint product of the object, on the one hand, and of its lightning, surroundings, and our changing vantage point, on the other'.[36] On the contrary, ontological, inherent form (*Daseinsform*) depended solely on the object and not on its changing appearance, and could only be abstracted from effective form. An artist, for Hildebrand, operated solely with effective form, exploring the laws of its formation and thus creating not objects, but their phenomenal impressions.

Translated into Hildebrand's terms, Ladovskii's revealing was an expression of *Daseinsform* through a *Wirkungsform*. Indeed, the Russian word for revealing, *vyiavlenie*, was comprised of the prefix *vy-* (signifying the movement outwards) combined with the root *iav'* ('reality') and meant revealing inner truth through phenomena. Dealing exclusively with physiological responses, revealing referred to producing in the beholder an experience of weight, mass, or geometrical shape of a building. It was opposed to another method of making architectural form unconsciously recognisable – expression or expressivity (*vyrazitel'nost'*), a term that referred to hyperbolising and otherwise accentuating properties of form in order to augment the viewer's emotional response. Less favored by the Rationalists, this method, they believed, was overexploited by Expressionism and was based on the notion of empathy, too literally comparing architecturally evoked sensations and human feelings. It was thus more appropriate for poetry than for architecture. In the words of Dokuchaev:

> *To express* [*vyrazit'*] *a form means to demonstrate its characteristic properties, that is, to make obvious its, say, geometrical structure – its rectangularity and proportionality, the commensurability of its surfaces, etc. In other words, here the artist-architect has to be, essentially, a geometer. To reveal* [*vyiavit'*] *a form means to make its structural properties – all the basic characteristics of form –*

> *visually clear and sharply perceived. In other words, an artist, an architect, wishing to endow the architectural form with certain qualities and properties, has to make these properties correctly perceived (according to his vision) by considering all possible impediments, such as: changing conditions of light, the distance and viewpoint from which the form is viewed, the impact and influence of the surroundings on the form, etc. Here, the artist has to approach the task as a composer.*[37]

Sublating the opposition of the conscious and the unconscious, revealing presented the major creative problem that could be solved by architectural means. According to Dokuchaev, it was the goal of composition – and as such, offered a middle ground between the Constructivists' preoccupation with physical structure and the Expressionists' concern with the creation of a legible and memorable geometric form.

Ladovskii formulated the assignment on the parallelepiped as a set of data that dictated both geometrical properties and the appearance of the object: its dimensions (20 × 20 × 30 metres), conditions of light (sunny), the spectator's viewpoint (movable, but no further than 30 metres away from the object) and speed of movement (no more than 15 metres per second). Among other properties to be revealed were: spatial orientation, the equality of sides, the relationship between the width and the height of the object, and the fact that all angles were right. In other words, looking at the figure from any point of view and under any natural conditions, the viewer had to be confident that its geometrical form was that of a parallelepiped of certain proportions. This could be revealed through vertical and horizontal articulations, chiaroscuro, and the texture (*faktura*) of surfaces, which divided surface into elementary forms. Each of these forms immediately affected the eye and provoked a familiar physiological sensation, acting not unlike Avenarius's philosophical generalisation. Describing a successful solution, by a student Petrov (Figure 4.3), Ladovskii clarified:

> *One must put an identity relator between each pair of the parallelepiped sides that are seen simultaneously, and consequently, between all of its sides. [In other words, one must demonstrate that the sides are identical – A.V.]*
>
> *This means that the articulations of all the sides of the parallelepiped must be identical. If, for example, we inscribe a circumference into each of the parallelepiped's sides in such a way that the spectator could, during the process of perception, define the equality of diameters of each pair of simultaneously seen circumferences, this would signify a certain degree of approaching the image to its geometric essence, and would demonstrate more clearly the equality of distances of separate ribs from the front rib.*
>
> *Having inscribed additional half-circumferences, we will comprehend the relationship between the base and the height: 1:½, the equality of sides and all its consequences – everything in a certain degree of approximation, which can be achieved with the help of these elements.*[38]

In its utter simplicity, Ladovskii's parallelepiped was – not unlike Le Corbusier's Maison Dom-ino famously analysed by Peter Eisenman – a statement about the

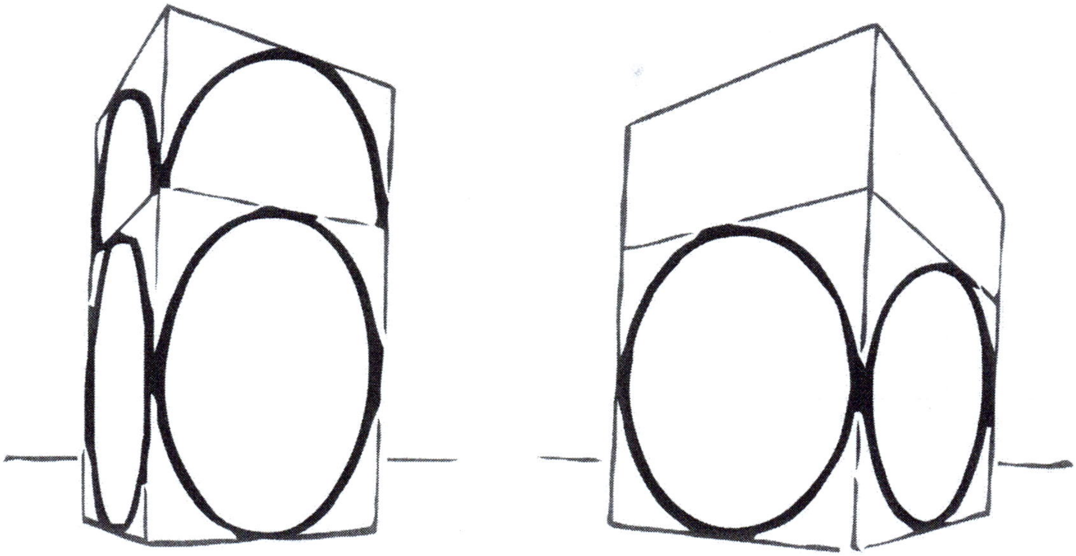

4.3 Above: Nikolai Ladovskii, Geometrical analysis of Petrov's project. Reproduced in *Izvestia ASNOVA* (1926, No. 1), p. 4, public domain. Right: V.A. Petrov, 'Parallelepiped'. Abstract assignment on the exposure of form (VKhUTEMAS, 1920). Reproduced in *Izvestia ASNOVA* (1926, No. 1), p. 5.

minimal conditions of architecture, a response to the problem of architectural disciplinarity, so central for modernist thought.[39] These conditions were found in revealing not the design process, but its result. The beholder of architecture, eliminated from consideration by the neo-modernists, remained the focal point of the theory of Ladovskii. But in contrast to the intentions of Eisenman's postmodernist discontents, the Rationalist reinstallment of the human in the centre of the universe did not rehumanise modernism, but rather dehumanised the subject.[40] The contingent, the accidental, and the atmospheric remained visibly present, and even fundamental, for Rationalist theory, which, however, saw them as a problem – in fact, the major problem that architecture faced. It had to free the subject's mind from the unpredictability bestowed upon it by the external environment with which it interacted, and assert stability, order and control within and thereby outside the human.

Typically for Rationalist pedagogy, an 'abstract' formal assignment was followed by a corresponding 'industrial' one, which intended to help students master technical and representational skills. In 1921 and 1922, the 'parallelepiped' was followed by a 'grain elevator', as an industrial assignment on the revealing and expression of architectural form. Technical requirements specified that the elevator had to possess a capacity of 3,580 cubic metres, and be divided into several separate cells for storing grain; the latter was received through pouring reservoirs and then lifted to the upper level where, after passing through purifying devices, it was poured down to separate reservoirs. At the same time, 'architectural requirements' specified that the form of the elevator had to be revealed and expressed as a holistic volumetric structure.[41] The solution of Mikhail Korzhev, a student and subsequently a teacher of 'Space' at the VKhUTEMAS, consisted of four equal cylinders arranged in a row (Figure 4.4). A contrast of rectangles and circles created within the composition a tension of dynamism and statics. On the one hand, the articulations of cylindrical sections made the 'façade' of the elevator read as a grid of horizontal rectangles, while the diagonals of the pedestal and the loft neutralised each other, conveying a feeling of dynamic monumentality, which was accentuated by a slight – almost unnoticeable – narrowing of the cylinders towards the top. On the other hand, the circles (wheels, quadrants, and the curves of the cylinders) emphasised rotation that lay at the heart of the elevator's functional program, making the beholder visually trace the movement of the grain: starting at bottom left, up the conveyor belt to the highest point of the structure, then moving downwards following the diagonal traversing the wheels, abruptly falling down into the elevator and slowly running toward the starting point, where the process, as it were, began anew. Ostensibly formalist and ideologically neutral, Korzhev's project nevertheless possessed an effect that transcended the boundaries of the formal. It singled out and emphasised particular processes and details, creating a complex ideological representation

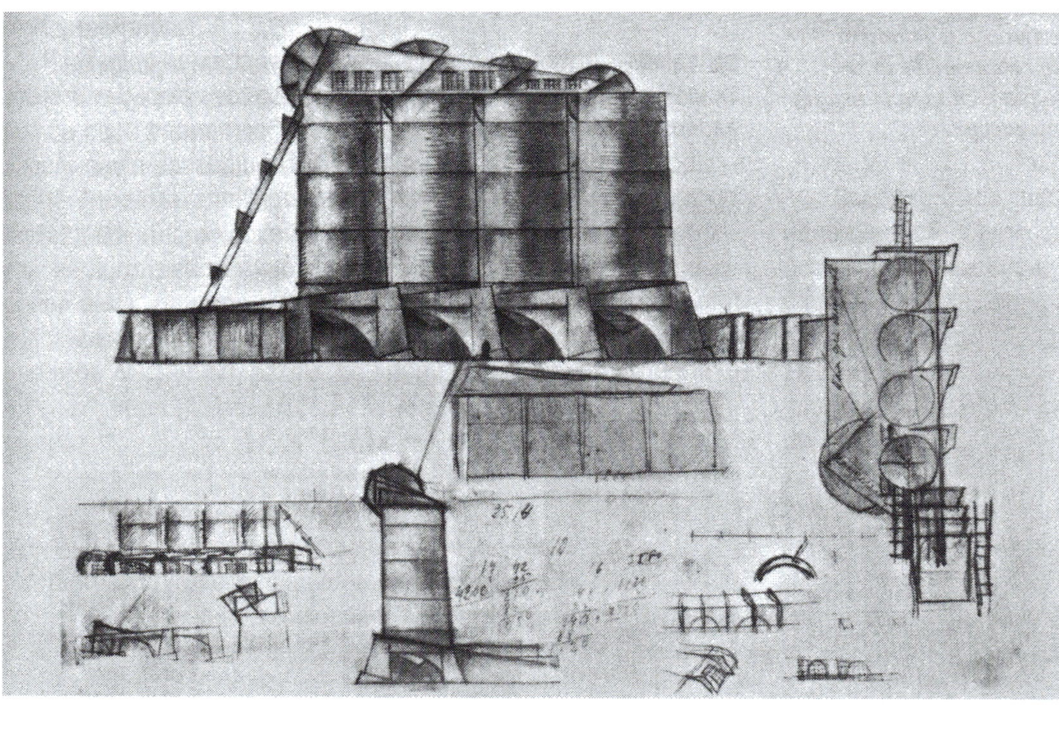

4.4 Mikhail Korzhev, 'Grain elevator'. Industrial assignment on the exposure and expression of form (VKhUTEMAS, 1922). Reproduced in S.O. Khan-Magomedov, *Ratsionalizm (Ratsio-arkhitektura) 'Formalizm'* (Moskva: Arkhitektura-S, 2007), p. 165, copyright owner unknown.

that unnoticeably shaped spectators' physiological responses, emotional stances, and ultimately their worldview. Registered only as a bodily sensation such as an intensified heartbeat or vertigo, it penetrated directly into their unconscious, freeing them from spending cognitive energy and thus rationalising their work on that elevator or elsewhere.

Not building materials nor representational techniques but the visual unconscious became the true medium of Rationalist architecture. Unlike the Freudian unconscious, the architectural unconscious of Ladovskii was not a static datum that was shaped once and for all during childhood years. Rather, similar to the interpretation that has been pertinent to techniques of social manipulation and management, such as public relationships and marketing – whose origins also date back to the 1920s – it was a dynamic and flexible material that could be effectively moulded and fabricated to control human behaviour while leaving the subjects unaware of the real triggers of their acts.[42]

If Constructivist artists embraced engineering principles to represent the construction of a new reality, the Rationalists – architects called to construct this material reality – adopted the principles of empiriocriticism in order to control its unconscious psychological representation. In this very embedment in economic reality they found the disciplinary particularity of architecture, distinguishing it from art, which remained transcendent to it. What distinguished architecture from engineering, economics and other non-creative disciplines was its preoccupation with the unconscious perception of form, which, according to the Rationalists, opened the way for design creativity. Rationalist architecture created ideal Platonic forms, which could finally be apprehended by humans. But ironically, these forms remained invisible to the mind, making humans lose that which has defined their identity since the Enlightenment: an ability to employ rational cognition. Moreover, the deified humans were deprived of the accidental, the moody, and the contingent, valued by contemporary postmodernist humanism. Gods turned into marionettes, used and manipulated by architects. But the marionettes, on the other hand, turned into gods: not a mere material of laboratory experiments, the beholders of Rationalist architecture were co-workers in the great common endeavor of the construction of communism. Deprived of individual experiences and judgements, they received a new, collective subjectivity, which transformed their minds and bodies to enable them to rationalise their efforts at surviving and prospering. And what, if not that, was the task of the modernist project?

NOTES

1 The renowned avant-garde school of art and architecture in Moscow, VKhUTEMAS (Higher Art and Technical Studios) was founded in 1920; in 1926, with some modification of its program, it was renamed VKhUTEIN (Higher Art and Technical Institute), which persisted until 1930.

2 Nikolai Dokuchaev, 'Arkhitekturnyi fakul'tet VKhUTEMASa', in *Arkhitektura: raboty arkhitekturnogo fakul'teta VKhUTEMASa, 1920–1927* (Moscow: Izd-vo Vkhutemasa, 1927).

3 Jacques Rancière, *The Aesthetic Unconscious*, trans. Debra Keates and James Swenson (Cambridge: Polity, 2009 [2001]).

4 On Freudianism in Russia, see: Alexander Etkind, *The Eros of the Impossible: The History of Psychoanalysis in Russia* (Boulder, CO: Westview Press, 1997); and Martin A. Miller, *Freud and the Bolsheviks: Psychoanalysis in Imperial Russia and the Soviet Union* (New Haven, CT: Yale University Press, 1998).

5 See Alexei Alexeyevich Kurbanovsky, 'Freud, Tatlin, and the Tower: How Soviet Psychoanalysts Might Have Interpreted the Monument to the Third International', in *Slavic Review*, 67(4) (Pittsburgh, PA: Association for Slavic, East European, and Eurasian Studies, 2008), pp. 892–906.

6 A remark made by comrade Stolpner during the discussion. Quoted in Alexei Alexeyevich Kurbanovsky, 'Freud, Tatlin and the Tower', p. 895.

7 B[ernard] Bykhovskii, 'O metodologicheskikh osnovaniiakh psikhoanaliticheskogo uchenia Freida' ('On the methodological foundations of the psychoanalytical teaching of Freud'), in *Pod znamenem Marksizma* (*Under the Banner of Marxism*) 11–12 (Moscow, 1923), pp. 158–77. Translation by the author.

8 Mikhail Bakhtin (pod maskoj) [(under a mask)], *Freidizm. Formal'nyi metod v literaturovedenii. Marksizm i filosofia iazyka. Stat'I* (*Freudianism: Formal Method in Literature Studies. Marxism and the Philosophy of Language*) (Moscow: Labirint, 2000), p. 117.

9 Eduard von Hartmann, *Philosophy of the Unconscious*, trans. William Chatterton Coupland, vol. 1 (London: K. Paul, Trench, Trübner & Co, 1893), p. 44.

10 Remark made by G.A. Kharazov during the discussion. *Vestnik Kommunisticheskoi Akademii* (*Journal of the Communist Academy*) 12 (Moscow, 1925), pp. 256–7. Quoted in Alexei Kurbanovsky, 'Freud, Tatlin and the Tower', p. 895.

11 Jonathan Crary, *Suspensions of Perception: Attention, Spectacle, and Modern Culture* (Cambridge, MA: The MIT Press, 2000), p. 172.

12 Anatolii Lunacharskii, 'Osnovy positivnoi estetiki' ('Foundations of positive aesthetics'), in *Ocherki realisticheskogo mirovozzrenia* (*Essays in a Realist Worldview*) (St. Petersburg: Izdatel'stvo S. Dorovatovskogo i A. Charushnikova, 1903), pp. 114–82.

13 See Aleksandr Potebnia, *Iz zapisok po teorii slovesnosti* (*From Notes on the Theory of Philology*) (Khar'kov: Parovaiia tip. i litografiia M. Zil'berberg, 1905).

14 Dmitrii Ovsianiko-Kulikovskii, *Voprosy psikhologii tvorchestva* (St. Petersburg: D.E. Zhukovskii, 1902).

15 Dmitrii Ovsianiko-Kulikovskii, 'Vvedenie v nenapisannuiu knigu po psikhologii umstvennogo tvorchestva (nauchno-filosofskogo i khudozhestvennogo)' ('Introduction to an unwritten book on the psychology of intellectual creativity [scientific-philosophical and artistic]'), in N.V. Os'makov, *Psikhologicheskoe napravleneie v russkom literaturovedenii* (*The Psychological Trend in Russian Literature Studies*) (Moscow: Prosveschenie, 1981), pp. 109–21 (p. 111).

16 See V. Kemenov, 'Dovol'no metafiziki! (Protiv idealizma Novitskogo)' ('Enough metaphysics! [Against Novitskii's idealism]'), in *Za proletarskoe iskusstvo* (*For a Proletarian Art*) 11–12 (Moscow: Ogiz-Izogiz, 1931), pp. 8–12; Aleksandr Gorelov, *Kontseptsiia nauki kak simvolicheskogo opisaniia v filosofii P.A. Florenskogo* (*The Conception of Science as a Symbolic Description in the Philosophy of P.A. Florenskii*) (dissertation, Russian Academy of Sciences, Institute of Philosophy, 2008); Charlotte Douglas, 'Mach and Malevich: Sensation, Suprematism, and the Objectless World', in *The Structuralist*, 49/50 (Saskatoon: University of Saskatchewan, 2009), pp. 58–65.

17 Nikolai Ladovskii, 'Osnovy postroeniia teorii arkhitektury (pod znakom ratsionalisticheskoi estetiki)', in *Izvestia ASNOVA* (*ASNOVA Newsletter*) 1 (Moscow, 1926), pp. 3–5 (p. 3).

18 Nikolai Ladovskii, 'Vyvody tov. Ladovskogo k analizu poniatii konstruktsiia i kompozitsia. Protokol No. 12 sektsiia otdela iskusstva INKhUKa' ('The analysis of the notions of construction and composition. Conclusions of Comrade Ladovskii. Proceedings No. 12 of the section of the INKhUK department of art'), Russian State Tretiakov Gallery, Manuscript Department, f. 148, op. 1, d. 87, l. 1. Translation by the author. The contributions of Ladovskii and Krinskii are discussed in Selim Khan-Magomedov, *Nikolai Ladovskii* (Moscow: S.E. Gordeev, 2011), pp. 84–8. For a comprehensive analysis of the discussion of construction and composition focussed in the Constructivists' approach see Maria Gough, *The Artist as Producer: Russian Constructivism in Revolution* (Berkeley, CA: University of California Press, 2005), pp. 39–59.

19 Nikolai Dokuchaev, 'Osnovy iskusstva arkhitektury (Kurs dlia khudozhestvennykh tekhnikumov)' ('Foundations of the art of architecture [A course for professional art schools]'), in *Sbornik materialov po khudozhestvennomy obrazovaniu* (*Collection of Materials on Artistic Education*) (Moscow: Gos. Izd, 1927), pp. 82–103 (p. 82).

20 The term 'Rationalism' allowed subsequent scholars to avoid using the derogatory 'Formalism', a nickname given to the group by the Constructivists, and frequently used in the 1920s and 1930s. The word 'Rationalism' was coined as a counterpart to 'Constructivism' by historian Selim Khan-Magomedov. See Margarete Vöhringer, *Avantgarde Und Psychotechnik: Wissenschaft, Kunst Und Technik Der Wahrnehmungsexperimente in Der Frühen Sowjetunion* (Göttingen: Wallstein Verlag, 2007), p. 42.

21 Nikolai Dokuchaev, 'Poiasnitel'naia zapiska k kursu 'iskusstvo arkhitektury' dlia khudozhestvennykh tekhnikumov' ('Explanatory note to the course "The Art of Architecture" for professional art schools'), in *Sbornik materialov po khudozhestvennomy obrazovaniu* (*Collection of Materials on Artistic Education*) (Moscow: Gos. Izd., 1927), pp. 79–81 (p. 79).

22 'Protokol zasedania rabochei gruppy arkhitektorov INKhUKa' ('Minutes of a meeting of the Working group of architects at INKhUK'), 26 March 1921, Selim Khan-Magomedov, *Ratsionalizm (Ratsio-arkhitektura) 'Formalizm'* (Moscow: Arkhitektura-S, 2007), p. 108. A similar dictionary of artistic terms had, however, been composed by GAKhN (The State Academy of Artistic Sciences), which also based its research methodology on psychophysiological aesthetics. The dictionary remained unpublished until recently.

23 Ernst Mach, *Contributions to the Analysis of the Sensations* (Chicago, IL: The Open Court Publishing Company, 1897), p. 22.

24 Ibid., pp. 2–3.

25 Ibid., p. 10.

26 Ibid., p. 3.

27 Quoted in Selim Khan-Magomedov, *Ratsionalizm (Ratsio-arkhitektura) 'Formalizm'*, p. 119. Translation by the author.

28 Selim Khan-Magomedov, *Mikhail Korzhev* (Moscow: Russkii Avangard, 2009), p. 32.

29 'Protokol zasedania programmnoi komissii rabochei gruppy arkhitektorov INKhUKa' ('Minutes of the meeting of the Program Commission of the Working Group of Architects at INKhUK'), in Selim Khan-Magomedov, *Ratsionalizm (Ratsio-arkhitektura) 'Formalizm'*, pp. 108–9.

30 'Protokol zasedania rabochei gruppy arkhitektorov INKhUKa', 26 March 1926, p. 108.

31 Selim Khan-Magomedov, *Viktor Balikhin* (Moscow: Russkii avangard, 2009), pp. 83–6. Translation by the author.

32 Nikolai Ladovskii, 'Osnovy postroeniia teorii arkhitektury (pod znakom ratsionalisticheskoi estetiki)', p. 4. Translation by the author.

33 Hildebrand lived in Munich, where he was likely to be known to both the future head of INKhUK, Wassily Kandinsky, and the future rector of VKhUTEMAS (between 1923 and 1926), Vladimir Favorskii (in 1906–7, a student in the Munich school of Hungarian painter Simon Hollósy). Together with N.B. Rosenfel'd, Favorskii translated Hildebrand's essay into Russian in 1914. Hildebrand's book was particularly popular among Russian modernist sculptors, among them Boris Korolev and Sergei Merkurov. See Nikolai Dokuchaev, 'Osnovy iskusstva arkhitektury', p. 88; Aleksey Mikhailov, *Gruppirovki Sovietskoi arkhitektury* (*Groups of Soviet Architecture*) (Moscow / Leningrad: OGIZ, 1932), p. 44.

34 Adolf Hildebrand, 'The Problem of Form in the Fine Arts', in *Empathy, Form, and Space: Problems in German Aesthetics, 1873–1893*, trans. Harry Francis Mallgrave and Eleftherios Ikonomou (Santa Monica, CA: Getty Center for the History of Art and the Humanities, 1994), pp. 227–80 (p. 245).

35 Ibid., p. 235.

36 Ibid., p. 233.

37 Dokuchaev's emphasis. Nikolai Dokuchaev, 'Osnovy iskusstva arkhitektury', p. 90. Translation by the author.

38 Ladovskii, 'Osnovy postroeniia teorii arkhitektury (pod znakom ratsionalisticheskoi estetiki)', p. 4. Translation by the author.

39 Peter Eisenman, 'Maison Dom-ino and the Self-referential Sign', in *Oppositions*, 15/16 (New York: Institute for Architecture and Urban Studies, Winter/Spring 1979), pp. 118–28.

40 See Sarah Whiting and Robert Somol in 'Notes Around the Doppler Effect and Other Moods of Modernism', in *Perspecta*, 33 (New Haven, CT: Yale University School of Architecture, 2002), pp. 72–7.

41 Nikolai Dokuchaev, 'Programma na izuchenie form dlia II-oi gruppy Osnovnogo otdelenia Ob'edinennykh masterskikh VKhUTEMASa', quoted in Selim Khan-Magomedov, *Mikhail Korzhev*, pp. 56–7; Selim Khan-Magomedov, *Ratsionalizm (Ratsio-arkhitektura) 'Formalizm'*, pp. 165–7.

42 On the history of these techniques, see Ellen Herman, *The Romance of American Psychology: Political Culture in the Age of Experts* (Berkeley: University of California Press, 1995); Stuart Ewen, *Pr!: A Social History of Spin* (New York: Basic Books, 1996). For an example of a contemporary use of the unconscious in marketing, see Douglas Van Praet, *Unconscious Branding: How Neuroscience Can Empower (and Inspire) Marketing* (New York: Palgrave Macmillan, 2012).

PART II
The Unconscious as a Discourse for Architecture of the City

5

Aldo Rossi and the Field of the Other

Lorens Eyan Holm

INTRODUCTION

One of the best ways to approach Aldo Rossi's project for the city is to understand it as a psychoanalysis of cities. That would explain the quote from Sigmund Freud's *Civilisation and its Discontents* comparing the unconscious to the Eternal City, with which Peter Eisenman prefaces Rossi's *The Architecture of the City*. It would explain the melancholy that prevails in the work; it would explain the shadow hand of an Other who witnesses the work but who – unlike the chorus in Greek tragedy – remains unannounced and absent. It would also explain the difference between historicism – with which Rossi is often associated by those who misunderstand him – and the retrospective glance that is the defining trope of psychoanalysis and which has nothing to do with nostalgia. In an analysis, the subject gazes at the unconscious with a kind of retrospective glance forward.[1]

A psychoanalysis of cities would aim to construct a city that is intelligible to its collective subject. We need to be careful what we mean by *intelligible*. Lacan insisted that the aim of analysis is not to interpret the unconscious, but to make sense of it. Lacan understood unconscious desire as a field; the aim of analysis is to give the subject a position, an orientation, and a direction within this field, rather than to provide an explanation of it that would appeal to the understanding of the ego. In French and Italian, the word 'sense' still carries this meaning of direction and orientation. In the streets of Rome, the '*senso unico*' signs mark the one-way system.

Rossi's architecture of the city is a vision of a certain form of continuity in which one might orient oneself, but the form of this continuity has little to do with the spatial continuity that got its iconic expression in the Nolli plan of Rome. Following Rossi, I will call it *analogic*. Rossi is rarely concerned with space *per se*, he is far more concerned with objects. His drawings and texts accumulate architectural and urban elements: the towers, arcades, bridges, basilicas that recur throughout history in different forms, uses, and contexts. He understands the city as an effect of historically situated economic, social, and political drivers. This materialist account

5.1 Aldo Rossi, 'Project for a municipal piazza' (1975). © Eredi Aldo Rossi / Courtesy: Fondazione Aldo Rossi, Milano + FFMAAM | Collezione Francesco Moschini e Gabriel Vaduva A.A.M. Architettura Arte Moderna. In which the architecture of the city is constituted of recurring elements, or the lexicon of the city of the dead.

of the city is never entirely resolved with the analogical city. The analogical city is a vision of the city as a material discourse that has the capacity to position and orient its multitudes. Discourse is something we inhabit. We can ask, what are the architectural elements and grammar of engagement that constitute this discourse, and what are the conditions that have to obtain in order for it to be intelligible to its multitudes? Lacan argued that the unconscious was not a language but was structured like a language. The architecture of the city *is not a language but is structured like a language*. The architecture of the city *is the field of the Other*.

Rossi moves quickly from the architecture of the city as a collective project of construction to the architecture of the city as constitutive of collective memory. The unconscious is never far from Rossi's text and it is the aim of this chapter to extend his argument by imposing a psychoanalytic model upon the city. This chapter will argue that in order for the city to function as the collective memory of its inhabitants, it must function like a language to them. It must constitute the exteriorised field of signifiers from which we are alienated – it is other to us – but which shapes our identities, defines what we want, positions us before our desire. We can ask to what extent this account of Rossi's city is recognisable in the world. We can also ask how this account of the unconscious in the material terms of the city may shed light on the unconscious. I want to argue that the unconscious is a collective space like the city, although unlike the city it is not public. The architecture of the city is not like the unconscious. This is not a metaphor or figure of speech. It is the unconscious, in so far as architecture is constituted in a signifying system called the analogous city.

THE ARCHITECTURE OF THE CITY: CONSTRUCTION

The Architecture of the City opens with the following statement:

> *The city, which is the subject of this book, is to be understood here as architecture. By architecture I mean not only the visible image of the city and the sum of its different architectures, but architecture as construction, the construction of the city over time. I believe that this point of view, objectively speaking, constitutes the most comprehensive way of analyzing the city; it addresses the ultimate and definitive fact in the life of the collective, the creation of the environment in which it lives (p. 21).*[2]

Rossi's understanding of collective memory is tied to a particular idea of the city constituted by an architecture that is always under construction. For Rossi, the city is constituted of innumerable acts of architecture, which are discrete and unrelated but collectively form a continuous, incremental, and piecemeal process of construction. This 'incomplete', 'interrupted work' (p. 18), is a 'collective artifact' and – we shall argue – it has a collective subject that is known in political discourse as the multitude. It is not an individual, neither exactly the generalised man on the street nor the figure of the city as it is embodied in a mayor or other public figure. Rossi's city is a continual process with no beginning or end: there is no empty site to mark its origins, and no ideal city toward which it aims. Its origin, like the origin of the species, is the process of evolution. And for all its attention to history, there is little nostalgia for or anxiety about origins in Rossi's work.[3]

Rossi creates a dichotomy between the city as 'visible image' and the city as construction; this trope runs through his thought and resurfaces when he discusses collective memory. He is here contrasting the image of the city – usually understood to be a thing – with the continuous process of construction, a contrast that is a caricature of, if not a formula for, the difference between conscious thought – the image, the whole – to the fundamentally unfinished flow of desire (Freud) or signifiers (Lacan) that constitutes the unconscious processes. We will see that this dichotomy will undermine the relation of the city as collective memory to its collective subject, a relation that seems to remain unresolved in Rossi's thought.[4]

THE ANALOGOUS CITY: SUBSTITUTION

> *To illustrate [the analogous city] I gave the example of Canaletto's fantasy view of Venice ... in which Palladio's projects for the Ponte di Rialto, the Basilica of Vicenza, and the Palazzo Chiericati are set next to each other and described as if the painter were rendering an urban scene he had actually observed. These three Palladian monuments ... constitute an analogous Venice formed of specific elements associated with the history of both architecture and the city. The geographic transposition ... constitutes a city that we recognize, even though it is a place of purely architectural references. [A] logical-formal operation could be transformed into a design method ... in which the elements were pre-established and formally defined, but where the significance that sprung forth ... was the authentic, unforeseen, and original meaning of the work (p. 166).*

Chiericati in Venice: the analogical city is introduced as an imaginary scene that has a compelling realism, is recognisable, and self-referential; elsewhere he describes architecture as 'the fixed scene of human events' and compares it to the theatre, which is for him the paradigmatic scene for experimentation with architectural elements and the social relations they house. But more important than the analogical scene is the analogical object, a term we coin for this chapter. Chiericati, the basilica, and the Rialto Bridge are analogical objects. One palazzo replaces another, one bridge replaces another. The analogical city is a city of substitutions based upon a form of free-association with objects such as what might happen in the analytic setting. The serial nature of architecture makes analogical thinking possible: the lexicon of 'pre-existing elements that are deformed by their context' and the analogical principle of substitutions. Analogy is based on likeness. The analogical process of substitution of objects is based on similarities and differences in form, use, and history.[5]

Rossi's drawings are an extended reflection in which he takes possession of his objects and organises them into the series that constitute the analogous city:

1. Cubes that could be fly-towers, ossuaries, apartment blocks, municipal offices.

2. Pyramids and cones that could be columns, church spires, lighthouses, landmarks, chimneys.
3. Rectangles that could be apartment slabs, office towers.
4. Extruded triangles that could be roofs, folded plate concrete beams, aqueducts, bridges.

Rossi's architectural elements are like words. We do not usually think of language as a serial phenomenon but at the level of its basic unit it is. The significance and originality of the text is derived from the combination of words. He attributes to architecture the symbolic fluidity of texts, to match the material fluidity of construction. Rossi calls it a 'compositional procedure' and a 'logical-formal operation' (p. 166).

The analogical object is always part of a substitution series with other objects and it is always deforming. Unlike Le Corbusier's *objets types* which are deforming towards an ideal – by industrial or other processes – the analogical object is just deforming. Each instance of the object contains traces of past and future instances. There is the trace of Rossi's beloved anonymous rural portico in Chiericati and in the municipal fountain at Segrate. The analogical object is thus quite strictly partial or incomplete. This is true even of Chiericati in Vicenza, where it is still marked by the traces of its potential others. There are thus two 'transpositions' or substitutions in the analogical city: a 'geographic' or spatial one and a temporal one. Nor are these substitutions simple. We could look at all the other ways Chiericati could be in Venice, e.g. part-whole substitutions (column-portico) or synecdoche; the condensation of several forms into one (metaphor); and the like.

In this context, Rossi's theory of types is understood as a formalisation of the architectural principles for substitution. The type is what repeats, what remains the same for each incandescent instance of the type, each of which flares brightly with its particular voice and history. In this regard it is akin to the building regulations which reconstitute architecture as the repetition of a code. The difference is that Rossi's code is much closer to the forms of architecture. If 'type is the very idea of architecture, closest to its essence' (p. 41), then we would expect collective memory to be externalised through architectural types. The type is 'permanent and complex, a logical principle that is prior to form and that constitutes it' (p. 40). '... it reacts dialectically with technique, function, and style, as well as with the collective character and individual moment of the artifact' (p. 41). The theory of types lifts architecture out of the material reality of its singular instances, and reconstitutes it as a symbolic order with the capacity to signify the same and the different, which will become important when we discuss collective memory.[6]

COLLECTIVE MEMORY

In *The Architecture of the City*, the city is the repository of collective memory.

> *One can say that the city itself is the collective memory of its people, and like memory it is associated with objects and places. The city is the locus of the*

> *collective memory. This relation between the locus and the citizenry then becomes the city's predominant image (p. 130).*

Rossi borrows the concept of collective memory from the sociologist Maurice Halbwachs's text *The Collective Memory* (1950). 'Halbwachs ... postulated that imagination and collective memory are the typical characteristics of urban artefacts' (p. 33). Rossi quotes Halbwachs twice:

> *When a group is introduced into a part of space, it transforms it to its image, but at the same time, it yields and adapts itself to certain material things which resist it. It encloses itself in the framework that it has constructed. The image of the exterior environment and the stable relationships that it maintains with it pass into the realm of the idea that it has of itself (p. 130).*

> *... the actual configuration of a large city can be seen as the confrontation of the initiatives of different parties, personalities, and governments. In this way various different plans are superimposed, synthesised, and forgotten, so that the Paris of today is like a composite photograph, one that might be obtained by reproducing the Paris of Louis XIV, Louis XV, Napoleon I, Baron Haussmann in a single image.*[7]

Halbwachs distinguishes autobiographical memory of the individual from collective memory. Individual memory is memory of events you have witnessed; collective memory is received from others, events that others have told you about. It is the personal memory of others, that has detoured through social codes, and is therefore an effect of historical processes. It is a difference of form and reception, if not of content, and has the essential characteristic for the subject, that it is externalised and materialised in these codes. Halbwachs's model is speech and bearing witness; someone tells you something that they witnessed, which you incorporate into your repertoire of experience. It is easy to see how this model could be transferred to architectural elements and urban artifacts. Instead of speech, an image; instead of an image, a distribution of objects in space.

The lesson Rossi draws from Halbwachs has to do with the identity of what he calls the 'collective', alternatively the 'citizenry of the city'. The image of the city is the image that the collective has of itself, to which he attributes the 'individuality' and 'significance of the urban structure'. But collective memory is more than a question of placed-based identity for Halbwachs because, in the section 'Economic Space', Halbwachs argues that price is a form of collective memory. The price of a product codifies the past trade relations between countries; relations between labour, raw materials, and manufacturers; relations between sellers and buyers.[8] The egress diagrams found in the Building Regulations, which appear in familiar and recurring plan forms, codify a history of building fires. For Halbwachs, memory is embodied in social codes. Language is the paramount code, but the money system, legal codes, liturgy, ritual, advertising, peer pressure, the taboo system ... are also codes. Lacan groups them as the 'field of the Other', alternatively the Symbolic Order, because they constitute the symbolic field within which the subject finds itself, and which collectively determines its reality, its identity, its desire.[9]

Collective memory is a history that we carry with us in our speech. It is in this sense a living history. We may not always be aware of it, but it is invoked in the use of our symbols. In addition to autobiographical and collective memory, Halbwachs had a third category. Historical memory is the past as it is represented or recorded in documents and monuments. It has the status of a reminder. Unlike individual and collective memory, it is dead. When I see Nelson's Column in Trafalgar Square, I may be reminded of Nelson's defeat of Napoleon's navy but it has no relation to the life of the collective; the Trafalgar Square under continual use whose form reflects land parcellisation, and whose edges are redefined by building projects, may qualify as the living memory of the collective. Rossi makes a parallel distinction with respect to monuments and permanent urban artifacts, between pathological and propelling permanences; the pathological ones are out of circulation, the propelling ones continue to be transformed through reuse.

Halbwachs's and Rossi's thesis has problems. They equivocate about the semiotic options for architecture. The collective imprints itself upon space; the city is an image of the collective. We might gaze into the city and see ourselves reflected in it but in neither case does this explain the symbolisation requisite for memory, collective or otherwise. In this regard, Lacan distinguishes the Symbolic and Imaginary Orders. Price is neither an imprint nor an image, but a symbolic object. There is a difference between a material object like a building, and a symbolic object such as what constitutes memory. Hence another gloss on the analogical object. In order to be a memory, something must be internalised, incorporated, even if it is held between the many. Your words penetrate my body, and their meanings penetrate my psyche. It is not the Parthenon that tormented Le Corbusier or that haunts modernism – that's just old rocks sitting on the Acropolis, dead memory, pathological – nor even images of the Parthenon, but the Parthenon as a symbolic object. And it is in the series of recurring architectural elements of which the Parthenon is one, that we expect their original significations to emerge. The Parthenon emerges as a symbolic object with the capacity to signify when an instance of the Parthenon is put into circulation.

FORGETTING ARCHITECTURE

We could speculate forever about Rossi's intent, except for an extraordinary detail in *A Scientific Autobiography*, where it becomes clear that for Rossi, collective memory is not about reflection upon self and identity, but is about symbolic objects within a signifying system.

> *In order to be significant, architecture must be forgotten, or must present only an image for reference which subsequently becomes confounded with memories (p. 45).*

> *Forgetting Architecture comes to mind as a more appropriate title for this book, since while I may talk about a school, a cemetery, a theatre, it is more correct to say that I talk about life, death, imagination (p. 78).*[10]

Forgetting is the flip side of remembering, and when something is forgotten, it is committed to the unconscious. Architecture cannot be committed to the

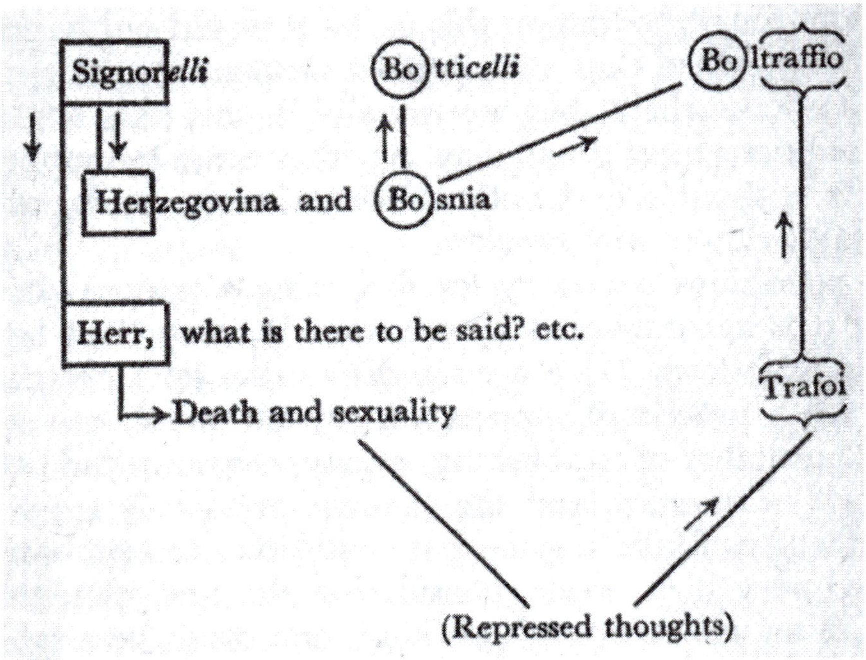

5.2 Freud's 'schematic diagram' of linguistic elements or signifiers, in their 'external associations'. © Bloomsbury Publishing. The lesson of this diagram is that symbolic objects are fluid even if words and buildings are not. Words vanish with their utterance, and buildings are fixed, but the significance of words and buildings to the subject are enduring and mutable. Imagine that this diagram is a plan of Rome or a section of Plug-in City.

unconscious unless it is symbolised. What is out in the world as a material object, enters the psyche as a symbolic one. We change our city through the continual construction of new objects that are deformations of existing ones, and we can change our symbols by committing them to the unconscious where they are subjected to processes of substitution, displacement, condensation. The lesson of the analogical city is that material and symbolic object coincide in the analogical object, but when they are forgotten, they seem to go their separate ways. When something is committed to the unconscious, we may retain its image, but its signification is released. The image is not a memory, but it is confounded with memory, and may be the point of access to its forgotten symbolisation. The image in the mind's eye is a model for consciousness, but it is no more the model for remembering than forgetting. When something is remembered, it returns from the unconscious with a new significance.

FREUD ON REMEMBERING/FORGETTING

School, cemetery, theatre signify life, death, imagination. The most spectacular demonstration of forgetting/remembering is Freud's essay 'The forgetting of proper names' (1901). In what could be a demonstration of Halbwachs's thesis that memory is mapped on to places, Freud struggles to remember the name of Signor*elli* and thinks instead of Botti*celli*, and Boltraffio. After interrogating the sequence of successfully remembered *wrong* names for the unsuccessfully remembered correct name, he concludes that Signorelli was associated in his mind with unconscious thoughts of 'death and sexuality' (p. 3),[11] the repression of which was necessary to maintain the equilibrium of his ego.

A little background: Freud had been talking to a companion about the health practices of the Turks in Bosnia and Herzegovina, who are respectful of doctors ('Herr Doctor') and for whom sex is so important they would rather die than abstain. In addition to being a 'delicate topic' unsuitable to his present company, it reminded him of an incident he would rather forget: one of his patients had killed himself rather than live with a sexual disorder, news which he recently received while staying in Trafoi. He wants to forget Turks and Trafoi (sex and death) by moving onto Signorelli (art). But what he wanted to repress, returns to disrupt his capacity to recall the name of Signorelli. When something is remembered it is plucked back from the gluey attachments of the unconscious (life and death), where it has been transformed.

To explain the 'substitute names' (p. 4) that comprise forgetting/remembering, he arranges the key terms of Signorelli and the names relating to the 'repressed topic' in an 'associative series' (p. 3) or 'associative connection' (p. 4). Hence:

> *Signor ... > Herr > Herzigovina, ... elli > Botticelli; Botticelli > Boltraffio > Bosnia; and Boltraffio > Trafoi.*

Freud keeps getting pulled back from Signorelli (art) to Trafoi (death and sexuality). He calls these links 'external associations' because they are linguistic. They relate not to the content of the words, but to their form, in the way that alliteration may be the linguistic principle for the slip of the tongue or type and place the architectural principles for Canaletto's analogic scene in which Chiericati appears in the place of an other (forgotten) palazzo. The unconscious content 'motivates' (pp. 4, 6) the substitutions ('I am forced to recognize the influence of a motive in the process' [4]) but does not determine them. In the language of twentieth century structuralism, they relate to the signifiers, not the signifieds. The signifier Signorelli is missing from the signifying chain and other signifiers – the names or parts thereof – slip along the chain according to linguistic rules of substitution that are autonomous of their content. In *Seminar VII*, Lacan attributes an originary status to forgetting. The subject of analysis, which in his reading of Freud is tantamount to the subject of the unconscious, is an elision in the signifying chain.[12]

LACAN AND THE FIELD OF THE OTHER

> *The unconscious is structured like a language (p. 203).*
>
> *The unconscious is the discourse of the Other (p. 131).*
>
> *Lacan,* The Four Fundamental Concepts of Psycho-Analysis[13]

Lacan and Freud invoke the city as a figure for the unconscious. For Freud, Rome is the eternal city whose history remains present to its inhabitants; for Lacan, we watch a cybernetic Baltimore from afar. The unconscious appears in Freud's thought as a plenitude from which nothing in the subject's experience disappears completely, everything leaves a trace. It is the reserve from which memory emerges. It appears in analysis as an inscrutable object of reflection that carries the subject's past with it, and to which the subject orients itself for future action. For Lacan, it appears as the field of collectively held signifiers. It is the public realm. The signifier chains and their syntax channel the subject's multiple histories. Freud sometimes attributes punctual qualities to it (like the navel of the dream), but for Lacan, it is the subject who is punctual and the unconscious the field which locates it. The question for both becomes one of signification. How do we make sense of it in ways that allow us to navigate it.

Lacan lifted Freud's thought out of its nineteenth century biologism and rewrote it for twentieth century structuralism. In 'The agency of the letter in the unconscious or reason since Freud' (1957),[14] Lacan insisted upon the central role of Freud's 'discovery' of the unconscious, and regarded his own work as a return to 'the truth of that discovery' (p. 163). Lacan is particularly attentive to the role of speech in Freud's investigations of unconscious formations like dreams and forgetting, and concludes that language has a determining role in structuring them. For example, when Freud argues in *The Interpretation of Dreams* (1900), that the meaning of the dream is an unconscious wish, Lacan shifts the focus from the content to the inter-subjective setting for interpretation. The significance of the unconscious wish in the life of the dreamer is made evident to the dreamer by a process of free association with the remembered dream images in an encounter with the free floating attention of the analyst. Lacan notes that this scene in which the unconscious emerges, is fundamentally inter-subjective, involving self and other. He notes that it is based in language, the rules of which run autonomously in the speech of the subject, due to relaxing the attention of subject and analyst.

Lacan insists that the unconscious is primarily a linguistic phenomenon. In 'The agency of the letter ...', '[T]he topography of this unconscious ... is ... defined by the algorithm: S/s' (p. 163). And, 'To pinpoint the emergence of linguistic science ..., it is contained in the constitutive moment of an algorithm that is its foundation: S/s which is read as: signifier over signified' (p. 149). Lacan is referring to the semiotic model for language. As if the meaning of a word lay under the word. This model describes the relation between dream image (signifier) and unconscious wish (signified), between Freud's series of misremembered names and his fears of sex and death, and between form and content in architecture. It shadows Rossi's relation between the remembered image and architecture's forgotten signification, and the seemingly paradoxical use of the city as the figure for the unconscious: the city which is a material spatial thing and the unconscious a symbolic one. Because the relation between signifier and signified is arbitrary, consensual, and historically and culturally determined – Saussure called it a social contract – architects have invoked it to dismantle the modernist dictate that form follows function.[15]

The unconscious is a paradoxical signified because, unlike meaning, it never appears to the subject. In the interpretation of dreams, interpretation is never complete. There is always a remainder that escapes. The signifier chain never arrives at a signified. This leads Lacan into poststructuralist territory in which signifiers are decoupled from signifieds. He pursues the signifier chains of the subject unencumbered by meaning. He is not interested in the meaning of the dream – he will never arrive at it – but only in the signification of the dream in the life of the dreamer, which will allow him to plot the subject's 'detours to death that make up the highway map of the psyche'.[16]

By insisting on the primacy of language, psychoanalysis seems to conflate epistemology and ontology. 'We only grasp the unconscious finally when it is explicated, in that part of it which is articulated by passing into words' (*Seminar VII*, 32). It is not the dream that is the road to the unconscious but what the dreamer says about the dream. This is not an admission that our access to the unconscious is limited by speech, but a statement that the unconscious is an effect of speech. 'The unconscious is the sum of the effects of speech on a subject ...' (*Seminar XI*, 126).

In *An Introductory Dictionary of Lacanian Psychoanalysis*, Dylan Evans writes that the Other designates a 'radical alterity, an other-ness that transcends the illusory otherness of the imaginary because it cannot be assimilated through identification' (p. 133).[17] Lacan identifies the Other with the Symbolic Order, the sum of symbolic

5.3 Aldo Rossi, '*Il Teatrino Scientifico* with the hand of a saint (1978)'. © Eredi Aldo Rossi / Courtesy: Fondazione Aldo Rossi, Milano + FFMAAM | Collezione Francesco Moschini e Gabriel Vaduva A.A.M. Architettura Arte Moderna. An inventory of architectural elements overshadowed by the hand of the Other; instead of Adam Smith's invisible hand driving the economy, or Halbwachs's subject of economic memory.

systems, which define the subject's identity and desire and mediate the relations of self and others (small 'o'). We touched on the Symbolic Order when we discussed Halbwachs's collective memory. 'The Other must first of all be considered a locus, the locus in which speech is constituted' (*Seminar III*, 274).[18] Lacan relates it to Freud's 'other scene' by which Freud referred to the dream scene of the unconscious. The Other is the scene of the Symbolic Order. We begin to understand its otherness when we contemplate the fact that speech does not originate in us but we are born into it and we have simply forgotten its originary strangeness. It comes from a place outside consciousness. Hence the unconscious is the discourse of the Other. Like Rossi's construction, this locus or field or scene of the Other is always incomplete, there is always a signifier missing.

Words, like buildings, have a life of their own. The paradigm of a discontinuity of the subject's discourse is the slip of the tongue. The unconscious resides in the gap between what you think you mean and what others think you said. Sometimes you don't say what you mean; sometimes the message you send to others is not received the way you intended it. What you say goes out into the world, and it returns to you in an unrecognisable form. Wittgenstein's language game is a game of Chinese whispers. Your unconscious is located in others because it is constituted by what they return to you. The lesson of Lacan is that the unconscious is always external and it is always collective. There are consequences for the unconscious as externalised and materialised in others by language: it is not that the city is like the unconscious but the unconscious is like the city.

TO CONCLUDE WITH THE HAND OF THE OTHER

The shadow of the hand of Sancarlone falls across a city that is otherwise empty. The personification of the Other returns to haunt Rossi's city, as an enigmatic witness.[19] Imagine a time-lapse film of the city. For Rossi, the architecture of the city is a temporal process, not a static array of objects. Like one of those films that documents a building under construction. Only instead of a single building, an aerial view of the whole city with many buildings under construction. It would capture the incremental acts of construction which transform the city, but which – unlike the individual building project – has no plan. Everyone contributes a piece to the mosaic, but no one has the cartoon. An image evolves, but it is not the image of any individual. The city is an alienating place. It seems to construct itself; it seems to speak without us. But in a sense it cannot, because we are building it. Nevertheless, except for tenuous frameworks like planning law, the norms of taste, and master plans, we build it without communicating: projects in different parts of the city are not coordinated with each other. How could these incremental acts be linked to make speech? And whose speech? If the city speaks, who is speaking through it and to whom is it speaking? Who, in other words, is the subject of the architecture of the city?

There is a similar constellation of truth, reality, history, and continuity in the discourses of Rossi and Lacan. We have drawn parallels between Rossi's architecture

5.4 The origin of architecture, in the Cesariano edition of Vitruvius, *On Architecture* (1521). Public domain. Or, the birth of the multitude, in which architecture and language, called together by fire, constitute the field of the Other. The multitude is born in the collective processes of construction and speech, and will remain a multitude so long as construction and speech do not terminate in objects of conscious self-reflection.

of the city and Lacan's field of the Other. We argued that the city functions as a collective unconscious. The city speaks to us, not directly, but in the oblique manner that the unconscious speaks to us, a speech marked by free association and forgetting/remembering. We need to now look at how strange and tenuous this subject of the city is. Rossi attributes agency to the collective. 'The collective memory participates in the … transformation of the space …' (*The Architecture of the City*, p. 130). Signifiers are necessarily the signifiers of a subject but that subject need not be an individual. I want to argue that the subject of the city is not me or you, but the multitude.

Let us imagine Vitruvius's primitive hut, which is one of the scenes in Rossi's scientific theatre. In this primal scene, men wandered aimlessly in the forest. This was their original Hobbsian condition. They were without *senso unico*. At a critical moment, they are drawn to a campfire for warmth and shelter, the remnants of a forest fire, perhaps the fire of creation, in any case, the real has intervened. Once gathered for the first time, they converse. Once conversing, they build. Speech came first, architecture second. Architecture is introduced as a communal form of inscription. The first hut is also the first writing. Speech and flame vanish in the utterance; but writing endures. The endurance of the material signifier is the principle of continuity that makes meaning and memory possible.

When Vitruvius's primitives wander in the forest in their isolation and lack of sense, they are simply individuals isolated in a kind of Brownian movement. They are automatons. Only when they start constructing, do they constitute a multitude. Converging around a fire does not form a collective space, because Vitruvius's people could still be solipsists. Nor does speech, because it vanishes. A multitude is formed when individuals participate in something that endures. The multitude shares a common orientation, not a common identity. Vitruvius's primitives remain a multitude so long as they are engaged in the process of building; they cease to be a multitude if they cease building. They either devolve to isolated individuals again, or they form a group that defends the house. When construction produces a finished building to which they identify, the multitude becomes calcified as a defended armored carapace, precisely what the city never was to Rossi.

Political discourse distinguishes the public or the people ('we the people …') from the multitude. One of the places where psychoanalytic and political discourse converge is in their respective concepts of the field of the Other and the multitude. In political discourse, the people are an imaginary body to which politics addresses itself; the multitude are the reality of individuals that exceed any attempt to name or identify them as a discrete whole. The group is an individual subject. In the present context, we regarded the image in Rossi's concept of collective memory as a distraction. It runs against the idea of the collective subject. The multitude never amounts to a unity. The image by which a public are identified, either by the politician or by the public itself, will always be inadequate to it. To impose it upon the multitude will always constitute a form of repression. There would be no unconscious without repression so it is not as if we can dispense with the image. The city as collective unconscious does not have a public, it has a multitude. This does not mean that the multitude does not have a certain power and orientation. To attribute to it an unconscious and to name that unconscious as a collective act of building, is to give it an orientation and power.

So long as our primitives keep the process of construction open, they will remain the real subject of the city as opposed to the imaginary subject of identity politics. We have to resist the narcissistic temptation of making objects with which we collectively identify, in other words, to regard construction as ending in complete objects, and façades as closure. Topping out is a pause and not an end in the construction of the city. The multitude is a collective subject, not a discrete group and not a disaggregate of individuals. If the unconscious is the discourse of the city, then this discourse is not mine, the speech that comes from me, the speech that I own; it is a speech that comes from elsewhere. Nor is it your speech – that's the speech of an other. It is the speech that I free up by construction, that comes to me from the clanging city. I am not its subject, except when I am the multitude.[20]

Construction opens up a form of collective space and time that may be political by nature because it is synonymous with a form of class consciousness that evades conscious reflection. We must distinguish this collective space from the space in which people gather to be heard and seen, like the piazza of the Renaissance city or the metro system of the industrial city, what Hannah Arendt in *The Human Condition* called the *space of public appearance*, where people exercise their political power. In his paper 'An Analogical Architecture', Rossi claims that 'architecture is transformed into autobiographical experience' and 'I am deformed ....' Although we may each make our own analogical city this does not undercut the collective nature of the project. The analogical city is a universal condition because we all do it, and we all do it according to the same shared linguistic-like laws of architecture.[21]

The architecture of the city is the field of material signifiers. It has a closer affinity to the written word than to the spoken one, a closer affinity to inscription than to voice. In his project to deconstruct *logos*, the word as it prioritises speech throughout the history of philosophy, Jacques Derrida shifts the focus from the living voice – breath of the speaker – as the bearer of a present meaning (Plato, *The Phaedrus*), to writing as the bearer of a deferred or delayed meaning in texts. Derrida coins the term *différance* (with an *a*) for this property of meaning; like Lacan's *objet a*, it speaks of a continual process of differing and deferring of meaning. For Derrida, this differing/deferring opens up a space between the subject and meaning, and gives it a temporality. Meaning is not present in the subject but is postponed for its realisation in the next act of speaking. There must be a trace that endures, something has to endure of this present conversation around the campfire, if there is to be meaning and memory. Construction is here assimilated to language, but the model for how it signifies is writing not speech, text not dialogue. Each new basilica is the re-inscription of the basilica type. Creation is writing. We are scribes.

In 'Freud and the Scene of Writing', Derrida argues that for all the attention to speech in psychoanalytic discourse and practice, the psychoanalytic model for speech is not living voice but inscription. Freud's metaphors relate to writing; Freud's model for memory is the path and the trace that endures.[22] The slip is of the pen, not the tongue. After the voice stops echoing around the consulting room, something must endure in order for the slip to be caught by others; something of the symbol must endure in order for it to be incorporated and worded/worked on by the unconscious. There must be some remainder once the voice is exhausted. For Rossi it is not the ruins that remain which make analogy possible (that's dead, pathological), but the field of construction, to which each building act contributes; it makes analogical thinking possible because it makes a certain form of recovery possible. In *Moses and Monotheism*, Freud argued that in the oral tradition, the word is not freed from the coercion of logical thinking, until it is written down and can be forgotten. Repression is here equated with freedom from logical thought that lets signification run its course. Rossi belongs to the tradition that resists logical thinking. Instead *ana*logical thinking produces *an*architecture. In the hands of Gordon Matta-Clark it led to cutting and a certain form of laughing out loud anarchy. For Rossi, it leads to the analogical city and the memory trace.

The city is the discourse of the Other; it speaks to the multitude. The aim of this chapter has been to deepen our relationship to the city, a relation that seems threatened by every attempt at closure, of which even this work is guilty.

In contemporary structuralist models of the unconscious, the unconscious is a relation between subjects, not an entity of dubious metaphysical status. It is:

- inter-subjective;
- shared;
- embodied by speech and by other material signifiers;
- depersonalised;
- the field of signifiers is not in us, we are in it.

The city as collective unconscious is a form of collective speech and collective space. We would like to speak of a speech of space and a space of speech. It is marked by the mistake. It exists because others exist and because something of the mistake endures. It is a form in which we all participate and from which we are all alienated; as such the city is the opposite of identity discourse.

Sodom and Gomorrah, Carthage, Dresden. We have great models for the material destruction of cities but few for their symbolic destruction. Rem Koolhaas said that the contemporary city is intelligible to those who understood development finance, which is tantamount to saying that it is not. When we erode the possibility of making sense of the city, we foreclose it to the multitude. We erode the class unconsciousness of the multitude which leads to a certain form of isolated individualism. The city offers a promise. It is like a home where nothing is lost, and if we could learn to return to it, to inhabit it, to be attentive to it, we would never be lost, never bereft, never without the love of others.

NOTES

1 Rossi is a frequent reference in the manifestations of the New Urbanism, the historicising styles and scales of which constitute an ill-conceived contextualism. Familiar advocates of New Urbanism include Leon Krier, Andres Duany, and Prince Charles.

2 Page references in this and the following three sections from Aldo Rossi, *The Architecture of the City*, trans. Diane Ghirardo and Joan Ockman (Cambridge, MA: The MIT Press, 1982), from *L'Architettura della città* (Padova: Marsilio, 1966).

3 Rossi is clear about the incomplete, temporal, collective nature of the architecture of the city: '*la fabbrica della città* ... means building in the sense of man's construction as it continues over time'. And '... architecture, or the *fabbrica* of the city, constitutes a ... collective artifact and derives from this its essential features' (*The Architecture of the City*, 18).

4 Gilles Deleuze and Félix Guattari reckon that Marx's capital and Freud's libido are the two seminal fluids of the twentieth century. For the treatment of the image as static in relation to the subject, see first, Lacan's discussion in 'The mirror stage as formative of the function of the I', in *Écrits: A Selection*, trans. Alan Sheridan (New York: W.W. Norton, 1977), pp. 1–7, and the discussion around his schema L diagram, in which the imaginary relation blocks – represses – the flow of signifiers between subject and Other. Freud's diagram of the psychical agencies in 'The Ego and the Id' (1923) shows a scrotum of desire (id, seat of the unconscious) with a shimmering outer image surface (ego), for which see Figure 1 on page 14 of Sigmund Freud, 'The Ego and the

Id' (1923), in *The Standard Edition of the Complete Psychological Works of Sigmund Freud*, vol. 19, trans. James Strachey (London: Hogarth Press and the Institute of Psycho-Analysis, 1962).

5 *Roma Interrotta* is a form of analogous city, in which different architects substituted their buildings for Roman ones.

6 Fifteen years later, Rossi used the 'Introduction to the First American Edition' of *The Architecture of the City* to reprise these themes of analogous city, continuous construction, and pre-existing elements. New York is 'an 'analogous city' of unexpected meanings' (Rossi's quotation marks) and defines the analogous city as a city whose architecture is 'constructed out of pre-existing elements that are ... deformed by their ... context' (p. 15). 'The analogous city is ... the city in its diverse totality; this fact is visible ... in the piecemeal structure of New York, and in the memories and analogies that every city ... offers' (p. 18). 'This overlapping of the individual and the collective memory, together with the invention that takes place within the *time* of the city, has led me to the concept of *analogy*. Analogy expresses itself through a process of architectural design whose elements are preexisting and formally defined, but whose true meaning is unforeseen at the beginning and unfolds only at the end of the process' (p. 18). 'This ... is the meaning of preexisting elements: the city ... presents itself through ... clearly defined elements such as house, school, church, factory, monument' (p. 18).

7 A quote remarkably like the quote from Freud's *Civilisation and its Discontents* with which Eisenman began his preface to *The Architecture of the City*. These quotes are from Chapter 4, 'Space and the Collective Memory', of Maurice Halbwachs, *The Collective Memory*, trans. Francis J. Ditter Jr. and Vida Yazdi Ditter (New York: Harper & Row, 1980 [1950]). Halbwachs is one of the theorists of place-based memory, identity, social formations.

8 These relations constitute the economic group, and are inseparable from an economic space constituting the spatial and temporal boundaries between seller and buyer (the checkout counter, when the auctioneer's hammer falls), the location of resources and factories, etc.

9 Roland Barthes articulated the linguistic and visual codes of advertising; Claude Lévi-Strauss articulated the visual and linguistic codes that constitute the customs, taboos, and rituals of societies.

10 The school at Fagnano Olona, the Modena Cemetery (the city of the dead), the Scientific Theatre. Page references in this section from Aldo Rossi, *A Scientific Autobiography*, trans. Lawrence Venuti (Cambridge, MA: The MIT Press, 1981).

11 Page references in this section from Sigmund Freud, Chapter 1, 'The Forgetting of Proper Names', in *The Psychopathology of Everyday Life: Forgetting, Slips of the Tongue, Bungled Actions, Superstitions and Errors*, trans. Alan Tyson, ed. James Strachey (New York: W.W. Norton, 1960 [1901]). In *Beyond the Pleasure Principle*, Freud argues that the life and death drives are the two fundamental drives that motivate the psyche; they are the flywheels of the psyche. If all content relates to sexuality and death (in Freud's terms, the unconscious is constituted by the 'ideational representatives' of the death and life drives), then content becomes indifferent and what becomes significant are the linguistic detours to arrive at it.

12 Jacques Lacan, *The Seminar of Jacques Lacan, Book VII: The Ethics of Psychoanalysis 1959–1960*, trans. Dennis Porter, ed. Jacques-Alain Miller (New York: W.W. Norton, 1992). 'A subject originally represents nothing more than the following fact: he can forget. Strike out that "he"; the subject is literally at his beginning the elision of a signifier as such, the missing signifier in the chain' (p. 224).

13 Jacques Lacan, *Seminar XI: The Four Fundamental Concepts of Psycho-Analysis*, trans. Alan Sheridan, ed. Jacques-Alain Miller (New York: W.W. Norton, 1981).

14 Jacques Lacan, 'The agency of the letter in the unconscious or reason since Freud', in *Écrits: A Selection* (New York: W.W. Norton, 1977) pp. 146–78.

15 Semiotics distinguishes two types of signs in addition to the symbol, based on the relation between signifier and signified. Words are symbols. An index is a sign in which there is a causal relation between signifier and signified, like the north star and north; for an icon, there is a visual likeness. Most images are icons. For an account of semiotic theory for architecture, cf. Geoffrey Broadbent, 'A plain man's guide to the theory of signs in architecture', reprinted in Kate Nesbitt (ed.), *Theorizing a new agenda for architecture: an anthology of architectural theory 1965–1995* (New York: Princeton Architectural Press, 1996). In discussing their work, Rodolfo Silvetti and Jorge Machado state that the relation between form and content in architecture is arbitrary and hence that meaning is inevitable. Cf. Rodolfo Machado and Jorge Silvetti, 'Banfire', in George Baird and Mark Lewis (eds), *Queues Rendezvous Riots: questioning the public in art and architecture* (Banff, Alberta: Walter Philips Gallery and Banff Centre for the Arts, 1994), pp. 18–27.

16 I have this phrase from the literary theorist, Harold Bloom, who argues that poststructuralist thought 'confuse[s] meaning with signification, a confusion … evident … in the most advanced models of post-Structuralist thought. For Emerson, meaning is concerned with survival, and signification is only an instrumentality of meaning …'. Harold Bloom, *Poetry and Repression: Revisionism from Blake to Stevens* (London: Yale University Press, 1976), p. 240. According to Bloom, signification is a function of language and bound by it; meaning transcends language. Lacan argued that meaning is imaginary. It is a reflective relation a subject has to itself; signification goes through the field of the Other.

17 Dylan Evans, *An Introductory Dictionary of Lacanian Psychoanalysis* (New York: Routledge, 1996).

18 Jacques Lacan, *The Seminar of Jacques Lacan, Book III: The Psychoses 1955–1956*, trans. Russell Grigg, ed. Jacques-Alain Miller (New York: W.W. Norton, 1993).

19 *A Scientific Autobiography* is interleaved with a portfolio of architectural images of significance for Rossi, the second of which (after the vault of Alberti's Sant'Andrea, Mantua) is the statue of San Carlone, Arona, whose hand appears in many of Rossi's drawings; it functions as an absent witness to the architectural scene.

20 Cf. Paolo Virno, *A Grammar of the Multitude: An Analysis of Contemporary Forms of Life* (New York: Semiotext(e), 2004), and Paolo Virno, 'Three Remarks Regarding the Multitude's Subjectivity and its Aesthetic Component', in Daniel Birnbaum and Isabelle Graw (eds), *Under Pressure: Pictures, Subjects, and the New Spirit of Capitalism* (Frankfurt: Sternberg Press, 2008), whence the following quote: 'The metropolis appears as a labyrinth of expressions, metaphors, proper names, and propositions, of tenses and moods of the verb; and saying this is no simple analogy. The metropolis actually is a linguistic formation, an environment that is above all constituted by objectivized discourse, by preconstructed code, and by materialized grammar. To find one's bearings in a metropolis is gaining linguistic experience' (p. 33).

21 Aldo Rossi, 'An Analogical Architecture', trans. David Stewart, in *Architecture and Urbanism* 56 (Tokyo: A+U Publishing, May 1976), pp. 74–6. Republished without the images in Kate Nesbitt (ed.), *Theorizing a New Agenda for Architecture: An Anthology of Architectural Theory 1965–1995* (1996). Another reprise, focussing on Rossi's own work.

22 Jacques Derrida, 'Freud and the Scene of Writing', in *Writing and Difference*, trans. Alan Bass (Chicago, IL: The University of Chicago Press, 1978). Derrida traces the metaphor of writing in Freud's account of memory, a path which begins in the *Project for a Scientific Psychology* (1895) and ends in the 'Note on the Mystic Writing-Pad' (1925). Freud conceives memory as a process of breaching (*Bahnung*, literally *pathbreaking*). 'Breaching, the tracing of a trail, opens up a conducting path' (Derrida, p. 200). The concept of pathbreaking is found in related contexts, like Le Corbusier's account of the primitive hut myth in *Vers une Architecture* in which man cuts a road through the jungle before erecting a tent.

6

Seducing God(s): Renaissance Ideal Cities as Mirror-images of Western Subjectivity

Francesco Proto

She can't pass a mirror without seducing it.

Sofia Coppola (dir.), Marie Antoinette

INTRODUCTION

In *La Società dei Simulacri* (1979), Mario Perniola ascribes Rome's political-military power to the practice of the *evocatio* (convocation, evocation), through which the *geniuses* of the cities with which they were at war were 'seduced' by being invited to Rome. Being the *conditio sine qua non* for the successful accomplishment of the *evocatio*, the designation of both the city and its genius with their original names, the Romans used to keep the original Latin name of their city secret, for only so could they avoid enduring this same ritual and prevent their genius from being seduced in return. The etymon of *sed-ducere* ('to seduce') is not by accident 'to lead astray', 'divide' or 'split'.[1]

The Romans knew very well that 'the real world begins, paradoxically, to disappear at the very same time as it begins to exist' and, according to a concern later reflected by the opposition between the iconoclasts and the iconophiles during the Byzantine era, did their best to sidestep any representation or materialisation of their divinity.[2] If the Romans could not be seduced for a long time, it was because their symbols and beliefs could not be either represented or materialised. In a fatal reversal of circumstances, this is exactly the destiny encountered by the Christian God at the time when Renaissance architecture first occurred.

By building on the homology that Jacques Lacan draws between the mirror stage (a fundamental aspect of subjective construction) and the optical model (a device with both a concave and plane mirror), this chapter argues that the Western city mainly unfolds as a projection of the prevalent subjective construction over different epochs and that, as such, it 'mirrors' back one of the Lacanian clinical structures of the subject (neurotic, pervert and psychotic) in the Lacanian theoretical model of the unconscious. The recourse to the poststructuralist historical technique of genealogy, through which such a condition is enucleated, is thus justified not just by the need to account for the predominant ideologies established since the inception of the so-called 'classic' age of modernity, but also by the very need to emphasise how the latter directly impacted the subjective construction of the self.[3] The latter is thus universalised and assumed as prevailing on the basis of an emerging, homogenising and all-encompassing visual culture. The image, into which most architecture comes to be translated, becomes the axiom that makes for certain principles to be postulated and disseminated.[4]

Renaissance Europe, and, in particular, fifteenth century Italy – where the new vision of Christ as omnipotent (*cunctipotent*, *pantocrator*) rather than suffering (*patient*) originally spreads to soon inundate the rest of the continent – is thus targeted as the geo-political area of interest for an analysis of the shift from a language-based construction of the unconscious to an image-based one, and according to a process that exceeds the very and more immediate fleshy embodiment that the Christian tradition made of God himself (Christ). By the time God is materialised through a complex system of mathematical ratios, geometrical proportions and perspectival apparatuses, such a God is also alienated from spiritual power (the Church). God and his most direct emanation – nature – are by now open to any possible manipulation.

It is therefore in this respect that the shift from Christ as the *Man of Sorrow* to the *Pantocrator* is of particular importance here: for if the former reflects the subject's passive acceptance of the fixed hierarchies regulating the universe, the appearance of the latter reflects an active mobility in the socio-political ladder.[5] In the newly born economic order – capitalism – not only is wealth a direct expression of God's benevolence (Protestantism), but so is genius. The architect is he for whom the ability to grasp the invisible 'correspondences' of the mundane becomes an outcome of the specific combination of observation (vision) and representation (craftsmanship).

By arguing that the emergence of bourgeoisie ideology over the Quattrocento produces a regression in the construction of Western subjectivity, this study draws on the Lacanian maxim 'man's desire is the desire of the Other', and, in order to both illustrate and exemplify the findings that Lacan extrapolates from the invention of the so-called optical model or double-mirror device, let ideal cities emerge as one of the most straightforward manifestations of such phenomena.[6] Hence the deconstruction of the Christian dogma on which the whole ideological apparatus came to be built ('man is made in the image and resemblance of God') and that, given its striking resonance with the 'mirror stage' (Lacan), is here addressed as the starting point of a process of *mise-en-abyme* that invests Western society in its entirety. Following this process, not only is the previous Symbolic order, as based on language ('In principium erat verbum') severely undermined, but pushed towards an Imaginary order whose underlying mechanism is also imposed to a new perception of the visible: just as man must aspire to resemble as much as possible his specular, ideal image in the mirror (Christ), so reality must aspire to resemble its specular image in its ideal representation (linear perspective).[7] That vanishing point on the horizon of the perspective window becomes the very utopia of Western civilisation.

In order to illustrate the shift from medieval ideology, as based on the Name-of-the-Father, to the Renaissance, as based on the imaginary reflection into a mirror, I will thus make use of the Lacanian theorisation of the mirror stage 'as formative of the function of the I'.[8] Since the aspect that I want to stress here is the way in which the mirror stage fits into the double movement of introjection (ego ideal) and projection (ideal ego) that constitutes the optical model, the emergence of the perverse structure of subjectivity, as anticipating the prevalent psychotic structure of Western subjectivity in the postmodern era, will therefore briefly be addressed in the conclusion of this chapter. The whole genealogy of the evolution of the relationship between Western subjectivity and its mirror-staging into the Western city will emerge as the incontrovertible evidence of a weakening of the Name-of-the-Father that Lacan first theorised via the 'capitalist discourse' during the 1970s. The latter is here taken into account as an effect of the establishment of a bourgeoisie ideology, and the consequent spreading of images, during the Renaissance.

'ADAEQUATIO REI ET INTELLECTUS': LACAN AND THE MIDDLE AGES

Lacan distinguished the ego ideal from the ideal ego in his optical model, where a concave and a flat mirror face each other to create the illusion of a bouquet fitting a vase (the two are, in reality, separated), and argued that while the ideal ego is the source of an imaginary projection, the ego ideal 'is the signifier operating as an ideal, an internalised plan of the Law. The guide governing the subject's position in the Symbolic order', the function of the ego ideal is to anticipate secondary (Oedipal) identification with the parental Other, the same that, by verifying and approving the child's mirror-image ('Yes! That's you, isn't it! Look at what a handsome boy you are!'), will later cause the child's internalisation of the mirror image as an ideal image of the self.[9] An introjection of the Symbolic order (its development depends on the parental Other's approval), the formation of the ideal ego determines the child's ability to judge himself on the basis of his caretaker's ideals and goals.

It is therefore in this respect that the evolution of the ego ideal satisfies the Lacanian motto according to which 'man's desire is the desire of the Other': by matching what the Other wants him to be, the child assumes 'the point of the ego ideal from which the subject will see himself [...] as others see him', thus abiding to the symbolic norm according to which the subject always desires what s/he thinks another subject wants him/her to desire;[10] just as it is in this respect that:

> *... the Biblical God is not the God that exists, but the speaking God [...] [,] [an] original character of God's Word [that] clarifies that God is a Father. The mundane encounter with him will not therefore be of a fusional kind, but crisscrossed by a distance, an 'in-between' that takes place primarily through listening.*[11]

Hence, the prevalent neurotic construction of the medieval subject as he who, by abiding to the principle of the *adaequatio rei et intellectus*, not only homologates the intellect of the knower to the thing to be known, but in so doing lets the superego emerge as the arbiter and witness of the subject's ego. A third agency verifying the subject's conformation to reality ('If you are inadequate you must abide; if you have failed you must improve; if you have sinned you must repent'), the superego, as a mirror image of the Church's authority, is there to stress and confirm an unbridgeable gap between macrocosm and microcosm, mundane and divine, God and man.[12]

Lacan made clear this linguistic condition of the Symbolic by addressing language as the symbolic dimension of intersubjective communication and desire. The moment the access to the mother is granted, for example by letting the child get trapped in a narcissistic identification with the ideal ego (or mirror image), at that moment the intersubjective domain collapses into a narcissistic, self-sufficient dyad unable to develop language as a means for articulating the desire for the Other (*objet petit a*); hence, the *No-of-the-Father*, i.e. the prohibition that the father sets in place in order to prevent the implosion of the linguistic domain into the visual realm of images.[13] The symbolic domain of the law is so established by the Name-of-the-Father.

This condition, unmistakably plausible in the Middle Ages (God acts as the Name-of-the-Father approving of man's reflection into Christ as a mirror-image), exemplifies the distinction between the ego ideal and the ideal ego that Lacan develops in the optical model, but that acquires its full meaning under the aegis of the Oedipus Complex.[14] Rather than the mirror image 'or the lowercase 'o' of the imaginary dyad' – which in the mirror stage stands for the mother's body and the incestuous desire to be merged with it, the ego ideal is the Oedipal drama that makes 'non-narcissistic inter-subjectivity become possible [...] through the introjection of the prohibition of the father'.[15] If the medieval God can act as a secondary identification (ego ideal) rather than a primary narcissistic identification as Christ (ideal ego), this is because, by means of a 'fundamentally linguistic phenomenon', the *logos* becomes guarantor of the successful access of the subject into the Symbolic order. By means of the introjection of the symbolic law (i.e. the word of God), the subject's superego (namely, the internalised law or prohibition of the father) is also born.[16]

It is in this regard that medieval theology is always a matter of hierarchy and of the incommensurability between the sensible and the intelligible worlds, which 'stand opposed to each other' and define each as the 'negation' or 'polar antithesis' of the other. If a relationship is possible between the two, the latter can only be accomplished on condition that the 'in-between' separating the two is either bridged or traversed by a medium that 'cannot be jumped over' but rather proceeds 'step by step in strictly ordered succession'; hence the spiritual and temporal power of the Church that, 'conscious of its own inviolable necessity', reflects the heavenly hierarchies in order to establish a 'moral-religious order of salvation'.[17]

It is exactly this fixed, unbridgeable realm of irreconcilable opposites, which the German humanist, philosopher and theologian Nicolas Cusanus (1401–64) summed up with the argument '*finiti et infiniti nulla proportio*' (the mundane and the metaphysical realms are incommensurable) that needs breaking; hence, the establishment of an 'inevitable assumption' that, by guaranteeing an immediate access to God (later reflected by Protestantism's belief in the Bible as a straightforwardly accessible source of authority), could also guarantee the bypassing of the medieval moral-religious order.

This 'inevitable assumption', which Cusanus himself singled out and that consisted in a condition of 'homogeneity' between the object of study and the unit of measurement applied, not only paves the way towards that *concidentia oppositorum* ('coincidence of opposites') that, brought to the fore by capitalist ideology, is also exemplified by the *perspectiva artificialis*, but which, by shifting the issue from God to the *knowledge of God*, *de facto* overcomes the alleged impossible overlapping of such distant and separate domains.[18] Through a play of mirrors, for which architecture provides the most powerful and shining of reflective surfaces, the realm of the visible is also appropriated and de-territorialised. Such a de-territorialisation, the mirror stage of the modern city, foresees the Imaginary order taking the upper hand over the Symbolic, and leading the way.

THE IMAGINARY ORDER

The Imaginary is a substantive that, in Lacanian theory, refers back to 1963, the same year when Lacan presented the mirror stage at the International Psychoanalytical Association in Marienbad, and has connotations of 'illusion, fascination and seduction as relating to the dual relation between the ego and its specular image'.[19] And despite Lacan's later development of this concept into one of the three orders constituting his tripartite scheme (Symbolic, Imaginary and Real), it has never lost its original connotation of 'illusion and lure'.[20] As the prototypical dual relationship that the ego and its counterpart form, they are in fact interchangeable and, for this very reason, of narcissistic nature: given the child's inclination to identify itself with deceptive illusions as derived by surface appearances and observable phenomena, the mirror stage leads the child to an imaginary identification with what Lacan defines as principal illusions of 'wholeness, synthesis, autonomy, duality and, above all, similarity'. The child remains captivated, as if hypnotised, by his own specular image and, contrary to other animals, which soon lose interest in the mirror image (they do so as soon as they realise that such an image is illusory), immediately transforms the latter into static fixations. From here is Lacan's firm belief that, 'in man, the imaginary relation has deviated [from the realm of nature]'.[21]

This fixation, which exemplifies the flip side – or ambiguity – of the Lacanian formulation 'man's desire is the desire of the Other', thus does not just exemplify Lacan's idea that, parallel to the subject's desire to match what s/he thinks another subject wants him/her to desire, lies the subject's desire for what another subject desires; but also the shift in the Renaissance ideological discourse of the inversion of the movement that, in the formation of human subjectivity, usually proceeds from the development of the ideal ego to the formation of the ego ideal.[22] By regressing the ego ideal into the narcissistic projection of the ideal ego, architecture makes of the ideal city the specular, abstracted mirror image of a simulated superego. The formation of the perverse subject, here exemplified by the emergence of both the modernist grid and the university discourse (predominance of science and knowledge), is well underway.

The ego ideal is not the ideal ego. For while the former refers to the symbolic Other, i.e. to language and discourse, the latter refers to the imaginary other, i.e. 'the image or picture of the other-equal in which the ego recognizes itself'.[23] Hence, the connotation in Lacanian psychoanalysis of the latter as 'imaginary': by serving a defensive aim, not only does the ideal ego install misrecognition, but in supporting the ego to achieve a generalised search for unity in the world, it plays a role in both primary and secondary identifications. 'An ever-present attempt to regain the omnipotence of the pre-Oedipal dual relation', the ideal ego – 'i(a)' in Lacanian algebra – denies the child's 'incapacity and internal chaos', thus distorting the experience of reality.[24]

It is by means of such identifications that my own study proceeds, and especially by singling out the pivotal role that architecture, following the imaginary identification that humanist philosophy stresses with Christ, plays during the Renaissance. By emphasising the role that both the development of geometric proportions and the *perspectiva artificialis* have in the Renaissance in establishing an imaginary identification with Christ, with God, with nature and, eventually, with the 'self' *tout-court*, the ideal city emerges as the outcome of the prevailing imaginary aspects of the formation of the ego over its symbolic ones; and according to a process though which not only language, as the discourse of the Other (God) is distorted, seduced, led astray, but ultimately weakened to the point of provoking the shift from a neurotic construction of subjectivity during the Renaissance to the perverse form of subjectivity impregnating the Second Industrial Revolution. The emergence of the modernist grid during the so-called heroic phase of modernist utopia becomes the reflection of the successful attempt at replacing a natural, God-made order with an artificial, man-made one.

The shift, or rather, the regression from the Symbolic order, where the individual can be finally subjectivised by voluntary subjugation to the realm of language (the discourse of the Other), to the Imaginary, where a dyadic, narcissistic relationship with the image is established, is not, however, here made exclusively dependent on the freezing of reality into a static, narcissistic image of itself (space holds a mirror to identity only on condition that the former is perspectivalised – Lorens Eyan Holm clarifies), but rather on the link that Lacan detects *apropos* of the relationship between the Symbolic and the Imaginary order via the linguistic sign ('[w]hereas the signifier is the foundation of the Symbolic order, the SIGNIFIED and SIGNIFICATION are part of the Imaginary order').[25] By the time Copernicus brings to public attention that the earth is no longer at the centre of the universe feelings of narcissistic omnipotence become the privileged defence mechanisms of a subject eventually trapped into a condition of 'divided representation'.[26]

THE MIRROR OF NARCISSUS: PRIMARY AND SECONDARY IDENTIFICATIONS IN THE RENAISSANCE CONSTRUCTION OF THE SELF

'Magnum Miraculum est Homo': Christ as Primary Identification

Despite constituting a corrosive attack on the *logos*, the Renaissance is strongly symbolic, and keeps the Name-of-the-Father in place. Like the mirror image reflecting back to the child a control over his bodily movement that he still lacks (as well as a sense of bodily coordination and wholeness which is also absent in his fragmented perception of his bodily parts), this omnipotent God, as embodied by the *Christus Pantocrator*, provides the subject with an imaginary sense of mastery; the very moment the image of Christ is assumed as man's own, at that very moment an imaginary triumph over nature is also accomplished. Nature becomes a reflection of the power that man can exert over reality exactly as man becomes a reflection of the power that religion can exert over society.

The manipulation of appearances, which follows this initial jubilation, is therefore a consequence of the successful attempt at replicating the process of God's creation on a smaller scale. Just as nature is a direct expression of God, so representation is a direct expression of man. Through the latter, nature is pushed to a higher level of intelligibility, and therefore reformulated, so to speak, in the image and resemblance of the subject.

To make clear that such an identification must now take place abruptly, rather than through the infinite mediations and intermediations ('from glory to glory') of the Church, Cusanus thus points out that a *visio intellectualis* (movement of the mind), rather than passive contemplation, must be mobilised; hence the materialisation, or seduction – in other words detachment of God – from the very mystery and impenetrability of that divine providence with which medieval theology used to endow divinity. God is made intelligible and graspable by the intellect.

It is in this respect that the development of linear perspective, which clearly stresses a shift from the *thing* seen (God's creation) to the *seeing* being (man), also represents the overthrowing of a well-established theological vision: despite Cusanus's alleged abjuration (the absolute being – God – is beyond 'any positive determination', he claims), the road is paved for a de-territorialisation of the visible;[27] so as it is in this respect that such a reinvention of the visible, which makes use of mathematics and geometry as privileged units of measurement, not only sublimates reality into 'a combination of volumes and surfaces', but, in so doing, also opens the way to a more direct comparison (or reflection) of the mundane with a higher level of divinity.[28] God's project can finally be appropriated, and exactly in terms of those human characteristics that the emergence of capitalist ideology makes cogent and persuasive.

The agreement sealed between man and divinity is so revealed in the Burlington House Cartoon (c. 1499), where Leonardo da Vinci freezes the Virgin Mary and the Baby Christ into a polaroid image of subjective splitting; and especially in the *perspectiva artificialis*, where the subject's obligation to abide by a number of set rules (for instance, the injunction to stand in a fixed position in front of the perspective window), still retains something of the medieval prohibition not to trespass the boundaries of the human. But it's a farce. Finally made commensurate and distinct, the macrocosm is now reinvented in the image and resemblance of its specular and (dis)proportionate counter-image. The *natura media* that stands half way between man and God, not only does Christ 'embrace [...] the finite and the infinite in one', but, in so doing, also elevates man 'up to the divinity'.[29] As Ernst Cassirer explains:

> *The regnum gratiae [the kingdom of grace] and the regnum naturae [the kingdom of nature] no longer stand opposed to each other, strangers and enemies; now, they are related to each other and to their common divine goal. The union has been completed not only between God and man, but between God and all creation. The gap between them is closed; between the creative principle and the created, between God and creature, stands the spirit of humanity, humanitas, as something at once creator and created.*[30]

'Finiti and Infiniti Nulla Proportio': The Secondary Identification with God

The proportioning system in architecture, and alongside it, the use of Platonic geometry and Pythagorean 'harmonies', as made available by translation into Latin of the writings of the Neoplatonic philosopher Proclus (412–85), satisfies this condition of knowledge of the 'absolute object', God, simply by establishing a principle of comparison, or unity of measurement, between two apparently irreducible realms. If all knowledge presupposes comparison, and such a comparison is prevented by one of the two objects of analysis having a different unit of measurement, then it is sufficient to reduce one quantity to another. Under the condition of *homogeneity* (Cusanus), microcosm and macrocosm are finally equated.

Brunelleschi's Spedale degli Innocenti and Santo Spirito in Florence, where space is subjugated by a standard unit, very well illustrate the birth of a unifying principle of equivalence through which the visible becomes suddenly intelligible; and so does Leonardo's reproduction of the Vitruvian Man, where it is made clear not only that man is now the measuring unit of the whole cosmos, but that this is due to the 'squaring of the circle' that Cusanus discusses in his *De Circuli Quadratura*. If man is inscribable within both a circle (Platonic symbol of God's creation) and the square (Platonic symbol of Mother earth), this is so because no irreconcilable discontinuity can be detected between the two. By abstracting two irreducible agencies (one, man, corporeal and finite; the other, God, immaterial and infinite) into equivalent geometrical constructions, not only does architecture become 'that reasoned harmony of all the parts within a [human] body' that reflects the structure of the cosmos; but also that man and God can now be reduced to the same equivalent substance.[31] And since God 'created all things in numbers, weight and measure [and] arranged the elements in admirable order', the emphasis is no longer put on the Demiurge's intellect (God) but rather on its mundane and finite counterpart (man).[32] The spreading of the so-called 'centralised plan' in sacred spaces, such as San Pietro in Montorio in Rome, as well as the diffusion of architectural treatises such as Leon Battista Alberti's *De re aedificatoria*, become the milestones of this ambitious process of divinisation (*divinatio*).[33]

'Quod Homo Imitatur Mundum in Figura Circularis': The Perspective Window as Secondary Identification with Nature

The development of the so-called *perspectiva artificialis*, invented by Filippo Brunelleschi and later theorised by Alberti (*Della Pittura*), represents one step further in the abstraction of Cusanus' theological speculations. This is not just because it eventually incorporates their definitive perversion into a rationalist ideology that, as argued by both Jean Baudrillard and Arnold Hauser, makes use-value the hegemonic factor at work in everyday reality;[34] nor is it because this embracement of humanistic values and proto-scientific truth proves the achieved disengagement of both art and architecture from religious subordination.[35] But rather because, as made clear by Cesare Vasoli, if 'perspective offers to bodies the freedom to materially unfold into space', it also reabsorbs and subsumes such bodies into the eye of the beholder.[36] *Perspectiva artificialis* expands the subject into the field of an imaginary appropriation of the visible.

By putting man at the apex of the visual pyramid emanating from Sense (lowest world) and God at the apex of the pyramid emanating from Intelligence (highest world), not only is a continuity between God and man ratified, but also and foremost one between nature and its illusory counterpart.[37] In the middle world of Reason, where Oneness and Multiplicity merge and unfold, nature can now conform to man's vision exactly as man, in the Middle Ages, used to conform to both God's and the Church's. The imaginary domain of *representation*, rather than the symbolic realm of *language*, is now the *natura media* of a rationalising subject.[38]

In this hydraulic model of communicating vessels, in which representation gains three-dimensional depth by stripping reality of one of its dimensions, the evidence of an attained mirror-staging with the Platonic Demiurge (God) is accomplished. 'We must venerate ourselves as Divine image of God, and turn into Him exactly as He has already turned into us' – Marsilio Ficino aptly epitomises in *De Christiana Religione*.[39] For not only can the Renaissance subject transform nature into an apprehensible, however impalpable, domain of unfolding sequences of geometrical figures; but, most importantly, unravel multiplicity from the simplest unity of the apex of the visual cone. Visual representation has become hegemonic.[40]

'Directe Contra Pupillam': The Secondary Identification with the Ideal City

The invention of the ideal cities during the 1400s very well illustrates the transition to a libidinal investment onto the ideal ego, and according to a process that, by reducing the gazing subject to an abstract pyramid of vision, contracts the former into the impalpable and invisible substance of subjective thinking (intellect). As a consequence of this, not only is hermetic magic thinking 'transmuted' into the sanitised, impersonal and Euclidian clarity of the new-born scientific belief; but ideal cities themselves become some sort of 'prototypical' scientific model through which the *res cogitans* (thinking matter), which René Descartes will theorise shortly afterwards in his *Principia Philosophiae* (1644), can be stripped of that organic substance (*res extensa*) that constitutes its physical and degenerated counterpart. Just as the built environment (and alongside it, the totality of physical reality through which God is not only prefigured, but actually embodied) starts making sense only if mirror-imaged by a 'pure Idea', so the subject, as a 'pure act of thinking', can be reflected in all of its newly acquired incorporeal glory. The city becomes an experiment in narcissistic subjective omnipotence.[41]

If the ideal cities – and I am referring here to the notorious Renaissance paintings such as those preserved at Urbino's National Gallery or the Gemäldegalerie in

Berlin – are empty, this is not so much because such paintings predate the utopian fulfilment of a future achievement, but rather because, projected from the vantage point of an omnipotent, monocular and punctiform subject, they are the evidence of a homological identification with the Eternal. Once the secrets of the 'Divine Artificer' (Pico della Mirandola) have been finally penetrated, 'Man the Beautiful' (da Vinci) can eventually 'procreate'.[42]

It again falls on Proclus, the Neoplatonic Greek philosopher from which most of the Latin translation of Plato's work derives, to provide the model for this successful operation. By reporting Plato's conception of 'the universe as being constructed in a geometrical progression from point to line to surface to solid' (i.e. from the simplest unity – 'the One' – to the 'potentiality of the Unlimited' that the One contains and entails), not only is God reduced to a geometrical element, the point itself, but such a point is endowed with the ability to originate the archetypal ideas of which matter is but a simulacrum or 'shadow' (Plato). From this moment on, not only does the perspective window reflect back to the gazing mind the narcissistic projection of a transcendental subject, but it also materialises, *hic et nunc*, the miracle of an omnipotent and, for this very reason, narcissistic subject: no longer shaped in the image and resemblance of God's physical appearance – Christ – but, *sic et simpliciter*, of God's intellect, the latter is finally reduced to that 'point in the eye's cone of vision [which] corresponds to the origin of all things'.[43] By reflecting both sensible and supra-sensible power, the ideal city becomes the greatest and ultimate transgression of the Name-of-the-Father.[44]

CONCLUSION: SEDUCING MIRRORS

If Lacanian theory is so strongly anti-ocularcentric, this is so due to the danger that Lacan averts in the mirror stage. Following identification with his own mirror image, the child could in fact either move towards the Symbolic order via introjection of the *non-du-père* or forever stay trapped within the Imaginary order (the fictional erection that his illusory upright posture generates in the mirror). Should the latter be the case, narcissistic feelings of omnipotence are likely to emerge.[45]

It is for this reason that Lacan relates the unconscious to the Symbolic order: via introjection of the Name-of-the-Father (*nom-du-père*), the subject is prevented from narcissistically identifying with the mirror image; and, to the same extent, it is for this reason that Lacan links the Imaginary order with the Real: by getting trapped in an imaginary identification with the mirror, narcissism, as a precondition for psychosis (psychotics have no unconscious), can be achieved. Halfway between the Symbolic and the Real, the Imaginary acquires a different meaning (of positive progress towards the identification with the ego ideal, of negative regression towards the identification with the ideal ego) according to the movement that the original alienation caused by the occurrence of the mirror stage produces.

Following identification with a number of primary and secondary projections, it is the latter case that Renaissance art and architecture let emerge: in Brunelleschi's experiment (in front of the Florence Baptistery, the reproduction of clouds via specular mirroring definitively testifies to an increasing process of disinterestedness towards the organic); in the libidinal cathexis with which architectural treatises are imbued (if in Filarete the process of 'patronage, design and construction' closely resembles an act of 'seduction', in Marsilio Ficino only incestuous 'copulation' leads to successful architectural accomplishments);[46] most and foremost, in da Vinci's cartoon at the British Museum in London, where the trapping of the characters into a narcissistic self-reflection (the Virgin Mary into St Anne, St John into Baby Christ) seems to allude to something more than an Imaginary contemplation. It is the latter that I wish to address.

The cartoon is singular. Just as St Anne, by pointing her index finger at the sky, invites the Virgin Mary to give up her maternal aspirations to a successful dyadic relationship with the child ('You need to let Him go' – St Anne tells her – 'that is God's will'), so Saint John informs Baby Christ that his future sacrifice – crucifixion – will separate the latter from his mother. The Oedipus Complex is, so to speak, fully operative. And yet, should this be the case, why do both the Imaginary and the Symbolic constructions of the ego co-exist? Why, in an image where the Father's injunction is so strongly and categorically imposed, is a mirror staging also so obviously and palpably exposed?

Quite surprisingly, the answer does not rest so much on the assumption that supports the ongoing thesis in this chapter (i.e. that da Vinci very well illustrates this transition, over the Renaissance, from a language-based unconscious to an image-based one); but rather that, exactly as it happens with the clinical construction of the pervert ego, the two orders overlap. By making of St Anne and St John the specular mirror-images of the Virgin Mary and Baby Christ, not only does da Vinci shift attention from the supposed dyadic couples inhabiting the drawing (Virgin Mary / Baby Christ, St Anne / St John) to an alleged ongoing introjection of the future ego ideal (St Anne and St John as the accomplished, omnipotent adults that Virgin Mary as a young woman and Baby Christ as child both wish to identify with); but, in so doing, he also makes a laughing stock of God's Word. As soon as the paternal prohibition comes into play (mother and son *need* separating), this very paternal prohibition is shredded into pieces. The *real event* – the dyadic self-reflection – is just happening elsewhere![47]

This position of the perverse subject, which Slavoj Žižek synthesises in the 'fetishistic' formula 'I know very well, but just the same ...', acquires here a disturbing relevance.[48] And not just because it reveals the newly-developed construction of the self during the Renaissance ('I know very well *that I'm not God*, but just the same *I act as if I were*'), but rather because it predates the radicalisation of the inadequacy of the Name-of-the Father as caused by the omnipotent, narcissistic and Imaginary self-empowerment of the modernist subject.[49] 'I know very well that I am shaped in the image and resemblance of Christ – the modernist subjective validation postulates – but just the same my brand new ego must now be shaped in the image and resemblance of science':

> *[T]hrown from his automobile one evening in 1909 into a factory ditch filled with water, the Italian avant-gardist poet Filippo Tommaso Marinetti emerges as if from amniotic fluid to be [re]born, without ancestors, a futurist.*[50]

6.1 Leonardo da Vinci (c. 1500), *The Virgin and Child with St Anne and St John the Baptist* ('The Burlington House Cartoon'). © The National Gallery, London.

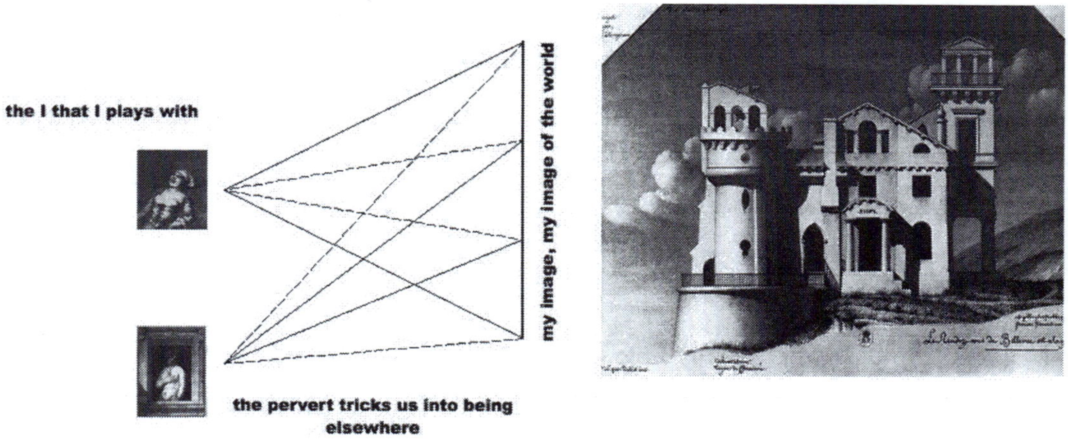

6.2 Lorens Eyan Holm, visual pattern of the perverse as gazing at the perspective window. Courtesy of Lorens Eyan Holm.

This weakening of the paternal function, of which Friedrich Nietzsche's 'death of God' can be seen both a cause and an effect, is what this study, as a long-term project, pursues. The modernist grid and Rem Koolhaas's *junk space* will thus be looked at as the consequence of a condition reflecting not just the modernist and the postmodern subjective positioning within space, but also and foremost the subjective positioning within the realm of the Other. The infamous *passage-a-l'act*, which for Lacan connotes psychosis in its accomplished and irreversible phase, will thus embody that generalised condition of the contemporary city where space, just as the Lacanian unconscious, rewrites itself with no end or finality. Subject and object, as always is the case with the incestuous connotation with which Lacan often invests the mirror stage, do not just become one, the specular image of the other, but rather do merge together into an unfathomable, inseparable realm.

NOTES

1 Mario Perniola, '*La Società dei Simulacri*', in *Agalma: Rivista di Studi Culturali e di Estetica* 221 (Roma: Mimesis, October 2010–April 2011), p. 110.

2 Jean Baudrillard, 'On Disappearance', in David Clarke, Marcus A. Doel, William Merrin, Richard G. Smith (eds), *Jean Baudrillard: Fatal Theories* (Abingdon: Routledge, 2009), p. 24.

3 Michel Foucault, 'Nietzsche, Genealogy, History', in Donald F. Bouchard (ed.), *Language, Counter-Memory, Practice: Selected Essays and Interviews* (Ithaca, NY: Cornell University Press, 1977).

4 I refer here to the works of the French philosophers Yves Michaud and Jean Baudrillard. If for the former aesthetic experience is a mental device for the apprehension of reality, for the latter reality is itself a byproduct of cultural practices, invented only through the use and abuse of (linguistic) representation/images. Reality is thus the leftover of ideological processes and mechanisms. This chapter offers a trans-disciplinary narration of the condition of the contemporary city, which is difficult, if not impossible, to grasp due to the number of concomitant factors at play. I have used the works of Lorens Holm and Gérard Wajcman to construct my argument. The understanding of the emergence of linear perspective as a device through which

modern subjectivity is formed, either though the freezing of space into an image (Holm) or through the creation of the notion of intimacy through the perspective window (Wajcman), is of utmost importance in establishing a relationship between the self and the city. The underlying argument of this chapter is the destruction of representation through an excess of representation and how it affects subjectivity and the construction of the self. The impossibility, for the postmodern subject, to make of the ideal ego the external referent for the construction of subjectivity is the final stage of my genealogical development of the contemporary city. The loss of an ideal, external standard of reference is the primary cause of a process of disintegration of both the self and the *forma urbis* to which the eruption of psychosis is attributed, in the city as a mode of configuration of the city itself and in the subject as a modality of (mis)apprehension of reality. The way genealogy is developed in the work of Jean Baudrillard in delineating his four orders of simulation assumes particular relevance as a discursive strategy. For Baudrillard, simulation is not just an account of the emergence of bourgeoisie ideology through the invention of the concept of reality, but also the way reality is produced through detachment of the 'referent' as the element grounding the signified into external reality. Just as in simulation this produces an arbitrary meaning of the image, so fixation with the ideal ego leads to the 'detachment' (i.e. the impossibility to develop a secondary identification) from the ego ideal. Psychosis emerges as an 'arbitrary' construction of the self with no grounding in the Symbolic order. According to Lacan's theorisation of the construction of the ego via the mirror stage, and further applications (Holm), the subject cannot make sense of himself other than by projecting himself onto an external referent (ego ideal, ideal ego); hence, the very idea substantiating this chapter that any paradigm shift occurring in the construction of Western subjectivity is immediately reflected in the perception of the city. As soon as, in postmodernity, the subject loses the ability to refer to an ideal image of the self, the city loses altogether its chance to be represented. See for this purpose: Gérard Wajcman, 'Intimate Extorted, Intimate Exposed', in *Journal of the Jan van Eyck Circle for Lacanian Ideology Critique*, 1 (2008), pp. 58–77. Available at: http://www.lineofbeauty.org/; Yves Michaud, *L'Art à l'État Gazeux: Essai Sur le Triomphe de l'Esthétique* (Paris: Stock, 2003); Jean Baudrillard, *Simulations*, trans. Phil Beitchman, Paul Foss, Paul Patton (New York: Semiotext(e), 1983); Lorens Holm, *Brunelleschi, Lacan, Le Corbusier: Architecture, Space and the Construction of Subjectivity* (London: Routledge, 2010); Lorens Holm, 'Space and its Assembled Subjects: The Neurotic, the Psychotic and the Pervert', in Louis Rice and David Littlefield (eds), *Transgression: Towards an Expanded Field of Architecture* (London: Routledge, 2014), pp. 40–56.

5 Rudolf Wittkower, *Architectural Principles in the Age of Humanism* (London: Alec Tirani, 1962), p. 30.

6 Slavoj Žižek, *Leggere Lacan*, trans. Marta Nijhuis (Torino: Bollati Boringhieri, 2009), p. 62. See also for this purpose Jacques Lacan, *Le Séminaire Livre XI, Les Quattre Concepts Fondamentaux de la Psychoanalyse* (Paris: Seuil, 1991).

7 'All of us, gazing with unveiled face on the glory of the Lord, are being transformed into the same image from glory to glory, as from the Lord who is the Spirit' (Paul, Cor. 13, *Second Letter to the Corinthians*).

8 Name-of-the-Father is the Lacanian expression to designate the Symbolic law or Symbolic domain of the Other. Jacques Lacan, 'The Mirror Stage as Formative of the Function of the I', in *Écrits: A Selection*, trans. Alan Sheridan (London: Tavistock, 1977).

9 Dylan Evans, *An Introductory Dictionary of Lacanian Psychanalysis* (London: Routledge, 2006), p. 53; Stephanie Swales, *Perversion: A Lacanian Psychoanalytic Approach to the Subject* (London: Routledge, 2012), p. 26.

10 Lacan in Stephanie Swales, *Perversion*, p. 27.

11 Enzo Bianchi, 'Parola di Dio, Parola a Dio. Approccio spirtuale', in *RCatT* 33/1 (Barcelona: Facultat de Teologia de Catalunga, 2008), pp. 41–52, p. 42.

12 Antonello Sciacchitano, *Scienza come Isteria: Il Soggetto della Scienza da Cartesio a Freud e la Questione dell'Infinito* (Pasian di Prato: Campanotto, 2005). As Sciacchitano clarifies, there is therefore a homology at work in the Middle Ages between the superego and the political/social function of authority that, from the influence of incontrovertible sources (*ipse dixit*) to the hegemony of the Church, mirror-images the subject's superego in all of its possible declinations. If the principle of reality is substantiated by the homologation of the subject to reality itself, Sciacchiatano expands, then a third agency must act to verify the success of this homologation; from here, the overwhelming power of both the Church (over society) and the superego (over the subject). By analogy, the reader should be able to grasp Lacan's definition of the neurotic as he who, by successfully accessing the Symbolic order, is constantly stuck in the self-enquiring question: 'To what extent does my desire match the desire of the Other?'

13 See Jacques Lacan, *Le Seminaire Livre III: Les Psychoses* (Paris: Seuil, 1981). A failure of the paternal function would in fact lead to the reduction of the latter to an 'image of the father', and therefore to the subject being caught in the Imaginary realm of self-fulfillment that Lacan first investigated through the mirror stage (narcissism/ psychosis).

14 It is here assumed that the medieval subject abides to the Law of the father (Symbolic order) by virtue of fixed hierarchies and limitation of knowledge imposed by his mundane condition.

15 Lacan in Stephanie Swales, *Perversion*, p. 26; Martin Jay, *Lacan, Althusser and the Specular Subject of Ideology* (London: University of California Press, 1994), p. 351.

16 The good city in the fresco by Ambrogio Lorenzetti in Siena is pervaded by words.

17 Ernst Cassirer, *The Individual and the Cosmos in Renaissance Philosophy* (Chicago, IL: The University of Chicago Press, 2010), pp. 9–10.

18 Ibid., p. 10.

19 Dylan Evans, *An Introductory Dictionary of Lacanian Psychoanalysis*, p. 84.

20 Ibid.

21 Lacan in Dylan Evans, *An Introductory Dictionary of Lacanian Psychoanalysis*, p. 118.

22 See also Jacques Lacan, *Le Séminaire Livre XI, Les Quattre Concepts Fondamentaux de la Psychoanalyse*.

23 Stijn Vanheule, 'Lacan's Construction and Deconstruction of the Double-Mirror Device', in *Frontiers in Psychology*, 2 (Lausanne: Frontiers, September 2011), p. 2.

24 Dylan Evans, *An Introductory Dictionary of Lacanian Psychoanalysis*, p. 53.

25 Lorens Holm, *Brunelleschi, Lacan, Le Corbusier*, p. 116; see also the 'Schema L' in Dylan Evans, *An Introductory Dictionary of Lacanian Psychoanalysis*.

26 I am here referring to Freud's assertion according to which three great wounds have been inflicted on humanity's pride and narcissism: Copernicus, Darwin and himself. While the Copernican revolution removed man from the centre of the universe, Darwin denied that humankind's existence is a unique art of creation. As for Freud, he proved that humanity is not the master of its own limited realm: it is the unconscious, rather than the mind, which determines human behaviour. See also for this purpose:

Sigmund Freud, 'The Libido Theory and Narcissism', in *Introductory Lectures on Psychoanalysis*, trans. James Strachey (London: Penguin, 1981); Sigmund Freud, 'On Narcissism: an Introduction', in *On Metapsychology: The Theory of Psychoanalysis: 'Beyond the Pleasure Principle', 'The Ego and the Id', and Other Works*, trans. James Strachey (London: Penguin, 1984). Also see for this purpose Dalibor Vesely, *Architecture in the Age of Divided Representation: The Question of Creativity in the Shadow of Production* (Cambridge, MA: The MIT Press, 2004).

27 Ernst Cassirer, *The Individual and the Cosmos in Renaissance Philosophy*, p. 8.

28 Régis Debray, *Vita e Morte Dell'Immagine: Una storia dello Sguardo in Occidente* (Milan: Elitrice, 2004), p. 192 (translation by the author).

29 Ernst Cassirer, *The Individual and the Cosmos in Renaissance Philosophy*, pp. 39–40. So as in the Lacanian mirror stage not only the child's specular image allows the latter to overcome his/her premature birth (but in so doing, indicates to the jubilant child a future of mastery and control over his/her own bodily movement that resembles the omnipotent parents' figures with which he will later wish to identify), so Christ, in Renaissance philosophy, becomes the literal identificatory substratum on which modern subjectivity can be built.

30 Ibid., p. 40.

31 Leon Battista Alberti, 'De Re Aedificatoria', in John Hendrix, *Platonic Architectonics: Platonic Philosophies and the Visual Arts* (New York: Peter Lang Publishing, 2004), p. 138.

32 Cusanus, ibid., p. 124.

33 For an account of the process of divination *(divinatio)* see Marco Pellegrino, *Religione e Umanasimo nel Primo Rinascimento da Petrarca ad Alberti* (Firenze: Le Lettere, 2012).

34 Arnold Hauser, *The Social History of Art, Vol. 2*, trans. Stanley Godman (New York: Vintage Books, 1951); Jean Baudrillard, *For a Critique of the Political Economy of the Sign*, trans. Charles Levin (St. Louis: Telos Press, 1981), p. 66.

35 Ibid., p. 70.

36 Cesare Vasoli, *Filosofia e Religione nella Cultura del Rinascimento* (Napoli: Guida, 1988), p. 56 (translation by the author).

37 See for this purpose Charles H. Carman, 'Meanings of Perspective in the Renaissance: Tensions and Resolution', in John Shannon Hendrix and Charles H. Carman (eds), *Renaissance Theories of Vision* (Farnham: Ashgate, 2010), pp. 31–44.

38 Erwin Panofsky in Cesare Vasoli, *Filosofia e Religione nella Cultura del Rinascimento*, p. 56.

39 Marsilio Ficino in Cesare Vasoli, *Filosofia e Religione nella Cultura del Rinascimento*, p. 58.

40 Alberto Pérez-Gómez and Louise Pelletier, *Architectural Representation and the Perspective Hinge* (Cambridge, MA: The MIT Press, 2000).

41 'The concept of infinity' – Panofsky writes – '[is] not only prefigured in God, but indeed actually embodied in physical reality'. Erwin Panofsky, *Perspective as Symbolic Form* (New York: Zone Books, 1997), p. 65.

42 Giovanni Pico della Mirandola, *Oration on the Dignity of Man*, in John Hendrix, *Platonic Architectonics*, p. 129.

43 John Hendrix, *Platonic Architectonics*, p. 158. It must be noted here the homology established, in the construction of one point perspective, between the vanishing point as posited on the horizon of the perspective window (God, the infinite) and the position of the monocular subject facing it. The principle of the communication

vessels is again at work here (not only do the finite and the infinite communicate, but actually swap).

44 Ibid., p. 159. This acquires particular relevance in Alberti's introduction to Book 2 of *Della Pittura*, the classic figure of Narcissus: 'the inventor of painting', he is the champion of Renaissance anthropocentric naturalism in his ability not so much to reflect himself in his own accomplishments (literally, one point perspective), but rather the metamorphosis that the latter entails. Just as the experience of self-reflection (into the water) turns Narcissus into a flower, so the experience of self-reflection into painting (perspective) elevates man into an upgraded version of himself. As Charles Carman discovers in his chapter on the 'Meanings of Perspective in the Renaissance', the emphasis in Alberti's metaphor should thus be put more on the transformative effects of art than on the narcissistic trap of a full immersion into sensory certainty (identification with nature) that perspective guarantees. And yet, the meaning implied in Alberti's metaphor should here be reversed and rather taken literally: for the narcissistic reflection that Alberti intends is not that of man into nature as a reflection of God, but rather of man as a transcended version of himself into himself. If a transformation is here implied, such a transformation is therefore only the result of that complex game of mirrors, or *mise-en-abyme*, that the mathematicisation of the visible through perspective and proportions – in other words through architecture – produces. This transcendental subject, ultimately only transcendent to himself, is the result of a complex machine that, by resembling Lacan's mirror device, shows the shifts into the Imaginary order accomplished by the Renaissance.

45 See for this purpose Freud on narcissism and the emergence of megalomania as a consequence of libidinal investment on to unreal objects (Sigmund Freud, 'On Narcissism: An Introduction', p. 79).

46 George Hersey, *Pythagorean Palaces: Magic and Architecture in the Italian Renaissance* (Ithaca, NY: Cornell University Press, 1976), p. 91.

47 Stephanie Swales, *Perversion*, p. 55. See for this purpose the 'perverse visual pattern' from Lorens Holm that inspired such an interpretation: by pretending to gaze at the visual plane from the position of a (symbolic) law-abiding subject, he is in reality gazing at it from where nobody would expect him to (the underlying question here is: from what position does the pervert gaze at the world? The pattern originally appears in Lorens Holm, 'Space and its Assembled Subjects'.

48 Slavoj Žižek, *Looking Awry: An Introduction to Jacques Lacan Through Popular Culture* (London: The MIT Press, 1992), p. 168.

49 I am indirectly referring here to the magic practices fashionable all over the Renaissance as made available by the diffusion of the *Pimander*.

50 Rosalind Krauss, *The Originality of the Avant-Garde and Other Modernist Myths* (London: The MIT Press, 1997), p. 157.

7

Unconscious Places – Thomas Struth and the Architecture of the City

Hugh Campbell

A large selection from *Unconscious Places*, the German photographer Thomas Struth's epic series of urban views, featured prominently at the 2012 Venice Biennale, curated by the renowned architect David Chipperfield under the title *Common Ground*. Facilitated in part by Chipperfield's friendship with Struth, the display at Venice was also intended to resonate with the theme of common ground. While, for Chipperfield, the term was meant primarily to suggest the discipline's shared

7.1 Thomas Struth, Sommerstrasse, Düsseldorf, 1980.

7.2 Thomas Struth, West Broadway, New York, Tribeca, 1978.

knowledge, it was also taken to connote a shared interest in the open, collective urban realm.

Begun in the late 1970s in Struth's native Düsseldorf, the photographs of *Unconscious Places* depicted mostly anonymous urban scenes. Struth used black and white film in medium and large-format cameras, usually aligned to a central vanishing point, to produce extremely calm, detailed and ordered images. From Germany the series extended to London and Paris, then to New York, where the streets of midtown and lower Manhattan proved particularly receptive to Struth's documentary method, and then to numerous cities in Europe and Asia. As the series extended Struth gradually embraced colour photography and eventually digital printing. The prints became larger; the viewpoint gradually became more varied.

From the earliest black and white photographs from 1977/78 to the most recent large-scale digital colour images, Struth's series has taken the urban realm as its unchanging focus. Even as the technique has changed and the range of cities depicted continuously expanded, Struth has remained dedicated to photographing the built fabric of the city because of its capacity to embody, and ultimately, to make visible an evolving collective identity. The title *Unconscious Places* – first conferred upon the series when it was published and exhibited in 1987 – was intended to convey the idea that this construction of collective identity was far from a conscious project, but simply the resultant of the ongoing development and occupation of urban space.[1] A much expanded and updated selection from the series was also published in 2012, with an accompanying essay by the renowned sociologist Richard Sennett. Sennett had first written about Struth's work in a catalogue essay of 1993.[2] He also played a key role in shaping Chipperfield's thinking on the theme of *Common Ground*, and contributed an essay on Struth to the accompanying publication.[3]

Accordingly, Struth's photographs became a kind of recurring register in the Arsenale, in which they were gathered in four successive groupings. Returning attention to the realities of built urban fabric, the calm photographs acted as both counterpoint and point of reference for what was being worked out in more demonstrative and three-dimensional form in the various architectural displays. This encounter might be interpreted as a rejoinder being offered to the excesses of architectural production. Struth has certainly cited a suspicion of, if not antipathy towards, the overly rational, instrumental approach of architects as among the initial motives behind the series.[4] A more optimistic reading might view Struth's images simply as reminders to architecture to pay attention to the given. In any case, it was hard to avoid the overriding impression that while other displays shouted more loudly, Struth's images ultimately spoke more forcefully. Most often, what they made visible were those aspects of the life and form of cities which emerge, continuously, over time and which usually exist beyond our attention. If, following William James, the unconscious is thought of as that which is sensed but not attended to, then at the Biennale, Struth's images were asked to stand for the collective unconscious of architecture – that which it does not attend to, but from which it ultimately derives, and to which it ultimately returns.

But the title of Struth's series can in fact sustain a number of interpretations, all hinging upon the relationship of urban places and the workings of the unconscious. Are we, in fact, intended to think that these are locations which are not, for the most part, the subject of our conscious attention, which are absorbed unthinkingly by the inhabitants of the city – places as unconsciously experienced? Or might we understand *Unconscious Places* as referring to the way buildings and spaces get built without being consciously thought about – places as unconscious products? Or are we to suppose that the very fabric itself is animate, imbued with latent selfhood, but not with awareness, and hence, to see these as places which are themselves unconscious? Or should we understand the visible fabric as a shared reservoir of meaning and memory for the urban populace – a collective unconscious? Or, finally, might we consider that in this exchange, it is in fact the camera which operates automatically – in other words, that these, ultimately, are scenes recorded and produced unconsciously? What sustains Struth's series is partly the manner in which it accommodates all these possible readings. But common to all is a sense that the city itself has some content, or some qualities, which equate to the unconscious, and which can be made visible through photography.

Both Sigmund Freud and Jacques Lacan explicitly drew analogies between the city and the unconscious. Quoted elsewhere in this volume are Lacan's remarks at a lecture in Baltimore:

> *When I prepared this little talk for you, it was early in the morning. I could see Baltimore through the window and it was a very interesting moment because it was not quite daylight and a neon sign indicated to me every minute the change*

> *of time, and naturally there was heavy traffic and I remarked to myself that exactly all that I could see, except for some trees in the distance, was the result of thoughts thinking themselves without knowing it, where the function played by the subjects was not completely obvious .... The best image to sum up the unconscious is Baltimore in the early morning.*[5]

In a scene drawn from Lacan's own experience, the early morning city becomes a convincing analogue for the unconscious. Earlier, Freud had also used the urban view, in a somewhat different way, as a point of comparison. In his famous 1930 essay *Civilisation and its Discontents*, he sought to explicate his assertion 'that, in mental life, nothing that has once taken shape can be lost, that everything is somehow preserved and can be retrieved under the right circumstances',[6] by offering an analogy with how the past development of a city can be discerned in its current form. Taking Rome as his example, he asks us to imagine that, instead of having to be understood through prior knowledge and study, every phase of the city's growth makes itself available to view, that 'all previous phases of development exist beside the most recent'. Almost immediately Freud acknowledges the spatio-temporal difficulties, if not absurdities, inherent in this analogy: 'if we wish to represent a historical sequence in spatial terms, we can do so only by juxtaposition in space, for the same space cannot accommodate different things'. Accordingly, he dismisses the exercise as 'an idle game: its sole justification ... to show how far we are from being able to illustrate the peculiarities of mental life by visual means'.

And yet, it is precisely this paradoxical combination of invisibility and enduring influence that proves the most compelling point of comparison between the unconscious and the urban past. Thus, the challenge of revealing the full extent and nature of the unconscious – the challenge addressed by Freud and Lacan – might find its equivalent in a project which seeks to discern and depict within the visible cityscape the hidden impulses and forces which have shaped it (from Freud's analogy), as well as the 'unthinking thoughts' which animate it (from Lacan's analogy). This chapter will argue that, in its ambitions and approach, *Unconscious Places* is precisely such a project.

Two crucial early reference points for Struth in defining his approach to photography were Walter Benjamin's essay 'Theses on the Philosophy of History' and Wolfgang Köhler's volume on *Gestalt Psychology*.[7] From the former he took a commitment to historical materialism as method, to the idea of bearing witness, to understanding the larger historical trajectory as defined not only by events but also by places. From the latter, he took an interest in how, in perceptual terms, elements come together to form a coherent whole. Accordingly, in his photographs, Struth became interested in discovering and revealing the coherence within a given urban location, and thereby allowing that discovered coherence to assume a socio-historical significance. His early series of New York streets can be seen to give real order and moment to what might otherwise go unnoticed, or at least undernoticed.

Having alighted upon a seemingly non-descript location, for instance West 44th Street, Struth establishes his large-format camera, not at a spot corresponding to the viewpoint of passers-by, but directly in the middle of the roadway. There,

7.3 Thomas Struth, West 44th Street (Mummenschanz), New York, Theater D, 1978.

for up to an hour, he balances the elements of the scene on the gridded ground glass. The decision-making is painstaking and deliberate – 35 years after this image was made, Struth remembers dwelling on how much of Yul Brynner to keep within the frame.[8] To something previously overlooked, untoward attention is being paid.[9]

Sennett describes Struth as 'taking his own good time to dwell in a scene before touching the camera'.[10] It is a process which in turn conditions the viewer response. For Maria Morris Hambourg:

> *Struth's cityscapes subtly guide the viewer towards a participatory model of occupying public space, in which the photographic image activates a critical understanding of one's environment ... Like the best mentors who teach without our knowing, these pictures sensitize us to our surroundings, encouraging us to listen to the particular tunes of all that is germane ....*[11]

In an early and typically perceptive review of the series, Peter Schejldahl conflates the making of and the experience of the images, describing how:

> *as with most of Struth's cityscapes, there is an initial disorientation, a compound of absolute specificity of place and seeming arbitrariness in point of view. It is as if we were walking with a companion who abruptly stopped at a spot with nothing obviously special about it, facing ostensibly nothing much. Following his gaze, we slowly register that we are seeing, for lack of a better word, everything.*[12]

In the early years of the series the feeling of 'seeing everything' is due, in part, to the strongly symmetrical, perspectival arrangement of the images. This pictorial strategy has often been seen as formal and objectifying, analogous to the uniform approach to the documentation of industrial and vernacular forms used by Bernd and Hille Becher, who were Struth's teachers at the Düsseldorf Academy. However, in his analysis, Armin Zweite prefers to use the term 'lateral inclusion' noting how the slightly disembodied and yet generic viewpoint allows all the scene's formal particularities to be revealed, with both sides of the street extending deep into the distance, detail intact.[13] Struth's reliance upon the centralised view is a result, not of a predetermined conceptual approach, but of a desire to incorporate and balance as much visual information as possible within the frame. Whereas the Bechers, at least initially, thought of their photographs more as information than as image, for Struth, the status and quality of the image is always of central importance.

In *Gestalt Psychology*, Wolfgang Köhler develops at length his theory of sensory organization, taking issue with William James's assertion that 'original sensory experience is uniformly continuous, and that all cuts and boundaries are later introduced into the field for pragmatic reasons' and arguing instead that the sensory field is composed of sensory units (constellations in a starry sky is the example he gives) which are immediately identified in relation to each other.[14] Thus the parts are, and remain, distinct within the whole they come together to form. Fritz Perls called this coherent whole the 'ultimate experiential unit', and focussed his Gestalt therapy on assisting patients in attaining a clear view of this 'ultimate unit'.

Although the unconscious does play a part in Gestalt psychology, it is considered more as something physiological than psychological – that is, it is raw sensation not yet registered as experience (there is a close correlation to the views of William James). It follows that the attaining of a coherent view is simply a matter of bringing to attention that which previously has escaped it. And whereas Freud would later maintain that, for the most part, the unconscious actively resisted being brought to light, Struth's pictures operate on the basis that, in bringing a view to attention, sensation can be translated into experience by virtue of being rendered pictorially.

Fritz Perls was equally concerned with the temporality of consciousness:

> *Nothing exists except in the here and now. The now is present, is the phenomenon, is what you are aware of, is that moment in which you carry your so-called memories and your so-called anticipation with you. Whether you remember or anticipate, you do it now. The past is no more. The future is not yet . . . . Nothing can possibly exist except the now.*[15]

The challenge, then, is to somehow abstract this 'now' from the continuum of time and assert its significance. In his essay *Understanding a Photograph*, John Berger describes the expectation of revelation as 'a human constant … a constituent of *the relation between the human capacity to perceive and the coherence of appearances*'.[16] It is precisely to the degree that it lends coherence to appearances that the photograph has the potential to be revelatory. Berger argues that it is an event's development in time which allows its meaning to be perceived and felt. If this movement is taken as an arrow, then normally the photograph cuts across this arrow, disrupting the event's development and confusing, or refusing, its meaning. Instead, Berger proposes that the significant photograph might be better understood as an expanded cross-section through the event – thus the photograph achieves something equivalent to duration by 'enlarging the circle beyond the dimension of instantaneous information'.

'A photograph which achieves expressiveness thus works dialectically' concludes Berger – 'it preserves the particularity of the event recorded, and it chooses an instant when the correspondences of those particular appearances articulate a general idea'. In Struth's case, he is looking for those locations which can express the city's inherent structure, its 'emblematic character', as he terms it.[17] Hence the particular is prevented from being merely anecdotal (the word is anathema to Struth) and becomes generic, in the sense that it typifies something.

In 'Theses on the Philosophy of History', Struth's other key reference text, Walter Benjamin contends that the 'historical materialist cannot do without the notion of a present which is not in a transition, but in which time stands still and has come to a stop. For this notion defines the present in which he himself is writing history'.[18] Taken together, this attending to the specifics of a moment both for its formal characteristics, and for its larger significance produces a specific quality that, once noticed, can be discerned again and again within the *Unconscious Places* series – a quality by means of which, paradoxically, a heightened sense of stillness, of things in arrest, makes evident the longer passage of time which has led to this particular configuration of urban artefacts being here at this particular moment. Each image is simultaneously a faithful record of a place and a moment, and something much larger and longer.

But besides the historico-temporal, there is another, more fugitive register at play in the images, a version of what Benjamin famously termed 'the optical unconscious'. Establishing the term in constrast to the 'instinctual unconscious' as proposed by Freud, Benjamin used it to refer to photography's capacity 'to reveal the physiognomic aspects of visual worlds which dwell in the smallest things, meaningful yet covert enough to find a hiding place in waking dreams'.[19] In his seminal 1931 essay 'A Small History of Photography', Benjamin discussed Eugene Atget's photographs of Paris in these terms:

> *The beholder feels an irresistible urge to search such a picture for the tiny spark of contingency, of the Here and Now with which reality has, so to speak, seared the subject, to find the inconspicuous spot where the immediacy of that long-forgotten moment the future subsists so eloquently that we, looking back, may rediscover it.*[20]

In Struth's project, there is an equivalent 'bringing to visibility' of the 'unconscious' qualities of the city – qualities of which it itself might be said to be unaware. This becomes conflated with the more avowedly formal and socio-historical aspects of the pictorial strategy. This artistic process, although proceeding from a close attention to the given, nevertheless opens up a gap between what confronted Struth on the ground and what is set before us in the resulting photograph.

7.4 Thomas Struth, Dallas Parking Lot, Dallas, 2001.

In his analysis of a well-known and beautiful image made in Dallas in preparation for the 2002 retrospective at the County Museum there, Armin Zweite contends that the picture gains its power precisely by virtue of the difference between what confronts the Dallas motorist looking for a parking spot on a morning, after rain, and what Struth's photograph shows us. How, from this bland and ungainly conglomeration of skyscrapers, has Struth managed to conjure such formal and tonal coherence, producing an image which is, to borrow a phrase from John Szarkowski, 'clear and lively' across its height and breadth?[21] The familiar qualities of crystalline lucidity and calmness are there. But more than this, there is a feeling that the buildings and structures gathered within the frame are, in some sense, animate – that they are holding still for the camera, waiting to be photographed. Indeed in the catalogue for the 2002 Dallas show, Douglas Eklund and Maria Morris Hambourg describe how 'like relatives posing for a group portrait, each structure in the street seems possessed of the same paradoxical mix of autonomy and interdependence'.[22] The insight picks up on a particular quality of the discontinuous American downtown, but more specifically, it connects the *Unconscious Places* series to another body of work which Struth has been making since the late eighties, the family portraits.[23]

It is not difficult to find significant correspondences between the two series. There is a clear similarity between the way in which, for instance, built forms arrange themselves before the camera in Struth's image of Shinjuku from 1986, and his photographs of the Shimada family from 1986 or of the Smith family from 1989. Struth himself has explicitly pointed to such parallels. 'The photograph of a single

7.5 Thomas Struth, Shinju-ku (die Hochhäuser), Tokyo, 1986.

7.6 Thomas Struth, The Shimada Family, Yamaguchi, Japan, 1986.

building has some similarity to an individual portrait', he told Benjamin Buchloch, before pursuing the analogy further. 'Buildings always tell the truth, it seems to me. They are the testimony of people's character, [they] express pride, anger, ignorance, love – everything that humans are capable of expressing'.[24]

The terms by which Struth judges the portraits – 'My idea of a successful photo is that it be readable, that everyone enters and plays his or her role, according to their momentary self-understanding. I believe that quite a bit can be read and is visible' – would apply equally to the cityscapes.[25] Struth explains how the portraits are made: 'I described the spatial limits and encouraged them to select their own place and position within the frame'.[26] He stands beside the large-format camera, allowing the sitters to become conscious of being photographed. In so doing (another paradox) they become less conscious of their demeanour and of how they dispose themselves within the space of the frame. Struth is ultimately interested in this arrangement of selves (thought of as animate bodies) in space. This dynamic is the true subject of the series: Struth has made very few individual portraits, being avowedly more interested in analysing relationships than in psychologising individuals.

The series in fact has its origins in a collaboration with the psychoanalyst Ingo Hartmann in the early eighties, in which they examined photos of family life contributed by a group of participants to see what they might reveal: 'What may be deduced from them about the dynamics of the group? Can one see anything at all?'[27] As Michael Fried notes in his detailed analysis of the series, each image combines a lateral axis of familial relationships which extends across the pictorial space with a perpendicular axis which extends out of it towards the viewer (in Fried's terms, a combination of absorption on the one hand, and theatricality on the other).[28]

It is perhaps not coincidental that it is when Struth begins making these portraits that he abandons the 'photographic uniform', as he terms of it, of centralised perspective used in the early works in *Unconscious Places*. He starts to allow the scene and the relationship between its elements to determine the viewpoint, the point from which the parts best cohere as a whole. The urban scene starts to acquire a greater sense of agency (a sense accentuated by the unavoidable inclusion of people in many of the images made in China and Japan around this time). It is also, determinedly, considered as a grouping, or gathering – a collective construct.

In his emphasis on social space, and on an internal dynamic of historical formation, Struth recalls Victor Hugo's famous assertion that:

> *the greatest products of architecture are not so much individual as they are social works; rather the children of nations in labor than the inspired efforts of men of genius; the legacy of a race; the accumulated wealth of centuries, the residuum of the successive evaporations of human society – in short, a species of formation.*

These lines are used by Aldo Rossi in *The Architecture of the City* as a means of developing his 'idea of the locus – a relationship between a certain specific location and the buildings that are in it'.[29] For Rossi, the locus might be considered equivalent to what 'Henri Focillon speaks of [as] psychological places, places without which the spirit of an environment would be opaque or elusive ...'.[30]

Whereas elsewhere in the book, Rossi attempts to understand the process of urban development in as 'scientific' a manner as possible, he concedes that the city is always more than an accumulation of empirically verifiable acts and artefacts: 'With time, the city grows upon itself; it acquires a consciousness and memory'. (It is worth noting that the passage from Freud cited earlier is quoted by Peter Eisenman in his introduction to the English translation of the book.) In *The Architecture of the City*, Rossi oscillates between ascribing these properties of consciousness and memory to the built artifact of the city in and of itself and to the urban population. In Struth's photographs, built form is presented sometimes as animate in and of itself, and properly the subject of a portrait, sometimes as a kind of proxy for social agents, who are effectively the absent subjects of the portrait. With Rossi, there is an equivalent dialectic at work between a regard for the autonomy of architecture on the one hand, and an emphasis on the social processes of urban formation on the other.

Rossi's overarching interest in an architecture which 'is transformed over time, of an architecture aquainted with immense spaces and delicate solutions and constituting the city'[31] would certainly align with Struth's concerns. It also resonated strongly with the aims of the 2012 Biennale, which, besides containing numerous references to the work of Rossi, included an exhibition – at which the opening address was given by David Chipperfield – of some of the design responses to Venice contained in the 1985 Biennale that Rossi had curated. Clearly, the architecture of the city remained an enduring concern, and the most substantial and valuable 'common ground' established at the 2012 Biennale was a shared commitment on behalf of the discipline to maintaining and strengthening the public urban realm. Struth's photographs offered testament to the qualities of that realm – qualities which were often quiet and almost anonymous. As this short chapter has hopefully shown, numerous aspects and varieties of the unconscious are at play in these calm, undemonstrative images. But in the particular context of the Biennale, their primary impact was to act as a kind of foil to the architectural project. Whereas architecture, inevitably, is a conscious product, the result of prolonged, close attention, Struth's *Unconscious Places* seemed rather to have emerged without conscious attention, or at least to have hitherto escaped it. If William James considered the unconscious to reside at the fringes or the margins of consciousness, then these places might be seen to reside in a similar relation to the mainstream of architecture. But while James did not think it possible to bring what was unconscious to attention without losing its intrinsic quality of nebulousness, Struth's images bring those indistinct margins sharply into view while preserving their mystery.

NOTES

1 The title deliberately referenced *Uncommon Places*, Stephen Shore's seminal photobook of 1982. Stephen Shore, *Uncommon Places: Photographs* (New York: Aperture, 1982).

2 Thomas Struth, *Unconscious Places* (Cologne: Schirmer Mosel, 2012). Sennett's first essay on Struth appeared in Thomas Struth, *Strangers and Friends: Photographs 1986–1992* (Cambridge, MA: The MIT Press, 1993).

3 Richard Sennett, 'Thomas Struth's City', in David Chipperfield, Kieran Long, and Shumi Bose (eds), *Common Ground – A Critical Reader* (Venice: Marsilio Editions, 2012), pp. 49–62.

4 Struth made the comment at a lecture in Dublin in 2013. *Constructing the View – A Symposium on Architecture and Photography*, 2 November 2013. See www.constructingtheview.com.

5 This intervention was published as 'Of Structure as the Inmixing of an Otherness Prerequisite to Any Subject Whatever', in Jacques Lacan, *The Languages of Criticism and the Sciences of Man: The Structuralist Controversy*, ed. R. Macksey and E. Donato (Baltimore, MD: Johns Hopkins Press, 1970), p. 189.

6 Sigmund Freud, *Civilisation and its Discontents*, trans. David McLintock (London: Penguin, 2002), pp. 8–9.

7 Cited in a lecture in the *Constructing the View* symposium, Dublin, November 2013, also noted in Maria Morris Hambourg and Douglas Eklund, 'The Space of History', in Douglas Eklund, Ann Goldstein, Maria Morris Hambourg, and Charles Wylie, *Thomas Struth 1977–2002* (New Haven, CT: Yale University Press, 2002), p. 156.

8 Struth lecture, *Constructing the View* symposium, Dublin, November 2013.

9 In an interview in *Uncommon Places*, Stephen Shore talks about how the use of a large format camera changes how the picture is composed: 'In the field, outside the controlled confines of a studio, a photographer is confronted with a complex web of visual juxtapositions that realign themselves with each step the photographer takes. Take one step and something hidden comes into view; take another and an object in the front now presses up against one in the distance. Take one step and the description of deep space is clarified; take another and it is obscured. In bringing order to this situation, a photographer solves a picture more than composes one'. Stephen Shore, interview with Lynn Tillmann, *Uncommon Places*.

10 Richard Sennett, 'Thomas Struth's City', in Thomas Struth, *Unconscious Places*.

11 Maria Morris Hambourg and Douglas Eklund, 'The Space of History', in *Thomas Struth 1977–2002*, pp. 161–2.

12 Peter Schjeldahl, 'Thomas Struth', in *Columns and Catalogues* (New York: The Figures, 1994). The review first appeared in the Village Voice, 1993.

13 Armin Zweite, '"... a certain sense of placelessness ..." Thomas Struth between Seoul, Cape Canaveral, Garching and Greifswald', in Anette Kruszynski, Tobia Bezzola, and James Lingwood (eds), *Thomas Struth Photographs 1978–2010* (Cologne: Schirmer Mosel, 2010), pp. 147–60 (p. 148).

14 Wolfgang Köhler, *Gestalt Psychology: An Introduction to New Concepts in Modern Psychology* (New York: Liveright, 1970).

15 Frederick S. Perls (Fritz Perls), *Gestalt Therapy Verbatim* (Lafayette, CA: Real People Press 1969), p. 41.

16 John Berger, *Understanding a Photograph* (London: Penguin Books, 2013), p. 121.

17 Thomas Struth, *Photographs 1978–2010*, p. 186.

18 Walter Benjamin, 'Theses on the Philosophy of History', in *Illuminations*, trans. Harry Zohn, ed. Hannah Arendt (New York: Harcourt, Brace and World, 1968), p. 262.

19 Walter Benjamin, 'A Small History of Photography', in Walter Benjamin, *One-Way Street and Other Writings*, ed. E.F.N. Jephcott and Kingsley Shorter (London: Verso, 1997), pp. 240–57 (p. 242). The term 'optical unconscious' was later appropriated by Rosalind

Krauss to guide the delineation of an alternative genealogy of modernism. Rosalind Krauss, *The Optical Unconscious* (Cambridge, MA: The MIT Press, 1994).

20 Walter Benjamin, 'A Small History of Photography', p. 241.

21 The phrase was used in a discussion of the work of Atget: 'The photographer's goal is simple in principle and seemingly modest in ambition: it is to find the place and moment from which some interesting aspect of the world can be converted into a photograph that will be both clear and lively'. John Szarkowski, *Atget* (New York: Museum of Modern Art, 2000), p. 50.

22 Maria Morris Hambourg and Douglas Eklund, 'The Space of History', in *Thomas Struth 1977–2002*, pp. 161–2.

23 This is a relatively small body of work, numbering about 35 images in total by the mid-2000s, but extensively exhibited and published.

24 Interview with Benjamin Buchloh, in Thomas Struth, *Portraits* (New York: Marion Goodman Gallery, 1990), p. 31.

25 Ibid.

26 Ibid., p. 29.

27 Ibid. Extended quote as follows: 'Another time I encountered the problem of the family portrait was this 'Family Life' investigation that I did with the psychoanalyst Ingo Hartmann eight years ago; on his initiative we collected photos in which family life was supposed to be represented. A group of about 40 or 50 people were each asked to submit three or four photos typical of their family life. We then reproduced and enlarged these, brought them to the same size in order to make them comparable, sorted them and then wondered, are these somehow readable? What may be deduced from them about the dynamics of the group? Can one see anything at all? Is there any kind of common reading in the photographs, or does everyone have a different opinion about them?'.

28 Michael Fried, *Why Photography Matters as Art as Never Before* (New Haven, CT: Yale University Press, 2008), Chapter 7 passim.

29 Aldo Rossi, *The Architecture of the City*, trans. Diane Ghirardo and Joan Ockman (Cambridge, MA: The MIT Press, 1984), p. 102.

30 Ibid., p. 106.

31 Aldo Rossi, *A Scientific Autobiography*, trans. Lawrence Venuti (Cambridge, MA: The MIT Press, 1984), p. 16.

8

X Marks the Spot that Will Have Been

Jane Rendell

Exiting the platform at Kennington Tube, after a particularly arduous day, I drag myself up the steps and along the curved corridor to the lifts. A woman flicks her hair just past my cheek and glances up at the curved mirror up in the corner to check her reflection. I start to follow suite … tilting my head upwards towards the image of her distorted face and the view back down the corridor disappearing behind her shoulder, but my gaze flickers over and is caught by a rather odd diagram, one I have not noticed before. This is a brand new, carefully framed and very well produced image. It is a simple black and white drawing of a circular labyrinth (or is it a maze?) divided into quadrants. Down at the bottom, next to the entrance (or is it the exit?) I see a small red cross. X marks the spot.

One of the earliest diagrams drawn by Sigmund Freud to show the unseen workings of the mind is 'Psychological Schema of the Word Concept',[1] originally published in

8.1 Mark Wallinger, *Labyrinth*, 2013 (Kennington Station). Commissioned by Art on the Underground / LUL, 2013. The work © the artist, courtesy of Hauser & Wirth. Photograph © Thierry Bal.

1891 as part of his research on aphasia. It shows the conscious and unconscious as two complexes – 'word-' and 'object-associations'. The diagram shows the division between the conscious and unconscious in terms of the two main branches of a tree, whereas in a later drawing, 'Schematic Diagram of Sexuality' (1894),[2] a line is used, sometimes dashed, to differentiate between two territories, one, un-named, located inside the boundary, and another labelled 'the external world' situated outside. In a subsequent diagram, 'The Architecture of Hysteria' (1897)',[3] Freud drew the relationship between inner and outer worlds from another point of view – rather than a drawing showing space two dimensionally like a section or plan – the various zones in this drawing appear to recede into the distance like a perspective.

For Freud, hysteria is associated with the return of a memory; the content of a recurring hysterical attack is the return of a psychical state, which the patient has experienced earlier.[4] Jean Laplanche and Jean-Bertrand Pontalis summarise how in *The Studies on Hysteria* (1893–5) Freud explores the way in which mnemic or memory-traces are stored in an archival fashion according to several methods of classification, including chronology, position in chains of association and accessibility to consciousness.[5] This archival system allows a single event to be stored in various places: connected with perception, memory and connected with the presentation of ideas or *Vorstellung*.[6] In 'The Project' (1895) Freud differentiated between perceptual cells and mnemic cells,[7] perceptual images (*Wahmehmungsbild*) and mnemic images (*Erinnerungsbild*).[8] Following Joseph Breuer, Freud reasoned that it was not possible for the same system to operate in terms of perception, as the 'mirror of a reflecting telescope', *and* in terms of memory, as a 'photographic plate', and instead he suggested that separate systems of registration existed.[9] Freud explained his thinking on this to Wilhelm Fliess in his letter of 6 December 1896 using a 'schematic picture' accompanied by the following written explanation:

> *As you know, I am working on the assumption that our psychic mechanism has come into being by a process of stratification: the material present in the form of memory-traces being subjected from time to time to a re-arrangement in accordance with fresh circumstances – to a re-transcription. Thus what is essentially new about my theory is the thesis that memory is present not once but several times over, that it is laid down in various kinds of indications. I postulated a similar kind of re-arrangement some time ago (Aphasia) for the paths leading from the periphery [of the body to the cortex]. I cannot say how many of these registrations there are: at least three, probably more.*[10]

In an essay accompanying a wonderful exhibition of Freud's drawings, curator Lynn Gamwell has argued that Freud's use of diagrams to map the space of the psyche needs to be connected to the development of science in a German context informed by the work of Kant and German Idealism where, rather than the rule of direct observation which was the norm in France, scientists in Germany were able to use 'theoretical models such as diagrams of unseen realms to guide their investigation'. She suggests that Freud 'moved back and forth between pictures based on observation and on theory in his pursuit of the elusive psyche'.[11] Writing in response alongside this set of Freud's drawings, Mark Solms' understanding is that the shift in Freud's drawings from 'representational pictures to abstract diagrams' parallels the change in his 'transition' from neuropsychology to metapsychology. Solms locates this transitional phase in that period of time when Freud had to abandon traditional methods of neuroscience based on clinical observation since many of the phenomena he was encountering, such as repression, could not be traced to visible causes, and in those drawings Freud prepared for Wilhelm Fliess including 'Schematic Diagram of Sexuality' (17 January 1895?).[12]

In 'The Interpretation of Dreams' (1900), Freud took a different visual turn, this time presenting the passage of communication between the exterior world and interior psyche through series of schematic diagrams comprising vertical bands, similar to an architect's cross-section through a substance. The final version shows perception (Pcpt.) at one end and the preconscious (Pcs.) at the other, with movement occurring from Pcpt. to Pcs. across a series of mnemic or memory traces followed by a dotted arc swinging under the vertical band representing the unconscious.[13] Later on in the written text, Freud supplemented his topographical account of the nervous system and the psyche, where the conscious, preconscious and unconscious were located in different places, with a dynamic one, where he argues a particular 'agency' is able to influence the structure.[14] Using the metaphor of a telescope, Freud likens the operation of the psychical system to the way in which beams of light are refracted to form an image when they enter a new medium.[15] The use of spatial metaphors to explain the arrangement of psychical structures and processes also appears in Freud's 'Introductory Lectures' of 1917. Here he uses architecture to position the role of censorship on the threshold between two rooms – conscious and unconscious – guarded by a watchman.[16]

> *Let us therefore compare the system of the unconscious to a large entrance hall, in which the mental impulses jostle one another like separate individuals. Adjoining this entrance hall there is a second, narrower, room – a kind of drawing-room – in which consciousness, too, resides. But on the threshold between these two rooms a watchman performs his function: he examines the different mental impulses, acts as a censor, and will not admit them into the drawing-room if they displease him.*[17]

Freud develops his understanding of the roles played by both the topographic and dynamic models of the psyche in his 1915 paper 'The Unconscious'.[18] At the start of Part IV, 'Topography and Dynamics of Repression', he employs the term repression or *Verdrängung*, to describe 'a process affecting ideas on the border between the systems Ucs. and Pcs. (Cs.)'.[19] In 'The Ego and the Id' (1923) Freud goes on to articulate activities on this boundary in terms of the ego – a 'frontier-creature' who 'tries to mediate between the world and the id'.[20] 'The Ego and the Id' contains a diagram, which repositions the systems or mental processes of the conscious, preconscious and unconscious, known as Freud's first topography, consolidated in 'The Interpretation of Dreams', with respect to what has become known as his second topography, a structural theory where the psyche is divided into the three new entities of ego, superego and id.[21] Freud places the ego below the preconscious and above the id circumscribed in a blob-like shape.[22] Ten years later, in 1933, in 'The Dissection of the Psychical Personality', Freud drew together these two triadic structures: 'the three qualities of the characteristic of consciousness [sic]' – the conscious, preconscious and unconscious, and 'the three provinces of the mental apparatus' – ego, superego and id; into one socio-spatial analogy using a geographical and cultural metaphor:

> *I am imagining a country with a landscape of varying configuration – hill-country, plains, and chains of lakes – and with a mixed population: it is inhabited by Germans, Magyars and Slovaks, who carry on different activities.*[23]

Literary critic Virginia Blum and geographer Anna Secor have argued that in his 1915 essay, 'The Unconscious', Freud posits that the unconscious and preconscious are not 'regions, territories or locations, whether anatomical or structure, but different relationships to the possibility of language'.[24] In Blum and Secor's view Freud's turn to structure in the second topography comes as a result of impasses presented by the Euclidean geometry of the topographical model itself, [25] as one 'inadequate to the task of mapping the psyche'.[26] They suggest that while Freud, in his early neurobiological writings and drawings, searched for the unconscious as an actual space that could be mapped, later, from 'The Interpretation of Dreams' onwards, he turned to the use of metaphors to indicate hypothetical places rather than real and locatable ones. Blum and Secor assert that for Freud, the spatiality of the psyche is 'caught between the topographical (having to do with regions and locations) and the metaphorical. Yet, the psychic processes Freud describes are in many cases arguably topological'.[27]

Some days later, along with an invitation asking if I would like to write an essay for a book on Mark Wallinger's artwork Labyrinth *for Transport for London, I receive a fascinating document that includes a set of intriguing drawings showing different kinds of labyrinth and maze. I join the dots ... the labyrinth I saw in the Underground at Kennington is part of an art commission. Of course, no other text positioned down there could have been so carefully framed, yet so speculative, except for an artwork. The lack of any visible explanatory context lets the mind wander. Mine has only just been relocated to this spot, with the help of a clue, which has repositioned me on the inside, at the centre of this labyrinth, a place where I have come to know things, including myself. Yet others stay on the outside, offered no revelation of the mystery, for them the labyrinth retains its status as an enigmatic figure. These are some of the spots that X marks.*

In my mind, a strange reversal takes place in Freud's drawings over time, from the early schemas which represent in an abstract fashion his search for a biological location to the unconscious, to the later figures where the various terrains of the psyche are drawn to resemble biological organs, such as the eye. Yet whether intending to represent the biology of the brain or to create more abstract diagrams of its mental processes, Freud's drawings attempt to make visible relations between interior psychic space and the exterior material world; in so doing they bear a striking resemblance to visual representations of labyrinths and mazes which also seek to link spiritual processes to physical geographies and have inspired Mark Wallinger's project for London Underground. Coming across Wallinger's *Labyrinth* in London's underworld makes it possible to imagine parallels between the spatial and bodily experience of traveling through these subterranean passages and the inner and often hidden workings of the mind.[28]

In everyday speech, both the labyrinth and the maze denote a complex and potentially confusing arrangement of pathways, yet structurally, philosophically, and mathematically, they can be distinguished. Structurally, a labyrinth is one path that winds its way from the start to the finish, two places that often coincide, whereas a maze has forks, dead ends and sometimes cycles. Philosophically, the labyrinth is a meditative and often spiritual path laid out with the intent of setting one free, while the maze presents a puzzle and a challenge, a structure designed to trap and to trick. Mathematically, while the same set of curves can be used to define a labyrinth or maze topology, labyrinths are the curves themselves and mazes are the spaces between. The eighteenth century mathematician Leonhard Euler (1707–83) was one of the first to analyze mazes mathematically, and in doing so he made the first significant contributions to the branch of mathematics now known as topology.

In 1735 Euler put forward a puzzle now famous in the history of mathematics called 'The Seven Bridges of Königsberg' whose negative resolution has been argued to set the foundations of graph theory and prefigure the idea of topology. The city of Königsberg in Prussia (now Kaliningrad, Russia) was situated on both sides of the River Pregel, and included two large islands, which were connected to each other and the mainland by seven bridges. A problem was set which was to find a walk through the city that would cross each bridge once and only once. Euler proved that the problem had no solution, but he was able to show that only the connective information was relevant; the pictorial representation of the graph could be distorted in any way without changing its properties, thus setting out a basic principle of topology that some spatial problems depend on the relations between objects – their continuities and cuts – not their exact shapes.

Blum and Secor describe how the field of topology focusses on the qualitative properties of space (as opposed to the geometric), and that:

> *topologically speaking, a space is not defined by the distances between points that characterize it when it is in a fixed state but rather by the characteristics that it maintains in the process of distortion and transformation (bending, stretching, squeezing, but not breaking).*[29]

For Blum and Secor topology deals with surfaces and sets of properties that retain their relationships under processes of transformation. Not only are topological figures often impossible to draw or construct, but highly theoretical topologists 'not only avoid anything like pictures of these things, they mistrust them', viewing them as mathematically meaningless.[30] Blum and Secor discuss how French psychoanalyst Jacques Lacan used topological operations to deal with psychic processes such as transference, condensation, displacement, and mourning put forward by Freud;[31] they draw attention to how Lacan's 'topology of the subject … allows the neurotic to situate people, events, and places that are apparently separated in time and space *in the same place*'.[32]

Blum and Secor explore how topology makes an early appearance in Lacan's teaching in the context of his address to the Rome Congress of Romance Language Psychoanalysts in 1953, and how his schemas (L, R and I), developed in his seminars between 1954 and 1957, provide a different kind of map from those of Freud's topographies.[33] They focus on how, in his Seminar IV (1956–7), Lacan made a very particular point concerning the schemas, that: 'It is not a matter of localizations, but of the relations between places'.[34] They go on to suggest that:

> *If many geographers have become convinced that the grid is not the whole story of space, Lacan can help us to understand how space works in non-Euclidean ways. We argue that it is because the subject is a topological figure that space as we live it is more-than-topographical …*[35]

According to Darian Leader, the thinking of the 1940s introduced a movement from the inductive study of objects to the refining of models, giving access to an understanding of 'structures considered as sets of relations between objects'.[36] In addition to the interest in algebra current, there was also a fascination in those structures of order, which deal with choices, hierarchies, classifications, topology and its concern with neighbourhood, proximity and barrier; such tools were emerging in anthropology and cybernetics. Leader considers Lacan's early schemas not as models; he notes that later, 'as Lacan moved from algebraic ideas to topologies and knot theory, he would come to see the diagram as something closer to the real, not as a representation of a structure but as the structure itself, understood in the sense of a set of relations of invariance',[37] a point of view close to Blum and Secor's description of Lacan's topology as 'at once psychic and material'.[38] Leader wonders then why 'diagrams should matter to psychoanalysis', and responds with the thought that, 'Where words fail something else is appealed to', noting how in his early work Lacan 'identifies this with certain privileged images'.[39]

It is possible to suggest that Harry Beck's innovative London Underground Tube Map might be one such privileged image. The map is used to assist navigation, and it is certainly topological, setting out clear relations between key points, despite the fact that their positions on his map bear little resemblance to their geographical coordinates. Many Londoners, as Wallinger describes, have this 'diagram' imprinted on their psyche, and strangely it is this abstract and imaginary representation of London which best describes the city spatially, providing a first visual clue for many visitors as to 'where things are', and remaining as a trace in the mind of residents long after they have realised the map's lack of physical accuracy.

From 1951, as psychoanalyst Bernard Burgoyne outlines, Lacan worked with the mathematician Georges-Théodule Guilbaud to examine forms of thinking and questions of structure.[40] Drawing on Elisabeth Roudinesco's biography of Lacan, theorists Ellie Ragland and Dragan Milovanovic give an account of how Lacan and Guilbaud 'in private indulged together in their shared passion, forever tying knots in bits of string'. They note how in his later work Lacan continued to be influenced by a number of mathematicians: Pierre Soury, Jean-Michel Vappereau and Valérie Marchande, who mentioned to him the heraldic display of the Milanese dynasty the Borromeos, which included the motif of three overlapping and linked rings.[41] During the 1950s and 1960s, Lacan developed several topological figures to illustrate the functioning of the human psyche, including the torus, the Möbius strip, the Klein bottle and the cross-cap; but from 1972, he turned to the theory of knots, a particular branch of mathematics, and in the last years of his seminar – 1975 and 1976 – he was specifically interested in the Borromean knot with respect to the symptom or '*le sinthome*'.

Lacan's interest in the symptom was tied to his fascination with writing and its relation to the real; he says: 'That the writing of little letters, that the writing of little mathematical letters, is what supports the real'.[42] Lacan focusses in particular on the use of language in James Joyce's work and in this seminar he refers both to Joyce's *Finnegan's Wake* (1939) and to *Ulysses* (1922) as key points of discussion. There are certainly strong similarities between the figure of the Borromean knot and its three intertwined rings and the figure of overlapping circles placed at the centre of *Finnegan's Wake*. But it is perhaps *Ulysses* which is more important for Lacan, for he starts the seminar by arguing that Joyce wrote the book in 'l'élangues', in other words in a style where 'the English tongue no longer exists', where signifier does not relate directly to signified, where words play off each other, creating different possibilities for meaning that are fluid and polyvalent, such that Lacan describes the work in terms of 'elation' or more specifically – in psychiatry – 'mania'.[43] In his musings around Joyce's *Ulysses*, at one point Lacan puts it most succinctly:

> *Ulysses bears witness to the way in which Joyce remains rooted in his father even as he disowns him; and it is this indeed that is, that is his symptom. ... I said he was the symptom. His whole oeuvre is one long symptom.*[44]

Ragland and Milovanovic explore how, in Lacan's work, the symptom is important topologically because it 'holds the subject together'; it is constituted through a basic unit of structure – the Borromean triadic associative unit of the Imaginary (identificatory), the Symbolic (language and social conventions) and the Real (effects whose cause is repressed excitation or trauma) – that 'functions topologically insofar as it is knotted by a fourth order: the order of the knot that belongs to each of the other three but also holds them together'.[45]

> *For Lacan, topology is not a metaphor; it is the precise way we may understand the construction and appearance of the subject. Topology provides an intuitive understanding of transformations. It encourages intuitive leaps and alternative conceptualisations. Often, multi-dimensional spaces, outside of our normal three space dimensions are employed.*[46]

I remember that I have been to this part of the Underground before, to this spot precisely, in a life that is past ... Last year I moved house and Kennington Underground station is now part of my morning ritual – leave home, unlock bike, cycle to Kennington, lock bike, go through barriers, run down spiral staircase, stand at far end of platform ready to exit near the steps at Euston – and again, in reverse, much slower, at the end of the day. But in 1992 as an architectural assistant just out of university, one of my first jobs was to survey the stations of the Northern Line from Kennington south to Morden. I was given a set of drawings issued by London Underground, and told to check that all the dimensions were correct. Arriving underground at Kennington one morning, I discovered a gap between what was drawn on the plans and the spaces I was experiencing. Dark lines, neat but fuzzy on the soft paper of the blue print, indicated the existence of a series of rooms and tunnels, some located parallel to the platforms, others hidden behind locked doors. When I started to investigate a group of men in white suits emerged from a circular shaft not marked on the map to block my entrance. Later I discovered by chance from a friend doing market research for a company X who wished to remain anonymous, that studies were being conducted to investigate the possibilities of burying nuclear waste under London, in the abandoned tunnels of the Northern line. … A buried history seen from another place today? A configuration that holds the relation between past, present, and future in terms of what will have been*? Perhaps X marks the relation between spots in time as well as space?*

X

Considered from another spot, a key aspect of Freud's shift from the first to the second topography can be understood to involve his conceptualisation of repression as 'a process affecting ideas on the border between the systems Ucs. and Pcs. (Cs.)'.[47] In psychoanalysis repression is linked to repetition and Freud's account of the compulsion to repeat is located in 'Beyond the Pleasure Principle' where he argues that while the pleasure principle's aim is to reduce agitation and return to an inorganic state, the compulsion to repeat works against this.[48] In their commentary on Freud's work, Laplanche and Pontalis posit that the 'defining property of the symptom' can be located in the manner in which it reproduces 'in a more or less disguised way' elements of past conflict, and the ways that 'the repressed seeks to 'return' in the present, whether in the form of dreams, symptoms or acting-out'.[49]

The temporal structure of deferred action, *nachträglichkeit* in the German original, *après coup* in the French translation, provides one way of understanding the distinction between conscious and unconscious, how one is separated from, but returns in the other. Laplanche has chosen the neologism 'afterwardsness' as his preferred English translation as he finds that this term is better able to embrace the double temporal direction – the 'to and fro' or back and forth – of retrogressive and progressive actions, as well as the processes of detranslation and retranslation he holds are central to the concept of *nachträglichkeit*.[50] According to Laplanche and Pontalis, it was Lacan who drew attention to this important concept of Freud's.[51] In 'The Function and Field of Speech and Language in Psychoanalysis' (1953) Lacan picks out the word *nachträglich* in Freud and discusses it in terms of turning points where the 'subject restructures himself'.[52] Lacan suggests that the meaning of symptoms comes, not from the past, as we might expect, but from the future, placing emphasis on the future anterior as the tense of what *will have been*,[53] the tense, with which as Lorens Eyan Holm writes, 'Lacan characterises the self-reflection of subjectivity'.[54]

It is perhaps in imagining the critical potential of the *will have been* in terms of city design and urban experience, as Holm does when considering Le Corbusier's early snapshots as un-yet-fulfilled objects of desire,[55] that we find the most suggestive spot in which to consider architecture's unconscious. A topographical approach offers a way of understanding the psyche spatially, if not materially, then certainly metaphorically. Such an approach allows us to think of the psyche in terms of spatial structures and processes, including repression and displacement, and at the same time, to consider architecture in psychoanalytic terms. A topological perspective goes a little further in providing an understanding of space, that, as Blum and Secor have described, is 'at once psychic and material',[56] and which positions 'people, events, and places that are apparently separated in time and space *in the same place*'.[57] This bringing together of past, present and future spaces and times in one place is certainly something conjured through the psychic workings of memory and creative design processes which imagine the future through speculation, projection and proposition, but an encounter with the unexpected which re-connects relations and experiences understood as already-separated also has something of the psychoanalytic process about it: to come at a familiar place from an unanticipated direction that renders it strange, to misrecognise and then to let yourself be reconfigured by what you had forgotten and wear again its well-worn forgotten intricacies.

If architecture does have an unconscious, then maybe we get closest to what this might be, through those urban experiences, which restructure us through spatio-temporal processes, like *nachträglich* and what *will have been*. André Green in discussing what he describes as the 'bidirectionality of language', its movements backwards and forwards,[58] between the processes of anticipation and retrospection, might call this '*associative irradiation*'.[59] And as John Shannon Hendrix and Holm write in the introduction to this book: it is in retrospective anticipation that signification occurs, 'at the 'anchoring point' (*point de capiton*), which is the point at which the subject inserts itself into language as absence'. X marks a spot, where for Lacan signifier and signified come together, if only to produce the illusion that together their meaning is fixed, an impression, which in its temporal dimension, only makes sense afterwards. Is this X in my mind? In the labyrinth? In the ink of the image under my finger? In the ground, right here, over there? Is this X that X? When will that X be this X?

The future anterior is at work in this very essay. Originally written as an invited response to Mark Wallinger's Labyrinth, *for a publication by Art on the Underground, just as the book was to go to press – all images commissioned, every grammatical error ironed out – I received an unexpected email. My essay had been dropped. The references to Freud and Lacan were unwelcome in not reflecting the artist's own influences. But no mention was made of my suggestion regarding the possibilities of storing nuclear waste under London and any role the then London Underground may have played in such plans. I was outraged, then upset, and finally somewhat baffled. I put the essay to one side, and when exiting the tube at Kennington walked up the 179 spiral steps to street level to avoid the red X in its spot. When a few months later I received an unexpected invitation to join a book on architecture and psychoanalysis and I sent Lorens and John an earlier version of this essay, along with a note on its provenance and current state of displacement, they offered to rescue 'X marks the spot', 'from the oblivion of a paranoid state'! So this writing exists somewhere in the relation between places and books, its X still carrying an imprint of what* might have been.

NOTES

1 For a reproduction of the original image see Sigmund Freud, 'Zur Auffassung der Aphasien' (1891, Vienna), translated as Sigmund Freud, *On Aphasia: A Critical Study*, trans. E. Stengel (New York: International Universities Press, 1953), p. 77, fig. 8. An extract from the 1891 text including the drawing relabelled is reprinted as 'Appendix C: Word and Things', in Sigmund Freud, 'The Unconscious' (1915), in *The Standard Edition of the Complete Psychological Works of Sigmund Freud, Volume XIV (1914–1916): On the History of the Psycho-Analytic Movement, Papers on Metapsychology and Other Works*, trans. from the German under the general editorship of James Strachey (London: The Hogarth Press, 1957), pp. 159–215, p. 214.

2 Sigmund Freud, 'Draft G. Melancholia' (1894), in *The Complete Letters of Sigmund Freud to Wilhelm Fliess, 1887–1904*, trans. and ed. Jeffrey Moussaieff Masson (Cambridge, MA: Belknap Press of Harvard University Press, 1985), pp. 98–105, p. 100.

3 Sigmund Freud, 'Draft M. The Architecture of Hysteria, 25 May 1897' (1897), in *The Complete Letters*, pp. 246–8, p. 245.

4 Sigmund Freud, 'On the Theory of Hysterical Attacks', and 'Sketches for the 'Preliminary Communication' of 1893', in *The Standard Edition of the Complete Psychological Works of Sigmund Freud, Volume I (1886–1899): Pre-Psycho-Analytic Publications and Unpublished Drafts*, trans. from the German under the general editorship of James Strachey (London: The Hogarth Press and the Institute of Psychoanalysis, 1966), pp. 145–54, p. 152.

5 Jean Laplanche and Jean-Bertrand Pontalis, *The Language of Psycho-Analysis*, trans. Donald Nicholson-Smith (London: Karnac and The Institute of Psychoanalysis, 1973), p. 247.

6 Ibid., p. 41.

7 Sigmund Freud, 'Project for a Scientific Psychology' (1895), in *The Standard Edition of the Complete Psychological Works of Sigmund Freud, Volume I (1886–1899)*, pp. 281–391, p. 299. This was first published in German in 1950, and then in English four years later. See editor's notes p. 283.

8 'A qualification is called for here in the case of '*W*' and '*Er*'. It will be found that these sometimes stand respectively for '*Wahmehmungsbild*' ('perceptual image') and '*Erinnerungsbild*' ('mnemic image') instead of for '*Wahrnehmung*' and '*Erinnerung*'. The only way of deciding for certain on the correct expanded version depends on the fact that the longer terms are of neuter gender whereas the shorter ones are feminine. There is usually an article or an adjective to make the decision possible; but this is one of those cases in which the reader must depend on the editor's judgement ....'. See editor's note in Sigmund Freud, 'Project for a Scientific Psychology', p. 288. The word *Wahrnehmung* is translated into English as perception and *Erinnerung* as memory.

9 Joseph Breuer, 'Theoretical Studies on Hysteria' (1893), in *The Standard Edition of the Complete Psychological Works of Sigmund Freud, Volume II (1893–1895): Studies on Hysteria*, trans. from the German under the general editorship of James Strachey (London: The Hogarth Press, 1955), pp. 183–251, p. 188, note.

10 Sigmund Freud, 'Letter 52' (dated Vienna, 6 December 1896), in *Extracts From The Fliess Papers: The Standard Edition of the Complete Psychological Works of Sigmund Freud, Volume I (1886–1899)*, pp. 233–9, pp. 233–4.

11 Lynn Gamwell, 'The Role of Scientific Drawings in 19th- and Early 20th-Century Research', in Lynn Gamwell and Mark Solms, *From Neurology to Psychoanalysis: Sigmund Freud's Neurological Drawings and Diagrams of the Mind* (New York: Binghampton University Art Museum and State University of New York Press, 2006), pp. 4–11, pp. 7, 9, and 11.

12 Mark Solms, 'Sigmund Freud's Drawings', in Lynn Gamwell and Mark Solms, *From Neurology to Psychoanalysis*, pp. 12–18, p. 16. Solms dates this drawing as 17 December 1894.

13 See figures 1–3 in Sigmund Freud, 'The Interpretation of Dreams' (1900), in *The Standard Edition of the Complete Psychological Works of Sigmund Freud, Volume V (1900–1901): The Interpretation of Dreams (Second Part) and On Dreams*, trans. from the German under the general editorship of James Strachey (London: The Hogarth Press, 1953), pp. 339–628, pp. 537, 538 and 541.

14 Ibid., p. 610.

15 Ibid., p. 611.

16 Sigmund Freud, 'Introductory Lectures on Psycho-Analysis' (1917), in *The Standard Edition of the Complete Psychological Works of Sigmund Freud, Volume XVI (1916–1917): Introductory Lectures on Psycho-Analysis (Part III)*, trans. from the German under the general editorship of James Strachey (London: The Hogarth Press, 1963), pp. 241–463, 'Lecture IX: Resistance and Repression', pp. 286–302, p. 295. Diana Fuss and subsequently Charles Rice have picked up on Freud's use of this domestic architectural metaphor to describe the relationship between the ego, superego and id, with Rice making the interesting point that it 'doubles the domestic situation experienced by Freud's clientele'. See Diana Fuss, *The Sense of an Interior: Four Rooms and the Writers that Shaped Them* (London: Routledge, 2004), p. 6, and Charles Rice, *The Emergence of the Interior: Architecture, Modernity, Domesticity* (London: Routledge, 2007), pp. 39–40.

17 Sigmund Freud, 'Introductory Lectures on Psycho-Analysis', p. 295.

18 Sigmund Freud, 'The Unconscious', pp. 159–215, pp. 173–6.

19 Sigmund Freud, 'The Unconscious', p. 180. See also Sigmund Freud, 'Repression' (1915), in *The Standard Edition of the Complete Psychological Works of Sigmund Freud, Volume XIV (1914–1916)*, pp. 141–58.

20 Sigmund Freud, 'The Ego and the Id' (1923), in *The Standard Edition of the Complete Psychological Works of Sigmund Freud, Volume XIX (1923–1925): The Ego and the Id and Other Works*, trans. from the German under the general editorship of James Strachey (London: The Hogarth Press, 1961), pp. 1–308, p. 56.

21 Ibid., p. 24.

22 Ibid.

23 Sigmund Freud, 'The Dissection of the Psychical Personality' (1933), in *The Standard Edition of the Complete Psychological Works of Sigmund Freud, Volume XXII (1932–1936): New Introductory Lectures on Psycho-Analysis and Other Works*, trans. from the German

under the general editorship of James Strachey (London: The Hogarth Press, 1964), pp. 57–80, p. 72.

24 Virginia Blum and Anna Secor, 'Psycho-topologies: Closing the Circuit between Psychic and Material Space', in *Environment and Planning D: Society and Space*, 29(6) (2011), pp. 1030–47, p. 1033.

25 Ibid., p. 1031.

26 Ibid., p. 1034.

27 Ibid.

28 See Steve Pile, 'The Un(known) City ... or, an Urban Geography of what Lies Buried below the Surface', in Iain Borden, Jane Rendell, Joe Kerr and Alicia Pivaro (eds), *The Unknown City: Contesting Architecture and Social Space* (Cambridge, MA: The MIT Press, 2001), pp. 263–79, for a much earlier psychoanalytic reflection on what lies under London.

29 Virginia Blum and Anna Secor, 'Psycho-topologies', p. 1034.

30 Ibid.

31 Ibid., pp. 1034–5.

32 Ibid., p. 1030.

33 Ibid., p. 1035.

34 Ibid., p. 1038.

35 Ibid., p. 1045.

36 Darian Leader, 'The Schema L', in Bernard Burgoyne, *Drawing the Soul: Schemas and Models in Psychoanalysis* (London: Rebus Press, 2000), pp. 151–166, p. 155.

37 Ibid., p. 152.

38 Virginia Blum and Anna Secor, 'Psycho-topologies', p. 1030.

39 Darian Leader, 'The Schema L', p. 153.

40 Bernard Burgoyne, 'Introduction', in Bernard Burgoyne, *Drawing the Soul: Schemas and Models in Psychoanalysis*, pp. 9–22, pp. 21–2, note 9.

41 Ellie Ragland and Dragan Milovanovic, 'Introduction', in Ellie Ragland and Dragan Milovanovic (eds), *Lacan: Topologically Speaking* (New York: Other Press, 2004), pp. xiii–xl, p. xxi.

42 Jacques Lacan, *The Seminar of Jacques Lacan, XXIII* (13.01.76), IV, 9. See http://www.lacaninireland.com/web/wp-content/uploads/2010/06/Book-23-Joyce-and-the-Sinthome-Part-1.pdf [accessed June 2014].

43 Lacan, *The Seminar of Jacques Lacan, XXIII* (18.11.75), IV, 2. See http://www.lacaninireland.com/web/wp-content/uploads/2010/06/Book-23-Joyce-and-the-Sinthome-Part-1.pdf [accessed June 2014].

44 Lacan, *The Seminar of Jacques Lacan, XXIII* (13.01.76), IV, 12. See http://www.lacaninireland.com/web/wp-content/uploads/2010/06/Book-23-Joyce-and-the-Sinthome-Part-1.pdf [accessed June 2014].

45 Ellie Ragland and Dragan Milovanovic, 'Introduction', pp. xiv–xv.

46 Ibid., p. xx.

47 Sigmund Freud, 'The Unconscious', p. 180.

48 Sigmund Freud, 'Beyond the Pleasure Principle' (1920), in *The Standard Edition of the Complete Psychological Works of Sigmund Freud, Volume XVIII (1920–1922): Beyond the Pleasure Principle, Group Psychology and Other Works*, trans. from the German under the general editorship of James Strachey (London: The Hogarth Press, 1955), pp. 1–64, p. 8.

49 Jean Laplanche and Jean-Bertrand Pontalis, *The Language of Psycho-Analysis*, p. 78.

50 See Jean Laplanche, 'Notes on Afterwardsness' (1992), in John Fletcher (ed.), *Essays on Otherness* (London: Routledge, 1999), pp. 260–65, p. 265. These notes are based on a conversation between Jean Laplanche and John Fletcher that took place in 1991.

51 Jean Laplanche and Jean-Bertrand Pontalis, *The Language of Psycho-Analysis*, p. 111.

52 Jacques Lacan, 'The Function and Field of Speech and Language in Psychoanalysis' (Paper delivered at the Rome Congress held at the Institute of Psychology at the University of Rome on 26 and 27 September, 1953), in Jacques Lacan, *Écrits: A Selection*, trans. Bruce Fink (New York: W.W. Norton, 2002), pp. 197–268, p. 257.

53 Jacques Lacan, *The Seminar of Jacques Lacan, Book 1: Freud's Papers on Technique, 1953–54*, ed. Jacques-Alain Miller, trans. John Forrester (New York: W.W. Norton, 1988), p. 158.

54 Lorens Holm, *Brunelleschi, Lacan, Le Corbusier: Architecture, space and the construction of subjectivity* (London: Routledge, 2010), p. 58.

55 Lorens Holm, *Brunelleschi, Lacan, Le Corbusier*, p. 70.

56 Virginia Blum and Anna Secor, 'Psycho-topologies', p. 1030.

57 Ibid.

58 André Green, *Illusions and Disillusions of Psychoanalytic Work*, trans. Andrew Weller (London: Karnac, 2011), p. 18.

59 André Green, 'Freud's Concept of Temporality: Differences with Current Ideas', in *International Journal of Psycho-Analysis*, 89(5) (London: Institute of Psychoanalysis, 2008), pp. 1029–39, p. 1038.

PART III
Fantasies, Desires, Diagnoses

9

Psychoanalytic Diagnosis in Architecture and Urban Design

Timothy D. Martin

The main purpose of this chapter is to address the field of architecture in a way that makes it more comfortable with psychoanalysis and its methods of diagnosis. Let me start off by saying that putting architecture together with psychoanalysis is different from putting it together with philosophy. On one hand, psychoanalysis isn't philosophy because it is a science. It was founded largely by neurologists and always keeps a close alliance to the field of medicine. And yet, because of this link to medicine, clinical psychoanalysis also carries a Hippocratic ethic that is not mandatory to philosophy. Psychoanalysis as a practice involves observation, diagnosis and treatment, and it is diagnosis that stands today as one of the more urgent and important interdisciplinary methodological hurdles between architecture and psychoanalysis. The benefits of jumping this hurdle are substantial

9.1 The Bingham Copper Mine, Utah. Public domain.

and so my objective is to introduce the method by setting out some definitions and examples, and along the way, to remind ourselves of how psychoanalytic diagnosis is already being used in the field of architecture.

Let me start my comments on diagnosis with a reminder of the many remarkable essays on architecture and art by psychoanalysts including Sigmund Freud, Carl Jung, Sabina Spielrein, Melanie Klein, Adrian Stokes, Jacques Lacan, Anton Ehrenzweig, Donald Winnicott, Wilfred Bion, Jean Laplanche, Julia Kristeva, and others.[1] These essays have been really important in raising an awareness of an unconscious in art and architecture. But, we should bear in mind that much of the core psychoanalytic literature on the arts, for example Freud's essay on Leonardo da Vinci, was produced after many steps that are not mentioned in the essay. Before writing, Freud had diagnosed da Vinci as a neurotic. This was a natural step for Freud, who was both a theorist and a practitioner, because psychoanalytic treatment *requires* diagnosis. Diagnosis, in any field that is medical in some way, is entirely normal and usually precedes treatment. It is sometimes the case, however, that diagnosis is made after experimenting with treatments, where success in the latter leads to the former. In psychoanalysis, diagnosis can seem quite complex and, if you were trained as an historian of architecture or art, or in a school of architecture, you were probably not taught to diagnose in this way. One exception to this may be the phenomenology of architecture, with its many studies of the ways that architecture creates shared experience and communal rites out of direct corporeal and mental phenomena.[2] Phenomenological enquiry deals with how things appear and how they affect our experience of the world, it grounds itself in observation, and it diagnoses based on types of *dasein*, the particular way of 'being-in-the-world' of an individual or a society.[3] Psychoanalytic diagnosis, with its hypotheses about the unconscious, arrived at a very different set of categories.

THE THREE PSYCHOANALYTIC CLINICS: PSYCHOSIS, NEUROSIS AND PERVERSION

I would like, therefore, to briefly introduce the diagnostic clinics using examples related to the fields of architecture and urban design. This could be a daunting task in itself. Any perusal of the DSM (the diagnostic and statistical manual for mental disorders) will show a dizzying variety of diagnostic categories and mental pathologies. I will only justify this in a footnote, but I want to simplify this down to three psychoanalytic clinics.[4] They are, Psychosis, Neurosis and Perversion. Among the psychoses are schizophrenia, paranoia and severe bipolar manic depression. Among the neuroses are hysteria, obsessionality, narcissism and phobia. Among the perversions are counted fetishism, sadism, masochism and exhibitionism. This list is not comprehensive, and not every school of psychoanalysis or psychiatry will agree with it. They accord most closely with Freud and Lacan and are adequate to most tasks. What I would like to do first in this chapter, then, is to describe something of the three clinics of psychosis, neurosis and perversion. I will use examples taken from case studies presented by practising analysts that include architecture in some way and ask, in each example, how architecture and the unconscious might be related. Because this review raises many questions about how to use diagnosis in architecture, I will conclude with a final example that draws some of these issues together.

Psychosis

Let me start, in no particular order, with the clinic of psychosis. This is quite a severe clinic. Freud, for example, largely stayed away from it (and the asylum). He ran a clinic of neurosis and was at his best as a theorist of neurosis. The better known psychodynamic theorists of psychosis are Lacan, Jung, and Gilles Deleuze and Félix Guattari. Jung was particularly apt with the visual side of psychosis whereas Lacan was particularly apt with the semiotic side. There are two main symptoms of psychosis. The first is hallucination, which may be visual or auditory. The second symptom is speech disorder. Florid psychotics (i.e. Judge Schreber) develop elaborate worlds, complex and lasting hallucinations that are logical but not rational.[5] The severe nature of the psychoses has long suggested an organic pathology and there are a wide range of drugs in use today. After this slender introduction, I won't say anything more to define psychosis. Obviously, to understand the clinic of psychosis would require further work.

One example chosen specifically from the field of architecture is the case of 'Anna', a French woman in her early thirties, daughter of a village butcher, who married a man from the city. Despite some reservations she decided to live in his home town, taking her away from a close knit community. She made friends and settled into domestic life rather slowly. She liked to go food shopping and, as is the norm in France, would regularly make an extensive walk around the neighbourhood to complete her task. It was only the butcher's shop, interestingly, that troubled her. It lay down a hill and the walk required that she pass by an unkempt four storey building on her descent and ascent. From the upmost storey of this building a rather perverted angry old man would shout insults at her. He said things like 'pig!', 'dirty sow!', and 'I'll cut you up!' It was often just one or two words and, whenever she looked up at the windows of the upper story, her assailant had already hidden. After several such episodes she became less upset and soon learned to ignore the unfortunate creep who taunted her.

Needless to say, after several years Anna began to develop some problems of a psychological nature which drew her into an analysis. These problems were not particularly severe and often seemed to stem from her isolation and loss of her childhood social network. She remained close to her husband and it was only in the course of casual conversation that she mentioned the creep that she encountered during her meat shopping. It turned out, after double checking, that the building in question was empty, and had been for almost a decade. It was entirely uninhabited (no vagrants in the loft). She was having auditory hallucinations, and this revelation obviously affected her diagnosis; she was of the clinic of psychosis.

Further analysis revealed that Anna had lived over her father's butcher shop. From her bedroom she could hear her father working below. Her father was a rather vulgar and coarse man who would shout, audibly through the floorboards, expletives such as 'sow' and 'pig'. After she married and moved away, Anna felt increasingly cut up, dismembered and fragmented, and what Anna heard from the upper window was what we could call her father's voice; she receives her own message as if it came from reality. For Anna, these words effectively came from herself but appeared in her father's name. This is why Lacan says of the psychotic that 'the-name-of-the-father' is foreclosed and, consequently, speaks from a hole in reality.[6]

How, in this case study, does architecture relate to the unconscious? We could say in answer that the architecture houses the unconscious. In psychosis you might say that the top of the head is open; the unconscious really speaks, out loud. The problem isn't how to find the unconscious. In psychosis it's not hidden; it's right there, providing you know where to look or listen. In this case study, architectural space becomes the space where a voice from the real resides. It speaks or displays itself as if it lived there. It got there by means of an extreme repression (foreclosure) and an equally extreme form of projection that is quite different from neurotic projection. Architecture, however, seems to have no particular privilege as a residence. There are plenty of examples of hallucinations that do not include architecture. It could be cars, trees or people. The thing to focus on is how architecture is accredited with a power of authority that speaks during hallucinations.

This is but one limited example of psychosis but one that is adequate, I hope, to the purpose of making clinical material a comfortable talking point within the architectural and urban design disciplines. It is important to be precise in the use of language. So many architects use the word 'paranoid' when they really mean 'suspicious'. Anna was paranoid but she did not constantly ponder other people's ulterior motives. And, just to say one thing about treatment, an architect could offer her greater opportunities to identify with certain people around her.

Neurosis

Let me go on next to the clinic of neurosis, which is also the largest clinic. Freud was its founder and it has seen many different schools develop in the last 100 years. This clinic treats hysteria, obsessionality, narcissism and phobias. The symptoms of neurosis are extremely varied. In general, neurotics have a buried unconscious thought that is rankling to come out. The more notorious defence mechanisms of neurosis include regression, rationalisation, denial, rejection and reaction formation. Diagnosis can examine dreams, free associations, and 'accidental' behaviour or irrational thoughts. Therapy often searches for a fundamental fantasy and seeks its traversal. The analyst does not know the unconscious fundamental fantasy any better than the analysand, but the accuracy of interpretations can often be judged by the beneficial reaction.

As an example I would like to cite the case of 'Peter', an architect who met his wife at university. She was studying a related design field and their student design collaborations became a part of their intimacy, a way they learned about each other. After six years of marriage and a successful design partnership it all went sour. The arguments particularly stemmed from attempts to design their own house, something they both had wanted to do for many years. Peter was bringing an increasingly anxious and dogmatic approach to the design of the house and to the design practice in general. He demonstrated a bitterness that was unusual. As a consequence of this wrangling, their professional design collaborations suffered and, partly for commercial reasons, they consulted a marriage therapist and then Peter consulted an analyst. He could see that he was initiating the conflict but didn't really understand why he felt so anxious.

You can imagine the tedium of the initial analytic sessions in which Peter talked endlessly of his concerns over which doorknob and which window casing to use. For many sessions all he did was rehearse his arguments over floorplan, location, size of the garden, how the kitchen and living room should relate to each other, etc. He brought the marital arguments to the analyst seeking affirmation of his views. His over-rationalisations, his 'love it or hate it' attitude, his insistence that it be 'just so' soon led to a diagnosis of obsessional neurosis. After this diagnosis, analysis helped him understand that his design dogmatism (the pleasure of making and following the rules) was a replacement pleasure. It was a metaphoric or replacement pleasure that stood in for the pleasure of something else, which turned out to be having children. As Peter later put it, 'Now I know that every time I feel like detailing the design of our house, I want to have another child'. This realisation alone restored a great deal in the marriage and the business. The message had, for a while at least, been decoded or excavated, enough that they built their house and had their children.

Although this is a very simple case study it is sufficient, I hope, to get the architectural fields to think about the ways they regularly get implicated in unconscious desires. In this case floor plans, elevations and models were, for Peter, a screen that blocked an unconscious thought. The architectural design process acted to hide the unconscious wish or thought; it was part of a repression and projection involving a swap or metaphor for desire. Although architecture is a visual art, architects need to be aware of the way many people are blind to their fundamental fantasy. This blindness can come in many places in the design process. This blindness can be big enough to hide an elephant in the room.

I had some scepticism myself about this kind of blindness until I saw a demonstration of hypnotism that was of such an architectural character that it is worth mentioning here. This hypnotism of a young man took place in a lounge area. The young man was given the suggestion that there was no furniture in the room and that he should go to the bar and get a drink. He did so with complete success. He didn't bump into any of the couches or tables. When he returned he was asked why he had taken several abrupt turns in a room that had no obstructions in it. He answered, in full belief, that he had merely turned to look at a painting, and turned again because he thought he saw someone he knew and then realised differently. He was able to completely rationalise his every move while remaining convinced that the room was empty of furniture.

Statistically speaking neurosis is the biggest of the three clinics, but be careful. Not everyone who wants it 'just so' is an obsessional. What a neurotic asks for, his demand, is a compensation or metaphor for what they do not know they want. In the clinic of neurosis, psychoanalytic method allows the architectural field to ask questions such as, 'what is the unconscious wish behind the architecture?' It is an interesting and valuable question and one that is refreshingly different from speculations about conscious intentions or ulterior motives. It complicates our understanding of architecture as a sublimation of unconscious thought and wishes.

An awareness of neurosis is quite evident in the conversations of architects. They often understand how architecture features as a screen for a wish that cannot be articulated, or which keeps appearing as if from someplace or someone else. Peter, for example, initially thought his wife was the neurotic. Sometimes it isn't necessary to see through the screen, it's enough to see that there is one and to ask what kind and what problems arise when it is too neurotic. I mention this because some architects, after what seems to be a diagnosis, design a kind of individual architectural treatment – a place that allows the fundamental fantasy to be present, if sublimated into something more 'acceptable'. These individual cases are very interesting although, as we shall see below, diagnosis can also be used by architects and urban designers when they are asked to mediate in a larger social sphere.

Perversion

The third and final clinic is perversion, which includes fetishism, sadism and masochism, exhibitionism and voyeurism, paedophilia and necrophilia. Many psychodynamic theorists have studied perversion, including Freud, who argued that childhood sexuality was polymorphously perverse; children had little sense of a pre-given natural order or understanding of the heterosexual biological purpose of sex.[7] One of the more common psychoanalytic diagnoses one hears when talking to architects is the term 'fetish'. It is often used correctly, yet without understanding the full implications of what they have diagnosed. For Freud the sexual fetish was a form of denial that conveniently alleviated sexual anxiety.[8]

Fetishism is an interesting topic in all the arts, but I would like to focus on sadism partly because it is such a fundamental question when considering the socio-political role of architecture. The problem is, this is a somewhat veiled clinic for a number of reasons. Sadists rarely ask for help because they do not generally see themselves as ill. They feel fine and often come into the clinic only on judicial order, because the acts of the pervert often break social norms. Sadism takes its name from the novels of the Marquis de Sade, which vividly describe bondage, debaucheries and orgies.[9] But, be careful, many would agree that de Sade was a masochist and that his novels were his fantasies of the life of a sadist. To Lacan, sadism was less a matter of non-normative acts and more a matter of a structure. Lacan was particularly struck by the way the sadist relates to 'the big Other'. A common example is the cruel teacher who makes the lives of his students miserable but does it 'for the greater good' or in the name of 'Discipline' or 'Order'. The pervert assumes the position of an object-instrument of the will-to-enjoy of the big Other, and this is why sadists have no guilt over treating people in the same way.[10] Paedophile scandals involving public media and religious figures often demonstrate one of the characteristics of perversion. Perverts have no difficulty committing dark deeds in the night and espousing high morals in the day. The sadist serves the Other's enjoyment yet refuses to see this Other in real people (usually neurotics). One of the sadist's favourite games is to figure out what people want (even if they do not know it themselves) and then taunt them by not giving it to them.

In contrast to the neurotic, the pervert knows what he desires. He thereby disregards the other's desire, not by forcing them to do something they do not want to do, but on the contrary, by calling forward the other's desire he can thereafter refuse to satisfy the demand.[11] Nevertheless, there are plenty of perverts who never end up in court, and quite a few non-perverts who do. This will be an important point to bear in mind when we consider the case study.

For a case study I want to take Bernard Tschumi's Parc de la Villette (1984), for the way this project used a clinical diagnosis of sadism. Located in northern Paris, La Villette was originally used for the slaughtering of animals. In the 1960s and 1970s the local area was treated to a Modernist functionalist redevelopment of low-income housing that left the slaughterhouses bordered with *béton brut* apartment blocks and an elevated highway. The relocation of the slaughterhouses in the 1980s offered an opportunity to create a public park for the surrounding housing and residents.

In 'The Pleasure of Architecture' (1977), Tschumi prompted architects to think of Modernist architecture as something fundamentally Apollonian, bound by reason, order and function. What Tschumi was getting at was that Modernist public housing can seem high-minded yet allow the instrumentalisation of individuals, a kind of Apollonian despotism. Following Friedrich Nietzsche, Tschumi proposed that, without the infractions of a second god Dionysus, Apollo would create functional rational structures that controlled and devoured everything, including the erotic pleasures of excess.[12] For Tschumi the danger was that Modernist architecture could be sadistic by over-regulating life; its paternalistic administration was quite faulty, cruel even, toward real people when it failed to give credence to the discourse of Dionysus.

Tschumi teases other architects, asking them whether they just accept the law, question it like the neurotic, or whether they accept the law and still do otherwise, like the pervert. This becomes more than a tease because when Tschumi starts work on La Villette, he suggests there is a lurking sadism in the public housing system. He does not lay this at Le Corbusier's feet but at the feet of French welfare state architecture. The system seemed to be quietly punishing the poor – and enjoying it. To some degree Tschumi's battle between two kinds of gods was a metaphor for two kinds of political administration, left and right wing. But, it went deeper than this. For Tschumi the rules of Apollo (a.k.a. Modernist functionalist rationalist architecture) were sadistic, and needed to be tied up and spanked in return, and yet left in place: no demolition, only remediation. In some respects Tschumi seems to fight fire with fire, to fight sadism with sadism; yet, this may not be the case.

What Tschumi is getting at is that the architect loves the rules but, unlike the sadist, he takes them with a pinch of salt. He does not want to destroy the rules but neither does he get off on them in an erotic way. He acts in the name of changing the rules, making them more responsive, inclusive and nuanced.

> *By stressing its transgressive nature, Tschumi insists that the pleasure of architecture does not result from the absence of rules but from their infraction. Rules, which are represented in forms and structures, are not simply destroyed but are preserved as faulty.*[13]

Tschumi put it like this:

> *... the game of architecture is an intricate play with rules that one can accept or reject. [...] These rules, like so many knots that cannot be untied, are generally a paralyzing constraint. When manipulated, however, they have the erotic significance of bondage.*[14]

What Tschumi found was a way of hijacking the sadist's fantasy to make binding rules that work for the general pleasure of residents, and for those who do not yet know what they want. Tschumi's plans called for a series of follies on a grid. Each folly was a composition of basic constructivist components assembled into a rudimentary architectural form. These follies were empty and incomplete as buildings, the product of a deconstruction of Modernist building components that Tschumi developed with Jacques Derrida.

Tschumi saw a sadistic eroticism in Apollonian Modernism and played it back, refused to be a victim, and looked for a way to take back the upper hand. Not in

9.2 Bernard Tschumi, Parc de la Villette, 1982–98. Photo by Tim Martin.

a violent way but in a pleasurable way. The lurking sadism can be deconstructed, dis-joined and reassembled.[15] But how do you do that? The parks' follies were architectural beginnings, partially completed structures that awaited the desires of the residents. It was for them to decide what to do with the follies, not the architect or the state. The deconstructed columns, beams, walls and floors of the follies have been likened to Rabelais' Gargantua who roughs out a beneficent order into social chaos.[16] For Tschumi you do it with metaphors that are incomplete, that await local public participation in the project of its completion. Among the preprogrammed follies are a burger shop, a children's theatre workshop, space for temporary exhibitions and dance, and an outdoor cinema. But many of the folly conversions were made at the subsequent request of the local community including an adult theatre workshop, and a medical clinic where the *sans papiers* may be seen without questions. Entirely unprogrammed is a small grove next to an empty folly, turned into a memorial site for local youths who have died from addiction, accident, crime and AIDS, their bodies cremated by the state. When a converted folly is no longer needed it is returned to its initial state as a folly, awaiting its next transgression into what is needed. According to Tschumi, La Villette is:

> *... that event, that place of shock, or that place of the invention of ourselves. The event is the place where the rethinking and reformulation of the different elements of architecture, many of which have resulted in or added to contemporary social inequities, may lead to their solution.*[17]

Tschumi's Parc de la Villette established two dialectics, Nietzsche's Dionysus and Apollo with Freud's Eros and Thanatos, in a relation that was rich in metaphors and ultimately an erotic game of binding and unbinding and rebinding, a playing with the rules that belonged somewhere near the clinic of sadism. At times he seems to pit sadism with masochism. In the end, however, I find that Tschumi turns sadism into a fantasy, turns it into theatre, and thus renders it into a neurotic structure, one that can allow local residents to re-establish a trust in the social bond, admit their lack, and seek to fill it.

In this case study, how did diagnosis feature in the architecture? Firstly, Tschumi diagnosed the architecture around the park and then used the park to treat the architecture. He found that the architecture around the park was unable to raise the question of what the other desires. It was built in the name of 'the Poor' without asking the poor what they wanted. 'The Poor' was just a puppet for an administration that was unable to put real people in the position of the Other. It is worth observing that Deconstruction was used therapeutically. By deconstructing the syntax of Modernist social housing, Tschumi opened up its possibilities. The unfinished follies were challenges to the veiled sadism behind paternalist social housing. The follies created a park for the neurotic, allowing local residents to decide how some of the follies would be developed according to their developing perceptions of their needs.

In this architectural case study from the clinic of perversion, where is the unconscious? Tschumi and Derrida had quite different beliefs in the unconscious. Tschumi was certain that the French public housing system served an unconscious sadism. Tschumi's certainty allows us to say something about how to spot the sadistic unconscious in architecture. When you find yourself uncertain that you have been threatened, unsure whether you remember a conversation or a place correctly as to its sadistic undertone, this was when Freud was most certain that he was in front of the unconscious of the pervert. The pervert's objective is to use threats to get people to wonder what they are, as objects, to be enjoyed by the big Other.

Tschumi's own unconscious was highly attuned to the unconscious strategies of the sadist. Tschumi's success lay in playing the role of the Other to the pervert because the pervert assumes the position of an object-instrument of the will-to-enjoy of the big Other. Yet, in Tschumi's hands the park produces a very different Other from what the pervert conjured. The Other in the park is not absolute; the Other is incomplete and requires and invites local participation in its completion.

Under the unconscious of the pervert, social bonds become suspect and untrustworthy. Under the unconscious of the paranoiac, there are hidden agendas at work no matter what anyone does or says. Under the unconscious of the park the social bond is incomplete. The follies are therapeutic to the neurotic precisely because they invite the traversal of a fantasy by presenting an incomplete desire. In one sense they mock the illusion that wishes can be fulfilled, or that one could 'breach want with a span'. And yet the joke is that the follies offer exactly that: a chance to breach want with a span and rise to the challenge of completing desire.

A study of the clinic of perversion helps show how architecture, if it is not careful, can get caught up in satisfying some rather disturbing social and psychodynamics. This can happen in the administrative relationship between architects and their clients, and the people for whom they both build. The master-slave relation can be suspected in any of these relations; there are examples of architects who treat their clients like slaves, and there are examples of clients who treat architects like slaves. In the case of the Parc de la Villette, the architect tried to provide a treatment in the belief that a sadistic system can be thwarted, deconstructed, and the foundations laid for a more neurotic structure. We are at a point here where we can see how psychoanalysis has offered the field of architecture a kind of ethics, in that Tschumi's park sought to tame the sadist for the benefit of the neurotic.

ISSUES OF DIAGNOSIS

Having briefly covered the three clinics of psychosis, neurosis and perversion, it might help to mention a few issues about diagnosis. One such issue is that you only get one clinic. In the diagnosis, if one clinic doesn't work, try another; don't get tempted by 'borderline' diagnoses. Another issue in diagnosis is that 'the symptom should not be confused with the structure'. A textbook example would be homosexuality, which can be an element in a neurotic, a perverse, or a psychotic structure. Another important thing is that diagnosis is made partly by the unconscious. Experience and study also feature in diagnosis, but in psychoanalysis 'it is the unconscious that interprets'. This is why knowing your own clinic helps so much. I think we need to keep a sense of humour about the benefits of knowing your own clinic and the good it will do. Woody Allan, for example, spent years in analysis dealing with his Oedipus complex. But it didn't stop him from marrying his adopted daughter. One final issue is also worth mentioning. There is a difference between being *in* a clinic and being *of* a clinic. Some are in a clinic; there is a problem, and so they attend. Everyone is of a clinic, which is to say that if problems arose, that is the clinic they would be in. Clinical diagnosis isn't always directed toward a pathology, it can simply be a way of understanding the structure of a person or a situation or a place.

INDIVIDUAL AND GROUP DIAGNOSIS: THE CASE OF ROBERT SMITHSON

Having given a brief introduction to clinical diagnosis, it is worth pointing out that the first two case studies dealt with the diagnosis and treatment of individuals. Parc de la Villette was an example of an upscaling from an individual to a group. Tschumi's park intervened on an urban scale and so he diagnosed on a social scale. Because this scale of diagnosis is perhaps the most difficult and the most important, I would like to finish with one further example of a social scale diagnosis, taken from recent history. This is the case of the earthworks and land reclamation parks of Robert Smithson (1938–73), the American sculptor, writer and architectural consultant. Because he may be less familiar than Tschumi, it could be helpful to give him a brief introduction.

As an observer of public space, Smithson was highly dialectical. He loved the incidental negative architecture of the quarries in his native New Jersey that had produced the stone for the buildings of New York City. For a generation that was consciously focussed on progress, his *Partially Buried Woodshed* (1970) (Figure 9.3) celebrated the dialectical opposite: a repressed pleasure in entropy and erosion. In his seminal earthwork *Spiral Jetty* (1971) he constructed a walk that was mirrored by the waters of a lake, a place that produced a psychoanalytic self-encounter, a mobius-strip of a journey that proceeded outward and ended inward.

When it comes to understanding a work of art or architecture, Robert Smithson said something in 1973 that still resonates today.

> *I think all perception is tainted with a kind of psychoanalytic reading. In other words, somebody who's having Oedipal problems, it's going to come out in the perception, or it's going to come out in the making, the kind of work they choose to do.*[18]

In his writings and earthworks he developed a method he called a 'psychoanalysis of landscape perceptions' in which he made clinical diagnosis of individuals and groups based on their perception of the landscape.[19] Smithson was a keen observer of the way unconscious thoughts were projected onto the external world, the way people made the landscape a portrait of their own unknown self. He noted, for example how much of the ecology movement held rather sentimental views of nature as pastoral and idyllic. They projected feelings about their mothers onto the

9.3 Robert Smithson, *Partially Buried Woodshed*, Kent State University, Ohio, 1970. © Estate of Robert Smithson / DACS, London / VAGA, New York, 2015.

environment, and unconsciously played out their Oedipus complex by attacking industrialists as if they were evil paternal rapists. Likewise, Smithson found among industrialists and miners a marked sadism. They extracted wealth from the land but had no feel for or connection to it. They threatened society with pollution and environmental degradation and yet the rule of profit blinded them to their role as agents of nature. The ecologists and the miners were increasingly at odds with each other in a social conflict, and they both needed an artist-analyst to shake them out of their fantasy (ecologists) or their denial (miners).

Perhaps the best example of Smithson's 'psychoanalysis of landscape perceptions' was his proposal for the reclamation of the Bingham Copper Mine in Utah, the largest man made hole in the world (Figure 9.1). No reclamation could restore the site to its original conditions without demolishing an entire mountain; Bingham demonstrated just how irreversible man's impact on nature could be. Smithson's Bingham proposal offered two paths down into the pit, one for each camp. The walk designed for the sadists offered a greater experience of their impact on the land and promoted a sense of responsibility for their actions. The path for the neurotics offered a chance to experience the inherent violence and drama of natural change and to clear their mind of their idealised view of nature. The design of each path was based on a diagnosis and provided a treatment of the person's perceptions of the landscape. Each camp went on their walk and, having undergone treatment, met at the bottom, where they might negotiate with each other in a more successful manner.

Like Tschumi's Parc de la Villette, Smithson's Bingham project asked questions about how the landscape had become a site of unconscious projection, how feelings that originated in childhood got transferred onto the world, and how large scale design projects could mediate in the conflicts between different clinics. Once they figured out the clinical picture of unconscious landscape perceptions they were then able to set out new forms that would change it, or move it on to a more mature state. The onus lay on the architect to find the solution to a conflict by offering each camp a set of experiences that addressed and redressed their pathology.

This chapter, by introducing methods of psychoanalytic diagnosis in a formal and structured way, pushes at interdisciplinary boundaries. Given the range of examples cited in this chapter it is clear that diagnosis has many applications and a considerable history in architecture. It can be applied in the office at an individual scale, it can be used to maintain and promote creativity, and it can be applied in understanding larger social dynamics. It provides a way to think about people outside the normal boxes of race, gender, religion, and social class. It is not a method limited to the design of mental health facilities, although it is clearly useful here too. The examples of Tschumi and Smithson show that this method can be applied where social issues and even sustainability issues prevail and that it can produce substantial results for architects who want an architecture that is capable of mediating social conflicts and environmental impacts.

NOTES

1 A general introduction to this topic can be found in Janet Sayers, *Freud's Art: Psychoanalysis Retold* (London: Routledge, 2007).

2 Examples include Dalibor Vesely, Christian Frost, Nicholas Temple, Jonathan Hale, and John Hendrix.

3 Ludwig Binswanger (1881–1966) is often considered the initiator of *dasein* analytical psychiatry.

4 The DSM includes developmental disorders such as autism, drug induced pathologies, eating and sleeping disorders.

5 Daniel Paul Schreber, *Memoirs of My Nervous Illness*, first German edition, 1903. See also Freud's 1911 paper on Schreber, 'Psycho-analytic Notes on an Autobiographical Account of a Case of Paranoia (*Dementia Paranoides*)', in Sigmund Freud, *Standard Edition, Vol. XII: The Case of Schreber, Papers on Technique and Other Works*, trans. J. Strachey (London: Vintage, 2001), pp. 9–79. Jacques Lacan, *Seminar III: The Psychoses* (1955–6), trans. Russell Grigg, ed. Jacques-Alain Miller (London: Routledge, 1993). Gilles Deleuze and Félix Guattari, *The Anti-Oedipus: Capitalism and Schizophrenia*, trans. Robert Hurley, Mark Seem, Helen R. Lane (London: Athlone Press, 1972).

6 Jacques Lacan, 'On a Question Preliminary to any Possible Treatment of Psychosis', in *Écrits: A Selection*, trans. Alan Sheridan (London: Tavistock, 1977), pp. 179–225.

7 Sigmund Freud, 'Three Essays on Sexuality', in *Standard Edition, Vol. XVIII: Beyond the Pleasure Principle, Group Psychology, and Other Works*, trans. J. Strachey (London: Vintage, 2001), pp. 165–6.

8 Sigmund Freud, 'Fetishism', in *Standard Edition, Vol. XXI: The Future of an Illusion, Civilization and Its Discontents and Other Works*, trans. J. Strachey (London: Vintage, 2001), pp. 152–7.

9 Notable novels by the Marquis de Sade include *Justine, or The Misfortunes of the Virtue* (1791) and *The 120 Days of Sodom, or the School of Libertinism* (1785).

10 Stephanie S. Swales, *Perversion: A Lacanian Psychoanalytic Approach to the Subject* (London: Routledge, 2012).

11 Kirsten Hyldgaard, 'The Conformity of Perversion', in *The Symptom*, Issue 5 (online journal for lacan.com, winter 2004).

12 Bernard Tschumi, 'The Pleasure of Architecture', in *Architecture and Disjunction* (Cambridge, MA: The MIT Press, 1996), p. 83.

13 Mark C. Taylor, *Disfiguring: Art, Architecture, Religion* (Chicago, IL: University of Chicago Press, 1992), p. 247.

14 Bernard Tschumi, 'The Pleasure of Architecture', p. 84.

15 Ibid., p. 83.

16 Danièle Voldman, 'Le Parc De La Villette entre Thélème et Disneyland', in *Vingtième Siècle. Revue d'histoire*, 8(8) (Paris: Presses de la Fondation nationale des sciences politiques, 1985), pp. 19–30.

17 Bernard Tschumi, 'Six Concepts', in *Architecture and Disjunction*, p. 258.

18 Lucy R. Lippard, 'Lucy R. Lippard Talks about Eva Hesse with Nancy Holt and Robert Smithson', in *Artforum* (New York: Artforum International Magazine, February 2008), recorded on 5 June 1973.

19 Ibid.

10

Architecture and the Unconscious: Fantasy, Construction, and the Dual Spatiality

Nikos Sideris

SUBJECTIVITY AND SPATIALITY

Subjectivity is imprescriptible in architecture.[1] 'Space is ... an effect of the relation between the subject and the world'.[2] The representation of space in childhood[3] and the alteration of spatial experience in regression and 'altered states of consciousness' establishes that spatiality and subjectivity are intertwined.[4] 'If the identity of the subject and its desire for objects is constructed by representations of space, then the subject and its space are not independent entities'.[5] So 'we are always already spatial, and ... architecture is always already subjective. The subject articulates its spatiality in architecture'.[6] '*With architecture, I space myself*'.[7]

In the elementary proposition *I am here*, the personal shifter *I* is in a relation of reciprocal definition with the spatial shifter *here*: *here* is by definition where the *I* places itself; and *I* is always, by definition, *here*. 'The shifter – I/you, here/there, this/that, now/then – is *the sign* of subjectivity'.[8] This duality of the linguistic status marks the splitting of the subject.

So, spatiality participates in any manifestation of the speaking subject, explicitly (at the level of the statement) or implicitly (as structural component of the conditions of possibility of any enunciation). This spatial component of subjectivity designates both the subject of the Conscious and the subject of the Unconscious, in its fleeting apparition-and-vanishing.[9] So, subjectivity itself is constructed through spatial determinants, and vice versa: 'We are led to the tantalizing possibility that space and the subject are constituted together, in relation to each other'.[10] Specifically '[t]he spatial form of identity and desire is everywhere around us, only we don't see it'.[11] This 'invisibility' of the spatial constituents of subjectivity is similar to a defining trait of ideology, that is, that in its constitution and functioning ideology denies its status as ideology. Such an 'occulted spatiality' resembles what a symptom represents, i.e. a metaphor denying its status as metaphor,[12] as illustrated in the case of the hysterical symptom, where an unconscious process is converted into a somatic manifestation; obviously, this bodily reality, through its physical literality, self-referentially affirms that 'it is body only', denying its psychical substrate. Similarly, the spatial components of subjectivity tend to occult their presence implicitly affirming that 'this is space only'.

The experience of being in space is mediated by many mechanisms. Among them, a strategic one is *body image* – that is, the representation of corporeity punctuated by the libidinal economy of pleasure and *jouissance*, acting as template of the Imaginary.[13] Moreover, the experience of the body itself has as its defining dimension spatiality. Also, body image and the Imaginary support the symbolic punctuation of space. So, body image, Imaginary and Symbolic relate spatiality and subjectivity in terms of reciprocal definition.

SUBJECTIVITY AND ARCHITECTURE

The zero degree of architecture corresponds to those 'ready-made', impersonal, alienating constructions sheltering humans and activities with no consideration for the personal experience induced by space. Those constructions represent a proliferation of egotic projections, that is, spatial statements excluding the subject of the unconscious. Actually, no subject of the unconscious, constituted through a singular combination of traces of a unique personal history, is identical to another subject of the unconscious. The absence of this subjective singularity is equivalent to repression or foreclosure of the signifiers specifically constituting and representing subjectivity. In this condition, the statement *I am here* could only mean *An ego is inhabiting this space in such a subjectively indifferent manner, that any other ego could also do the same, subjectivity never recognizing itself in this faceless spatial frame and the only relation of the subject to this zero degree of spatiality being that of malaise.* In such a condition of spatial exile, the subject is reduced to its sole needs and becomes object of exploitation, control and manipulation by spatial means, with no provision for the spatial configuration defining it as subject of the unconscious desire. This condition engenders characteristic symptoms: *malaise,* alienation, *Unheimlich,* coldness, sense of being excluded from the space of one's own life, feeling aggressed by one's own impossible presence in an intimate *here,* and finally aggressivity towards space itself. The impasse of such an architecture of need-only spatial statements indicates that architecture beyond its zero degree equals construction for/of subjectivity. The question now is, how is subjectivity transcribed into architectural act and space?

ARCHITECTURE AND SUBJECTIVITY AS IDENTITY

Subjectivity in architectural creation does not arise from disparate elements of the psychical system nor is it embodied in disparate elements of the building. In the work of distinct architects, subjectivity is obvious as structural derivative of the building itself, as structural effect of its own design, as component of the global architectural *Gestalt* embodied in the construction and its integration in space.

This subjectively felt sense of subjective presence and breath is inferred through the experience of the encounter with the building, qualifying the work as creation of an architecturing subjectivity irreducible to other architecturing agents or to any trend of the epoch, any *Zeitgeist* or other impersonal source of inspiration: Le Corbusier or Gaudí do not need to sign their work in ways other than its creation itself. Such work signed by the architect's *style* corresponds to the *signifying building*:[14] The building incorporates in its design not only functional imperatives, but also spatial signifiers representing the subjectivity of its creator, as well as a treasure of semiotic material, functioning as a field offering spatial voice and the capacity to recognise themselves in spatial signifiers to its users.

ARCHITECTURE AND FANTASY

The appearance/disappearance of the vanishing subject of the unconscious and of the implied split subjectivity[15] is not a random process; it is not an aleatory parade of fleeting signifiers in the stage of the subject's experience. The Unconscious is a semiotic system, open to the influx of information from corporeity (drives), other subsystems of the psychical system, as well as from multiple versions of otherness (symbolic, imaginary or real) and governed by its own rules and codes – the primary process.[16] The same holds for its particular modality, 'subject of the unconscious'. This is not a disparate succession of irruptions into / disruptions of the conscious flow of the psychical system. The Unconscious and its subject are marked by systemic coherence. Underlying their phenomenologically proteiform manifestations (in dreams, slips and other formations of the Unconscious), and supporting their persistent, recurrent epiphany, there exists a structural stability assured by powerful homeostatic processes. Repetition – the persistent return of certain signifiers – is but an aspect of this internal logic, framed by a clear principle of coherence: the fugitive appearances of the subject of the unconscious are governed and formatted by the field of forms and forces supporting its manifestations – fantasy. Specifically, by the *fundamental fantasy*[17] (see below), defining the locus and the modus operandi of subjectivity in its relation with the objects of desire and *jouissance*. The *forms* of such manifestations can vary *ad infinitum* – as in any semiotic system, verbal or nonverbal, like language or painting. But the underlying structure (fundamental fantasy) and functional – syntactical and grammatical – rules (primary process, in the case of the Unconscious) rigorously constrain and direct any such manifestation. Such apparitions are then equivalent to transformations of the original axiom / fundamental fantasy (Lacan – see below) in such a way, that each derivative is *compatible* with the original, since it is derived from it through definite transformational algorithms: this is, *stricto sensu*, the rationale underlying the *interpretation of the dream* in psychoanalysis. This transformation of an *original proposition* to *compatible derivatives* presents clear affinities with Noam Chomsky's transformational grammar, which is the most adequate linguistic analogon for the functioning of the psychic system.[18] John Forrester[19] studies the particular modalities of this process in the field of psychoanalysis under the heading *propositional analysis*. In architecture a similar procedure is proposed by Peter Eisenman through the term 'transformational relation' and systematically discussed (and practised) by John Shannon Hendrix.[20]

In this sense, subjectivity formatted and supported by fundamental fantasy reformulated as architectural space constitutes the principle of coherence and of specific identity of the personal architectural work. 'Something with the essential property of defining the conjunction of identity and difference – that is what seems most appropriate to me [Jacques Lacan] to structurally account for the function of the subject'.[21] Actually, this embedded in the work subjectivity manifests itself in two complementary ways. Synchronically, as clear diversity of the architectural solutions proposed by different architects for the same building program. Diachronically, as coherence of the distinctive style characterising the architectural agent, paradigmatically illustrated by the unique, eventually inimitable style of eminent architects: example, Le Corbusier or Gaudí.

A NOTE ON FUNDAMENTAL FANTASY

Given the strategic function of fundamental fantasy in the psyche and in the creative process and the analytical importance of the concept in our approach, a brief note on it might prove useful. There are many fantasies, conscious or unconscious, roaming and acting in psychical reality. The fundamental fantasy is the original formulation of this phenomenon. A comprehensive review of the concept and its place in Lacanian psychoanalysis is presented by Bruce Fink.[22]

Object a represents the remainder produced when the hypothetical mother-child unity breaks down, as a residual trace of that unity, a perpetual reminder of the mythology of the Thing. 'By cleaving to that rem(a)inder, the split subject, though expulsed from the Other, can sustain the illusion of wholeness; by clinging to object a, the subject is able to ignore his or her division. That is precisely what Lacan means by fantasy, and he formalizes it with the matheme $◊a, which is to be read: the divided subject in relation to object a'.[23] In his *Seminar VII*, Lacan refers to 'the fantasm ($◊a), which is the form on which depends the subject's desire'.[24]

Each person has a fundamental fantasy, which defines the template for 'the myriad intrusive thoughts, scenarios, daydreams and masturbation fantasies' representing permutations of the fundamental fantasy. All variance of fantasmatic work in the mind 'boils down or cooks down to a 'single' fundamental fantasy'.[25] 'The subject comes into being as a form of attraction toward and defense against a primordial, overwhelming experience of what the French call *jouissance*: a pleasure that is excessive, leading to a sense of being overwhelmed or disgusted, yet simultaneously providing a source of fascination'.[26] 'Fantasy stages the position in which the child would like to see itself with respect to the object that causes, elicits, and incites its desire'.[27]

As Lacan posits it in his *Seminar XIV*, *The Logic of Fantasy*, the fundamental fantasy is an axiom. That is, a formulation not proven and not needing proof; it just is there, as a starting point which 'in conjunction with other axioms and definitions, generates all of the allowable statements within a certain field'.[28] The subject 'sees the world through the lens of [his/her] fundamental fantasy'.[29] That is, the fundamental fantasy represents the map, the navigation system and the modus operandi of the subject; the matrix for the modalities of any appearance-and-vanishing of the subject of the unconscious; eventually, the cardinal mediation between the structural subject of the unconscious and the active manifestation of the subject's desire in its world.

ARCHITECTURE AS FANTASY REFORMULATED

Architecture, as creative gesture and as work created, corresponds to subjectivity reworked, re-elaborated, transposed and transcribed in the building. The question is, which modality of subjectivity carries and modulates this transcription in the field of architectural spatiality, and through which specific process? Picasso, in 1926, states: 'I think the source of all painting lies in a subjectively organised vision ....'[30] Freud,[31] discussing sublimation and its pleasure, notes: 'A satisfaction of this kind, such as an artist's joy in creating, *in giving his phantasies body* ... has a special quality ...' (my italics).

Lacan[32] considers sublimation as redefinition of the status of the object in the field of the fantasy – an operation elevating the sublime object to the dignity of the Thing. This transition 'from the desired imaginary object to the enshrouded void of the Other ... is related to the three registers of human reality: the Symbolic, the Imaginary and the Real ....'[33] This process is evident in architecture, 'the paradigmatic art of sublimation inasmuch as it creates a void ....'[34] As sublimation, 'the art of building manages to bring us into a relation with our own emptiness as subjects of desire. Both organise the void by creating emptiness'.[35]

Architecture, then, enters the stage. Let's hear its voices.[36] Rem Koolhaas:[37] 'If there is to be a 'new urbanism' it will not be based on the twin fantasies of order and omnipotence ....' Alan Colquhoun:[38] 'The Art Nouveau movement ... disintegrated with the decline of a certain set of bourgeois and nationalistic fantasies'. Also: 'The [Russian] Rationalists, starting from the architectural fantasies of Expressionism ....'[39]

The term 'fantasy' is then present in modern architectural discourse. But what happens to 'fantasy' as a concept? In psychoanalysis, fantasy is a scenario created by imagination, where the subject is present and desire is staged as fulfilled.[40] Thus[41] fantasy is a dramatic creation of the mind, constituting the fundamental work of the psyche, the most important semiotic syntagm in the realm of psychic reality. Anything that acquires a personal value, an emotional investment – any version of subjectivity – takes shape and functions in the psyche through fantasy. However,[42] the point is that, as a rule, even where the word appears in modern architectural discourse, the concept is not employed in an epistemologically rigorous and analytically valid way, as operational tool, concerning architectural creation.

This conceptual void becomes obvious when it appears, indirectly and symptomatically, as circumlocution.[43] The more strategic this lack, the more circumlocutions appear, ineffectually trying to compensate for it. So, William Curtis repeatedly attempts to consider the incidence of the architect's fantasy without resorting to the concept of fantasy: '[A new tradition in architecture] … lies in the special intellectual chemistry of the individual work of a high order';[44] '(Scarpa) had a myth and a language of his own';[45] 'A great architectural creation is like a symbolic world with its own empires of imagination, its own mental regions and its own inner landscapes';[46] '[A]uthenticity is inconceivable without … shapes pregnant with meaning embodying a mythical interpretation of the world'.[47] Clearly, these remarks reflect unsuccessful attempts of thought, discourse and language to compensate for a conceptual void. Such figures of speech, however, can just designate the locus of a question and along with it the impossibility to answer it without resorting to an appropriate concept. Therefore, these rhetorical symptoms bring into light the fundamental question: *How can the thing I want to say be said? Does that thing have a shape and a name? If the answer is yes, where can we find them? If not, how are we to invent them?*

Creation always entails personal involvement and subjective gestures. It is the act of creating a personal signifier – eventually, a name for the subject. It represents a reformulation of a crucially subjective *something* into a common code, shared with other people.[48] This *something of the subject* supporting its act as creation of new signifiers of subjectivity corresponds to the signifiers of subjectivity as composed by the syntax of fantasy. On the other hand, the way that that *something defined by and defining subjectivity through fantasy* is reformulated into a common, shared code, determines the specificity of any art and creation. Thus, the poet and the novelist reformulate their personal sense of things into a common, shared code – words. The musician does the same thing with the modulated sound; the actor with his/her performance; the film-maker with the camera … And *the architect with the punctuation and formation of space through construction.*

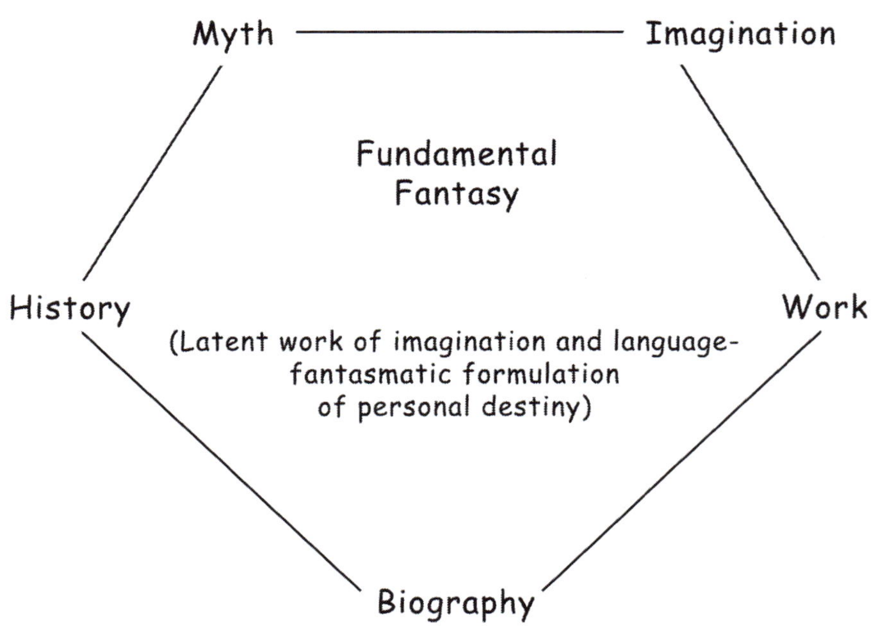

10.1 Man's Encounter with History. Courtesy of Nikos Sideris.

Our analyses so far as well as other studies[49] converge to the same conclusion: in creation, *work is the subject's fantasy formulated in the language of his/her art or practice*. The system of causal determinations and subjective gestures that constitute the environment and the work's mode of production are illustrated in Figure 10.1.

Creation is the result of the interaction between five fields – Myth, History, Biography (personal history), Imagination and Work. Their interplay ultimately constitutes *the singular psychic formulation of one's sense of the world and personal destiny* – his fundamental fantasy. The creating subject, more than anyone, feels that s/he has a personal destiny forcing him/her to live through one's art. Le Corbusier, for instance, experienced 'periods of exaggerated confidence when he sensed he must have some Olympian destiny'.[50] Actually, great artists are not 'free' vis-à-vis their art, but rather possessed by their art – by every sense of the word 'possess', not just Apollonian or Dionysian, but also its demonic[51] connotations. Every creator is most specifically governed by the particular feeling that s/he incarnates a 'plan of fate'. This *fundamental fantasy* amounts to a foundational representation of the subject's world and a formulation of its place in it, hence of one's personal destiny. For example: the savior, the creator, the enchanter, the victim, the fatal, and so on. Subjectivity is constituted, assumed, functions and manifests itself through the mediation of the fundamental fantasy.

It is an endopsychic mechanism – a powerful, fateful machine that constrains or even dictates every essential subjective attitude or choice. A syntactic machine relating in many variants a signifier, as sufficient representative of the subject, to another signifier, as sufficient representative of his/her object, in the frame of an imaginary scenario assuring the realisation of desire. This compositional machine is constantly diffusing its derivatives in every instance of the psychical system, thus guiding everyone's life, even if we do not consciously know where to and how. Creation – a paramount versant of subjectivity – is a specific mode of integration of the fundamental fantasy of the subject in the field of the socially shared world. That is, *artistic creation is the product of an encounter between a powerful, fertile fantasy (amounting to the fundamental fantasy) and a common, shared code (an art's specific language)*. In the case of architecture, what is the element defining the specificity of this artful creation?

$$A = (\mathrm{fa})^{\mathrm{lc}}$$

10.2 Architecture = The Architect's Fantasy (Re)Formulated (Elevated) in the Language of Construction. Courtesy of Nikos Sideris.

This 'quasi-formula', represents the proposition 'Architecture = the architect's fantasy (fa) formulated in the language of construction (lc)'. This could be rephrased, in an epistemologically more prudent way, as follows: architecture reformulates the architect's fantasy in the way of the construction. Because construction is not just a language. It is, above all, a way, a manner, a modus operandi broader than any language, since it embraces, beyond language, *jouissance* and the Real.

The theorem 'architecture reformulates the architect's fantasy in the manner of construction' reveals the underlying subjectivity at work in architecture; it relates this work to the *differentia specifica* between creation in general and architectural creation in particular, which is *the manner of the* τέκτων. As τέκτων is the builder, architecture as αρχιτεκτονική is a practice of the τέκτων guided by a specific principle (αρχή) – the architect's fundamental fantasy. '[Mies van der Rohe and Louis Kahn] focus ... upon the irreducible nature of tectonic construction and upon its sublime interaction with light, as the two transhistorical conditions of architecture'.[52]

The language of construction corresponds to the historically determined and specific, according to place and time, set and system of material and mental contexts, terms, rules, possibilities, limitations, constraints, acts and tools, in the field of which the architectural work is designed and constructed. This language embraces facts, determinations, operations and codes, which are physical, material, technological, technical, practical, aesthetic, communicational, psychological ... defining the field, the environment and the way which allows the architectural work to be designed and constructed. That is, the language of construction designates the set of mental, material and cultural resources rendering possible the conception and realisation of the building. In this frame, subjectivity is encountering versions of otherness which simultaneously enable and constrain its unfolding as architectural act.

To resume the subjective process in the context of the supra-subjective conditions of its transcription in architectural act: fantasy represents the semiotically efficient device forming the foundation of one's personal mythology supporting desire. Actually, in creation, architectural or other, the subject has the sense that (t)his world is not sufficiently complete[53] and/or modulated[54] and a complement to its lack is anticipated and wished. Both aspects (constative and performative, respectively) are determined, fed, supported and configured as signifier-engendering act by the fundamental fantasy. The work of Giorgio de Chirico *The Archeologists* shows what is meant here: there always are certain ruins deep inside the architect. There must be something ugly, rather formless (άσχημος in ancient Greek, where σχήμα, form, means both shape and beauty), some kind of traumatic imperfection, for the creators to interfere. The artist does not complete the beautiful and pleasurably livable world; s/he does not reproduce the 'good form'. The artist aesthetically reshapes a world usually unlivable or, in any case, incomplete or semi-complete.

In architecture, those ruins, designating the subject's position as the one having to care about the world's imperfection, clearly correspond to the status of fantasy as *l'envers* of the subject's world: 'fantasy is the reverse of the world, always present to support it';[55] actually 'it is fantasy which for and through the subject supports the world, because it makes the world 'interesting', discovering in its various elements the object a'.[56] Le Corbusier's compulsion to reform the inhuman metrics of the modern world through his Modulor illustrates the spirit and the deep psychical roots of the creative function. Each major architect struggles, using his/her distinctively personal manner (style and view of things), historically evolving but coherent, in order to realise that 'plan of fate' s/he deeply feels determines his/her destiny.

The template for this 'conjunction of identity and difference' (Lacan, *Seminar VII*, see p. 9), for this existential singularity, differentiation and coherence, corresponds to the architect's sense of the world as determined by his/her unconscious fundamental fantasy. This paradoxical 'compulsory freedom' is also an indication about the work of sublimation concerning the death drive, implicit in any act of creation. So, the fundamental fantasy is the cardinal mediation between the structural subject of the unconscious and the active manifestation of the subject's desire as architecture. Accordingly, architecture is the architect's fantasy reformulated in the language of construction. The leading function in this process is the encounter with the Other, and its outcome presents itself as the signifying building (see page 182, 'Architecture and Subjectivity as Identity').

THE ENCOUNTER WITH THE OTHER

Actually, the language of construction involves: material-technical and historical potentialities, determinants and constraints, such as those mentioned, as well as

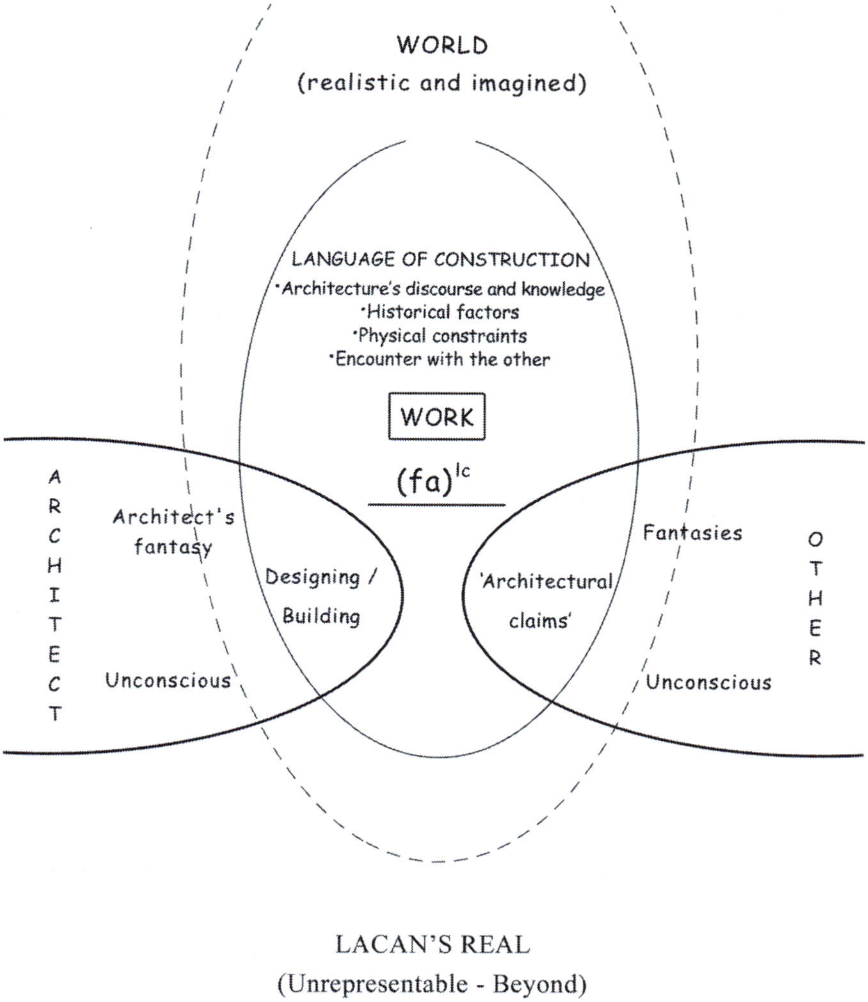

10.3 The Architect and the Other. Courtesy of Nikos Sideris.

architectural discourse and knowledge, with their own particularities, potential and limitations, productive and blind points, hierarchies, authorities, etc. (Every architect functions within the context of an architectural community, with given structures, principles, systems of representations and practices …). That is, architectural praxis implies multiple discourses, fitting or not fitting with one another, as well as with circumstances and context. These discourses are part of the environment in which the architect encounters the other in its version of a being (personal or impersonal) who wants and seeks and, ultimately, negotiates.

Essentially, the other comes (see right ellipsoid in Figure 10.3) with architectural claims and demands. And s/he tells the architect – an example – to make a chalet in a picturesque fishermen's village in southern Greece (this really happened in Finikounta). A Swiss chalet at the beach (admittedly, something unbelievably fascinating) shows how fantasies underlie the other's demand. It is notorious how many strange things people ask from the architects. All these are clearly fantasies of the other – of the architect's prospective client as interlocutor having power.

In principle, architectural demands are first formulated by the other, while the architect comes into the encounter with a toolbox with design and construction patterns, models, tools and instruments inside; a practically inexhaustible repertoire of possibilities and capacities of architectural practice. The architect and the other meet, within the environment 'language of construction'. The work occurs as a built version of the underlying formula – the architect's fantasy formulated in the language of construction. In this dialectical encounter with the other, the whole environment is activated and the outcome is a built thought[57] – a spatial thought, which is the architectural work. Thus, the work, as a signifying building, represents built subjectivity.

THE DUAL SPATIALITY

Fantasy represents the semiotically efficient device framing the interplay between the subject and its objects. An inference here is inevitable: if architectural space metaphorically reformulates the unconscious construction of fantasy, then it also refers to an unconscious spatiality. And if architecture inscribes its work in the language of construction, then it also refers to a conscious spatiality ('also' here meaning 'at least'). This minimalist view is but a local formulation of a more general principle: that the architectural space is represented, conceived, designed, constructed, felt, lived and experienced in the specifically human environment of *Dual Spatiality*, that is conscious and unconscious. This duality of the subjective spatial functioning is crucial for theorising and practising architecture in general and, in particular, for the articulation of the architecture of need (heavily present and probably dominant in conscious spatiality) and of the architecture of desire (constituting the field and modality of unconscious spatiality).

Dual spatiality is not reducible to familiar dipoles of attributes such as realistic/nonrealistic, useful/experiential, real/imaginary, natural/aesthetic, functional/fantasmatic, practical/pleasurable, domesticated/savage, instrumental/poetical, and so on. It is founded upon the distinction between conscious and unconscious experience and functioning of spatiality. Conscious spatiality can comprise both poles of the dipoles already mentioned, typically under the auspice of the first term, while Unconscious spatiality as a rule comprises the second terms, with the primary process assimilating anything of the first terms entering its realm. *Conscious spatiality* is governed by the reality principle, functions in terms of the secondary process, and its constitution is based on the conventional operational 'solid' space under the Euclidian dominant, on the encounter-co-presence-interaction of persons and things, on practicality and on aesthetics. *Unconscious spatiality* is governed by the pleasure principle and its beyond (*jouissance*), functions in terms of the primary process, and its constitution is based on virtual, fluid, topological spaces, on performative and plastical parameters, on the figurative representation of things, on personal-asocial soliloquy, on non-shared experience, and on fantasy.

Both aspects of spatiality always necessarily coexist, because they are not springing from particularities of the external realities, but from the constitution itself of the split subject. This coexistence can be unilateral, with one aspect sometimes almost atrophic – for example, realistic space in dreams or video games, or imaginary fluid space during statics calculations for the building. However, their co-occurence and coexistence, eventually their interpenetration (yin-yang could be an illustrative analogon) is inevitable, even in conditions where one aspect is overfed or presents itself in poor, distorted, suppressed or abject forms, as well as in conditions of conflict between the two.

The fertile dialectics between need and desire, formulated in terms of dual spatiality, is a possible designation of the aim of architecture as art. On the other hand, the concept of dual spatiality is necessary for any reflection on the theory and practice of architecture. We could invoke many cases supporting this claim. However, I will prefer to illustrate this necessity through the aporias arising in the field of a rigorous theoretical analysis, exploring space and subjectivity without the concept of dual spatiality.

Lorens Eyan Holm,[58] in his masterful book on architecture, space and the construction of subjectivity, offers profound insights about them. His descriptions are full of subtlety and sensitivity as well as solidity of the argument. The culminating point of his investigation corresponds to his effort to unearth the deepest roots of the inherent propensity of humans to be (in) space, eventually hypothesizing the existence of a *space drive*. Here is the quintessence of his point: 'In so far as architecture has any relation to subjectivity, it is a symptom of the drive to be space. We need a verb: to space the subject. *With architecture, I space myself*.'[59]

> *Architecture is but the narcissistic fantasy of space: whole, well-formed, everything in its place and a size for everything ... It screens the space of the drive that lies beneath it, whose wild conflation of categories – repeating, at once brittle/resilient, trajectorial/flowing – constitutes an originary condition of indeterminacy ... We can ask what sort of space this is: this font of signifiers, this vortex of Becoming organized around the real object. A theory of the spatial drive would look at how I disengage from the architectural space that locates my body to assume a richer spatiality derived from the relations and situations that architecture stages ...*[60]

> *Architecture lures us away from recognizing a form of spatiality that is so quotidian and familiar that we simply do not see it, except in the fleeting glimpse afforded by an encounter on the Acropolis, and its immediately apparent but seemingly purloined intelligibility. Drive space recovers for architecture something archaic that corresponds to originary gestures in other discourses which tarry with the intractable and inexpressible, and whose effect upon the discourse is more likely than not to threaten it. To Le Corbusier's ineffable space we can add such diverse instruments as the confluence of natural and symbolic disorder in King Lear ..., Freud's comments on the oceanic [feeling], Derrida's non-concept of différance, Plato's concept of Chora or Klee's cosmogenetic moment. What is alluded to in these works, but never fully represented, is space returning to an archaic, more indeterminate form.*[61]

Almost every phrase here points to the experience of dual spatiality. The *other scene* of spatiality makes its echo more than audible: a necessity. However, despite the richness of its representation, this revelation of the duality of the spatial experience cannot adequately reach the sharpness, clarity and fecundity of a concept shedding light to the phenomenon under study. Instead, aporias arise at the points of conceptual blurring, indicating that what is conceptually lacking manifests itself as discursive symptoms. For example: introducing, even as metaphor, a space drive, adds unnecessary complication to the effort of conceptual clarification, for a number of reasons, among them not the least being that, according to Freud '[T]he theory of the drives is, so to say, our mythology. Drives are mythical entities, magnificent in their indefiniteness.'[62]

'We can ask what sort of space this is: this font of signifiers, this vortex of Becoming ...': both formulas proposed as a reply to the (pertinent) question posed are circumlocutions and rhetorical tropes which cannot claim the status of concept. This concept, however, is clearly evoked here – that of the unconscious component of the dual spatiality. '[E]xcept in the fleeting glimpse afforded by an encounter ...': this point is crucial. Because the metaphor 'fleeting glimpse' implies that the spatial experience in question is organised as sequential succession of perceptions in the linear flow of time; that punctual, fleeting moments of escape from the linearity of conscious spatial experience are the only available glimpses revealing the other side of dual spatiality. This functional linear representation contrasts with the structurally parallel spatialities simultaneously and continuously experienced in terms of dual spatiality, as in spatial settings so familiar such as the dancing hall or in more sophisticated spaces like Peter Zumthor's baths in Vals.

'Drive space recovers for architecture something archaic that corresponds to originary gestures in other discourses which tarry with the intractable and inexpressible, and whose effect upon the discourse is more likely than not to threaten it': here the reference to unconscious spatiality is direct, but the relation of the two aspects of dual spatiality has a tint of mutually exclusive experiences. The metaphor 'threat' implies something more than the conflictual difference of psychical status; it denotes a relation of bilaterally threatening exteriority, instead of a dialectical relation whose representation could fairly correspond to the two-in-one and one-in-two faces of a band of Moebius.

'What is alluded to in these works, but never fully represented, is space returning to an archaic, more indeterminate form': the term 'returning' again risks to evoke mutually exclusive exteriority with temporal incidents of transition from the one to the other aspect of the dual spatiality, thus blurring the conceptual representation of the phenomenon. So, it is rather inevitable to conclude that, even if the description of the phenomenon is rich and evocative, the conceptualisation remains distorted by the absence of a concept like that of dual spatiality (and/or another equivalent or alternative).

ANTONI GAUDÍ, THE MASTER-COPPERSMITH

The case of Antoni Gaudí eloquently illustrates our approach.[63] The architect's style, his architectural signature, is known and haunting. It represents a particular spatial object with tangible affinity with the *fine-broidered artifact*.

Antoni Gaudí was 'born into a family of coppersmiths', so he 'always proudly cited this family trade as the origin of his personal vision and understanding of space'.[64] He writes: 'I get this capacity to feel and see space from the fact that I am the son, grandson and great-grandson of a coppersmith. All these generations have prepared me. The coppersmith is a man who makes a three-dimensional object from a flat surface; he has seen the space before he starts

10.4 Casa Batlló.
© Casa Batlló S.L.U.

10.5 Casa Batlló. © Casa Batlló S.L.U.

his work. All the great Florentine artists of the Renaissance were carvers who created three-dimensional works from a plan'.[65] 'More than a theorist, Gaudí was the combination of an artist and a craftsman, maintaining he had learnt to handle complex surfaces – hyperboloid, helicoid, paraboloid, hyperbolic and conoid – watching his coppersmith father work with metal, hammering plates of copper and steel, curving them, bending them, thus deriving the miracle of volume'.[66]

This clearly shows *the genealogy as fantasy* Gaudí places himself in: not just a lineage of coppersmiths, but also the lineage of the Renaissance Great Masters. It substantiates the significance Gaudí ascribes to origin and genealogy, as well as the way this kind of references and affinities, institutional or intellectual, participate in the constitution of his fantasy. Here is, then, an architectural program that the architect himself has connected to his personal history, at a level meaning 'I work as a coppersmith in the language of architectural construction (and not with the tools of the coppersmith)'. For Gaudí architecture is the continuation of coppersmithing through the means of construction, and architectural space is fashioned in image and likeness of family coppersmithing. This is an explicit formulation of the personal mythology of a unique artist, the expression of his fantasy, of the way this mythology is transcribed into architectural creation of spatiality: exactly what *dual spatiality* refers to. I already find this an exemplary illustration of the statement 'Architecture is the fantasy of the architect formulated in the language of construction' – the process of this reformulation drawing from both registers of dual spatiality.

In the light of this idealised reference of Gaudí to origin, institutional and intellectual, there vividly emerges the deeper, fantasmatic meaning and significance of two pivotal elements. First, his emblematic maxim 'Being original means going back to your origin'.[67] Obviously, this is not a simple pun, but rather a deeply determinant sense of the world of an artist who was arduously seeking for the meaning of tradition and art 'since its very beginning'.[68] Actually, Gaudí elaborated, a synthesis of the three great Mediterranean traditions – Byzantine, Gothic and Islamic – 'under the auspices of Greece, the only civilization that can be called 'classical' according to Gaudí, who was convinced that he did what the Greeks would do if they had been able to continue'.[69] Thus, it is not a mere figure of speech, but a deep psychic construction when Gaudí defines the Sagrada Familia as 'the Hellenic temple of Mediterranean gothic'.[70] It is a definite proof that Gaudí, in terms of fantasy, thinks that he derives his origin not only from the Gaudí family of coppersmiths and the Great Masters of the Renaissance, but also from all the spiritual families converging in the Mediterranean, under the auspices of the supreme spiritual origin represented by Ancient Greece.

Second, numerous of the architectural elements in his work (pillars, in particular, surfaces, whole buildings – like the Casa Milà ...) 'seem to grow from the ground'.[71] The common observation here is that Gaudí resorts to organic forms provided by nature, etc. However precise this description is, it does not touch the deepest question, which is what personal inclinations and forces animate and orient Gaudí in this recourse to the birthing land? Simply formulating the question like that makes the answer emerge clearly. The unique and inimitable way of Gaudí, his sui generis sense of the world, is also expressed here as a consequence of his fundamental fantasy: originality through recourse to descent, to origin. Obviously, there is no metaphor more adequate, in architectural terms as well, for this descent, than the birthing land and its creatures – trees, plants, animals ...

To sum up, Gaudí's work is a great lesson about the place of fantasy in architecture. His whole life – inseparable from his architectural function – seems to be summarised in the fact that, in his last twenty years, Gaudí lived in fusion with the Sagrada Familia – the Holy Family: can't we assume that his sublimation in the signifier 'Holy Family' is not another verbal coincidence, but rather the ultimate, till death, fulfillment of what he felt was his personal destiny, in the place and in the name most appropriate for such a destiny? And, as such, that his symbiotic merging with the building illustrates that he lives what he creates as incarnation of his fantasy pushed to the ultimate origin – the Holy Family, (the family of) God? Thus transcribing in terms of personal destiny and *jouissance* what is a cosmical destiny and founding mythology? At the same time, this transcription as process whose key is *code-switching* (from the primary process in the fantasy to the language of construction in the building, and vice versa, recurrently), magisterially illustrates the meaning and the incidence of Dual Spatiality on sublimation, architectural praxis and the experience of architectural space.

THE SECRET FORMULA

A final question is, what could be the contribution of the theorem 'Architecture is the fantasy of the architect formulated in the language of construction' in theorising and practising architecture? I think the answer is tangible in the development of the argument so far. However, there is a concise formulation of this answer pronounced not by a great architect or writer, but from a young architect. In the School of Architecture of the National Technical University of Athens, I had the pleasure to comment on the thesis of Angela Kouvelis. Her thesis ends with the phrase I wish to cite: 'In architectural design, everyone uses a secret formula through which s/he designs. The aim is to be able to re-examine it, not in order to flatter one's narcissistic side, but rather to be able to move forward, keep pace with others, not talk in solitude'. This formula is precisely what I wanted to substantiate: *The secret formula according to which an architect designs is his/her fantasy formulated in the language of architectural design and construction*. Eisenman and Hendrix,[72] investigate the formal procedures of those transformations in highly theoretical frames. And Angela confirms it intuitively, through her experience as a young architect: it is constructive.

NOTES

1 Lorens Holm, *Brunelleschi, Lacan, Le Corbusier: Architecture, Space and the Construction of Subjectivity* (London: Routledge, 2010), passim.

2 Ibid., pp. 9–10.

3 Jean Piaget and Bärbel Inhelder, *The Child's Conception of Space*, trans. F.J. Langdon and J.L. Lunzer (London: Routledge and Kegan Paul, 1956), passim.

4 Nikos Sideris, 'Ασυνείδητο και Χωρικότητα' ['Unconscious and Spatiality']. Teaching documents, Postgraduate Program of the School of Architecture of the National Technical University of Athens. Last modified 4 April 2013. Available at: http://courses.arch.ntua.gr/113353.html.

5 Lorens Holm, *Brunelleschi, Lacan, Le Corbusier*, p. 35.

6 Ibid., p. 38.

7 Ibid., p. 208.

8 Ibid., p. 30.

9 Bruce Fink, *The Lacanian Subject: Between Language and Jouissance* (Princeton, NJ: Princeton University Press, 1995), p. 41.

10 Lorens Holm, *Brunelleschi, Lacan, Le Corbusier*, p. 35.

11 Ibid., p. 36.

12 Nikos Sideris, 'Πλάνη και σαγήνη του συμπτώματος' ['Deception and Seduction of the Symptom']. Paper presented at the sixth Pan-Hellenic Conference of the Hellenic Psychological Society, Athens, Panteion University, 29 May–1 June 1997.

13 Paul Verhaeghe, 'Subject and Body: Lacan's Struggle with the Real', in Paul Verhaeghe, *Beyond Gender: From Subject to Drive* (New York: Other Press, 2001), pp. 65–97.

14 Ibid., 'The Encounter with the Other'.

15 Bruce Fink, *The Lacanian Subject*, p. 41.

16 Nikos Sideris, Η Εσωτερική Διγλωσσία [*Inner Bilingualism*] (Athens: Kastaniotis, 1995), pp. 112–14.

17 Bruce Fink, 'Fantasies and the Fundamental Fantasy: An Introduction', in *Virtualia* 13 (Revista digital de la Escuela de la Orientación Lacaniana, Junio/Julio 2005). Available at: http://virtualia.eol.org.ar/013/pdf/fink-en.pdf [accessed 27 September 2015]; Nikos Sideris, *Architecture and Psychoanalysis* (Kindle edition, 2013), 'The Concept of Fantasy'.

18 Nikos Sideris, Η Εσωτερική Διγλωσσία, pp. 224–5.

19 John Forrester, *Language and the Origins of Psychoanalysis* (London: Macmillan / New York: Columbia University Press, 1980).

20 John Shannon Hendrix, *Architecture and Psychoanalysis: Peter Eisenman and Jacques Lacan* (New York: Peter Lang, 2006), pp. 20, 43 and passim.

21 Jacques Lacan, *Le Séminaire de Jacques Lacan, Livre XIII: L'objet de la Psychanalyse, 1965–1966* (unpublished typescript, 12 January, 1966).

22 Bruce Fink, 'Fantasies and the Fundamental Fantasy', pp. 2–9.

23 Bruce Fink, *The Lacanian Subject*, p. 59.

24 Jacques Lacan, *The Seminar of Jacques Lacan, Book VII: The Ethics of Psychoanalysis, 1959–1960*, ed. Jacques-Alain Miller, trans. Dennis Porter (New York: Routledge, 1992), p. 99.

25 Bruce Fink, 'Fantasies and the Fundamental Fantasy', p. 4.

26 Bruce Fink, *The Lacanian Subject*, p. xii.

27 Ibid., p. xiii.

28 Bruce Fink, 'Fantasies and the Fundamental Fantasy', p. 6.

29 Ibid.

30 Enrique Mallen, 'Pablo Picasso and the Truth of Greek Art', in *Athens Journal of Humanities and Arts*, 1(4) (Athens: Athens Institute for Education and Research, October 2014), pp. 283–98.

31 Sigmund Freud, *Civilization and its Discontents, S.E., XXI*, trans. James Strachey (New York: W.W. Norton, 1989), p. 79.

32 Jacques Lacan, *The Seminar of Jacques Lacan, Book VII*, p. 112.

33 Viviana M. Saint-Cyr, 'Créer un vide ou de la sublimation chez Lacan', in *Recherches en psychanalyse* 13 (Sorbonne Paris Cité: Psychoanalytic Studies Faculty of the University Denis Diderot, 2012), pp. 14–21.

34 Ibid.

35 Ibid.

36 Nikos Sideris, *Architecture and Psychoanalysis*, 'Creation and Fantasy'.

37 Rem Koolhaas, 'Whatever Happened to Urbanism?', in Rem Koolhaas and Bruce Mau, *S M L XL* (New York: The Monicelli Press, 1997), p. 969.

38 Alan Colquhoun, *Modern Architecture* (Oxford: Oxford University Press, 2002), p. 33.

39 Ibid., p. 122.

40 Jean Laplanche and Jean-Bertrand Pontalis, *The Language of Psycho-Analysis*, trans. Donald Nicholson-Smith (London: Hogarth and the Institute of Psycho-Analysis, 1973).

41 Nikos Sideris, *Architecture and Psychoanalysis*, 'The Concept of Fantasy'.

42 Ibid., 'Creation and Fantasy'.

43 Ibid.

44 William Curtis, *L'achitecture modern depuis 1900* (Paris: Phaidon, 2006), p. 275.

45 Ibid., p. 482.

46 Ibid., p. 636.

47 Ibid., p. 689.

48 Nikos Sideris, *Architecture and Psychoanalysis*, 'Creation and Fantasy'.

49 Nikos Sideris, Ο ερωτισμός στην τέχνη – Εικαστικές φαντασιώσεις [*Eroticism in Art – Pictorial Fantasies*] (Athens: Metaixmio, 2010).

50 William Curtis, *L'achitecture moderne*, p. 164.

51 This demonic possession and its mechanisms, illustrating the process here described, is the theme of the novel by Patrick Süskind, *Perfume: The Story of a Murderer*, originally published in German as *Das Parfum* in 1985. The main character of the novel is a perfume apprentice in eighteenth century France. He was born with no body scent himself; later he tries to realise his fantasy murdering virgins in order to obtain their essence and thus to create the 'perfect scent', the absolute *Perfume*.

52 Kenneth Frampton, *Modern Architecture: A Critical History* (London: Thames and Hudson, 1992), p. 306.

53 Bruce Fink, *The Lacanian Subject*, pp. 59–60.

54 Nikos Sideris, *Architecture and Psychoanalysis*, 'Le Corbusier: The dispersion of the Creator'.

55 Alain Juranville, *Lacan et la philosophie* (Paris: Presses Universitaires de France, 1984), p. 193.

56 Ibid.

57 Nikos Sideris, *Architecture and Psychoanalysis*, 'An Illustration: A Country House in Western Peloponnese'.

58 Lorens Holm, *Brunelleschi, Lacan, Le Corbusier*.

59 Ibid., p. 208.

60 Ibid., pp. 208–9.

61 Ibid., p. 209.

62 Sigmund Freud, *New Introductory Lectures on Psycho-Analysis, The Standard Edition*, trans. James Strachey (New York: W.W. Norton, 1990), p. 95.

63 Nikos Sideris, *Architecture and Psychoanalysis*, 'Antoni Gaudí, the Master-Coppersmith'.

64 'Gaudí', The website of Barcelona city. See http://w110.bcn.cat/portal/site/Turisme/menuitem.7e257cdd389697aa58cb0d3020348a0c/?vgnextoid=0000000630858164VgnV6CONT00000000000RCRD&lang=enGB [accessed 27 January 2014].

65 Philippe Thiébaut, *Gaudí: Builder of Visions* (New York: Thames and Hudson, 2001), p. 33.

66 Isidre Puig Boada (ed.), *Antoni Gaudí: paroles et écrits* (Paris: L'Harmattan, 2002), p. 16.

67 Ibid., pp. 18 and 80.

68 Ibid., p. 18.

69 Ibid., p. 27.

70 Philippe Thiébaut, *Gaudí*, pp. 79 and 95.

71 Rainer Zerbst, *Antoni Gaudí: Toute l'architecture* (Cologne: Taschen, 2002), p. 29.

72 John Shannon Hendrix, *Architecture and Psychoanalysis*.

11

Shadows of Venice: Adrian Stokes, Aldo Rossi and 'Interior Darkness'

Stephen Kite

In this chapter exploring the shadows of the unconscious we shall be in Venice: sometimes looking at Early Renaissance, and sometimes at twentieth century buildings, but always through a twentieth century Freudian lens – and specifically that offered by the British School psychoanalytic aesthetics of the analyst Melanie Klein (1882–1960) and art-writer Adrian Stokes (1902–72). The first part of this chapter asks: how can the psychoanalytic aesthetics of Klein and Stokes inform our understanding of architecture, shadow and the unconscious? Within these interpretative frameworks the second part explores shadow and the unconscious in the work and ideas of Aldo Rossi (1931–97) – focussing on his *Teatro del Mondo*, Venice.

Architecture and the unconscious might be examined in many aspects and sites to illustrate the inventions of an operative architectural unconscious. In coupling shadows and architecture in Venice through two powerful twentieth century protagonists in shadow-thinking and shadow-making – one a distinctive art-writer (Stokes), one both architect and theorist (Rossi) – I hope to shed light on particularly powerful realisations of the unconscious in architecture. From Plato's cave of shadows, to John Locke's image of the mind as *camera obscura*, this shedding of light has been characterised as within, or into, a mind conceived in itself as darkly spatial, architectonic, and mostly undescribable. As for Venice; for Margaret Plant it readily gives rise:

> *to those qualities that Klaus Theweleit elicited in Male Fantasies – fluidity, malleability, close proximity to the unconscious, 'a life of emotion rather than intellect', in short, the dangerous state of the oceanic that Freud had described.*[1]

Even preceding his analysis with Melanie Klein from 1930, Stokes's engagement with psychoanalysis and architecture was an intimate one. But it was only in texts from 1945 – such as the *Venice: An Aspect of Art* (Faber and Faber) focussed on here – when he ventured into full psychoanalytical terminology. He was right to be circumspect about this; as a result he lost Faber and Faber as a publisher, and a number of admirers of his earlier, more immediately poetic books. In these aspects, it would be unfair to expect the same theoretical rigour from an architect and often allusive writer such as Rossi – especially the author of the oneiric *A Scientific Autobiography* which is his core text for this essay. The Italian's theory of the unconscious, though clearly informed, is that intuitive engagement of the creative mind. Stokes and Rossi also share an intimacy with Venice based on deep knowledge of its architecture and emotional commitment. We shall use Stokes to interpret Rossi, but to my knowledge it is not known if Rossi read Stokes. Both however also approached Venice through John Ruskin's *Stones of Venice* (1851–3); Stokes sometimes in *oedipal* rejection of his towering antecedent; Rossi sometimes with a Modernist rejection of the Victorian's Picturesque – but neither escaped the powerful aura of *Stones*. Moreover – as commentators such as Stephen Bann have pointed out – there is much in Ruskin's psychologised evocations of architecture that foreshadows Freud:

> *Ruskin wrote* The Queen of the Air *over 30 years before Freud published* The Interpretation of Dreams. *Yet Ruskin's tracing of the history of purple through 'the fantastic course of dream' shows to what extent he anticipated the mechanisms of condensation and displacement ....*[2]

To begin with Stokes: in his book *Venice: An Aspect of Art* of 1945, Stokes interprets a plate of the façade of the Ca' Dario of circa 1487 in these terms:

> *The reader will have felt for himself the interchange between the rows of windows and the wall-space studded with dark circles as if the interior darkness were summed and embossed there, so that everything is held on the one level. The second storey balcony is evocative of the same effect, part ironwork showing white stone through the interstices, part white stone embossed with dark marbles.*[3]

Stokes wants us to note the drawing out of a shadowy 'interior darkness' to a firm outwardness in the dark circles of porphyry. In the preceding plate of the Manzoni-Angaran palace he finds that particular quality in fifteenth century Venetian architecture he capitalised as Quattro Cento, namely 'a compulsive solidifying of what is successive'[4] wherein the fluxing 'brightness and darkness of the water' is 'converted into stone. There is light and dark: all is precious, all weighty; nothing obtrudes. This architecture solidifies the continuity of water'[5] to a reassuringly weighty stability. There are many hints here of the fluid proximity of the unconscious, translated to outward synthesis in a satisfying work of architecture; yet to this point in this war-time book, even the most intent readers of Stokes would scarcely suspect the influence of Melanie Klein. Klein's examination of the roots of the adult world in the inner world of infantile unconscious fantasies, was her major contribution to her field, together with her emphasis on the function of hate and envy in these early stages – along with love for the mother. As compared to Freud, and reflecting her observation of children, Klein's concept of the unconscious is dynamic with no sharp distinction between conscious, unconscious and preconscious:

> *For Klein, what is unconscious is the biological and affectual condition of the human being. In essence, by the time of her later writings, the unconscious is equivalent to the instincts: to the life drive and death drive and their effects. The unconscious exists as a condition and from it emerge preconsciousness and consciousness.*[6]

Klein, herself, did little to develop a psychoanalytic aesthetic, but in giving meaningful life and spatiality to the unconscious, as a container full of contents rather than another system of thought, she created the potential for others – such as Stokes – to do so.[7] Stokes had shown interest in Freud as a schoolboy, he was analysed by Melanie Klein for over six years from January 1930, and Freudian-Kleinian ideas are latent in earlier texts. But it is only in the final 'Envoi' section to *Venice* that he first fully 'outs' his Kleinian sympathies, when he writes:

> *Consciousness is no more of the mind than the surface is of the sea. And just as the surface of the sea lies opposite to the sky and, indeed, is thus defined, so does consciousness lie opposite to the external world. Mental processes, unknown in themselves, obtain entry to consciousness through speech. Symbolic substitution, even before speech, is natural to the infant. The basis of speech is substitution, the basis of all projection. To create is to substitute.*[8]

Klein's stress on 'the influence of unconscious phantasy on art ... and on the activities of every-day life'[9] encouraged Stokes to study the role of substitute objects, and symbol formation, in creativity.[10] Thus in his first psychoanalytical paper 'Concerning Art and Metapsychology' – also of 1945 – he praises how 'the artist and the aesthete would appear to have found cause for celebrating the mechanism [of subsititution] in and for itself. But the aesthetic substitution is especially distinguished by the power to synthesize meanings. A synthesis of inner meaning put outwards to be on its own, as it were, in the open world, always characterises the work of art'.[11] This is that paramount quality of outwardness the readers of *Venice* might have felt for themselves in contemplating Stokes's account and plate of the Ca' Dario above. In another architectonic image from the same paper Stokes describes how:

> *the generating relations of a work of art have the air of a set-out finality, of a diverse expression that is single, of a phantasy that has been detached from its originator to become an object, as if he were able to make of his mind a stone which yet displays and manifests the content of his mind.*[12]

As Paul Tucker has explained – in examining his manuscripts of this period – Stokes's goal in this paper, in so valorising art and architecture, and the practices of the artist and architect, is to 'present a major challenge to Freudian theory in so far as this subsumes [art] under an idea of sublimation understood in terms of illusion and of a turning inwards, away from the external world'.[13] Therefore Stokes quotes the Freud of 1911 to refute his opinion of the artist as 'originally a man who turns away from reality ... and who then in phantasy-life allows full play to his erotic and ambitious wishes'.[14]

11.1 A house, seventeenth century, from Adrian Stokes, *Venice* (1945), Plate 17. © Estate of Adrian Stokes.

This brief contextualisation may help those, who cannot imagine a Venice without colour, to be less surprised now by the strongly tonal city Stokes presents: 'Venice excels in blackness and whiteness; water brings commerce between them. Italians excel in the use of black and white, white stone and interior darkness'.[15] The black and white comes from the materials of Venice, especially the remarkable Istrian stone which: 'bleaches in the light, blackens in the shade, many columns and projections upon Venetian building are most dramatically most intensely light and intensely dark. This darkness that radiates evenly has inspired as well the characteristic chiaroscuro of Venetian painting, the extensive use of dark-coloured discs and circular holes in Venetian architecture, common in all periods'.[16]

Note that this is a 'darkness that radiates'. Stokes concludes his *Venice* book with Giorgione's *Tempesta* (c. 1505–6) as an example of this 'characteristic chiaroscuro'. The detail he gives from this painting (his plate 48) captures the intense chiaroscuro of the approaching storm against the spectral light on the Veneto architecture; in the foreground stand the fragments of the new Early Renaissance Venice then under construction. Stokes stresses that this is *not* the dramatic Tenebrist chiaroscuro to come of artists like Caravaggio; rather it is a radiant enabling chiaroscuro where local colour flowers between these tonal extremes.[17] If none of the foregoing imagery is explicit enough, then in Stokes's next semi-autobiographical book *Inside Out* (1947) (pointedly subtitled *an essay in the psychology and aesthetic appeal of space*) he explicitly metaphorises our 'insides' – the figures and objects of our Kleinian unconscious – as the dangerous, yet potential, shadows and depths of a Piranesian underworld:

> *Yet even vast spaces are informed with our feeling, with images, maybe, of our own insides. A film of Les Misérables shows once more the sewers of Paris. The hero, pursued, squanders his failing strength carrying the girl, foundering in the subterranean mud and cataracts, in the slipping silky waters of dirt. Many the dangers from this tomb of suffocating, purposeful yet silent water. His head submerges. The vast under-waterway, with its occasional arches, with dim lights from above, holds firmly on the imagination, magnifies, indeed intensifies, images of the inside of the body.*[18]

SANTA MARIA DEI MIRACOLI

In *Venice* Stokes gives three plates and a full reading of the casket-like church of Santa Maria dei Miracoli (1481–9); greatly symbolic of the good mother as a new foundation created to hold a miracle-working image of the Virgin Mary.[19] Stokes writes:

> *Respiration is … suggested by the black space of the open windows beneath. Interior life is dark within these wide connections with the outside world. Like the sense apparatus of the human body, windows bring what is inside in communication with what is without: like consciousness they are the exit upon the external world of the life within. … Such building, then, is a vast and concrete symbol of inner-outer life.*[20]

Darkness is not always described in such renewing terms. In the 'negative sublime' of Mark Rothko's last works Peter Fuller finds 'within the boundaries of his canvases deep black spaces of beckoning nothingness which seem to invite you, the viewer, to annihilate yourself in them'.[21] In a trajectory opposed to Rothko's, Fuller gives a case, from a significant early paper of Klein's of 1929, of the healing effect of artistic creativity. Klein discusses the artist Ruth Kjär who made masterly portraits of her relatives in response to a 'compelling urge' to heal deep early anxieties and to repair the blank spaces she felt without and within.[22] At the Miracoli Stokes finds a similar reparation, that even the 'last of the *inner* darkness ... has squeezed through to be a still and static outward thing'.[23]

INCRUSTED CAVES

The cave metaphor – productive of much sublime imagery – connects the unsettling shadows of the unconscious with the outer light at the aperture.[24] For Stokes:

> *Aperture ... existed first, then the skeleton, then the walls that withstand the water. ... And if the remaining apertures suggest caves, then the circular discs, so often in attendance upon Venetian windows, are stones that have been rolled away from these entrances.*[25]

This echoes a famous Ruskin theme:

> *The whole early architecture of Venice is architecture of incrustation. ... The Venetian ... built his houses ... as if he had been a shell-fish, – roughly inside, mother-of-pearl on the surface. ... You might fancy early Venice one wilderness of brick, which a petrifying sea had beaten upon till it coated it with marble ....*[26]

These themes of rough cave or shell, and smooth revetment, are laid out in Stokes's *Smooth and Rough* (1951):

> *We partake of an inexhaustible feeding mother (a fine building announces) ... though we thought to have lost her utterly, to have destroyed her utterly in fantasy and act. We are grateful to stone buildings for their stubborn material .... . Much crude rock stands rearranged; now in the form of apertures, of suffusion at the side of apertures, the bites, the tears, the pinches are miraculously identified with the recipient passages of the body, with sense organs, with features; as well as with the good mother ...*[27]

Transactions take place between inner and outer, as well as many negotiations between the objects of Klein's inner world. In a paper of 1959, 'Our Adult World and its Roots in Infancy', Klein emphasises the 'sense of persecution' along with the 'capacity to love' in the infant's relationship with the mother – the rough as well as the smooth: 'Love and hate towards the mother are bound up with the very young infant's capacity to project all his emotions on to her, thereby making her into a good as well as dangerous object'.[28] An inner world of 'unconscious fantasies':

> *is built up which is partly a reflection of the external one. The double process of introjection [taking into the self the situations and objects of the outer world and making them part of the 'inner life'] and projection [the 'capacity in the child to attribute to other people around him feelings of various kinds, predominantly love and hate'] contributes to the interaction between external and internal factors. This interaction continues throughout every stage of life.*[29]

As has been indicated, Klein is more positive than Freud in suggestively stressing the role of unconscious fantasy in the making of art, but it was largely left to followers such as Hannah Segal, Marion Milner, and Adrian Stokes to develop the aesthetic implications. The first months of life – characterised as the paranoid-schizoid position – exhibit 'the tendency of the infantile ego to split impulses and objects', for 'persecutory anxiety reinforces the need to keep separate the loved object from the dangerous one ....'[30] Growing integration of the ego at around the fifth and sixth months of life leads to a greater synthesis of the good and bad aspects of the object, to attain the second 'depressive position'. So called because the baby now:

> *becomes afraid of the harm his destructive impulses and his greed might do, or might have done, to his loved objects. ... He experiences feelings of guilt and the urge to preserve these objects and to make reparation to them for harm done.*[31]

Klein also stresses the continuities of these early infantile fantasies and emotions into adult life.[32]

Hanna Segal saw artistic creativity as essentially a resolution of the later depressive situation. But Stokes moved from a similar standpoint, to the recognition that the artist sought *both* an ideal object merged with the self (as in the paranoid-schizoid position) *and* an object perceived as discrete and independent (as in the depressive position),[33] reinforcing our earlier points that Stokes posits these shadowy unconscious spaces as radiant and creative. For – although they certainly contain fearful objects of hate and destruction – they also contain objects of goodness and harmony; in these dark spaces, and in creative transactions between inner and outer objects, an integrated personality can be achieved and the good mother restored.

ALDO ROSSI'S *TEATRO DEL MONDO*

Stokes writes of S. Maria dei Miracoli as 'the grandest of Venetian vessels'; of how the church 'seems to move towards us ....'[34] In common fantasy the buildings of Venice do appear to float, but now a real boat-building sails into the second part of our story, created by an architect much concerned with shadows and the unconscious – Aldo Rossi. For the 1979 Venice Biennale his *Teatro del Mondo* was towed across the lagoon to the Punta della Dogana, adding its baptistery-like form to the triumphant setting of the Salute's domes. As Rossi says, it was moored at 'a place where architecture ended and the world of the imagination began'.[35] Rossi's oneiric *A Scientific Autobiography* maps the unconscious with its repetitions and strangely shifting memories.[36] Here Rossi writes:

> *What pleases me above all is that the theatre is a veritable ship, and like a ship, it is subject to the movements of the lagoon, the gentle oscillations, the rising and sinking ....*[37]

In youthful memories of the Adriatic the sea seemed to Rossi:

> *a coalescence capable of constructing a mysterious, geometric form made up of every memory and expectation. Perhaps it was really a verse from Alcaeus that led me to architecture when I was in secondary school: 'O seashell / daughter of stone and the whitening sea / you astonish the minds of children'. ... In [these lines] are contained the problem of form, of material, of imagination – that is, of astonishment.*[38]

And he returns to Alcaeus' verse when thinking about the theatre:

> *Yet inside and outside are also part of the meaning of theatre, and I rediscovered the other meaning of the seashell ... which Alcaeus had written about ... Astonishment has a hard crust made of stone and shaped by the sea, like the crust of great constructions of steel, stone, and cement which form the city.*[39]

Rossi's invocation of Alcaeus maps quite perfectly onto our earlier exploration of the inner and outer transactions of the unconscious, and the incrustation of the petrifying ocean. I do not know if Rossi read Stokes, but he was certainly familiar with the psychologising of Ruskin's *Stones of Venice*.[40] Given these promising sanctions of the interpretative potential of the Ruskin-Klein-Stokes frameworks, I want to now probe further into the nature of this inner-outer binary of Rossi's, along with those of shadow and light, the irrational and rational, and the unconscious and conscious.[41]

ANALOGICAL ARCHITECTURE AND THE UNCONSCIOUS

In fantasy, the *Teatro del Mondo* also floats into one of Rossi's 'Analogous' compositions, grouped with two other Venice projects.[42] Its arrangement exactly rhymes with Canaletto's Palladio *capriccio* of Venice with which Rossi illustrates the concept of the 'analogical city'.[43] To further define the concept of analogy Rossi quotes from a letter of C.G. Jung to Freud of 2 March 1910:

> *... 'logical' thought is the thought expressed in words, that addresses itself to the outside world as a discourse. The 'analogous' of fantastic thought is sensible, figurative and mute, it is not a discourse but a rumination [on] material of the past, an act of revolt. The logical thought is 'thinking in words'. Analogical thought is archaic, unconscious and practically inexpressible in words.*[44]

For that key interpreter of Rossi's unconscious, Peter Eisenman, analogy is the 'shadow of logic', his 'conscious images exist only as a key to their shadow imagery. It is their intrinsic, often unconscious content which confronts the more problematic and perhaps fundamental reality of the extrinsic cultural condition today'.[45] While:

> *In Rossi's drawings the shadows themselves … take on material solidity. … [They] become another figure. In their highly exaggerated, pitch black shadow they assume a graphic presence that overpowers the actual literal shape of the building. As such they become objects which cannot share the same qualities as the buildings. … They become the negative image of positive reality.*[46]

But we saw how for Stokes 'the basis of speech is substitution, the basis of all projection. To create is to substitute'; the artist bodies the unconscious forth through language and articulate form. In this regard, the muteness of Rossi's dislocated analogical forms and shadows, places his work in the realm of the unconscious or pre-conscious owing to its apparent resistance to synthesise inner meanings outwards. As Manfredo Tafuri emphasises, 'Rossi elaborates an alphabet of forms that rejects all facile articulation'; he deploys 'a syntax of emptied signs'; his is 'an emptied sacrality' and 'a language of emptiness and silence'.[47] Tafuri adds that 'the emptied sign is also the instrument of the metaphysics of de Chirico' in a connection many have made between the Surrealist artist and Rossi's architecture. For, as Frances Butler has explained:

> *de Chirico's shadow did not symbolize the power residing in fixed taboos, or in the traditional styles or structures of knowledge, but power without known consequences. He used shadow to make exactly that point about the mind, the ultimate source of human power in the modern era, that its power had no fixed pattern and no prefigured consequences. de Chirico not only liberated shadow from its source … [he made] the consequence of power, the cast shadow, project over an empty stage.*[48]

Butler shows how de Chirico 'returned to the extended vertical axis of pre-literate thought'; in the face of the collapse of collective discourse, his collage-like processes revisited the 'primitive thinking tactic' of parataxis, and he used 'shadow to disconnect objects from the myths of significant placement; to isolate and disconnect them from sense'.[49] For Tafuri the same social angst that produces Rossi's:

> *removal of form from the sphere of the quotidian … is not because of any incapacity on the part of the architect, but rather because that 'centre' has been historically destroyed, because that 'source' has been dispersed into multiple streams, each without beginning or end.*[50]

Rossi's shadows represent a cultural condition irrevocably altered by the events of the Second World War, by mass-destruction, the Holocaust, and the atomic bomb.[51] He imagines 'photographs of cities during war, sections of apartments, broken toys',[52] and talking of the fragmentary character of drawings such as his *L'Architecture Assasinée* (1975) declares his belief 'that today we live in a world that cannot be repaired, a world of psychological and human fragments'.[53] Conceiving the Cemetery of San Cataldo, following a major road accident in 1971, he even 'saw the skeletal structure of [his own] body as a series of fractures to be reassembled'.[54] Klein would define this acute sense of fragmentation as 'depressive anxiety', when the ego:

> *finds itself confronted with the psychic reality that its loved objects are in a state of dissolution – in bits – there is anxiety how to put the bits together in the right way and do away with the bad ones ....*[55]

Confronted with the impossibility of restoring the good whole-object, much modernist art and architecture has resorted – like de Chirico – to collage composition. Composed of what are in actuality disembodied part-objects, the collage nonetheless preserves aspects of the whole-object. Alluding to analogous architecture, Rossi describes it as a 'singular type of collage in which ... the ultimate meaning itself remains unknown ....'[56] If the various projects that compose the analogous drawing of Venice are not themselves shattered to the extreme extent of *L'Architecture Assasinée*, they are wilfully displaced, nonetheless, as elements that cannot 'constitute a dialectic: ... projected into the infinite as timeless anecdotes'.[57] In fact the denuded echoes of such classical typologies as the stoa only intensify this sense of displacement.

Within his desire for outwardness, Stokes is acutely aware of a cultural fragmentation which he places a whole century earlier – to the mid-nineteenth century and the full emergence of the industrial city. His *Invitation in Art* (1965) describes modern art's struggle to 'reach a compromise with our disjointed urban environment, with the illimitable enveloping quality of the startling chaos around us'.[58] For Stokes, our hostile environment makes whole-object relationships unsustainable, condemning us to 'hypnotic envelopment by part-objects'. His section on 'Collages' in *Reflections on the Nude* (1967) captures the surrogate, yet illusory, whole-object nature of the shadow-world of the analogous city:

> *The employment in collages and assemblages of actual objects points not only to the reiteration of whole-object nature in a void created by the abandonment of representations that truly imitate them, but also to our particular hunger in the modern environment for surrounding objects that we may contemplate in their possession of the wholeness and self-sufficiency of which the nude was once the presiding symbol.*[59]

SHADOWS OF THE IN-BETWEEN

Accordingly, Rossi's shadows image sometimes an 'extreme melancholy' equal to the mood Étienne-Louis Boullée describes in his 'Architecture, Essay on Art' when 'on the edge of a wood in the moonlight ... the shadows of the trees etched on the ground made a most profound impression'. 'Nature offered itself to [his] gaze in mourning' and Boullée proceeded to seek a new type of architecture composed of the 'effect of shadows'. Rossi says how the work of translating this passage on shadows into Italian in 1967 'allowed [him] to understand the complexity of the irrational in architecture'.[60] As in the case of Tafuri above, commentators habitually invoke the paintings of de Chirico to read these shadows of Rossi; thus Sheila O'Donnell brackets de Chirico's *The Mystery and Melancholy of a Street* with a view of Rossi's housing at Gallaratese, Milan.[61] But Rossi himself rather disavows the de Chirico connections visited on his work, as in this interview of 1990:

> *Certainly there is a de Chirico-like element in my drawings, but I always find it strange that critics fixated on an immediate association with de Chirico. Because the truth is that my great influence and love is with Sironi and with Morandi. In fact, what Morandi does with his precise bottles and still lifes is part of what I aim to do in my architecture.*[62]

A *Domestic Architecture* (1974) drawing of Rossi's rhymes the shadows of a Giorgio Morandi-like grouping of coffee-pot, mug and utensils with those of the elevation of the residential development at Gallaratese. It illustrates Rossi's feeling for the inner and outer, and his uncannily oneiric mixing of scales. In *A Scientific Autobiography* he writes of his love for the receptacles of the kitchen as 'miniatures of the fantastic architecture that I would encounter later. Today I still love to draw these large coffeepots, which I liken to brick walls, and which I think of as structures that can be entered'.[63] For – as Michael Hays points out – 'dimensions are of no importance in analogical thought since the order of the city is cognitively embedded in all architectural types of any scale'.[64] As described in Rossi's *The Architecture of the City*, a single building such as Diocletian's Palace at Split can come to 'refer *analogically* to the form of a city'.[65]

11.2 Gallaratese housing, north Milan, 1969–70. Photo by Stephen Kite.

So, if we imagine the *Teatro del Mondo* as a large kitchen receptacle that has found its way into St Mark's Basin, then equally Morandi's still-lifes are deeply implicated in the artist's home-cityscapes of Bologna, in its famously endless colonnades, and tall medieval towers. The critic Carlo Ludovico Ragghianti says that Morandi's interest in still life is 'wholly architectural, so much so that it should prompt us to think of cathedrals rather than of bottles'.[66] The city of Bologna – held in the hands of St Petronio in a Lorenzo Costa altarpiece – might be compared with a Morandi Still Life of 1956 where the paired bottles seem to echo Bologna's famous medieval Due Torri, soaring above the general urban fabric – represented by three boxes in the Still Life.[67]

Reviewing Morandi's Legacy Paul Coldwell describes Bologna as 'an artificial environment where the vertical forms of the towers have a counterpoint in the horizontal colonnades, measuring out the city in units of column and shadow'.[68] The bars of shadow thrown by the pilasters and columns of Bologna's passages would have syncopated every step Morandi made through his home city.[69] Thus – in more plausibly subtle parallels than with de Chirico – it is fascinating to compare Bologna's colonnades with those at Gallaratese (Figure 11.2) and then to examine the in-betweens in Morandi's townscape/table-scapes – those dark alley-like fissures bidding us to the in-betweens of inner and outer.

Coldwell says that Morandi's drawings 'tentatively delineate the outline of tree, house and shadow as being of equal value. They deliberately create a jigsaw of positive and negative ...'.[70] This pattern is particularly striking in some of the *Still Life* watercolours of 1959 where form is entirely described by the negative shadow-shapes.[71] To reiterate Eisenman's points, here Rossi could learn how shadows might take on 'material solidity' and the 'negative image of positive reality'. This material solidity of shadow comes out even more strongly in some of Morandi's etchings. *Still Life, 1931*[72] is a misty city silhouette of cross-hatchings that might be paralleled with an etching-like hatched drawing of the *Teatro del Mondo* from *A Scientific Autobiography* where only the octagon's crowning globe glints out of a dense matrix of criss-crossed marks.[73] As in Bologna, surely shadowed colonnades should invite life:

> *In the last few days I saw the first open windows, clothes hanging out to dry in the loggias – the first timid signs of the life it will assume when people move in. I am confident that the spaces reserved for this daily life – the big colonnade, the ballatoi – will bring a sharp focus to the dense flow of daily life and the deep popular roots of this residential architecture ....*[74]

This is Rossi talking about his hopes for the Gallaratese project in 1974, though in images at any rate, his colonnades are weirdly devoid of any such life. Here, a red notice placed by the *amministratore* forbids games of football and tennis – *sui piazzali e nei passaggi comuni sono vietati i giochi del Pallone e del tennis.* Is Rossi's confidence in the invitation of his colonnades 'reserved for this daily life' knowingly disingenuous given the muteness of an 'archaic [and] unconscious' analogous architecture so lacking in gesture? His inscrutable white liner docked in the embrace of Carlo Aymonino's expressively articulated residential blocks makes a bemusing sight. Tafuri contrasts the 'hieratic purism of [Rossi's] geometric block, which is kept aloof from every ideology' with Aymonino's wish 'to underscore each solution, each joint, each formal artifice'.[75] Aymonino's objects 'are full of 'memories'', but in Rossi 'memory is contracted into hieratic segments'.[76] Rossi's colonnades belong too much to the private unreal dreams of the analogous city; here the unconscious inner has made insufficient connection to the outer to establish a viable in-between. Stokes saw such shaded in-betweens as *potentially* realms to be desired, as in his essay 'Living in Ticino, 1947–50':

> *As I walk under the arcade of Locarno's main square, I see in a clear and liquid shade a café table with a light-blue cloth that touches a stone pier. I think I would be entirely safe there: leaning against the pillar I would be able to partake utterly of every thought: I would be immobile, provided for, as in the womb yet out-of-doors ....*[77]

Stokes would progressively stress the role of the first 'paranoid-schizoid' position in creativity *together with* the second 'depressive' position, as in his paper 'Form in Art' (1955) where he argued that the infant's 'homogeneity associated with idealization (the inexhaustible breast), is harnessed by the work of art to an acute sense of otherness and actuality'.[78] Celebrating Stokes's reification of the in-between, Colin St John Wilson finds in the art-writer: 'The extraordinary conclusion: that it is uniquely the role of the masterpiece to make possible the *simultaneous* experience of these two polar modes; enjoyment at the same time of intense sensations of being inside and outside, of envelopment and detachment, of oneness and separateness'.[79]

THE LIGHT OF LOW WINDOWS

More positively, the *Teatro del Mondo* seems to be corporeal, in a more received humanist sense; though a short-lived project that may be why it has endured in memory as one of Rossi's most popular works. It is a body whose inside can be entered like the San Carlone colossus at Arona, which Rossi writes of often.[80] In its internally skeletal structure the *Teatro* is also machine-like, comparable to the many festively elaborate *macchine del mondo* that preceded it.[81] Its controlled modulation of shadows and light also make it another kind of *macchina* – a looking machine such as a camera obscura.

Musing on the interior of his *Teatro* Rossi agrees with those who write of:

> *a pre-monumental Venice, a Venice not yet white with the stone of Sansovino and Palladio. It is the Venice of Carpaccio, and I see it in the interior light, in the wood, and I am reminded of certain Dutch interiors which evoke ships and are near the sea.*[82]

Rossi writes also of Dutch painters who 'cover tables [with Persian carpets] and display their Oriental colours in the light of a low window'.[83] Two celebrated pictures that bring together this southern and northern imagery are Carpaccio's *Vision of St Augustine* and Vermeer's *The Astronomer* (1668). They also evoke that camera obscura image of the mind in Locke's *Essay Concerning Human Understanding* (1690):

> *External and internal sensations are the only passages that I can find of knowledge to the understanding. These alone, as far as I can discover, are the windows by which light is let into this dark room. For, methinks, the understanding is not much unlike a closet wholly shut from light, with only some little opening left ... to let in external visible resemblances, or some idea of things without ....*[84]

A line from Stokes's *Smooth and Rough* seems apposite to these apparently cerebral, but also moody dark spaces: 'The candle of reason, brighter, steadier, longer than heretofore, discloses a nearer and more active darkness: we are ringed by emotion'.[85] In conclusion to the first chapter of his *Venice*, Stokes returns to his plate 9, a detail of the Torre del'Orologio in the Piazza San Marco, and the gateway to the Merceria (Figure 11.3). For him this photograph is 'the one that is most beautiful' for it is seen to 'exemplify a perfect harmony of inner and outer things'. Stokes says:

> *I attribute to the reflections of the piazza, to the street beneath the dark archway, to the stone building, the quality of a visual parable of unconscious, pre-conscious and conscious. For the Quattro Cento building, by itself expresses the solution of manifold directions, manifold movements of the spirit as might a vigorous face.*[86]

In conclusion – against these more affirmative shadows of the *Teatro* – it has to be admitted that Rossi's darks are rarely as radiant as those of Stokes's Quattro Cento palaces. At the same time, Rossi is certainly among those few significant architect-thinkers to have rehabilitated shadow as an operative figure within the architecture of modernism – or rather postmodernism – against prevalent ideologies of transparency and over-illumination. As we have seen his shadows often partake of a sinister, surreal quality – one in fact more like de Chirico or the Fascist artist Mario Sironi, than Morandi's more benign influence. Thus, the mourner at Rossi's New Cemetery of San Cataldo at Modena (1971–8) – after passing along the supportively corporeal and humanised neo-classical colonnades of Cesare Costa's earlier structures (1858–76) – broaches a small door to be 'set adrift in [Rossi's] immense stoa, shadowed and featureless'.[87] And one might add, more or less functionless in any practical sense.

In making positive figures of what is normally negative, on occasion Rossi's shadows become so materially solid that they take on a spooky life independent of the objects that cast them – becoming in fact part-objects that might be sensed as 'bad'. Reminders, therefore, of nightmarish tales such as that one of the devil who seized Peter Schlemihl's shadow.[88] With all his love for the total integration of the inner and outer represented by such a work of architecture as Mauro Codussi's Torre del' Orologio, Stokes recognised the deconstructed nature of the modern condition and the artist's need to work through collage and the fragment – the condition Rossi articulates in the silence of *his* shadows. Stokes increasingly explored beyond Klein's stress on the role of the 'depressive' existential state in

11.3 Detail of clock tower, St Mark's Piazza, Venice, from Adrian Stokes, *Venice* (1945), Plate 9.

11.4 Stoa, New Cemetery of San Cataldo, Modena, 1971–8. Photo by Stephen Kite.

creativity, to understand *The Invitation in Art* (1965) which attracts the artist or architect to plunge into the dark unconscious of oceanic feeling, and to play with depth and with harsh chiaroscuro.[89] Problematizing the collage, we discussed the use, in the post-humanist condition, of whole-objects as fragments – a situation intensified if an object's shadow becomes yet another part-object, as in de Chirico, and often in Rossi. But we have also pointed to the enabling darks of Carpaccio's painting of *St Augustine* in the *Scuolo San Giorgio degli Schiavoni* in connection with Rossi. These final words from Stokes speak of the possibility 'to savour the counting house gloom dim with warmed stones' of these *Scuole* of Venice, whose 'great windows of black bottle glass give out upon the sea like portholes'.[90]

NOTES

1 Margaret Plant, *Venice: Fragile City 1797–1997* (London and New Haven, CT: Yale University Press, 2002), p. 339.

2 Stephen Bann, 'The Colour in the Text: Ruskin's Basket of Strawberries', in *The Ruskin Polygon: Essays on the Imagination of John Ruskin*, ed. J.D. Hunt and F.M. Holland (Manchester: Manchester University Press, 1982), pp. 123–36, p. 133.

3 Adrian Stokes, *The Critical Writings of Adrian Stokes, 3 vols*, ed. Lawrence Gowing (London: Thames and Hudson, 1978). Subsequent references in the form: *CW, vol. 2, Venice*, p. 103.

4 *CW, vol. 2, Venice*, p. 102.

5 Ibid., p. 101.

6 Juliet Mitchell, 'Introduction to Melanie Klein', in John Phillips and Lyndsey Stonebridge (eds), *Reading Melanie Klein* (London: Routledge, 1998), pp. 11–31, p. 24.

7 Nicky Glover, *Psychoanalytic Aesthetics: An Introduction to the British School* (London: Karnac, 2009), p. 25.

8 *CW, vol. 2, Venice*, pp. 137–8.

9 Melanie Klein, 'Our Adult World and its Roots in Infancy', in M. Masud and R. Khan (eds), *Melanie Klein: Envy and Gratitude and Other Works* (London: Hogarth Press, 1975), pp. 247–63, p. 251.

10 See Glover, *Psychoanalytic Aesthetics*, p. 37.

11 Adrian Stokes, 'Concerning Art and Metapsychology', in *The International Journal of Psycho-Analysis* 26 (London: Institute of Psychoanalysis, 1945), pp. 177–9, p. 178.

12 Adrian Stokes, 'Concerning Art and Metapsychology', p. 179.

13 Paul Tucker, '"A Summing Up of All I Have Ever Thought": Adrian Stokes's "In Short" (1942) and his Other Writings of the Period', in *Tate Papers*, 20 (London: Tate, 19 November 2013), pp. 1–13, p. 9.

14 Sigmund Freud quoted in Adrian Stokes, 'Concerning Art and Metapsychology', p. 179.

15 *CW, vol. 2, Venice*, p. 88.

16 Ibid., p. 91. (The adjective 'intensely' light and dark is only in the original 1945 edition.)

17 Ibid., p. 131.

18 *CW, vol. 2, Inside Out*, p. 163.

19 Richard J. Goy, *Venice: An Architectural Guide* (London and New Haven, CT: Yale University Press, 2010), pp. 183–6.

20 *CW, vol. 2, Venice*, pp. 98–9.

21 Peter Fuller, *Art and Psychoanalysis* (London: Writers and Readers, 1980), pp. 222–3.

22 Peter Fuller, *Art and Psychoanalysis*, p. 223. Melanie Klein, 'Infantile Anxiety-Situations Reflected in a Work of Art and in the Creative Impulse', in *The International Journal of Psycho-Analysis*, 10, pp. 436–43.

23 *CW, vol. 2, Venice*, p. 99.

24 See, for example, James B. Twitchell, *Romantic Horizons: Aspects of the Sublime in English Poetry and Painting, 1770–1850* (Columbia, MO: University of Missouri Press, 1983), pp. 74–84.

25 *CW, vol. 2, Venice*, p. 91.

26 E.T. Cook and Alexander Wedderburn (eds), *The Works of John Ruskin* (London: George Allen, 1904–13), vol. 9, p. 323.

27 *CW, vol. 2, Smooth and Rough*, p. 241.

28 Melanie Klein, 'Our Adult World and its Roots in Infancy', p. 248.

29 Ibid., p. 250.

30 Ibid., p. 253.

31 Ibid., p. 255.

32 Ibid., p. 262.

33 Hannah Segal, 'A Psychoanalytic Approach to Aesthetics', in John Phillips and Lyndsey Stonebridge (eds), *Reading Melanie Klein* (London: Routledge, 1998), pp. 203–22, p. 220.

34 *CW, vol. 2, Venice*, p. 100.

35 Aldo Rossi, *A Scientific Autobiography*, trans. Lawrence Venuti (Cambridge, MA: The MIT Press, 1981), p. 66.

36 Ibid., p. 111.

37 Ibid., p. 67.

38 Ibid., p. 25.

39 Ibid., p. 66.

40 John O'Regan, and Aldo Rossi (eds), *Aldo Rossi: Selected Writings and Projects* (London: Architectural Design, 1983), p. 51.

41 Jean La Marche, *The Familiar and the Unfamiliar in Twentieth-Century Architecture* (Urbana and Chicago, IL: University of Illinois Press, 2003), p. 76.

42 '*Aldo Rossi. 'Analogous' composition, with the entrance gate for the Architectural Exhibition at the Venice Biennale, the Teatro del Mondo, and a project for a hotel in Cannaregio-West, Venice, Italy. 1981*', Black ink on tracing paper, 52.3 x 95.4 cm, Canadian Centre for Architecture Collection, AP142.S1.D42.P3.1.

43 Aldo Rossi, 'An Analogical Architecture', in John O'Regan, et al., *Aldo Rossi*, pp. 58–64, p. 59.

44 Quoted in Peter Eisenman, 'The House of the Dead as the City of Survival', in Kenneth Frampton (ed.), *Aldo Rossi in America 1976 to 1979* (New York: The Institute for

Architecture and Urban Studies, 1979), pp. 4–15, p. 6. See also the chapter on 'Analogy' in K. Michael Hays, *Architecture's Desire: Reading the Late Avant-Garde* (Cambridge, MA: The MIT Press, 2010).

45 Peter Eisenman, 'The House of the Dead as the City of Survival', p. 9.

46 Ibid.

47 Manfredo Tafuri, *The Sphere and the Labyrinth: Avant-Gardes and Architecture from Piranesi to the 1970s*, trans. Pellegrino d'Acierno and Robert Connolly (Cambridge, MA: The MIT Press), p. 273.

48 Frances Butler, 'The Shadow Does Not Know: Disconnected Power', in David Murray (ed.), *VIA 11, Architecture and Shadow* (Philadelphia, PA: University of Pennsylvania, 1990), pp. 116–23, p. 118.

49 Frances Butler, 'The Shadow Does Not Know', pp. 120–21.

50 Manfredo Tafuri, *The Sphere and the Labyrinth*, p. 274.

51 See Peter Eisenman, 'The House of the Dead as the City of Survival', p. 5.

52 Aldo Rossi, *A Scientific Autobiography*, p. 8.

53 Carlos Jimenez, 'Mystic Signs: A Conversation with Aldo Rossi', in *Cite* 24 (Houston, TX: Rice Design Alliance, The Architecture + Design Review of Houston, Spring, 1990), pp. 16–17, p. 16.

54 John O'Regan et al., *Aldo Rossi: Selected Writings and Projects*, p. 82.

55 Quoted in R.D. Hinshelwood, *A Dictionary of Kleinian Thought* (London: Free Association Books, 1989), p. 145.

56 Aldo Rossi, 'My Designs and Analogous Architecture', in Kenneth Frampton, *Rossi in America*, pp. 16–19, p. 19.

57 Ibid.

58 *CW, vol. 3, Invitation in Art*, p. 287.

59 *CW, vol. 3, Reflections on the Nude*, p. 317.

60 Aldo Rossi, *A Scientific Autobiography*, p. 52.

61 John O'Regan, et al., *Aldo Rossi: Selected Writings and Projects*, p. 10.

62 Carlos Jimenez, 'Mystic Signs. A Conversation with Aldo Rossi', p. 17.

63 Aldo Rossi, *A Scientific Autobiography*, p. 2.

64 K. Michael Hays, *Architecture's Desire*, p. 37.

65 Aldo Rossi, *The Architecture of the City*, trans. Diane Ghirardo and Joan Ockman (Cambridge, MA: The MIT Press, 1984), p. 174.

66 Quoted in Siri Hustvedt, 'Not just bottles', in *Modern Painters*, vol. 11, no. 4 (New York: Louise Blouin Media, Winter 1998), pp. 20–25, p. 22.

67 See Siri Hustvedt, 'Not just bottles', p. 22.

68 Paul Coldwell, *Morandi's Legacy: Influences on British Art* (London: Philip Wilson, 2006), p. 10.

69 For a detailed study and images of these arcades, see Andrea Santucci, *Il Mirabile Artificio, colonne, archi e capitelli dei portici di Bologna* (Bologna: Gli Inchiostri Associati Editore, 1997–8).

70 Paul Coldwell, *Morandi's Legacy*, p. 17.

71 See Ernst-Gerhard Güse and Franz Armin Morat (eds), *Giorgio Morandi: Paintings, Watercolours, Drawings, Etchings* (Munich: Prestel, 1999), plates 57, 58.

72 Ernst-Gerhard Güse and Franz Armin Morat (eds), *Giorgio Morandi*, plate 103.

73 Aldo Rossi, *A Scientific Autobiography*, p. 107.

74 Aldo Rossi quoted in Peter Arnell and Ted Bickford, *Aldo Rossi: Buildings and Projects* (New York: Rizzoli, 1985), p. 75.

75 Frances Butler, 'The Shadow Does Not Know', pp. 120–21.

76 Manfredo Tafuri, *The Sphere and the Labyrinth*, p. 276.

77 Richard Wollheim, *The Image in Form: Selected Writings of Adrian Stokes* (Harmondsworth: Penguin Books, 1972), p. 316.

78 Adrian Stokes, 'Form in Art', in Melanie Klein, Paula Heimann, and Roger Money-Kyrle (eds), *New Directions in Psycho-Analysis: The Significance of Infant Conflict in the Pattern of Adult Behaviour* (London: Tavistock Publications, 1955), pp. 406–20, p. 414.

79 Colin St John Wilson, 'The Natural Imagination: An Essay on the Experience of Architecture', in *Architectural Review* 185 (London: Emap Limited, 1989), pp. 64–70, p. 66.

80 Aldo Rossi, *A Scientific Autobiography*, p. 3.

81 Aldo Rossi, *Teatro del Mondo*, ed. M. Brusatin and A. Prandi (Venice: Cluva Librería Editrice, 1982).

82 Aldo Rossi, *A Scientific Autobiography*, p. 68.

83 Ibid., p. 69.

84 Quoted in Jonathan Crary, *Techniques of the Observer: On Vision and Modernity in the Nineteenth Century* (Cambridge, MA: The MIT Press, 1992), pp. 41–2.

85 *CW, vol. 2, Smooth and Rough*, p. 234.

86 *CW, vol. 2, Venice*, p. 111.

87 Peter Blundell Jones and Eamonn Canniffe, *Modern Architecture Through Case Studies* (Oxford: Architectural Press, 2007), p. 194.

88 See Victor I. Stoichita, *A Short History of the Shadow* (London: Reaktion, 1997), p. 169.

89 See Nicky Glover, *Psychoanalytic Aesthetics*, pp. 96–7.

90 *CW, vol. 2, Venice*, p. 95.

PART IV
Case Study: Maison de Verre

12

Projection: On Approaching the Maison de Verre

Andrew Ballantyne

The Rue Saint-Guillaume is a narrow street off the Boulevard Saint-Germain. If it does not seem quite fashionable then it is only because it is too central in Paris ever to go out of fashion. There are some interesting shop windows, and some stretches of the street are quiet. There are more people in the street than cars, and students are hanging around the entrance to Sciences Po, among them the politicians and political journalists of France's future. For the time being they are waiting for a lecture to begin, for friends to show up, or passing the time of day with other students before they disperse. Next door, in a building that is much like any other, there is a large secured door or gate that opens, on the rare occasions when it does open, into a low space that gives into a courtyard surrounded by five-storey buildings. It feels more open than the street, and quieter. Across the cobbles there is the facade of the Maison de Verre: plate glass floor-to-ceiling on the ground floor, and above that the whole wall is an uninterrupted screen of glass blocks, a grid of compact squares.[1]

It is inscrutable but it is now very famous, so it looks familiar. The house was built between 1928 and 1932, and it was the first house anywhere to have a glass block facade, so it has a place in the history books; but its real claim on our attention here is because of its compelling presence. It is a house, but it does not seem to go out of its way to look like a house. From the courtyard it seems more institutional than that, and there is something mesmerising about the wall, which has a degree of transparency but does not allow a view through it. The dense skin is substantial in a way that is quite different from the taut thinness of plate glass. When I approached the house for the first time I did so as an architectural tourist, and I already knew something of what I would find inside. The best-known view of the house is its grand salon, two storeys high with a wall of shimmering blocks that makes a luminous backdrop to the activity within, screening out the world's bustle. It is a large house, and its generous proportions and gentle stairs give it a palatial quality that is quite at odds with its industrial aesthetic: exposed steel girders rather than stone columns, and a studded rubber floor. It is set up for entertaining, and the most glamorous parties could happen here. However the building was also the consulting room and surgery for the original proprietor, Dr Jean Dalsace, who was a pioneer of birth control, and whose patients were all female. The building, as Kenneth Frampton said, 'defies any accepted form of classification'.[2] For as long as he was in practice most of the visitors to the building came not to the house but to the consulting room, which is on the ground floor.

Part of the reason for the success of the design was certainly that for the patients who approached, it had the aspect of a pioneering medical establishment. The medical practice had most of the ground floor to itself, and the waiting room had controlled glimpses of the garden at the back, so there would have been calm and privacy away from the street. Had the facade had a clearly domestic character, then the medical practice would have seemed to be very tucked away, almost invisible beneath the dwelling. In fact if we approach it as a respectable bourgeois house, uncertain about the novel business of contraception, which was not then quite established as respectable, and which could border on the illegal, we can feel reassured by the building's blankness. No one is watching us as we approach, and the building seems to be a substantial three-storey clinic. Maybe this seems like a trick or a deception, but it is a direct consequence only of the blankness. The building will accept the interpretation that I project on to it according to what I imagine I will find. The facade is a mask, perhaps, but more importantly it is a screen.

The projection of ourselves and our ideas into the world is something we do often and without thinking about it. We see faces in the clouds, and in the moon, and imagine that other people are in some ways like ourselves. In the literature of psychoanalysis, projection comes into the discussion with Sigmund Freud's discussion of paranoia. In paranoia there is an:

> *abuse of psychical mechanism which is very commonly employed in normal life: the mechanism of transposition or projection. Whenever an internal change occurs, we can choose whether we shall attribute it to an internal or an external cause. If something deters us from accepting an internal original, we naturally seize upon an external one.*[3]

Melanie Klein (1882–1960) is particularly associated with the analysis of projection, where we displace our own responses and feelings outside of ourselves, into the objects that seem to be causing them (for example the 'good breast'). There is a corresponding mechanism, introjection, where we take these objects and our feelings about them back into ourselves, so we feel that they are part of our identity.[4] Projection is one of the mechanisms that we deploy from early infancy, and is one of the fundamental ways that we make sense of the world. Klein saw 'paranoid' and 'schizoid' phases in normal infant development, but in adults we notice the mechanisms most clearly when something has gone wrong.

If paranoia uses projection to excess, it also helps us to bring it into focus. For example Captain Ahab in Herman Melville's novel *Moby Dick* is perhaps the most celebratedly paranoid character in literature. In the past, before the narrator (call him Ishmael) encounters him, Ahab has been injured by the white whale, Moby Dick, and has become obsessed by him. Ahab wants to hunt him down and kill him, and is not confused about that, but Ahab is convinced that his feelings about the whale are reciprocated by the whale, and that the whale is stalking Ahab, trying to kill him. Of course this is madness. It is Ahab's obsession with the whale that draws him close to it and makes it a danger to him. He cannot really know how the whale feels, but his obsession is such that he cannot feel that the whale is indifferent to him. The malignancy is all Ahab's, but Ahab projects it on to the screen wall of the whale and feels that the whale is malignant. He says:

> *To me, the white whale is that wall, shoved near to me. Sometimes I think there's naught beyond. But 'tis enough. He tasks me; he heaps me; I see in him outrageous strength, with an inscrutable malice sinewing it. That inscrutable thing is chiefly what I hate; and be the white whale agent, or be the white whale principal, I will wreak that hate upon him.*[5]

There is a corresponding introjection that is less acknowledged, as Ahab has internalised the whale as his destiny. As a character he is defined by his relation with the whale. Without Moby Dick the captain of the whaler is not Captain Ahab. The paranoia that projects his personal feelings out into the world, also internalises this part of the world, the whale, as part of Ahab's psychology, his 'becoming-whale', as Gilles Deleuze and Félix Guattari put it.[6]

Guattari studied psychoanalysis and was himself analysed by Lacan. In his books with Deleuze the two of them repudiate some Freudian ideas about the unconscious, but others (like projection) are quietly adopted. In their book *Mille Plateaux* they develop an idea, 'faciality' (*visageité*), that takes a white wall, such as the whale's, as its starting point. In their hands it becomes a more general principle, a white screen that accepts our projections. Like Ahab, we might have an intuition that there is something beyond the wall, but in fact we cannot know it. The other component of their face is the 'black hole' of the eyes. A white wall reflects everything, whereas a black hole absorbs everything. Again we know nothing about what has gone into the black hole – nothing escapes it, not even light, that is why it is black. It is the mechanism of the other's introjection, seen from the outside. The white wall is the place of signification, where signs are inscribed or projected, while the black hole is the place of subject-formation, where we infer that the other is taking in information, and stimuli that through empathy and projection we register or infer from the screen.[7]

When we interact with others we might use facial expressions as a way of signalling, and actors (some actors) have developed very articulate ranges of expression that signal their states of mind and enhance the expressive power of their words. It is no straightforward thing to analyse what it is that we respond to and we ourselves feel when we watch what we know to be an actor's performance. We understand that the character feels anxious, and if we have formed a bond with the character then we perhaps feel anxious through the mechanism of empathy. This play of inside and outside, of expression and projection, is given a special intensity in Robert Bresson's analysis of cinematography. Bresson (1901–99) invented the term '*cinématographe*', published in his *Notes sur le cinématographe* of 1975.[8] He had been making films since 1934 (*Les affaires publics*) and devised a way of working that produced films with a power to fascinate, and aesthetic qualities that set them apart from being films of stage works. The aim, as the notes make clear, was to avoid anything like stagecraft. He never employed actors in his films, because he thought that they would not be able to stop themselves acting. The people he did employ, he used in only one film each, so that they would not see themselves on screen and therefore start to modify their behaviour into a performance. He used the term 'model' rather than 'actor' in the notes, and the aim was to catch 'automatic' responses on film – reflexes, rather than acting – aiming for an affectless delivery of lines.

> *Cinematographic film, where expression is obtained by relations of images and of sounds, and not by a mimicry done with gestures and intonations of voice (whether actors or non-actors). One that does not analyze or explain. That re-composes.*[9]

So this idea of cinematographic film, is utterly unlike a theatrical film (made of carefully nuanced performances by actors). One of Bresson's key techniques is the use of the reaction-shot, in which the model's face is more-or-less blank. Depending on the sequence of shots the reaction might look serene, anxious, wary, baffled: whatever. The effect is caused by the viewer's projected understanding of how the character would be feeling, and the viewer's empathy is engaged with the character. The model is not 'performing', but the film director is editing so as to make the character seem alive, and the film works through the viewer's engagement by way of projection and empathy. As a formula for film-making this sounds as if it could go badly wrong, and in the hands of someone without Bresson's sensibility and fine judgement it would be a recipe for dullness, and yet in his hands it produced films of mesmerising power that are held in very high esteem.

For example *Pickpocket* (1959) from the middle of his film-making career, is presented quietly and calmly, with extensive use of a reflective voiceover, and a sparing use of stately baroque music – typically there is no musical accompaniment, but the sounds of amplified footsteps or traffic. The opening shots are dominated by people's backs, and careful observation of movements of hands and money. An atmosphere of anxiety is quickly established, and it remains in place for much of the film. The story is a free adaptation of Dostoyevsky's *Crime and Punishment* (1866), a psychological novel if ever there was one, but *Pickpocket* makes no attempt to analyse the pickpocket's state of mind. It makes us experience through empathy the anxious tension in which the character dwells, and to which he seems to be irresistibly drawn – at least at the stage of his life when the 'drama' unfolds (he has reached a different state of mind by the end of the film, and in the period when he recorded the narrative voiceover).

One of the most obviously dramatic moments is not in the film at all. The pickpocket is at a cafe with two friends, and he notices that someone else at the cafe is wearing a good watch. The friends go away for a few minutes, leaving the girl's jacket on the back of a chair. The man with the watch leaves, and the pickpocket decides to follow him. Then we see the friends return and pick up the jacket. They wonder where their friend has gone, and we see him return to his squalid little room. His clothing is scuffed, and his hands. The friend arrives and wonders why he left the cafe. He can't explain. Why is he hurt? 'It's nothing. I ran. I fell'. In the hands of a different film-maker the snatch of the watch and the chase would have been a big exciting scene, but the mood would have been out of kilter with Bresson's film. There would have been fast action and a rush of adrenaline. Instead the mood of quiet anxiety is maintained. The dialogue is banal, and there is a sense that the friend is less trusting than he was before. He already knows that the pickpocket is doing something he shouldn't, though he does not quite know what it is. He remains his friend nonetheless. In the exchange as the friends part the subtext, which becomes clear on repeat viewings, is about the girl and her affections. It is on that issue that the friends are rivals without quite knowing it, and the scene concludes with the revelation that the pickpocket has the watch, which is beautiful (he remarks that the watch is beautiful). This is misdirection, as we think that the story of the watch has reached a happy ending, whereas the more important story is taking shape without our noticing it.

Part of the beauty of the film is in its showing of the sleights of hand and misdirection involved in the petty heists: the rehearsal of the deft removal of a wristwatch from a table leg, the perfectly timed substitution of a rolled up newspaper for a snatched bag, so that the bag-carrier does not immediately notice her loss, the precisely choreographed passing of stolen goods from one person to another, each with averted gaze so they all seem to be about different business. One of the themes of the film is how we do not look where we should look to see what is going on. We read suspicion and apprehension in the movements of eyes, which are often in this film downcast, and every glance is telling, but these are things we project on to the faces. Bresson told his models not to emote. They shot and re-shot scenes, so that the action became automatic. He told the models where to look and when, and then cut things together when he was editing, so an involuntary twitch is read as a suppressed reaction. The glances are cut together so they seem to be responses, but for the models when they were being filmed they were affectless movements of the eyes.[10]

Cinema works usually by intercutting between images that we take to be temporally and spatially related to one another. Sometimes there are changes of time and place, which can be confusing if they are not signalled. Routinely there are changes of time and place to which we are blind, as we unconsciously piece the fragments together into coherence. So for example we can hear a conversation, and see the faces of the people who are conversing, and it feels as if we are maybe in the room with them, switching our attention from face to face, but the participants' faces may have been filmed on different days, maybe with a stand-in, and the dialogue in the soundtrack recorded afterwards, and then the sound effects added to give a sense of the space in which the conversation was supposed to happen. The extreme artificiality of the process is not evident to a naive viewer, and even a child can watch a film without feeling spatially at sea. We learn about and internalise a sense of spatial coherence at an early age, and unconsciously draw on it when we watch films, which in fact give very little spatial information. The illusions that are possible because of photographic or painted backdrops work only because we cannot accurately gauge the space between the actor and the background. Similarly punch-ups in films typically show a fist that stops short of hitting a body, but which seems to connect because of the sound of a real fist (much amplified) hitting a slab of meat on the soundtrack, and the actor recoiling from the apparent blow. The soundtrack conveys much more than the visual image about the space, whether it be through the acoustics or the sounds of things like traffic, birdsong or rustling fabrics. In films the sounds that give these spatial cues tend to be amplified so that we hear them more clearly than we would in real life: even if our attention is focussed elsewhere we pick up the cue about the space. We make something coherent out of the subliminal messages that we are given.

There is a film by Peter Strickland, *Berberian Sound Studio* (2012), which gives very deliberate demonstrations about the way we fuse sound and image. It shows a sound engineer who is involved with some horror films, making sound effects that accompany images that for the most part we do not see. What we do see is him slicing into vegetables, tearing handfuls of leaves apart, hacking at cabbages and melons, to the accompaniment of bloodcurdling screams from the actors impassively standing at microphones. Later in the film we see images and hear sounds that seem to belong together, and even though we have been taken through the process by which they are artfully made we cannot help but respond to them viscerally, and it is only on reflection that one sees what has been done. The fused sound and image bypass the processes of reasoning, making the viewer uneasy or horrified in response to things that are not at all clear. The experience in viewing the film is partly unconscious, and that is made very apparent here. We make sense of things without noticing that we are doing so. Our experience of the film takes cues from images and sounds, and though we might engage with a plot or a conversation in a conscious way, there are other things going on that turn out to be the things that really matter, and we find ourselves moved to tears or recoiling in horror in response to things of which we are not altogether aware as the story unfolds. The assemblage of sounds and images is traditionally credited to the film's director, but often the editor will have as great an influence on judging the effects. As viewers of films, we tend to be unaware of the film editor's role, and we allow the events to make sense before us without even knowing that there is such a person making judgements about the things to which we are responding.

There are times when we allow similar slippages in our apprehension, and our language seems to collude in misdirecting us. We do not hesitate to say that something is beautiful – a flower, a sunset – when the beauty is more precisely understood as a feeling within us. We project the feeling onto the cause of it, and imagine that the beauty is objective and set apart from ourselves.[11] In a normal conversation it would be awkward to say that a flower or a building produces in me a feeling of beauty, because our ways of speaking have inculcated a different way of describing things. It is more comfortable to say that the building or the flower is beautiful, but then we find ourselves analysing the objects in order to find the cause of their beauty, when we should be analysing ourselves. Rather than ask 'Why is this beautiful?', I should be asking 'Why do I find this beautiful?'. Serious works of art in the twenty-first century seem rarely to be aiming to stir a sense of beauty (they are more routinely described as 'challenging') and beauty has migrated to a more commercial world of advertising and fashion. The pickpocket's sleight of hand as his gaze directs our attention elsewhere, is no less skillful than that of the advertiser who attracts our attention with a beautiful model and then associates the fantasy of a product with the arousal of desire. If we have the means to buy the product, we can do so and feel that we are satisfying the desire, living the dream. The advertiser's role like the film editor's is often invisible to us, and we might not notice what made the product so appealing and why we somehow feel attached to a particular brand of car or perfume, which does much the same as its competitors. The sights and other sensations in an event fuse with our feelings about the event to make a coherent whole that can, on reflection, be dissected, but in the lived moment everything is fused together and we respond to that fusion, which is as much a projection as it is actual stimulus.

Going back to the Maison de Verre and its glass block facade: there are no traces of conventional domesticity in the signification here. When the house was built (1928–32) there was no domestic precedent for such a facade, and the glass blocks from which it was built were developed with the idea that they would be used in pavements, in order to bring illumination to underground spaces. If we search for other uses of glass blocks in external walls, the one that resonates most strongly is that of the entrance front of the Finsbury Health Centre (1935–8) designed by Berthold Lubetkin, where the main entrance doors lead into a foyer that is illuminated by the wall of glass blocks. Again this is a medical building, though the foyer space did not have a specifically medical use. It was set up before the National Health Service, and was designed to educate a working-class population to be healthier by participating in a club that encouraged healthy living as well as offering cures for infections.

The image of the Finsbury Health Centre was used, for example, in disseminating the knowledge that the disease rickets, which left children with malformed bones, could be avoided by making sure that one had adequate exposure to sunlight. The foyer was a social space for conversation, board games and cups of tea, as well as a waiting room for doctors' appointments.[12] The glass block wall here separates the health centre's interior from the outside, but allows the interior to be flooded with health-giving sunlight. The connection between rickets and sunlight was a scientific discovery of the 1920s, and prompted the connection between large areas of glazing and healthy living.[13] In the Netherlands in Amsterdam and Hilversum there were schools designed in the 1920s with large areas of glazing and scope for fresh air. Their architects were Johannes Duiker and Bernard Bijvoet, and Bijvoet collaborated with Pierre Chareau on the Maison de Verre.

The glass wall already had a connection with the idea of medical health, and that idea would be consolidated in the years that followed. In the twenty-first century the ideas are less securely linked, as glass walls have been used very widely, especially in commercial office buildings and showrooms. Moreover the idea of automatically connecting sunlight and health has been undermined, as we are more aware of the skin cancers caused by over-exposure to sunlight, and there are cases of modern rickets caused by over-use of sun-block.[14] Moreover the ultraviolet light that generates vitamin D is filtered out of sunlight by glazing, so a light-filled interior is not really a cure for rickets. The apparent healthiness of the glass wall in 1928–31 was a projection from scientific findings that did not quite apply. There are other aspects of the house that reinforce the idea of healthy living, such as the expressively overabundant plumbing, and the arrangement of bedrooms that gives every member of the family access to an outside balcony well away from the street, with fresh air and unfiltered sunlight.[15]

The white screen-wall of the Maison de Verre accepts the projection of medical connotations, but there is more than healthcare in the life that goes on around it. It is not, like Captain Ahab's version of the whale, just a reflection of the feelings that we bring to it. The wall is translucent, and some limited information comes from beyond it, but the most apparent transmission from the interior to the exterior is audible. If the house is quiet we might not notice it, but when there is a party in the grand salon and music is played, then it is not only the salon itself that is filled with the mood of the event. The music and chat drift through the wall and reterritorialise the exterior space as a *cour d'honneur*. On such an occasion one approaches the same wall with a different set of expectations and indeed will be heading for a different space, up the palatial stairs and into the grand receptive space. Its substance is the same as before, but animated by the sounds and perhaps with an idea of movements beyond the screen, if there are lights on inside for a soirée.

Also if one approaches with the expectation of reaching the event, there will have been an invitation and a set of anticipations will already be in place. The mechanism at work is projection, and of course when it works well like this we think of the shift as intuitive and commonsensical, but for it to be able to work the designer has to have held back from the over-articulate expression of any one of the purposes to which the screen wall might be put. Like Bresson's models' blankness, which looks like finely nuanced acting when it has been put into an appropriately judged sequence of sounds and images, expectations and echoes, the facade seems to shift from that of a medical facility to that of a place of entertainment, through a shift of expectations and projections that a more deliberately expressive facade would not be able to bring off.

Imagine a more traditional facade, with masonry and windows, and the same arrangement of spaces within. Some of the projection of meaning would be possible, and the movement and sound, the use that one made of the building would ensure that the building seemed to be quite appropriate for the life that went on in and around it. If the facade were very clearly legible in a way that meant we could see only and exactly the truth of what was going on beyond the façade – a medical practice tucked in below an impressive house – then the building would have been less successful that it actually is, through being rather blank but able to accept the different projections. There is a corresponding process of introjection going on, through the back holes that are our eyes, seen by another. The act of projection and assimilation of the building-as-experienced, turns us into a different sort of person. Approaching the medical facility one is territorialised as a patient, prepared for a certain kind of acquiescence in behaviour that would to someone not mentally prepared seem violating and intrusive. Without preparation there will be panic and degradation, but if one allows the building to do its work of assurance that this is a respectable place and that any loss of dignity will be temporary and hidden away, then one can leave the place with decorum. The building helps to change the visitor. Similarly if I approach for a soirée, I compose my features differently, expecting to smile and to be vivacious. I expect to make sounds, rather than try to suppress them. I expect to be open rather than guarded. The building has done different work on me.

How much this is a lesson that can or should be generally applied is open to question. There is still a role in film-making for actors who can act and emote, and those actors sometimes connect with mainstream audiences through barnstorming performances. Often, though, the audience identifies with a less histrionic character whose role is to take us to witness the showier performer's spectacle. In this understated style of performance we see the reaction-shots onto which we project our own emotions and therefore feel that this is a sympathetic character. What we might learn from this is that while there can certainly be a role for the extravagantly wrought and expressive monocultural buildings that punctuate our cities, there is also something to be said for the understated underdetermined buildings that seem to shift in character as they shift in use. Perhaps it is those buildings, which have seen a wider range of people and have accommodated a wider range of lives, that seem more like rounded characters. There are great attention-seeking egomaniacs, whom we might admire if they are doing something remarkable, and there are quieter more accommodating characters who seem better to adapt and understand, who seem better suited to the lives that we find ourselves to be leading. And perhaps it is those characters, on whom we can project our sense of appropriateness and ease, with whom we can most comfortably live, and with whom we most completely fall in love.

NOTES

1 This chapter developed from a symposium held at the Maison de Verre on 9 May 2014, and I would like to take this opportunity to thank the owners of the house, Robert and Stéphane Rubin, for supporting it. Kenneth Frampton, 'Maison de Verre', *Perspecta* 12 (1969), pp. 77–128, reprinted in *[Re]Reading Perspecta: The First Fifty Years of the Yale Architectural Journal*, ed. Robert A.M. Stern, Alan Plattus, Peggy Deamer (Cambridge, MA: The MIT Press, 2004), pp. 268–75; Dominique Vellay, *La Maison de Verre: Pierre Chareau's Modernist Masterwork* (London: Thames and Hudson, 2007).

2 Kenneth Frampton, 'Maison de Verre', p. 268.

3 Sigmund Freud, Draft H, 24.1.1895, 'Paranoia', in Sigmund Freud, *The Origins of Psycho-Analysis: Letters to Wilhelm Fliess, Drafts and Notes: 1887–1902*, ed. Marie Bonaparte, Anna Freud, Ernst Kris, trans. Eric Mosbacher and James Strachey (London: Imago, 1954), pp. 109–115, p. 111.

4 Melanie Klein, 'Notes on Some Schizoid Mechanisms' (1946), in *The Selected Melanie Klein*, ed. Juliet Mitchell (New York: Macmillan, 1986), pp. 176–200.

5 Herman Melville, *Moby-Dick or The White Whale* (New York: Harper, 1851), Chapter 36; there are many editions, for a page reference: *Moby-Dick* (London: Everyman, 1991), p. 164.

6 Gilles Deleuze and Félix Guattari, *Mille Plateaux: Capitalisme et schizophrénie tôme 2* (Paris: Minuit, 1980), trans. Brian Massumi as *A Thousand Plateaus: Capitalism and Schizophrenia volume 2* (Minneapolis, MN: University of Minnesota Press, 1987), pp. 167–91.

7 Ibid., p. 168.

8 Robert Bresson, *Notes sur le Cinématographe* (Paris: Gallimard, 1975), trans. Jonathan Griffin as *Notes on Cinematography* (New York: Urizen, 1977).

9 Ibid., p. 5.

10 There are accounts in interviews with 'The Models of *Pickpocket*' included in the supplementary material on the 2-DVD edition issued in 2005.

11 See Freud's writings about art and literature in Sigmund Freud, *Art and Literature: The Penguin Freud Library Vol. 14*, ed. Albert Dickson and Angela Richards (Harmondsworth: Penguin, 1985). This is distinct from the tradition of philosophical aesthetics; see for example Denis Dutton on empirical psychology in Denis Dutton, 'Aesthetic Universals', in Berys Gaut and Dominic McIver Lopes (eds), *The Routledge Companion to Aesthetics* (London: Routledge, 2001), pp. 206–10. My position here is aligned for example with David Hume's conviction that when we discuss beauty we are discussing feelings: David Hume, *Treatise on Human Nature*, ed. L.A. Selby-Bigge and P.H. Nidditch (Oxford: Clarendon Press, 1978 [London, 1739]), p. 471, without his conviction that human nature is universal.

12 John Allan, *Berthold Lubetkin: Architecture and the Tradition of Progress* (London: Artifice, 2013).

13 Jeffrey L.H. O'Riordana and Olav L.M. Bijvoet, 'Rickets before the Discovery of Vitamin D', in *BoneKEy Reports, the Journal of the International Bone and Mineral Society* (Chicago, IL: International Bone and Mineral Society, 8 January 2104), online doi: 10.1038/bone key.2013.212. The key article connecting sunlight with rickets was A.F. Hess and L.J. Unger, 'The Cure of Infantile Rickets by Sunlight', in *Journal of the American Medical Association* 77(1) (Chicago, IL: The American Medical Association, 1921), pp. 39–41.

14 See online http://www.telegraph.co.uk/news/health/children/10052972/Six-year-old-diagnosed-with-rickets-after usingsunscreen.html; http://sunlightinstitute.org/factor-50-sun-block-gave-woman-rickets/; http://www.dailymail. co.uk/news/article -2323506/Struck-rickets-sports-mad-boy-played-garden-smothered-sun-block.html

15 Mary Vaughan Johnson, *L'Art de Vivre Moderne in the Toilet Rooms of the Maison de Verre* (Virginia Tech, unpublished PhD thesis, 2016).

13

Imaginative Enclave in the Maison de Verre

Kati Blom

INTIMATION

This chapter discusses the relationship between spatial imagination and the unconscious in architecture. Spatial imagination relies on spatial perception and architecture's concrete qualities, which interact with our body, our unconscious and become noted in the associative intimation which we have with objects around us. For Sigmund Freud the personal sensuous experiences (percepts) are embedded in the unconscious. Any mental image has its origin in the perceptual, objectual world: 'all mental images stem from – are reproductions of – perceptions'.[1] In his second topographical model of the unconscious Freud concentrates on the super-ego, ego, and the id. One form of consciousness, consciousness of percepts, is associated with the skin and other sense organs. The skin mediates between the sensations of internal and external impulses. According to Freud memories do not surface into consciousness non-altered, rather they surface in a converted manner in the shape of preconscious mental images, dreams or other distorted sensuous data of which we were once conscious and now become again aware.

> *The reproduction of a perception as a mental image is not always a faithful copy; it can be modified by omissions or by fusion of various elements.*[2]

Personal experiences are vital to discharge the enormous energy which lies in our unconscious. Experience happens at the bodily level; it does not happen in our minds, but in our embodied minds. 'Embodied mind' is a phenomenological concept which is used for instance by Shaun Gallagher to describe the fusion of the personal and sensual (preneotic) unknown mechanism of the body.[3]

Similarly James Gibson argues for an ecological approach to visual perception. He asserts that the human body reads environmental phenomena either as negative or positive affordances, and this reading is automated, it does not need our conscious consent.[4] Objects invite us to do something or we feel the need to detach ourselves from them (withdraw, run away, turn around). In this respect the body is assumed to have functions of which we are not aware. Architects influence whether buildings are read as habitable (positive affordance) or non-habitable (negative affordance). The filtering and evaluative process of the unknown is a constant in architectural experience; sometimes these evaluations cause our body to reject a place, sometimes to feel relief when residing.

We could ask what qualities in architecture trigger mental images to surface. Because this is a relation between object and subject, it has a special concrete acuteness and particularity to it. Gaston Bachelard's poetic image is a specific materially based on the mental image, which does not rely on our memories but our body's muscular relation to the object or space which reverberates in us. Bachelard thinks these images are functions of the intimate sense (*sens intime*).[5]

This *sens intime* is a concept for which I do not find a definition in Bachelard. According to the translators of *The Imagination* by Jean-Paul Sartre, Kenneth Williford and David Rudrauf, the term had been used by Pierre-Françoise Maine de Biran, and it does not refer to 'inner sense' but 'denotes the immediate self-knowledge of consciousness that grounds our explicit reflective knowledge and cannot be identified with or reduced to the knowledge acquired from sensory organs'.[6] I am attracted to it because of its vagueness. When 'intimation' is used in social life it means to imply, hint; it refers to the hidden (unknown, or almost known, as in preconscious daydreams or mental images) and to the one who is aware of the hidden and wants to share it with someone else. Intimation in this sense is sufficient to trigger imagination because its minimal oblique expression requires more or less conscious interpretation to become fully revealed, hence its connotation of the political unconscious. I find this notion appealing. According to Jonathan Webber, who translated *The Imaginary* by Jean-Paul Sartre, this term 'the connotation of 'intimate' should be borne in mind. Sartre means to indicate our awareness of what is closest to us'.[7] The rareness and the fleeting smallness of this term attracts. The same applies to Bachelard's poetic images; they are oblique and withdrawing at the same time as they emanate an aura of synaesthesia compatible to vivid experiences of architecture.

Maurice Merleau-Ponty, in his commentary on Sartre's *The Imagination*, uses the *sens intime* in the first paragraph when he summarises the difficulties of integrating the image into our mental faculties. He sketches the scenario that Sartre, like Hume, Descartes and Leibniz, have each returned to the question of the relation between the thought and image, the common denominator being that image is a revived perception. Nevertheless, no psychology so far has disputed the existence of the image.

> *As a modification of thought or a received impression, [the image] is a real part of the thinking being. In a word, it is a thing within. Experimental psychology will never challenge that conception. It will never confront it with the data of the intimate sense (sens intime).*[8]

To have intimate knowledge of an environment is to gain and renew it at any moment, but more specifically, in some specific moments of inner turmoil or enjoyment of which we become aware. Architectural intimation also has a hint of the gestures we find in the environment, its provocations or silent suggestions in the form of 'affordances' or 'kinaesthetic gestures' or 'figures' which 'reverberate' in us. On the other hand, we also bring to the environment our own hidden passions, emerging affective dispositions, and motile intuitions. We visit and inhabit places, only to return to or reject them in our real life, or in our daydreams or dreams, due to their significance to us.

Consequently, instead of the word 'spatial image' I am arguing for the notion of 'architectural intimation', which is an event in between and in connection with the mind and the body, in the shared thin or limited Freudian surface or 'skin'. Architectural intimations cannot be reduced to sensations, because our intense personal relations project toward external real buildings and evocative objects, and consequently reflect certain qualities, strange objects, and partial objects of the environment.

THE MAISON DE VERRE

To exemplify the complexity of spatial images as architectural intimation, I take the case of imaginative enclave implied by Kenneth Frampton when he writes about the Maison de Verre, Paris (1928–32) by Pierre Chareau. In spring 2014, I wanted to read something about the house before visiting it in order to test the idea of preconceptions and refutations, as this was the theme for an intimate meeting of the Architecture's Unconscious Network in Paris. I read texts about the Maison de Verre in order to imagine the spaces emerging from the text. When I then visited the 'real' Maison de Verre I could reflect upon my preconceptions while seeing it in the flesh.

According to Kenneth Frampton the Maison de Verre is a project about furnishing rather than spatial design.[9] This remark by Frampton, which is noted by Sarah Wigglesworth[10] as being dismissive of Pierre Chareau's talent as an architect, could be an expression of the puzzlement of Frampton toward the incremental and delicate interior which transcends anything a standard design practice would provide. I interpret Frampton to mean that this building is like furniture in the context of the site. The steel frame structure was erected but no working drawings existed, as Chareau and his client Mrs Dalsace worked using models to make communication easier. This spontaneous practice is like an artistic installation.

This intuitive design process of Chareau exemplifies how architectural processes work like an unconscious matrix, which allows us to do certain things, but not others. We are not fully in control of the process. The specific locality of this particularity encases it in the influence of the old building and its occupancy of the attic, as the prehistory or pathological circumstance we cannot fully know, but the consequences of which we meet in the Maison de Verre.

TEXT AS INSPIRATION

Reading Frampton's article, my thoughts started to revolve around several puzzles, all indicating lighting conditions. Among the notes about Pierre Chareau's masterpiece, I stopped for a while at the paragraph about the glass brick walls. When imagining the effect of the famous luminous façade, I realised that one can discriminate between various different 'seeing-light' conditions in architecture. Architecture is experienced in the continuum of daylight/twilight/darkness.

The liminal case, where light-discrimination has a crucial role in spatial imaging, is the phase of twilight. At the Maison de Verre, the peculiar in-between phase of reduced illumination became an interest of mine: mainly a diffuse light, as in viewing outdoors when indoors. The instances of twilight and other in-between illumination phases are enhanced, I argue, by spatial imagination. I argue that the condition of seeing-as – in other words noticing the imaginative elements – interferes with the physiological act of sensing, thus making these moments in space more memorable. In these peculiar moments, intimations interfere with the normally unconscious way we live as bodies in space.

THE LIGHT ARRANGEMENT ON THE STAGE OF THE MAISON DE VERRE

I come from a functionalist view of light in architecture, and initially I was unwilling to dwell in these complex in-between luminous instances. The lighting conditions can be interpreted from a practical point of view: when designing, we engage with the variations of the shadows according to the angle of sunlight falling on objects. On the surface, this functionalist view dictated the design of Chareau's masterpiece. In the quarters demolished in order to construct what became the Maison de Verre, the lighting conditions were dark indeed, and consequently a lot of light was desired, to flush away the memory of the past darkness. The light on the three new floors, underneath the floor left untouched, was crucial to its new function as a doctor's practice and for the social life of the lady of the house. One could not use skylights to illuminate the floors below. The answer was to use glass bricks on the façades. Also, other manufactured building parts were used, such as train windows at the rear and the steel columns. Frampton states 'The original two floors had been so dark that the employees of the asinine old lady, who would live to be 100, were compelled to do their work during the day by artificial light'.[11] Frampton condenses two interesting cues here – attention is first given to the miserable light conditions of the old building. The second part of the jigsaw is the old lady who remained living on the second floor which made it impossible to demolish the old structure entirely. What Frampton calls 'asininity' is a combination of her old age and the prevailing dark conditions on the floors below her. This forced the designer to work around the obstacle of the second floor, which had to stay as it was. The narrative of the Maison de Verre has its mythical as well as 'rational' sides to it, adding to the surreal atmosphere which surrounds this place. We will leave the lady for a while and continue to uncover the functional reasons for Chareau's lighting manoeuvres.

When Frampton's text continues things start to look more puzzling than my rationalist view allowed – the text and my imagination guided me into a building which I had never visited before. He mentions the glass brick wall with 'translucent Nevada lenses' which diffuses the light and makes one experience the condition of the outdoors when indoors, intensified by the fact that the 'real' outdoors is invisible, when in the living room.

> *This light diffusion simulates a quality of illumination comparable to that experienced in the open air, thus contributing to the experience of the house as a 'world within the world', enclosing its own hierarchy of public and private spaces (emphasis mine).*[12]

Frampton's text continues to analyse the house's different grids and elementary spatial and furniture constellations; that obviously being his 'world within the world'.

The text acts as a trap for the spatial imagination. In what ways are the diffused light conditions outdoors and indoors comparable? To which grades of seeing-as does he refer? As-outdoors, or as-if-outdoors? Or only partially the same: almost-as-outdoors? In which capacity then could the indoors be as the outdoors? The only thing for sure is the fact that there is no visual connection to the outdoors, and that makes this enclosure prone to the imagination, which – to borrow Frampton's words – is another kind of 'world within the world', i.e. an imaginative enclave, more like a claustrophobic cell than breathing or bathing in light. It is truly a *mise-en-scène* of the eradication of darkness. The actual description, and indeed also my experience once in the Maison de Verre, suggests that the light, which illuminates the reception room, is diffuse and disorientating, even nauseous. The light is not diffuse in a flickering manner but rather ambient or homogeneous. This condition may have been different earlier, as the original 'Nevada bricks' have a more textured and uneven colour finish.

According to Mary Vaughan Johnson, many visitors feel claustrophobic in the reception hall (Architecture's Unconscious Network second meeting, 9 May 2014). This is because of the effect of the glass bricks. First, the screen dominates, as its area is the same as that of the floor. Second, the diffuse light condition is a very particular one. The light, when diffused, is like that of a cloudy day, where the endless muted reflections of the sun's rays through the clouds make the environment shadowless. The illumination is not full of scintillation but damped. The glow of the diffuse reflective light is similar to that on the street in the seventh arrondissement.

It is possible to experience very similar conditions in a forest or jungle where the source of the light is undefined. According to old photographs, Mme Dalsace had large plants inside, just behind the glass brick wall, and that may have enhanced the idea of being as-if-outside when being entertained in the living room. Similarly, the light conditions in dreams possess the quality of an undefined light source, similar to the morning shimmer just before the sun actually rises. These conditions are all exceptional, short lived, or imaginary. They are liminal experiences which heighten the intensity of absorption in the sensory system.

In order to induce make-believe, the owners lit the 'floodlights' in front of the garden and front façades in the evening to prolong this condition. The floodlights are more powerful than any of the lights used inside, and the glass bricks reflect back some of the light from the floodlights so that the façade's surface is effectively a translucent skin. Frampton, continuing the sentence cited above implying the imaginative, 'as-outdoors', enclave of the Maison de Verre, states, 'This condition

Photo: Editions du Salon des Arts Ménagers.

13.1 The reception hall. In Kenneth Frampton, 'Maison de Verre', *Arena, The Architectural Association Journal*, 81(901) (1966), p. 262. The Architectural Association, Éditions du Salon des Arts Ménagers. À hauteur de la reproduction: Les Arts Décoratifs, Paris / Musée des Arts Décoratifs. Dans la rubrique crédit photographique: photo distr. Les Arts Décoratifs, Paris.

is maintained at night, when the interior of the house is again illuminated by light diffusing through its glass from the flood-lights mounted off the forecourt and garden facades'.[13] This text reinforces the conjecture that once you are in, you are in the phenomenal 'outdoors', without temporal interruption, without seasonal or nocturnal cessation which normally is experienced when 'in the open air'. The delicate condition of sensing the descending and diminishing daylight is replaced by eternal in-between-ness. The conscious image or setting of the outdoors, is rendered atmospherically stable but its effect is surreal and unsettling. The impossible task of capturing and keeping safe the passing light is felt in the hugeness of the living room and its symmetrical cubistic void which illuminates the cultured objects of the owners with a mystical inner glow (Figure 13.1). Artificiality is part of its lure and enigmatic attraction.

THE STAGE AS UNSTABLE IMAGINATIVE ENCLAVE IN DIFFUSE LIGHT

Certainly, the reasons for the use of these glass bricks are complex; one of them being the need for privacy for both the clients of Dr Dalsace and the visitors in Mme Dalsace's salon. Furthermore, the social niche of the inhabitants and their guests or clients is physically present in the exclusiveness of the huge imposing front façade, not ever found before. The psychological need for a social enclave or difference may be seen in the urge for the modern, avant-garde. The knowledge of this peculiar house's role in the life of high-class ladies or cultural personalities is, of course, part of the informed visitors' aesthetic appreciation; at the same time it covers this house with an overstated sense of social exclusion. The Maison de Verre operates as a hostile fortress, or a confrontational 'object'.

What I imagined when reading the text is that once you are in this building, it enclaves you within a certain local atmosphere. It is due to the glowing paraphernalia. The objects and the rubber floor become thinner in the prevailing artificiality. Instead, twilight gains materiality: its quasi-objective character is explained by Gernot Böhme when he studies the atmospheric qualities of twilight: 'Furthermore, the twilight has a character of a something, almost something which counters us'.[14] According to Böhme, what is remarkable about twilight is that once noted it has a certain thingness about it, hence it becomes quasi-objective. You can understand quasi-objective in two ways – either it is a thing we encounter outside ourselves that is other to us, or it is about the diffuse light as concrete volume.[15] It is the unconscious becoming pre-conscious in the sensing of the space. The quasi-stuff of the never-ending twilight and consequential artificiality resides over the furniture and planes of the living room.[16] The diffuse illumination circumstance is, in effect, darkness-in-waiting, and the ghostly images or mirages start to overcome the reality; the architectural intimation becomes eerie.

Let us continue with Böhme's phenomenology. Further, in 'Das Atmosphärische der Dämmerung', Böhme notes that the twilight is sensed before it is perceived, and we automatically change our mannerisms. Like darkness, so twilight is a limiting factor, not because we choose this but because we are affected by the miniscule changes in sensual input. Unconscious bodily nerve impulses seep into our mindset, saturating it with intuitions of rest or the cessation of daily activities. Encountering the twilight means noticing not only it, but also the changes it makes in social and natural life.

SEEING-AS: THE MAGIC OF SPATIAL THEATRE

On the day when I visited the Maison de Verre, one remarkable encounter happened, which made me think of the French National Library and W.G. Sebald's image of it as an ocean-liner.[17] The stairs from the ground floor leaving the reception hall have no handrails. They are quite wide, and the partial walls are further away. When ascending you have to look down to your feet, and the stairs reveal their structure, which is not bolted, but rests on hooks. You are elevated from the ground level and you ascend into a different world altogether. The feeling of voyage or travelling on sea is emphasised by some window features reminding you of industrial origins. Kinaesthetically, when entering the living room, the guest is boarding a ship, not the home of Mrs Dalsace.

13.2 Fujiko Nakaya, Veil (2014), in Philip Johnson's Glass House (1949). Courtesy of Richard Barnes, 2013.

The disappearance of the interior which is replaced by a make-believe outdoors or ocean ship deck is part of the operation of re-figuring or relocating the outdoors, reinforcing one's unsettling location. Are we in a phenomenal outdoors? Or somewhere in imaginative space? Before I can answer the question, let me point out a parallel case.

When you enter Philip Johnson's Glass House (1949), the interior seems to disappear – it seems to become empty, while you are perceptually transported outwards. In normal situations, being inside the house means that one may be drawn visually outside. This translocation was made apparent when fog was introduced in 2014 by artist Fujiko Nakaya in an installation on the premises (Figure 13.2). The temporal circumstances might have locked the spectator inside the house when transparent glass suddenly became opaque. Inside the glass box which is circumscribed by the fog the spectator realises the existence of the indoors, which enclaves him, similarly to the Maison de Verre. Are you here, but amidst the fog also in the imagined outdoors? The light conditions may be similar, and you are not only connected to the outdoors visually: this must be a make-believe enclave of the outdoors. The imaginative enclave is unstable and free in its interpretations. The unconscious seeps into the real concrete world. In constant checking of the outdoor-indoor constellation you are in an intimate relationship with architecture. This is an intimation which has more seen-as than as-if qualities, because the connections between the outdoors and indoors are severed (Figure 13.3).

13.3 Enclave in fog of Philip Johnson Glass House. Courtesy of Kati Blom, 2015.

PHENOMENAL EPISODE

'Inattentional blindness' is a condition where the subject fails to notice a fully visible but unexpected object because her attention has been engaged by another object. The word describes a normal condition, which makes one's brain discard information one is not focussed on for the moment. In the recent exhibition *Inattentional Blindness* (2014) in Galeri Zilberman, Turkey, Liddy Scheffknecht presented a work 'Crop' where the shadow from the window display could be misread as a shadow of a plant (Figure 13.4). The shadow is wrongly read as attached to the plant which acts as if it were an obstacle in between the sun and the floor. The 'real' shadow is in its normal position on the other side of the pot. The blurred, 'real' shadow and the sharp, 'surreal' shadow co-exist. As such, there is nothing alarming in this because it represents the usual state of affairs where there are many light sources present. But the existence of the non-rational in this topological puzzle is made clear when you see the white 'shadow' on the glass pane. The irrational link is established – the virtual enclave created. The surreal condition creates a subspace where the enigmatic conditions prevail, and even if we understand that we have erred, it is hard not to notice the surreal. To realise the error one must pause and solve the puzzle consciously. In the unconscious there are, according to Freud, no negations or contradictions, but when we start to verbalise these preconscious 'impossibilities', the negation (*Verneinung*) marks the presence of the unconscious – we must halt to pay attention.[18] This also shows the blindness of the unconscious to causality. In such an instance, the artwork becomes a miracle.

13.4 Liddy Scheffknecht, CROP, 2013. Lambda print, 100 × 130 cm, *Inattentional Blindness*, 10 January–22 February 2014, Galeri Zilberman, Beyoğlu/ Istanbul, Turkey.

Vivian Mizrahi, in a recent symposium about shadows, images and transparencies, claimed that air, glass, water and mirrors are all mediating substances. She observes that the glass pane of the window, which causes the sharp shadow, goes unnoticed. We are not sure of the ontological status of the white figure – it could be yet another shadow caused by the mystical redirection of the sun's rays hanging in the air like a ghost or phantom. We can understand the transmission of the rays via glass only rationally, for the glass-sun link is not concretely present. It is certain that glass's subliminality or non-phenomenality contributes to the increased sense of the surreal in the cast shadow. Similarly, the glass bricks of the Maison de Verre do not phenomenally contribute to the twilight which remains unexplained. Consequently, also the glass bricks become enigmatic. The surreal is, according to Merleau-Ponty, the attachment we have to objects in their infancy, in pre-perceptive directness. He refers to André Breton's view on objects of desire, in vertiginous proximity.[19]

OBJECTS OF DESIRE OR REPULSION

In the Maison de Verre, the supporting columns are 'odd objects' of which we become aware in the diffuse light. The old photo (Figure 13.1) shows clearly how

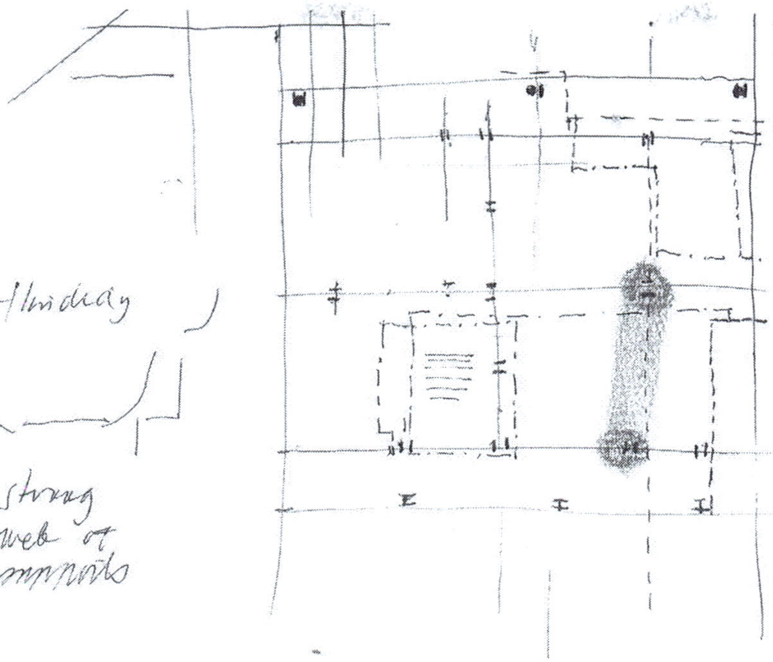

13.5 Oddly located columns which do not coincide with anything in the hall. Courtesy of Kati Blom, 2015.

13.6 The living room: no signs of the columns identified in the plans. One particular column disappeared (the one on the right, close to the bookshelves). In Kenneth Frampton, 'Maison de Verre', *Arena, The Architectural Association Journal*, 81(901) (1966), p. 261. Courtesy of Michael Carapetian, 1966.

the industrial pillars stand out among the bourgeois comforts. The columns are a structural necessity but their position in plan appears random. Before visiting the Maison de Verre, I found myself intrigued by the immaculate minute design, where some elements in the drawings are incomprehensible. I could not, for instance, understand the meaning of the columns which are present in the drawing (Figure 13.5), but I felt no trace of them in the interior photo credited to Éditions du Salon des Arts Ménagers (Figure 13.6). Things did not align. These absurd permutations may have resulted either from the hidden and open function of the structure but also from the associative dialogue between Mrs Dalsace and Pierre Chareau.

In my aesthetic consideration, I take into account the facts of which I am aware. Relating back to the old asinine lady and the darkness of the living quarters, the persistence of the condition remains in the unstable image of the prolonged twilight or diffuse light condition. The presence of the not-belonging parts (columns, glass bricks and the repeated encounter with them elsewhere in the house) work as the white shadow in Liddy Scheffknecht's artwork – they are not integrated into the experience and thus interrogate the stable nature of the concrete architectural configuration. Their irrationality invites other images or poetic explanations to enter; Bachelard's singular material imaginings take place. The ghost of the lady is everywhere, in the luminous façade and in the way glass bricks are used inside close to the doctor's surgery. Her existence is not private, for it is very concretely part of the house. The Maison de Verre probes the darkness and twilight, the origin of which is located in the repository of the former second floor.

This is repeated and recreated in the unconscious of the architectural pilgrims who take photographs and always try to frame the picture to include only the new façade, and eliminate the attic as non-existent. Even for me, it took a while to realise the upper area did exist, although I had seen several hundred pictures of the house, both professional and amateur. The sections or plans suppress the upper floor, and Frampton's second visit as described in his article 'Maison de Verre' (1969) is no exception, by framing out the unnecessary relic (Figure 13.8). In contrast, Frampton's cross-section from 1966 shows boldly the empty, ghostly upper residence (Figure 13.7).

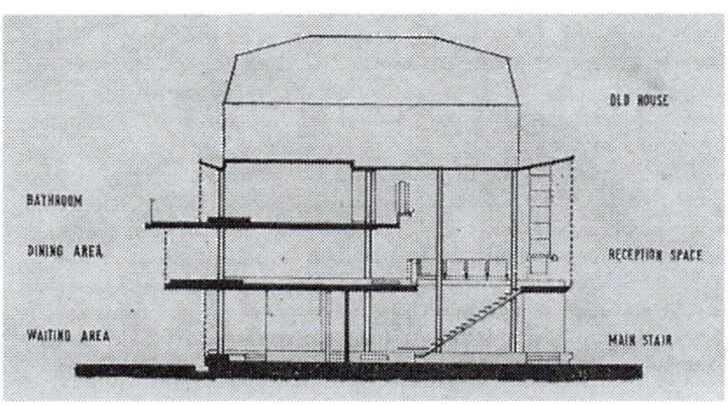

13.7 Cross-section. In Kenneth Frampton, 'Maison de Verre', *Arena, The Architectural Association Journal*, 81(901) (1966), p. 258. Kenneth Frampton, 1966.

The mixture of my preconceptions in the form of the images was reinforced by other unsettling objects in the actual building. The real encounter with the glass house is a mixture of different thoughts, memories, images, allusions and prenominal acts. All these mental and visceral elements contribute to the whole house to become an intimation as the stairs, cupboards and glass walls rise up to remind the visitor of the magic initiated. It is not only the details which invigorate us; we agree that the building itself is vibrating (Figure 13.9).

The image of the Maison de Verre is a configuration of things we already know or have experienced, or can imagine from Frampton's texts. This architectural intimation is a fragile conglomeration of both percepts and imagined entities. According to Edmund Husserl, the imagined entity (image) is embedded in the

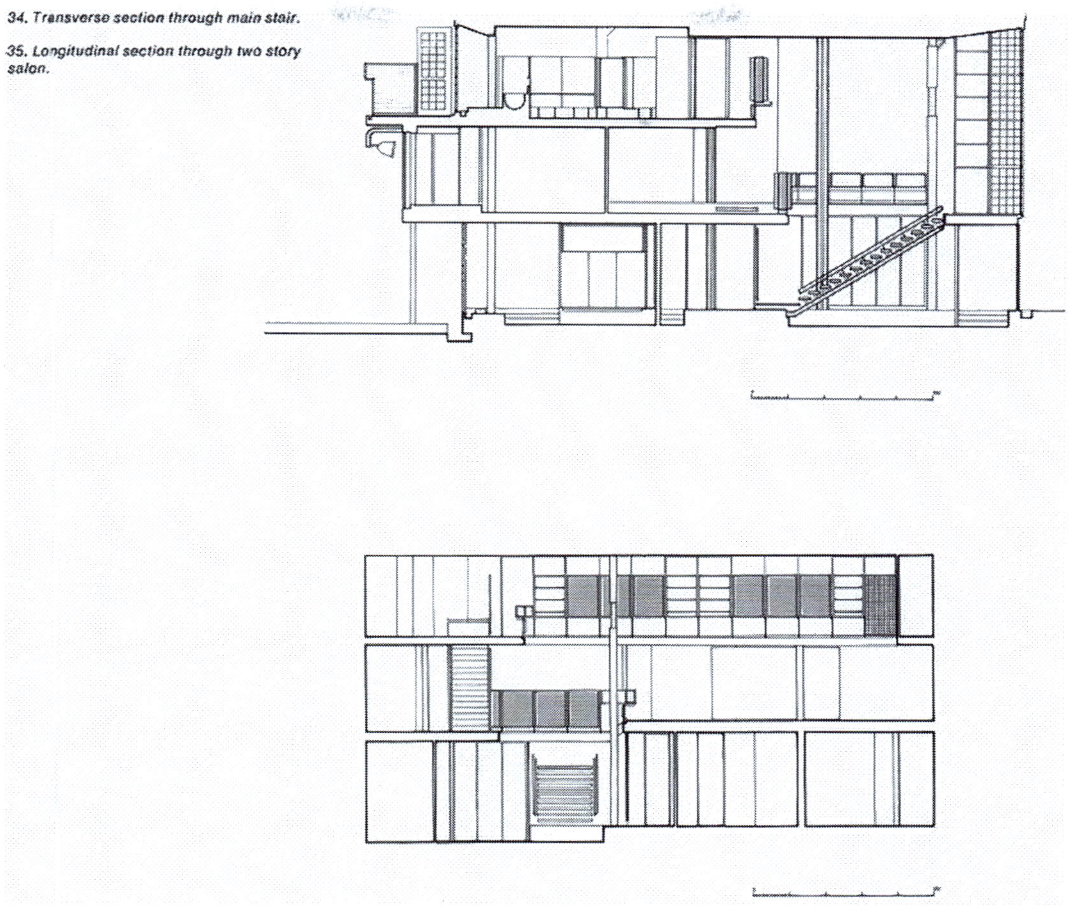

13.8 Cross-section. 'Maison de Verre', *Perspecta*, 12 (1969), p. 91. Kenneth Frampton, 1969.

perception: the perceptual conflict assures we are dealing with a mental image. (What is it? An image or an object?)[20] For Gaston Bachelard the material imagination is a creative process initiated by conflicts.[21] The unconscious, according to Freud, is an accumulation of perceptions (sensual input) either repressed or not: there is no mental image (presentation, i.e. *Vorstellung*) which has not been once a percept.[22]

One similar description can be found in Sartre's *The Imaginary*. A female actor, Françonay, mimics Maurice Chevalier (1888–1972); as the spectators know, it is a woman giving the impression of the famous male comedian and singer.[23] With a straw hat tilted diagonally over her head, the reality of a woman is changed to the illusion of a man not present. The image to which we agree is attended by a strong feeling of the presence of Chevalier. There is a conscious shift from the real woman to the impression of Chevalier. The physiognomy of 'Chevalier' affects one's body at the same time as one is conscious of the contradiction. Sartre asserts that the two realities, the real woman and the memory of Chevalier, are synthesised, and thus give a certain joyfulness and depth to the experience of the imitator's performance. 'This is ultimately because only a formal will can prevent consciousness from slipping from the level of the image to that of the perception'.[24]

13.9 'Forecourt night view of house, illuminated both internally and externally'. The blackness of the attic is another noticeable feature. 'Maison de Verre', *Perspecta*, 12 (1969), p. 93. Michael Carapetian, 1969.

Percepts and illusions co-exist or are very close to each other. Husserl notes this closeness of fantasy and perceptions, and ponders about different possibilities of one phenomenon existing in either of the worlds; thus, some phenomena would be in the process of 'becoming' to exist in either of the realms, in an in-between zone.[25]

It is up to the observer to maintain the illusion of a man instead of the reality of a woman. The state is not that of the equilibrium. It is a very fragile intimation alternating between reality and imagination. The Maison de Verre has a simultaneous double life. We feel that the pretension in the setting reveals something, which is hard to maintain except by will. And the imagination adds to this physicality, infused by the sustained outdoor lighting, some precise artificiality and haunting beauty.

IMAGINATIVE ENCLAVE IS AN ENCLOSURE IMAGINING CONNECTIONS

In the case of the Maison de Verre, the space is really a place. Hence it is a limited, Aristotelian enclosure. The glass brick wall and especially the surfaces, a luminous miracle, comprise the borders of the sensuous locality. All surfaces in the living room, as the screen of the Maison de Verre suggests, are impenetrable vertical surfaces with some notion of penetrable partitions. The visual connections are terminated; there is no way of any substantial sensuous testimony of the reality of outside. The only thing reminding me of the existence of the reality is diffuse light. The persistence of the otherwise short-lived twilight is disturbing and contributes to the realisation of the increasing artificiality of the space. The real vertical walls are mysteriously torn apart when the visitor starts to imagine the outdoors, trying to make sense of the peculiar stage, doing away with the real verticals to reinforce the fictional as-if image of the outdoors; getting to grips with the material reality which is vanishing in front of the observer is an example of vertiginous proximity, as Merleau-Ponty notes. So the connections in this enclave are imaginative, not real.

SCINTILLATION AND ARCHITECTURE: CONTRASTS IN SENSING BRIGHTNESS

Let us return to the focus of my interest in Frampton's 1966 article about the Maison de Verre, the illumination. Frampton assumes that the glass brick façade was used to create a light condition inside the house compatible to that outside. He especially mentions the diffuse light, which is prolonged in the evenings by light fixtures located outside the façades. Before visiting the house, I investigated the photos to detect the diffuse light conditions, which had been referred to in the text.

The photo (Figure 13.6) reveals a peculiar artificiality, as the living room is photographed from a spot in the balcony close to the façade, facing towards the objects, furniture and the surfaces, which are bathed in this indirect, shadowless light. Why is this so peculiar that it further animates me, and later even causes nausea? One explanation is that what I imagine does not correspond to anything I can express verbally, even if it was influenced by Frampton's text. I wanted to see what the text implies, because the text itself was full of fictional or poetic imagery (old asinine lady, her 100 years of life, darkness of the previous living quarters, etc.), which revives an oneiric presence.

I have one line of inquiry in order to study further the dullness or dead quality of the light in the photo. It is obviously important to eliminate direct sunlight, but consequently this setting dampened the possible glittering or iridescence, and consequently, even if not intentionally, minimised the variations of lustre in the interior of the Maison de Verre. The lustre of the surfaces is a key to this growing uneasiness due to the diffuse light.

The nature of the surface has deeper significance to our visual perception than the form or shape of an object. According to James Gibson, surfaces are detected by human sight with absolute and astonishing accuracy; we are able to distinguish the texture, viscosity, reflectivity, density or edibility of the things around us, to the extent that Gibson denies that the human visual system is capable of 'seeing' depth or three-dimensionality space.[26] The information we gain is dependent on the sensed stimulus but also on the grade of illumination, as homogeneous ambient brightness and darkness may fail to stimulate sight receptors, and consequently no information is available to the visual system.[27] The percept is then that of 'nothingness' if the condition prevails.[28] The dullness or lifeless appearances of things are unconsciously noted, and without doubt the glossiness or iridescence; and the possibility of observing them is an important psychological factor. Lack of direct sunlight makes the observation of the grade of brightness of things more difficult.

In architecture, the shadow or lack of shadow is of interest, for it has an impact on the way we perceive space. Consequently, the dullness of diffuse light in the Maison de Verre eliminates sharp shadows and direct sunlight, and contributes to the ghostly artificiality of the setting. The glimmer or flickering translucency is minimised, as noted earlier in this chapter, due to the newer, more perfect glass bricks. Even if the earlier ones also eliminated the sharpest differences, they seemed to maintain some of the flickering quality of the light coming through the foliage, for instance. The light entropy contributes to the claustrophobic or unsettling impact that the Maison de Verre's light condition has on some visitors.

Finnish architect Juha Leiviskä for instance notes how sharp corners, and accordingly sharp shadows, are important in architecture, as round corners or curved walls eliminate the shadow and the spatial clarity is lost.[29] He does not approve of the concave walls in Reima Pietilä's Student Union Building (1966) of the Dipoli Conference Centre on the Otamiemi Campus of Aalto University in Espoo, Finland. In contrast, Juhani Pallasmaa muses enthusiastically about the chiaroscuro of Alvar Aalto's round walls:

> *The emotive impact of light is highly intensified when it is perceived as an imaginary substance. Alvar Aalto's lighting arrangements frequently reflect light from a curved white surface and the chiaroscuro of the rounded surfaces give light an experiential plasticity, materiality, and heightened presence.*[30]

Juha Leiviskä's designs create a different, optically vibrant spatial experience, where the planes are cut precisely to punctuate the space, which then radiates and results in an undulating light condition, a bit like in the play of light in water, never still, rather scattered rhythmically. The sharp corners are in contrast with shimmering white planes giving the rooms a distinct spatiality.[31] In the Finnish language there is a word for 'water glimmer', a short-lived *vedenvälke*. For me the presence of life in the form of glittering or vibration is an important quality in the environment. It has been said that in Nordic architecture, the light has a central role, and possibly this is due to the sensitiveness to radiance or 'coldness-incandescence' in snow and ice. Nordic people can tell when the ice no longer supports them by its radiance. This is due to decreased glossiness, which in turn is caused by the consistency of ice becoming more liquid. Radiance changes in all living things. We can unconsciously know the presence or absence of living energy.

DISCUSSION

In the architectural intimation we fuse previous knowledge or memories with the acuteness of the concrete object-world in order to create a personal, subjective relationship with an environment. The surreality is triggered in the intimation if the real qualities are substituted by mental images surfacing mainly from our unconscious. These preconscious surreal images are in conflict with our day-time consciousness, causing doubt or hesitation, even nausea in the environmental experience.

Psychoanalyst and author Christopher Bollas describes well how the everyday environment becomes part of our daily associative thinking. Each evocative object resonates in us in a particular way, either causing attachment and enjoyment, or dejection. As in Freud's dream work where free association and creative imagining are crucial, orientating ourselves in a human environment can liberate our kinaesthetic and emotive being, and create new connections and amplify spatial intimations.

According to Bollas, monumental buildings symbolise patriarchal stiffness, and some of them may be created as 'archi-excrement' by architects. Consequently, the public experiences them as offensive.[32] Buildings, when they are designed as identifiable monuments, evoke memories or mental images similar to other evocative, smaller objects.[33] More precisely, this term 'evocative object' refers to inner associations: 'The term "evocative object" was used in psychology to refer to the self's capacity to evoke an internal mental representation of the object'.[34] In the Maison de Verre, the ambiguous columns and glass bricks in the square outer wall were evocative objects to me. The vague disposition of the columns in the photo and their disappearance in the actual nauseating diffuse light conditions, present in the photo, made certain other associations surface from my unconscious.

Such an object in this sense may not always revive good memories, or even any mental images which linger in the preconscious. The significance of 'ugly buildings' or revolting objects is also to discharge some unconscious energy to dejection (melancholia); the attitude or pose towards this particular building or object may not ever change, or may change during one's lifetime.[35] The most important factor that contributed to the emergence of the fragile paradoxical architectural image was the diffuse and dampening light conditions which I could sense in the old black and white interior photos, and also when I visited the house. Absence of iridescence and oscillating natural light intensified the artificiality of the interior and made the twilight itself quasi-objective and surreal, enclosing me rather than connecting me to the world outside.

In the case study of the imaginative enclave caused by the Maison de Verre, I have also pointed out that the architectural processes themselves can be seen to reflect unconscious acts from our side (the way we photograph or redraw this particular building without its attic, or the way we design buildings in an ad hoc manner). Also the prehistory of any building, like the partly demolished ancestor of the Maison de Verre, can haunt the existing building. The Maison de Verre's specific made-up construction is a phantom of a specific trauma of not being able to reject the dependency of the earlier occupancy. I have explained how this prehistory is felt at a personal level, during a fleeting architectural intimation.

NOTES

1 Sigmund Freud, *The Unconscious*, trans. Graham Frankland, with an introduction by Mark Cousins (London: Penguin Books, 2005), p. 91.

2 Ibid.

3 Shaun Gallagher, *How the Body Shapes the Mind* (Oxford: Oxford University Press, 2005), p. 2.

4 James J. Gibson, *The Ecological Approach to Visual Perception* (Hillsdale, NJ: Lawrence Erlbaum Associates, 1986), pp. 127–43.

5 Gaston Bachelard, *The Poetics of Space*, trans. Maria Jolas (Boston, MA: Beacon Press, 1969), pp. 100–102.

6 Kenneth Williford and David Rudrauf, 'Translators' Introduction', in Jean-Paul Sartre, *The Imagination* (London: Routledge, 2012), p. xxxviii.

7 Jonathan Webber, 'Notes on Translation', in Jean-Paul Sartre, *The Imaginary: A Phenomenological Psychology of the Imagination* (London: Routledge, 2004), p. xxx.

8 Maurice Merleau-Ponty, '*Review of L'Imagination*', in Jean-Paul Sartre, *The Imagination*, pp. 162–71, p. 162.

9 Kenneth Frampton, 'Maison de Verre', in *Perspecta*, 12 (Cambridge, MA: The MIT Press, 1969), pp. 77–128, p. 77.

10 Sarah Wigglesworth, 'Maison de Verre: Sections through an In-vitro Conception', in *Journal of Architecture*, 3(3) (London: Routledge, The Royal Institute of British Architects, 1998), pp. 263–86, p. 265.

11 Kenneth Frampton, 'Maison de Verre', in *Arena, The Architectural Association Journal*, 81(901) (London: The Architectural Association, 1966), pp. 257–62, p. 258.

12 Ibid., p. 259.

13 Ibid.

14 Gernot Böhme, 'Das Atmosphärische der Dämmerung', in *Anmutungen: Über das Atmospärische* (Stuttgart: Editions Tertium, 1998), pp. 13–34, p. 19: 'Vielmehr hat sie selbst [die Dämmerung] den Charakter eines Etwas, fast eines Gegenstandes'. Translated by the author.

15 This is repeated in Jean-Paul Sartre, *The Imaginary*, p. 90, when he claims that 'images' are not things, i.e. precepts of actual things, but quasi-objective 'melanges'.

16 It is worthwhile mentioning that the quasi-objective stuff over the objects when perceived in exceptional light conditions reveal quickly how depth is relative to us, and loses its 'objectual' character. The reflections from the objects' surfaces compromise 'voluminosity', the thickness of air full of undefined redirected sun rays from undefined sources. See for instance Maurice Merleau-Ponty, *Phenomenology of Perception*, trans. Colin Smith (London: Routledge, 2002), p. 310. Oliver Sacks counts these instances when we become aware of the undefined depth as pre-perceptions: Oliver Sacks, *A Leg to Stand On* (London: Picador, 2012), p. 113.

17 W.G. Sebald, *Austerlitz*, trans. Anthea Bell (London: Penguin Books, 2002), p. 387.

18 Sigmund Freud, *The Unconscious*, pp. 4, 70, 91–2. Furthermore, Freud states that: 'recognition of the unconscious by the ego is always expressed in negative formulations' (p. 92).

19 Maurice Merleau-Ponty, *The World of Perception*, trans. Oliver David (London: Routledge, 2004), p. 66.

20 See John B. Brough, 'Translator's Introduction', in Edmund Husserl, *Phantasy, Image Consciousness, and Memory (1898–1925)*, trans. John B. Brough (Husserliana, vol. XXIII) (Dordrecht: Springer, 2005), pp. xxix–lxviii, pp. xlvii, xlix.

21 Gaston Bachelard, *The Poetics of Space*, pp. 88–9.

22 Sigmund Freud, *Johdatus narsismiin ja muita esseitä* [*Introduction to Narcissism and Other Essays*], trans. Mirja Rutanen, ed. Ilpo Helén and Mirja Rutanen (Helsinki: Love Kirjat, 1993), pp. 130–31.

23 Jean-Paul Sartre, *The Imaginary*, pp. 25–9.

24 Ibid., p. 29.

25 Edmund Husserl, *Phantasy, Image Consciousness, and Memory (1898–1925)*, p. 141.

26 James J. Gibson, *The Ecological Approach to Visual Perception*, pp. 22–32, 83.

27 Ibid., p. 54.

28 Ibid., pp. 150–51.

29 Juha Leiviskä, 'Rakennustaiteen keinot tänään' ['Contemporary means for the art of building'], in *Arkkitehti, Finnish Architectural Review*, (5) (Helsinki: Finnish Association of Architects, 1976).

30 Juhani Pallasmaa, 'Tangible Light: Integration of the Senses and Architecture', in *D&A* (07) (Hørsholm: Velux Group, 2008), pp. 8–13, p. 13.

31 Kati Blom, 'Undulating Light', *Arkkitehti, Finnish Architectural Review*, (3) (2004), pp. 72–85.

32 Christopher Bollas, *The Evocative Object World* (London: Routledge, 2008), p. 68.

33 Ibid., p. 52.

34 Ibid., p. 86.

35 Ibid., pp. 90–94.

14

Part-architecture: The Manifest and the Hidden in the Maison de Verre and the *Large Glass* (or Towards an Architectural Unconscious)

Emma Cheatle

INTRODUCTION

At the opening of the twentieth century Sigmund Freud wrote that the role of psychoanalytic research is 'to uncover connections by tracing what is manifest back to what is hidden'.[1] Some 50 years later Jacques Lacan developed Freud's thinking on the part-object and unconscious. This chapter traces my own critical architectural research method, 'part-architecture', which develops a framework for analysing and recovering the hidden or repressed past to a piece of architecture. Part-architecture is heavily influenced by Lacan's psychoanalytic ideas and the art historiography of Rosalind Krauss.[2]

14.1 Pierre Chareau, Maison de Verre, 1928–32, 'Nevada' glass lens to front façade. Photo by Emma Cheatle, 2012. With permission of Robert Rubin.

In my doctoral thesis, 'Part-architecture: The *Maison de Verre* through the *Large Glass*', I use part-architecture to draw out the hidden aspects of Pierre Chareau's Maison de Verre (1928–32) through its relationship to Marcel Duchamp's artwork the *Large Glass* (1915–23).[3] The two works are not chosen for their similarity, but appear to already be aligned. My approach is not a dialectical one. Rather than oppositional or contrasting, I argue each proposes and contextualises the other. They are works within works, or doubles. Rather than merely providing evidence to reinforce the other, a joint critique produces new constructions; heterogeneous yet related spaces.

Designed for progressive gynaecologist Dr Jean Dalsace and his wife, Annie Dalsace, the Maison de Verre combines a family home with a gynaecology clinic in a 'free-plan' enclosed by translucent glass curtain walls (Figure 14.2). In the 1930s numerous women visited the clinic, seeking sexual health treatments, including illegal contraception advice and abortion. There are, though, no records of their presence.[4] The enigmatic artwork, the *Large Glass*, was constructed by Marcel Duchamp between 1915 and 1923. Nearly three metres high and two wide, it is divided horizontally into two glass panels on which a narrative of unconsummated sex between the Bride above and the Bachelors below is played out. Their relations are composed through figures (instruments and bodies) made of oil, varnish, lead foil, lead wire, silver and dust applied painstakingly to the back surface of the panes of glass. Duchamp's notes, an integral part of the artwork, suggest a complex discourse on sexuality in the early twentieth century.[5] The figures appear to be floating or trapped on its flat transparent surfaces. Looking at them, in elevation, in perspective, through the glass, they spatialise Duchamp's resistance to the Parisian social mores of marriage and procreation.

Twentieth century historians reinforce a functionalist image of the Maison de Verre.[6] Focussing on structure, form and architectural detailing, the interior is described empty of historical inhabitation, or social context. Presented as a house, the clinic is overlooked. Further, there is little archival material through which to reassess it. Reacting to this, part-architecture uncovers the history and inhabitations hidden beneath the image of the building. Physically entering the spaces, I analyse interiors, materials and objects as transitional connections between the building and the body, to tell a fragmented and ambiguous story of progressive sexuality in the 1930s. The *Large Glass* acts as a relational device. A response to the sexual constraints of 1910s and 1920s Paris, it appears to anticipate the building, especially the relations between domesticity and sexuality. The *Large Glass* presents these themes in three ways: firstly, through its use of glass as a medium to register otherwise concealed corporeal experiences; secondly, through dust as a collection of past body fragments; and, thirdly, with a discourse on air as an underlying communicative system.

This chapter is composed of two parts. Firstly, a theoretical part explores Krauss and Lacan's work on the unconscious, 'L Schema' and part-object. Here, I build the method of part-architecture – its identification of the enticement of a specific building or artwork, the yearning to understand it beyond the limitations of available material and connect with it as a corporeal subject – towards an architectural unconscious. Secondly, following the glass, dust and air themes offered by the *Large Glass*, I present some fragments of part-architecture writing which recover the Maison de Verre. Written and visual descriptions combine history, theory, narrative and design to explore past inhabitations and desires, in the present.

14.2 Pierre Chareau, Maison de Verre, Paris, 1928–32. Photo by Emma Cheatle, 2009. With permission of Robert Rubin.

1. PART-OBJECT

In *The Optical Unconscious* Rosalind Krauss employs an interdisciplinary approach to rethink art history. In particular, she adopts Jacques Lacan's diagram, the L Schema – a psychoanalytic construction of the relations between the subject and his objects – and the associated concept of the part-object, to explore the way certain art objects stimulate, through their 'optical unconscious', a corporeal response in the spectator.[7]

Lacan used numerous schemata to give topological and mathematical accounts of his psychoanalytic theories. First drawn in the 1950s, the L Schema describes the way a subject, the person in question, is not a single unified concept, but 'symbolised' or composed over time as a number of interrelated parts or objects (Figure 14.3). These parts are given the following notations: (Es) *S* is the subject; *a'* (usually termed by Lacan as *objet petit a*), is the 'little other' or part-object; *A* is the 'big Other', or society; and *a* is *moi* or the ego. The subject, (Es) *S*, comes into knowledge of himself during what Lacan terms the mirror stage.[8] On recognising himself in the mirror line, or imaginary relation, he splits into his part-objects, *a'*, and his ego, *a*.[9] He measures himself against the imperatives of society, *A*, forming repressions, which are inscribed on, but hidden by, the other parts/objects. The schema is not static, but describes a dynamic movement, through the unconscious, from one object to the other, a continuous rotation along the direction of the arrows.

Lacan's key is the *objet petit a*, the part-object. This is any object of desire – a body, part or sound even – split from but connected to the subject. It recalls yet rephrases the earlier theory of Freud and Melanie Klein.[10] In 1917, Freud wrote that the subject's 'pleasure drive' leaves a 'lost object' or 'little thing'.[11] Oscillating between the instinctual, internal drive and a real physical figure, the breast, Freud's object has a circularity which he explains as: 'The finding of an object is in fact a refinding it', that is, it was already there.[12] For Klein although initially associated with the mother's breast, the part-object has two developmental phases, from the 'introjected' breast to an exteriorised reality. Once it becomes the latter, the part-object is no longer attached to the mother but manifests as an idea, separable from the body, and hence displaced and replaced by other real objects, 'people and things'.[13] For Klein this separation, driven by guilt, causes the subject to embark on a creative relationship with the world, where 'creative impulses which have hither been dormant awaken and express themselves in such activities as drawing, modelling, building and speech'.[14]

14.3 Jacques Lacan's first L-Schema. The subject (ES) *S* is proposed as an effect of the discourse of the unconscious between the big Other (A), the little other (*a'*) and the ego (*a*). The imaginary relation is the mirror line.

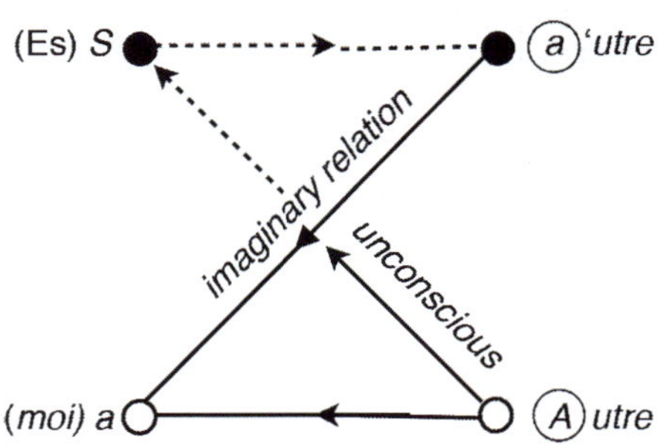

Lacan's part-object is developed across a number of papers and seminars.[15] Following Freud (and Klein), it is a concept between interior feeling and exterior figuration. It associates with parts of the body, interior feelings and memories, and physical objects that are identified outside the body from those associations. Settling on a definition that includes any object which sets desire, the 'drives', in motion for the subject, the part-object is positioned between loss and creativity, and manifests as speech, waste products, body parts, or the act of seeing.[16] Like a 'bump in the fabric of something else', the desirous part-object signifies a present absence.[17] Most importantly, it is, for me, the figure representing the *process* of the L Schema, a dynamic discourse of objects over time. For Lacan the process is one of deception: it is through the subject's 'imaginary relationship with his semblable', his image in the mirror, that he is 'making himself into an object in order to deceive the Other', or those outside himself.[18] The L Schema depicts the subject playing a spatial game of hide and seek with his objects.

In *The Optical Unconscious*, Krauss presents Freud's lost object, Lacan's *objet petit a* and Klein's exteriorised part-object as interchangeable.[19] She also suggests that the part-object always signifies relations within the L Schema. Performing the work of the unconscious, the part-object is established as the signifier in the process of the spectator's unfolding experience. This suggests to me that the part-object, whether body part or object that associates with the body, is also already a memory in the mind of the spectator which re-emerges (Krauss uses the term 'pulses'), through his or her experiential interaction with the art object, through an 'optical unconscious'.[20]

Krauss identifies certain works of art as allusions to this process. Referring to Duchamp's spinning glass discs, the *Rotoreliefs* (1935), and the pieces of collaged body floating in the spaces of Max Ernst's *La femme 100 têtes* (1929), she says:

> *Sometimes the apparition is accompanied, or even substituted for, by a wheel-like form suggesting a turning disc, a circle that [...] resembles Duchamp's optical machines, or his rotoreliefs, with their obvious allusion to the part-object: the breast, the eye, the belly, the womb.*[21]

SPATIAL EXPERIENCE

Krauss' analysis suggests to me that the work of the unconscious is a spatial experience. The artworks described split the body into parts across a space to create a network of body interactions. For instance, it is not merely the way in which the *Rotoreliefs* transform into breast, eye or belly but the way in which, as I stand watching them in the room, I perceive my breast, eye or belly to be separated from my body and reincorporated into the space of the spinning disc. By watching, part of me becomes spinning glass. A spatial severance occurs for the subject: I am split between the space I occupy here, and the *Rotorelief* over there. As Krauss acknowledges, there is a discomfort to this scattering, 'those part-objects belonging to the subject are similarly parts lost to the subject'.[22] Recognising the part-object is therefore a spatial and temporal process of identifying and losing parts/pasts. For Lacan the part-object is not reabsorbed into the subject. It, he says, 'can never be swallowed as it were [but] remains stuck in the gullet of the signifier. It is at this point of lack that the subject has to recognize himself'.[23]

I argue that the spatialisation of the body, split between here and there, is the very essence of the L Schema. It is a two-dimensional diagram – a 'mental framework' – that represents the three-dimensional physical reality of experiences over time.[24] The subject is set out through a number of exteriorised parts which the schema houses. The subject is therefore not a spectator outside the schema looking in, but an occupant inside it. He is not only defined by the schema in an abstract way but inhabits it. It is his home, built over time.

The L Schema, then, spatialises the subject's object history. It shows that, as objects appear and become lost in the mind of the subject over time, an architecture is being formed as a space-time narrative. The L Schema is the psychoanalytic form of the subject's 'house' – its objects repressed/remembered in rooms, against walls, floors, windows, in relationship to each other.

PART-ARCHITECTURE

The subject's physical home is the parallel real space on which he leaves marks, sees/masks himself, positions, loses and recalls objects. He is looking, walking around, taking a bath, leaving traces, sleeping amongst his objects. Lost and found, they bear the traces of and hide his past. But how, as a historian, do I examine a space that is not my own (house)? As many before me, I have been pulled into, beguiled by the Maison de Verre and the *Large Glass*. In a similar manner to Krauss' *Rotoreliefs* description, *I see myself in them*. This way in which we develop empathy for a work could be described as an *architectural* unconscious. The architectural unconscious can be defined as the recognition of the self in a particular architecture or artwork. I find myself in the space despite its historical removal, lack of archival material, or repressions. It has a hold over me.

On its flat surface the *Large Glass* depicts particular subjects engaging in activities in space over time. It is the Bride and Bachelor's house, the place in which they play out their relationship. Yet what we are seeing is a section through the proceedings, with the rest of the space absent. The actual house of the Maison de Verre can be described, in reverse, as a whole house yet with its original inhabitants and visitors absent. It is a building of numerous parts and materials – glass lenses, glass panels, steel columns, sliding screens, sanitary ware – in spatial arrangements, on which each inhabitant is located as a mark or trace made by touch, association, event, love and memory. As a three-dimensional schema, the Maison de Verre has event and memory pressed into it, its objects and spaces clues to recovering former inhabitations and their interactions. So, where the L Schema is a general diagram describing the specificities of experience, the Maison de Verre is a specific place which has housed particular lives. My work writes a new architectural form which, like the *Large Glass*, frames the house at a particular moment in history. For this framing and writing a set of lost relations through an architectural unconscious, I coin the term part-architecture.

The process of part-architecture can be made into a diagram or mental framework – a plan. If the architectural plan generally operates as a projection to a future construction, the diagram of part-architecture describes the opposite process of engaging the past, or 'what was there'. The plans we have of the Maison de Verre were drawn decades afterwards, a record of what physically remains.[25]

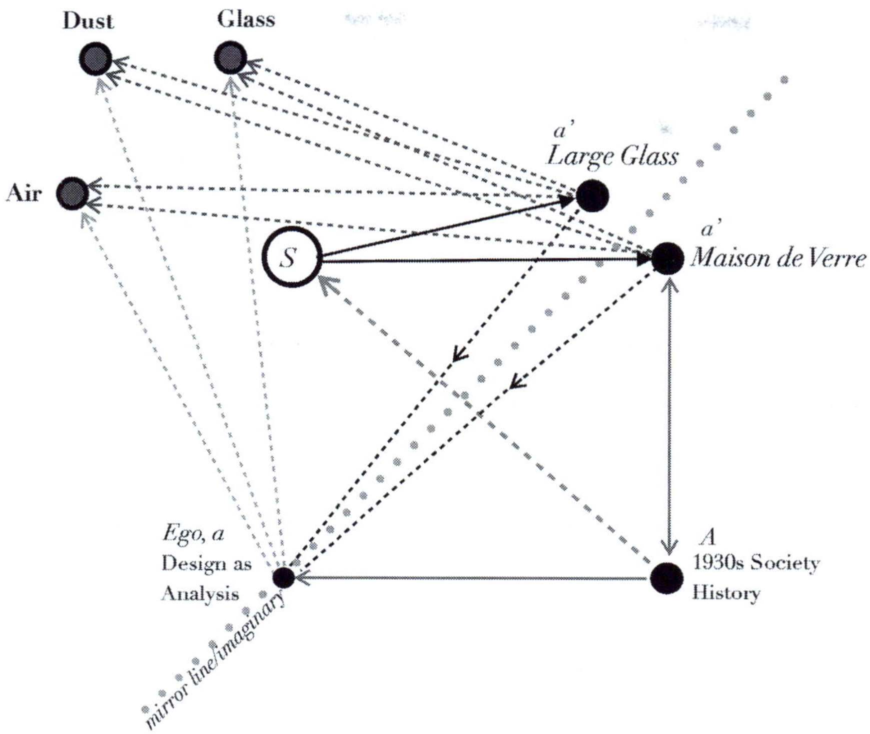

14.4 Part-architecture schema, 2012, Emma Cheatle.

The part-architecture diagram is an alternative plan, a schema which describes the looking backwards and the building of a story from the existing house. It maps the retrospective analysis, recollection and reconstruction of its architectural events (Figure 14.4).

Like the L Schema, the part-architecture schema is based on a square, with 'objects' in the four corners. It then extends with further extrusions hovering above (or below). It is my occupation of the Maison de Verre and the *Large Glass* – and their occupation of me – that inspires this text, therefore the subject (*S*) is, at the outset, me. My analysis is instigated through three mechanisms: the material presence of the Maison de Verre and the *Large Glass* as objects of desire or part-objects (*a'*); my creative writings and drawings (ego, or *a*); and their formation or resistance to the society in which they are found (*A*). Through the middle lies an invisible diagonal plane, the imaginary (mirror line as a reflective device – at times the plane of the *Large Glass* itself). All are interrelated by further lines indicating the play of the work of the architectural unconscious, repressing, relating and retrieving the past. The architectural unconscious is not a neutral process. It demands the writer rethink relations to the object, and hence the nature of architectural history. It prioritises what may be thought of as marginal research – social, feminist, sexual, medical, material (drives).

Here, from the process of the parts of the schema enacting on each other, three related writings emerge, 'Glass', 'Dust', 'Air', like 'bumps in the fabric'. In the *Large Glass* and the Maison de Verre, glass, dust and air are intrinsic and connected materials. Glass predominates, forming a medium for dust collected intentionally on the *Large Glass* or as a byproduct in the Maison de Verre; air, contained within the glass walls, both activates their interior life, whether metaphorically (the *Large Glass*) or literally (the Maison de Verre), and oxidises their materials causing further dust. Each material signifies sexuality, domesticity and modernity prompting a different understanding of history and inhabitation: glass signifies visual interaction, or the visuality of sexuality; dust suggests the past, bodies, unwanted matter, decay, cleaning and archiving; and air the breath of life and the carrying of sound and smell.

The three writings, with analytic drawings, are investigative, subjective studies of the *Large Glass* and Maison de Verre. Each analyses the history, role and signification of the material to the architecture, to recover it as an inhabited space of the 1930s. The writings are partial, open-ended and contingent. Through them, the status of *S* changes. Initially me, the writer, it incorporates the past lives of others, and ultimately becomes you, the reader of the work in the present.

2. GLASS, DUST, AIR

The themes of glass, dust and air underlay the *Large Glass* and the Maison de Verre. Lacan's *objet petit a* can be considered through three parallel concepts: the visual (glass), the remainder (dust), and the voice (air). Firstly, with the visual, Lacan notes that the object is rooted in looking. Initially he follows Jean-Paul Sartre's phenomenological 'look', which acknowledges the existence of the other in the process of looking: looking at the other contains the possibility of being seen, and looked back at.[26] Lacan develops this by separating the eye from the gaze. On one side the eye exists which looks at the object; on the other side the gaze of the object looks back: 'You never look at me from the place from which I see you', he says.[27] Gaze and eye are not in the same place.

Secondly, with the remainder, Lacan argues that objects are always partial, or incomplete, 'not because these objects are part of a total object, which the body is [incorrectly] assumed to be, but because they only partially represent the function that produces them'.[28] They are part of the body and its physical biological function, yet embody desire. Lacan indicates that when desires are met the object can be partially missed, slipping out onto the margins, forgotten. He uses the French term *reste* repeatedly, to indicate this 'leftover' or 'remainder' of desire.[29] In this way, the object is a remainder dropped away from the body. As he says, 'the remainder is always fruitful', it is 'slag', waste indicating the subject.[30]

The third definition expands the part-object – usually thought of as another body or part of the body, often the breast or phallus – to include temporary registers, in particular the voice, but also 'the phoneme, the gaze, [...] faeces and flow of urine and the nothing'.[31] Lacan goes on to say that these objects in common: 'have no specular image, or, in other words, alterity. It is what enables them to be the "stuff", or rather the lining – without, nevertheless, being the flip side – of the very subject that one takes to be the subject of consciousness'.[32] The voice, critical in forming the subject, is invisible, always a remainder or by-product, and therefore lost.

Importantly, this three-way split does not indicate three separate objects but different framings of the same subject, reunited by the systematic movement of the L Schema. The following excerpts from my writings 'Glass', 'Dust' and 'Air' – titled 'Clinical Glass', 'Slips', 'Dark Room' and 'Transmission' – are kinds of architecture, written and drawn, which, as they combine, reconstruct the Maison de Verre for you to enter, walk around in.[33] Through these fragments you may glimpse the ghosts of the building's past inhabitants, their concerns, experiences, objects.

GLASS

Clinical Glass

Glass is the prevalent material of the Maison de Verre, constructing various complex spatial interactions. Dr Dalsace's clinic was a modern practice, promoting

14.5 Surgery, at the front of the Maison de Verre. Photo by Emma Cheatle, 2009. With permission of Robert Rubin.

female sexual health for its potential for pleasure, and hence dismantling the inevitability of its procreative imperative. Lit at each end by a glass wall, the clinical suite is along one edge of the building (Figure 14.5). It comprises three sequential spaces: the doctor's consultation room; examination room; and surgery. Dalsace's medical practice worked through the sequence of the architecture, unfolding the gynaecological body through the three spaces. A glass vitrine at the centre of the clinic, embedded in the wall between examination and surgery rooms, housed historic gynaecological instruments. Lit from within, the instruments are shadowy imprints on the glass. A blank window, it is a negative exposure, an x-ray, envisaging the interior of the body.

Light was key to seeing into the body. The lighting and materiality of the architectural features of the three spaces, consultation, examination and surgery, unfold the gaze of the gynaecologist. The first room, for consultation, was cerebral. Dalsace's books and records were kept in a glass cabinet. He seated himself with his back to the lit garden wall to discuss treatment with the patient. The light behind him caused his face to be in darkness. An illuminator for displaying radiographs hung lit against this wall of glass.

In the examination room, a completely internal room when its sliding wall is closed, the white walls are lined with sheets of white glass. Various pipes, sockets and light fittings are attached. The surface is highly reflective and, if the sliding wall is open, picks up shapes and outlines of the moving bodies as well as a quavering reflection of the glass lenses from the rear façade. If shut, the bodies in the room are still reflected dimly, absorbed into the glass between the equipment and the architecture. This room was for looking inside but not further intervening.

The final room of the clinic, the surgery, used its vitrine-like qualities in an extraordinary way. The end wall of glass lenses faces onto the courtyard (Figure 14.5). The gynaecological table was positioned in front of it to expose the interior of the body. The clinic's new innovative pieces of technical and architectural equipment, previously hidden, were, like the body, completely exposed, presented both lit, and silhouetted against the glass. A figure entering the building can be seen silhouetted on the outside – can he see me? These instances, like gynaecological instruments for looking, establish the building's *raison d'être*, the viewing of the body and need to moderate procreation in the pursuit of pleasure.

Although there is no explicit information on which clinical practices he pursued at the Maison de Verre, I maintain that the glass architecture, completed by the laying bare of the medical suite itself, references Dalsace's medical advances and his support of enlightened sexual politics. The three-roomed gynaecology clinic, though contained in plan along one edge of the building, is reached through the shared spaces of the entrance and ground floor of the house, setting up a tension. The waiting area of the clinic, a delay itself, is visible to the free-plan of the rest of the building. The patient is caught there between the front and back walls of glass.

Slips

In 1901 Sigmund Freud outlined his interest in 'slips of the tongue', or 'parapraxes'.[34] Rereading Freud, the slip connotes the slippery interstitial space between the body and its communication. Tongue can mean the corporeal organ or the language formed by it. To slip is to be caught in the act of sliding between two states, or two spaces, between the body and language, text and image, interiority and exposure. Between intended meaning and error lies a kind of unspeakable gap, related to a stutter; a betrayal, as Freud puts it.[35] A space which resists categorisation, linked to suggestion, feeling and corporeality; a space marked out by Freud's 'little errors of speech as symptoms of unconscious desire'.

The slip offers a description of parts of the Maison de Verre. As the house of a married couple, Annie and Jean Dalsace, their spatial interchanges suggest a different story of domesticity and marriage to that feared by Duchamp. The clinic installed in the house signifies a space of emptying out procreation, returning the body to a 'pure' state. The Dalsaces were then free to practise a form of consummation outside procreative imperatives.[36] The architecture reflects this in the parts of the building furthest away from the clinic on the first and second floors. At these points there is a slippage in the notation. Materials, spaces and elements become interchangeable, between transparency, translucency and opacity, depending on their position. Glass, perforated metal, mirror and lacquer reflect, reveal or mask. Window, frame and door merge. Rooms are paired. It is in these shifts of architecture, and here between the text and diagram, that an erotics may occur, a creative non-procreative domesticity, an alternative sense of dwelling, outside the political imperatives of the contemporary milieu.

One such slip occurs in the junctions between Madame's boudoir and Doctor's adjacent office on the first floor – a 'sexually suggestive set of staggered doors'.[37] The potential is in the arrangement of two sliding doors and four separate layers of fixed roughcast glass fixed in a T shape in plan (Figure 14.6 [5]). These recall Brassaï's description of the brothel '*Suzy*' of 1930s Paris: 'there could be a whole system of sliding doors, curtains, trap doors [...] to protect one customer from ever meeting another'.[38]

Here, the first sliding door (3), is wired glass and allows access from the dining room into Madame's boudoir. It slides through the cross shape of glass panels into the doctor's room. When the door is open to the boudoir, his view of the winter-garden is obscured. Or she may slide the door closed behind her – to listen to music, or receive guests – revealing to him the projecting winter-garden through transparent framed glass (6). As well as a communicative device, it is potentially a tease as Madame retreats with her guests. Further, I/she can assess her husband's movements by entering the corner winter-garden, and looking across into his office or down toward his consulting room. If he is in his office, their eyes may meet across the void to the floor below. They cannot speak as the layer of clear glass lies between them.

The second sliding door, opaque, is to the side of the Doctor's office (4), and perpendicular to the boudoir door (3). When both are open a last diagonal view connects the two rooms. These doors act as interchangeable silent or visual signs of communication and suggestion. The occupants become the erotic glass planes slipping between outer and inner, opening and closure, presence and absence, knowing and seeing.

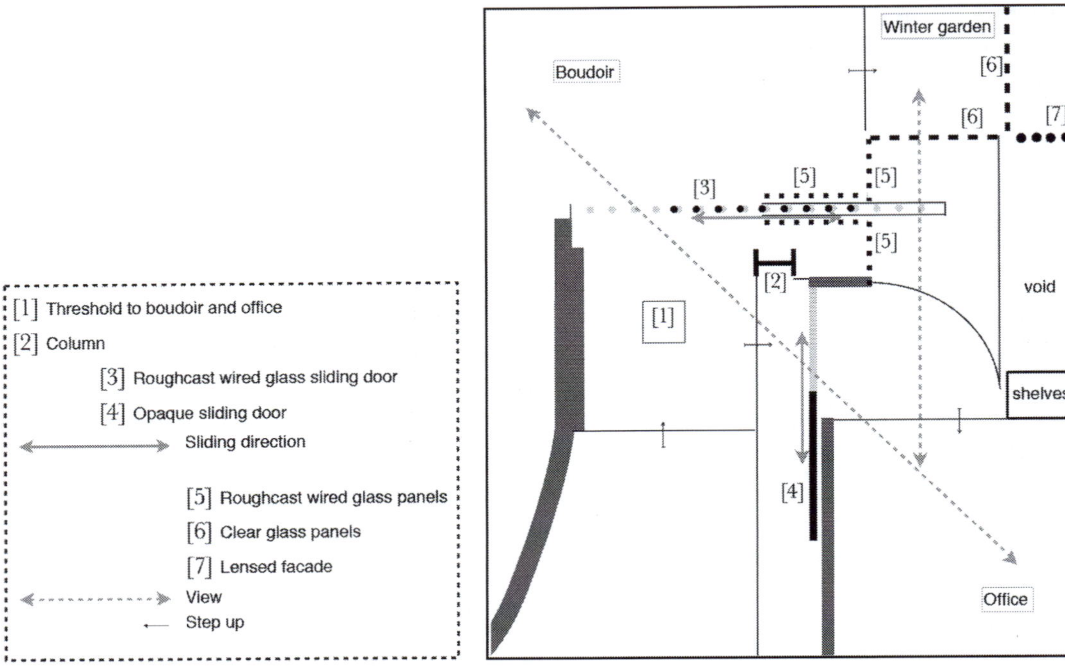

14.6 Plan of the junction between Mme Dalsace's boudoir and winter garden and Dr Dalsace's office, on the first floor at the Maison de Verre. Drawn by Emma Cheatle, 2008.

DUST

From the visual understanding implied by glass, dust is a material that can be seen yet challenges vision. A mélange of tiny remnants left over from the built environment and the body, it was deliberately collected onto the *Large Glass* as 'Dust Breeding',[39] a sign of passing time. Its default presence in the Maison de Verre acts as a challenge to its hygienic programme – an anathema to modernity, and a metaphor for the body and its occupation of the building. An indication of time, dust is always of the past – history.

Dark Room

Carolyn Steedman proposes that dust is the 'idea' of the archive.[40] Dust signifies both literal dust, collected as deposits of the 'past' on the materials of the archive, and a critique of the primacy the archive is afforded.[41] Steedman argues that contemporary history writing is still reliant on the nineteenth century practice of trying to create unambiguous factual events from the past, rather than places of memory and ambiguity.[42] There is no official archive to the Maison de Verre. Surviving design drawings and notes describing Chareau's intentions are few.[43] I here analyse the only existing plans, dated 1927 and 1928, against the house itself. Bearing little relation to the final building, the differences offer clues to the development of the clinic in the house. The house and its dust are primary materials to be understood, as witnesses and remainders to past events.

The architectural drawing is a kind of skin of a building. It indicates the future, and is left behind. In the 1927 and 1928 plans no medical suite or live-in servant

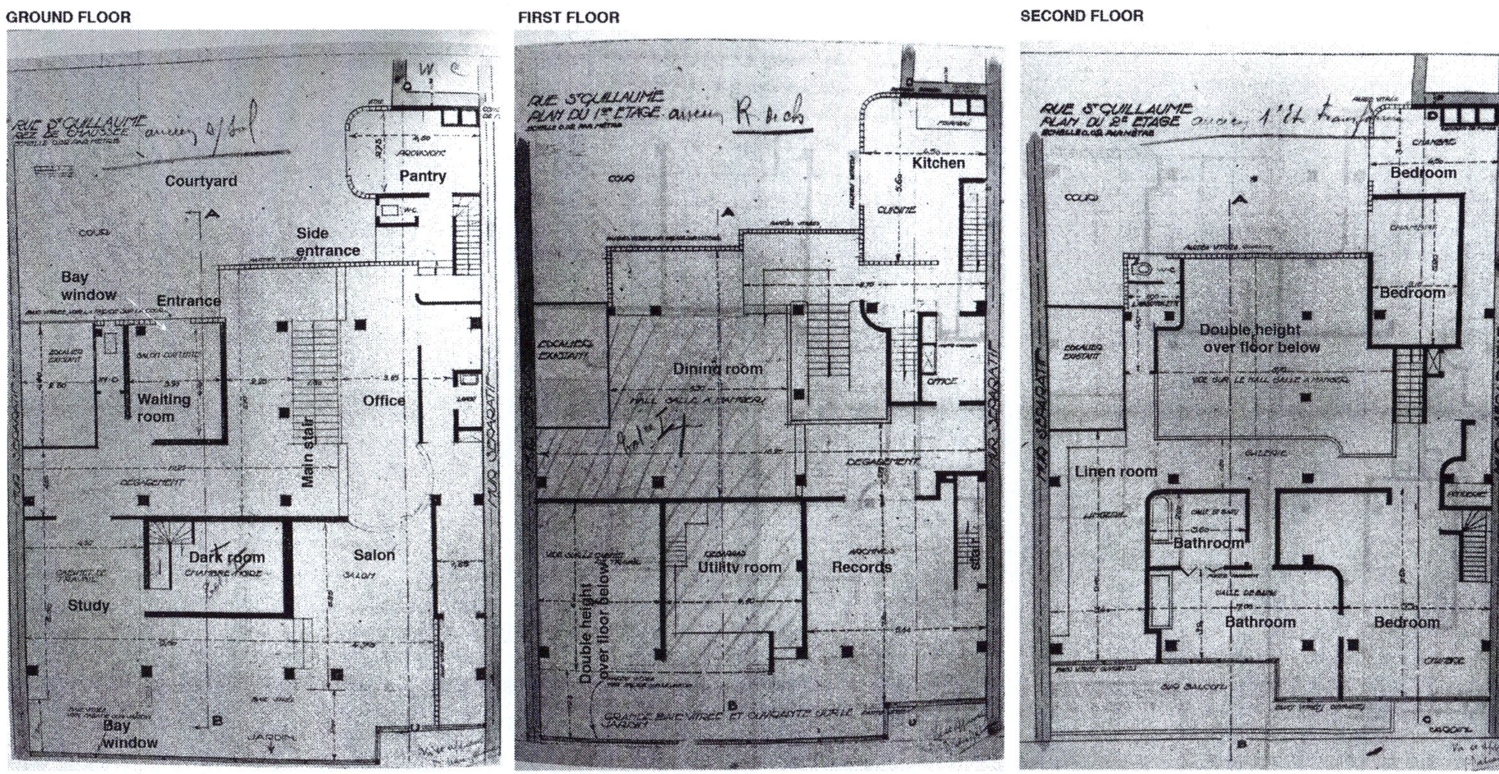

14.7 1928 plans of the Maison de Verre, re-annotated by Emma Cheatle, 2010.

spaces are drawn. The 1928 plans, submitted for planning approval just before the work started on site, label a *salon d'attente* (waiting room), *archives* (archive/records), a *débarras* (utility) and a *chambre noir* (dark room).[44] My supposition is that, as the Dalsaces could not afford to be overt about the inclusion of the clinic, these four rooms were intended as clinical spaces and labelled otherwise to distract the authorities. The dark room signified an examination/x-ray room, the *archives* and *débarras* other medical spaces. If the dark room and archive were indeed stand-ins for clinical rooms to distract the authorities, they indicate the siting of the non-domestic female body in the house. Indeed, the paper records no longer exist, substituted as they were by the bodies of the women themselves visiting the clinic.

In the end the clinic was not only secreted into the interior, but also overlooked by the rest of the house, with the entrance and ground floor continuous and largely open plan. Only the examination and surgical rooms cannot seen by the other occupants inside the house. In contradiction, the surgery with its glass wall to the front of the house is almost visible to the public outside (Figure 14.5). The examination room, then, is the true dark room of the house.[45]

AIR

Glass might be thought of as the motif of modernity.[46] The development of large sheets of transparent glass suggested a utopian immateriality. As I have argued elsewhere, dust and dirt, as well as reflection and translucency, betray the invisibility of glass.[47] Instead air is modernity's true motif, fully reflecting its desire for invisibility. Duchamp suggests in his notes to the *Large Glass* that a system of 'Illuminating Gases' forms the (invisible) communications between Bachelor and Bride.[48] In the Maison de Verre, as everywhere, air is an invisible necessity, allowing the combination and transmission of sounds, smells, atmospheric conditions, and tension through space.

Transmission

Sound – like light, colour and smell – is ephemeral and unpredictable. It resounds off the material of objects and buildings, measuring each sensory quality at a different rate, speed and weight, creating 'air-casts' of spaces.[49] In her essay 'Flesh Colors' Luce Irigaray notes: 'the speed of sound and light are not at all the same'. She stresses that in the psychoanalytic setting, the voice is emphasised. Time and patience mean that: 'everything has to pass through sound'.[50] The voice – formed from complex combinations of timbre, intensity, pitch, travel, shade and tone, and shaped by the throat and mouth, gender and culture – is formed and forms space. Its sound leaves the moistness of the mouth and lips, moves and is shaped across the air in the room, against its harsh, soft, dense materials, to the interior of the ear. It incorporates feeling as it pulses across its flesh, scooped from the outer ear into its orifice, into the darkness of the cochlea.

As we trace the circulation of gas through Bride, Bachelors, Sieves, Chocolate Grinder, Draughts and so on, the *Large Glass* converts the visual into the heard.

Bachelors grind, wheeze and 'splash-crash'; Bride blows, oozes and sputters. As Duchamp notes, the *Large Glass* is a 'sculptured sound form', 'to be heard (or listened to) with one ear', while 'looked at with a single eye'.[51] Sound appears as an 'infrathin', a new space/word/feeling between the spoken and heard.[52]

The cracks (cuts) on the glass, made during transportation in 1926, allowed air to seep in for a period, undoing its communications. Duchamp's work is riddled with homophones, and word traps that transport the spectator/hearer from one thought or place to another. With examples including 'Aiguiser l'ouïe (forme de torture) [Sharpened hearing (form of torture)]',[53] I have the idea that 'cut' sounds like 'cunt' if heard quickly.

Building materials carry sound into the present. The Maison de Verre's palette of rubber, render, glass, steel, aluminium, timber, and travertine is sounded and felt, bouncing through the air: round, flat, slow, light and dark. Combinations of materials, colours and senses occur: off-white rubber, round and absorbent; black slate, dark and warm; flecked terrazzo, creamy and shrill; black terrazzo walls, grainy, cold; burnt umbre mahogany floor strips, slow and light; flat grey duralumin, dull; thick greenish glass lenses, turning milky as they cup light, scooping and amplifying each noise; mottled greyish glass screens of dark cracks; perforated metals, sound streamed into each hole. Painted materials recall flesh as they convey their sound: glistening black doors as reflective as the pupil of the eye, bouncing the voice off their curve; orange painted columns, tense sinews pulled up through the building, with muffled pockets in the reveals.

The material colour-sound of the building is fluid and overlapping except in two spaces: the only two completely enclosed windowless rooms – the examination room and telephone booth (the latter is discussed elsewhere).[54] These two rooms register the past encoded into their strange materials and atmosphere. The examination room, *the dark room*, is closable from both ends by a heavy sliding duralumin wall from the Dr's consultation room, and pivoting white painted valve doors to the surgery. The two-sided vitrine of instruments and experiments glows in the wall between. The room has a stillness when closed off. It is dark except for task lighting, and pumped with warm air through the circular changing booth floor. An interior space for the folded quiet interior of the naked female body, its materials are hard, deflective. The floor of pale, flecked travertine and the walls lined with reflective milky glass sheets, easy to wipe clean, are sharp in sound and image. Yet overall, the examination room baffles sound. Fitting the functions occurring within, when the doors are closed, the room cannot be heard.

CONCLUSION

The excerpts laid out in the previous sections demonstrate a new form of architectural history written through the method of part-architecture. Set in motion through the mechanism of an architectural unconscious, part-architecture reads architectural space in a fundamentally different way. The method was born from a dialogue between the Maison de Verre and *Large Glass*. It was fine-tuned to this dialogue. Scrutinising the house and artwork through repeated visits, I approached their materials as clues to now absent bodies and scenes, social and sexual, political and artistic. Specific themes, writing styles and drawings emerged from the analytic process.

The results are partial versions of history in two ways. Firstly, by their very definition, they remain incomplete, repetitious and linguistic. Like the slip between boudoir and office, they acknowledge the slippery, invisible, elusive nature of the unconscious itself.[55] Secondly, they deal with the desires of subjectivity. To restate Lacan's 'partial because it partially represents the desire that produced it', my desires are spatialised through those of the original inhabitants. With the hold the works' objects have over me, I find I am reflected in them. I see myself in the house.

Part-architecture is applicable as a new method of architectural scholarship, and can be retuned to new subjects. It offers ways of rethinking spatial situations, particularly those derived from or associated with marginal subjects such as gender, sexuality, class, or practices such as cleaning and birthing. It realises its potential as a method when the limits of archival material are reached, whether through absences, repressions or the fact that memory and subjectivity cannot be archived. It suggests different, experimental and personal forms of writing history, that make absence present. If the role of the writer is to use research to create experience, part-architecture proposes that architectural history research, rather than being circumscribed by its perceived limits, expands into an original form of critical, creative enquiry.

Finally, part-architecture speculates on what constitutes an architecture. Is it a building, design or writing – where are the boundaries between the various combinations of functional, idiosyncratic, drawing, building and writing? Cross-disciplinary – between design and fiction, history and theory, art, architecture and society – each part is brought to bear on the other, proposing an architecture as reflexive space, built through writing about the history of an inhabitation. Its partial stories are propositional in reverse, offering a newly written architecture in the present.

NOTES

1 Sigmund Freud, 'Contributions to the Psychology of Erotic Love' (1910–18), trans. Shaun Whiteside, in *The Psychology of Love* (Harmondsworth: Penguin, 2006), p. 257.

2 See Jacques Lacan, *The Four Fundamental Concepts of Psycho-Analysis*, trans. Alan Sheridan (Harmondsworth: Penguin, 1991); Jacques Lacan, *Écrits: A Selection*, trans. Alan Sheridan (London: Routledge, 1991); Jacques Lacan, *Écrits: A Selection*, trans. Bruce Fink (New York: W.W. Norton, 2002); Rosalind E. Krauss, *The Optical Unconscious* (Cambridge, MA: The MIT Press, 1994).

3 Emma Cheatle, 'Part-architecture: The *Maison de Verre* through the *Large Glass*' (unpublished doctoral thesis, University College London, 2013). Forthcoming in book form, Emma Cheatle, *Part-architecture: The Maison de Verre, Duchamp, Domesticity and Desire in 1930s Paris* (Farnham: Ashgate, 2016).

4 There are no surviving records of the activities taking place in the clinic. Perhaps due to their illegality at the time, they were unrecorded, removed, or destroyed.

5 Marcel Duchamp, 'The Box of 1914', trans. Elmer Peterson; 'The Green Box', trans. Cleve Gray; 'À l'infinitif', trans. Cleve Gray, in Michel Sanouillet and Elmer Peterson (eds), *The Writings of Marcel Duchamp* (New York: De Capo, 1973). Also see Marcel Duchamp, *Marcel Duchamp, Notes*, trans. Paul Matisse (Paris: Centre national d'art et de culture Georges Pompidou, 1980); Marcel Duchamp, *From the Green Box*, trans. George Heard Hamilton (New Haven, CT: Readymade Press, 1957); Marcel Duchamp, *Manual of Instructions for Étant donnés: 1° – la chute d'eau, 2° – le gaz d'éclairage* (Philadelphia, PA: Philadelphia Museum of Art, 1987). For key analyses see Jean-François Lyotard, *Les Transformateurs Duchamp* (*Duchamp's TRANS/formers*) (1977), trans. Ian McLeod (Leuven: Leuven University Press, 2010), p. 179; Rosalind E. Krauss, *The Optical Unconscious*, pp. 81, 122; Rosalind E. Krauss, 'The Story of the Eye', *New Literary History*, 21(2) (Winter 1990), p. 292; Penelope Haralambidou, *Marcel Duchamp and the Architecture of Desire* (Farnham: Ashgate, 2013).

6 Kenneth Frampton, 'Maison de Verre', in *Arena*, 81(901) (London: The Architectural Association, 1966), pp. 257–62; Kenneth Frampton, 'Maison de Verre', *Perspecta*, 12 (Cambridge, MA: The MIT Press, 1969), pp. 77–125; Kenneth Frampton, 'Pierre Chareau: An Eclectic Architect', in Marc Vellay and Kenneth Frampton (eds), *Pierre Chareau: Architect and Craftsman 1883–1950* (London: Thames and Hudson, 1985), pp. 235–48; Brian Brace Taylor, *Pierre Chareau: Designer and Architect* (Koln: Taschen, 1992).

7 Rosalind E. Krauss, *The Optical Unconscious*, pp. 22–7, 36, 74–5. Lacan's L Schema was first published in 'On the Possible Treatment of Psychosis' (1955); see Jacques Lacan, *Écrits: A Selection* (1991), p. 193. See also Rosalind E. Krauss, 'Sculpture in the Expanded Field', in Hal Foster (ed.), *The Anti-Aesthetic: Essays in Postmodern Culture* (Seattle, WA: Bay Press, 1983), pp. 31–42.

8 See Jacques Lacan, 'The Mirror Stage as Formative of the Function of I as Revealed in the Psychoanalytic Experience', in Jacques Lacan, *Écrits: A Selection* (1991), pp. 1–8. This essay was based on an earlier paper 'Le stade du miroir' (1936). See Ellie Ragland Sullivan, *Jacques Lacan and the Philosophy of Psychoanalysis* (Beckenham: Croom Helm, 1986), p. 315, n. 33.

9 Here Lacan explains (although confusingly he switches the symbols a' and a): 'This schema signifies that the condition of the subject, S [...] depends on what unfolds in the Other, A. What unfolds there is articulated like a discourse (the unconscious is the Other's discourse [discours de l'Autre])'. He continues to say that S is party to his own discourse, his form 'reflected in his objects [a' and a]'.

10 Although Lacan dismissed Klein as a thinker, it seems impossible that he ignored her 1930s definition of part-object.

11 See Sigmund Freud, 'Melancholia' (1917), in *On Murder, Mourning and Melancholia*, trans. Shaun Whiteside (Harmondsworth: Penguin, 2005), p. 207. See also Catherine Clément, *The Lives and Legends of Jacques Lacan* (New York: Columbia University Press, 1983), p. 98; Sigmund Freud, 'Three Essays on the Theory of Sexuality' (1905), 'Fetishism' (1927), and 'Female Sexuality' (1931), in Sigmund Freud, *On Sexuality: Three Essays on the Theory of Sexuality and other works*, trans. James Strachey (Harmondsworth: Penguin Books, 1977).

12 Sigmund Freud, 'Three Essays on the Theory of Sexuality' (1977), p. 222.

13 Melanie Klein, 'Love, Guilt and Reparation', in Melanie Klein and Joan Rivière, *Love, Hate and Reparation* (1937) (London: Hogarth, 1953), pp. 61, 91, 107; Melanie Klein, 'A Contribution to the Psychosis of Manic Depressive States' (1935), in Juliet Mitchell (ed.), *The Selected Melanie Klein* (Harmondsworth: Penguin, 1986), pp. 116, 118–19. Also see Jay R. Greenberg and Stephen A. Mitchell, *Object Relations in Psychoanalytic Theory* (London: Harvard University Press, 1983), pp. 119–150.

14 Melanie Klein, 'Love, Guilt and Reparation', p. 107.

15 For example, Jacques Lacan, 'Function and Field of Speech and Language'; 'The Treatment of Psychosis'; and 'Subversion of Subject and Dialectic of Desire' in *Écrits: A Selection* (1991), particularly pp. 59–63, 349; 'From Interpretation to the Transference'; and 'In You More Than You', in *The Four Fundamental Concepts of Psycho-Analysis*, pp. 256–9, 267–70. Also see Bruce Fink, *Lacan to the Letter: Reading Écrits Closely* (Minneapolis, MN: University of Minnesota Press, 2004).

16 Jacques Lacan, *The Four Fundamental Concepts of Psycho-Analysis*, p. 168; Jacques Lacan, *Écrits: A Selection* (2002), p. 693. Also, Jacques Lacan, *Écrits: A Selection* (1991), p. 360. Lacan translates the drive or instinct from Freud's Treib, dérive (drift) in French, suggesting a more circuitous route than Freud's instinctual urge.

17 Jacques Lacan, *The Four Fundamental Concepts of Psycho-Analysis*, pp. 257, 270.

18 Jacques Lacan, 'Seminar on "The Purloined Letter"' (1956), in *Écrits: A Selection* (2002), p. 40.

19 Krauss also refers to the part-object in Rosalind Krauss, 'The Story of the Eye', p. 293; Yve-Alain Bois and Rosalind E. Krauss, *Formless: A User's Guide* (London: The MIT Press, 1999); Rosalind E. Krauss, *Bachelors* (London: October Books, 1999), p. 60.

20 Krauss' schematic remapping of Lacan's L Schema can be seen in Rosalind E. Krauss, *The Optical Unconscious*, pp. 22–7, 36, 74–7.

21 Rosalind E. Krauss, *The Optical Unconscious*, pp. 79, 81. See also Yve-Alain Bois and Rosalind Krauss, *Formless*, pp. 152–61.

22 Rosalind Krauss, *The Optical Unconscious*, p. 75.

23 Jacques Lacan, *The Four Fundamental Concepts of Psycho-Analysis*, p. 270.

24 The schema as mental framework comes from Jean Piaget, *The Origin of Intelligence in the Child* (1936), trans. M. Cook (London: Routledge, 1953).

25 No original plans of the final building exist.

26 Jacques Lacan, *The Four Fundamental Concepts of Psycho-Analysis*, p. 84; see also Dylan Evans, *An Introductory Dictionary to Lacanian Psychoanalysis* (New York: Brunner-Routledge, 1996), p. 73; Jean-Paul Sartre, *Being and Nothingness* (1943), trans. Hazel E. Barnes (London: Routledge, 1969), pp. 259–61, 277.

27 Jacques Lacan, *The Four Fundamental Concepts of Psycho-Analysis*, p. 103.

28 Jacques Lacan, 'Subversion of Subject and Dialectic of Desire in the Freudian Unconscious', in *Écrits: A Selection* (1991), p. 349.

29 Jacques Lacan, 'Seminar on "The Purloined Letter"', in *Écrits: A Selection* (2002), p. 56; Jacques Lacan, *The Four Fundamental Concepts of Psycho-Analysis*, pp. 17–64.

30 Jacques Lacan, *The Four Fundamental Concepts of Psycho-Analysis*, p. 134.

31 Jacques Lacan, *Écrits: A Selection* (2002), p. 693. Also, Jacques Lacan, *Écrits: A Selection* (1991), p. 360.

32 Jacques Lacan, *Écrits: A Selection* (2002), p. 693.

33 The full chapters of 'Glass', 'Dust' and 'Air' appear in my forthcoming book Emma Cheatle, *Part-architecture*. Also see Emma Cheatle, 'Recording the Absent in the Maison de Verre', in *IDEA Journal* (Interior Design / Interior Architecture Educators Association, 2012); and Emma Cheatle, 'To Look at the Maison de Verre (from the Other Side of the Glass) with One Eye, Close To, for Almost an Hour, Again', in Emanuel de

Sousa and Kirk Wooller (eds), *Propositions: Ideology in Transparency* (London: AA PhD Publications, 2011).

34 Sigmund Freud, *The Psychopathology of Everyday Life* (1914), trans. Alan Tyson (Harmondsworth: Penguin, 1975), pp. 71–114.

35 Ibid., p. 112.

36 The Dalsaces had two children. The house was carefully constructed: the two child bedrooms have fixed beds, suggesting there was no intent to have more.

37 Anne Troutman, 'The Modernist Boudoir and the Erotics of Space', in Hilde Heynen and Gülsüm Baydar (eds), *Negotiating Domesticity: Spatial Productions of Gender in Modern Architecture* (London: Routledge, 2005), p. 308. She does not elaborate.

38 Brassaï, *The Secret Paris of the 30s* (1931–9) (London: Thames and Hudson, 1976), unpaginated.

39 Duchamp writes about the deliberate collection of the dust: '[12. DUST BREEDING] To raise dust on Dust-Glasses for 4 months. 6 months'. See Marcel Duchamp, 'The Green Box', in Michel Sanouillet and Elmer Peterson (eds), *The Writings of Marcel Duchamp*, p. 53.

40 Carolyn Steedman, *Dust: The Archive and Cultural History* (Manchester: Manchester University Press, 2001), pp. ix, 70. *Dust* is a dialogue with Jacques Derrida, *Archive Fever: A Freudian Impression*, trans. Eric Prenowitz (London: University of Chicago Press, 1996).

41 See Carolyn Steedman, *Dust*, pp. ix, 70.

42 Ibid., pp. x, 7, 164.

43 Sketch plans from 1927 and 1928 are published in Brian Bruce Taylor, *Pierre Chareau*, pp. 30–31; several perspectives and sketches are in Kenneth Frampton, 'Maison de Verre', in *Perspecta*, 12, pp. 83, 117.

44 See Brian Bruce Taylor, *Pierre Chareau*, p. 28. Permission to build the proposed plans was received just after the building work had started.

45 A further internal room does exist: the Doctor's tiny telephone booth.

46 Walter Benjamin, 'The Return of the Flâneur' (1929), in Walter Benjamin, *Selected Writings, Volume 2, 1927–34*, trans. Rodney Livingstone (London: Belknap Press, 1999), p. 264.

47 See chapter 'Glass', in Emma Cheatle, *Part-architecture*.

48 Pierre Cabanne, *Dialogues with Marcel Duchamp* (1971), trans. Ron Padgett (New York: Viking Press, 1987), pp. 48–9. Marcel Duchamp, 'The Green Box', in Michel Sanouillet and Elmer Peterson (eds), *The Writings of Marcel Duchamp*, pp. 49, 50.

49 For these 'air-casts' see chapter 'Air', in Emma Cheatle, *Part-architecture*.

50 Luce Irigaray, 'Flesh Colors', in Luce Irigaray, *Sexes and Genealogies*, trans. Gillian C. Gill (New York: Columbia University Press, 1993), pp. 153–4. Also see Luce Irigaray, *The Forgetting of Air in Martin Heidegger*, trans. Mary Beth Mader (London: Athlone, 1999).

51 Marcel Duchamp, 'À l'Infinitif', in Michel Sanouillet and Elmer Peterson (eds), *The Writings of Marcel Duchamp*, pp. 75–6.

52 Duchamp coined the word 'infrathin' in 1930 to describe the idea of 'becoming' or being between two states; Marcel Duchamp, *Marcel Duchamp, Notes*, note 1, unpaginated.

53 Marcel Duchamp, 'The Green Box', in Michel Sanouillet and Elmer Peterson (eds), *The Writings of Marcel Duchamp*, p. 31. See Marcel Duchamp, 'Rrose Sélavy & Co.', trans. David Ball, Ron Padgett, Roger Shattuck, Trevor Winkfield and Elmer Peterson, in Michel Sanouillet and Elmer Peterson (eds), *The Writings of Marcel Duchamp*, pp. 105–19.

54 'Air' in Emma Cheatle, *Part-architecture*.

55 As Lacan puts it, 'the unconscious is structured like a language', in Jacques Lacan, *Écrits: A Selection* (1991), p. 65; and 'the unconscious closes up again', in Jacques Lacan, 'Seminar XI', in *The Four Fundamental Concepts of Psycho-Analysis*, p. 144.

Bibliography

Agrippa, Heinrich Cornelius, *De occulta philosophia libri tres*, ed. Perrone Campagni (Leiden: Brill, 1992).

Allan, John, *Berthold Lubetkin: Architecture and the Tradition of Progress* (London: Artifice, 2013).

Anderson, James William, Elizabeth A. Danze, and Jerome A. Winer (eds), *Psychoanalysis and Architecture* (Catskill, NY: Mental Health Resources, 2005).

Arnell, Peter and Ted Bickford, *Aldo Rossi: Buildings and Projects* (New York: Rizzoli, 1985).

Bachelard, Gaston, *The Poetics of Space*, trans. Maria Jolas (Boston, MA: Beacon Press, 1969).

Bakhtin, Mikhail (pod maskoj) (under a mask), *Freidizm. Formal'nyi metod v literaturovedenii. Marksizm i filosofia iazyka. Stat'I* [*Freudianism. Formal Method in Literature Studies. Marxism and the Philosophy of Language*] (Moscow: Labirint, 2000).

Bal, Mieke, *Looking In: The Art of Viewing* (Amsterdam: G+B Arts International, 2001).

Bann, Stephen, 'The Colour in the Text: Ruskin's Basket of Strawberries', in *The Ruskin Polygon: Essays on the Imagination of John Ruskin*, ed. J.D. Hunt and F.M. Holland (Manchester: Manchester University Press, 1982), pp. 123–36.

Barthes, Roland, *Semiology and Urbanism*, Colloquium Op. 10 (Naples: University of Naples Institute of Architectural History, 1967).

Baudrillard, Jean, *For a Critique of the Political Economy of the Sign*, trans. Charles Levin (St. Louis: Telos Press, 1981).

———, *Simulations*, trans. Phil Beitchman, Paul Foss, Paul Patton (New York: Semiotext(e), 1983).

Benjamin, Walter, 'Theses on the Philosophy of History', in Walter Benjamin, *Illuminations*, trans. Harry Zohn (New York: Harcourt, Brace & World, 1968).

———, 'The Work of Art in the Age of Mechanical Reproduction', in Walter Benjamin, *Illuminations*, ed. Hannah Arendt, trans. Harry Zohn (London: Fontana, 1973).

———, 'A Small History of Photography', in Walter Benjamin, *One-Way Street and Other Writings*, ed. E.F.N. Jephcott and Kingsley Shorter (London: Verso, 1997).

———, 'The Return of the Flâneur' (1929), in Walter Benjamin, *Selected Writings, Volume 2, 1927–34*, trans. Rodney Livingstone (London: Belknap Press, 1999).

Berger, John, *Understanding a Photograph* (London: Penguin Books, 2013).

Bianchi, Enzo, 'Parola di Dio, Parola a Dio. Approccio spirituale', in *RCatT* 33/1 (Barcelona: Facultat de Teologia de Catalunga, 2008), pp. 41–52.

Blom, Kati, 'Undulating Light', in *Arkkitehti, Finnish Architectural Review*, 3 (Helsinki: Finnish Association of Architects, 2004), pp. 72–85.

Bloom, Harold, *A Map of Misreading* (Oxford: Oxford University Press, 1975).

———, *Poetry and Repression: Revisionism from Blake to Stevens* (London: Yale University Press, 1976).

Blum, Virginia and Anna Secor, 'Psycho-topologies: Closing the Circuit between Psychic and Material Space', in *Environment and Planning D: Society and Space*, 29 (6) (2011), pp. 1030–47.

Blundell Jones, Peter, and Eamon Canniffe, *Modern Architecture Through Case Studies* (Oxford: Architectural Press, 2007).

Boada, Isidre Puig (ed.), *Antoni Gaudí: Paroles et écrits* (Paris: L'Harmattan, 2002).

Böhme, Gernot, *Anmutungen: Über das Atmospärische* (Stuttgart: Editions Tertium, 1998).

Bois, Yve-Alain and Rosalind E. Krauss, *Formless: A User's Guide* (London: The MIT Press, 1999).

Bollas, Christopher, *The Evocative Object World* (London: Routledge, 2008).

Boring, Edwin G., 'Editor's Introduction' to Gustav Theodor Fechner, *Elements of Psychophysics*, trans. Helmut E. Adler, ed. Davis H. Howes and Edwin G. Boring (New York: Holt, Rinehart and Winston, 1966).

Bowie, Malcolm, *Lacan* (London: Fontana Press, 1991).

Bragdon, Claude, Bragdon Family Papers (BFP), Department of Rare Books, Special Collections and Preservation, Rush Rhees Library, University of Rochester, NY, 1890–1912.

———, 'Mysticism and Architecture', in *Interstate Architect and Builder* (Cleveland, OH: Builder's Exchange of Cleveland, 13 and 20 July 1901).

———, 'Maeterlinck', in *Critic* 45 (New Rochelle: G.P. Putnam's Sons, August 1901).

———, 'The Beautiful Necessity: Being Essays upon Esthetics', in *House and Garden* (New York: Condé Nast, January–June 1902).

———, 'The Modern Note', in *Reader Magazine* 3 (Indianapolis, IN: Bobbs-Merrill Co., December, 1903).

———, 'The New Mysticism', in *Reader Magazine* 4 (Indianapolis, IN: Bobbs-Merrill Co., July, 1904).

———, 'The Art of Architecture from the Standpoint of Theosophy', in *Theosophic Messenger* (San Francisco, CA: American Theosophic Society, May 1909).

———, 'The Theosophy of Architecture', in *Theosophic Messenger* (San Francisco, CA: American Theosophic Society, June–November 1909).

———, *The Beautiful Necessity: Seven Essays on Theosophy and Architecture* (Rochester, NY: The Manas Press, 1910).

———, 'Did the Words Come from Beyond the Grave? Students of the Supernatural are Interested in the So-Called Communications from the Spirit of Professor William James', in *New York Herald*, Sunday 20 November 1910, Magazine Section.

———, 'The Language of Form', in Ralph Adams Cram, Tomas Hastings, and Claude Bragdon, *Six Lectures on Architecture: The Scammon Lectures at The Art Institute of Chicago* (Chicago, IL: University of Chicago Press, 1917).

———, *Architecture and Democracy* (New York: Alfred A. Knopf, 1918).

———, 'A Voice Out of Russia', in *Theosophic Messenger* 7 (San Francisco, CA: American Theosophic Society, December 1919).

———, 'Ouspensky on Love', in *Theosophic Messenger* 7 (San Francisco, CA: American Theosophic Society, March 1920).

———, *Four-dimensional Vistas*, 2nd edn (London: G. Routledge & Sons, 1923 [1916]).

———, 'A Dissertation on Dynamic Symmetry', in *Architectural Record* 56 (New York: McGraw-Hill, October 1924).

———, *The New Image* (New York: Alfred A. Knopf, 1928).

———, *The Secret Springs: An Autobiography* (London: Andrew Dakers, 1938).

———, *A Primer of Higher Space, The Fourth Dimension* (to which is added *Man the Square, A Higher Space Parable*) (London: Andrew Dakers Limited, 1939 [1913]).

———, *The Arch Lectures (Eighteen discourses on a great variety of subjects delivered in New York, during the winter of 1940)* (Great Neck, NY: Core Collection Books, Inc., 1942).

———, *Projective Ornament* (Seattle, WA: Unicorn Bookshop, 1972 [1915]).

Brassaï, *The Secret Paris of the 30s* (London: Thames and Hudson, 1976).

Bresson, Robert, *Notes on Cinematography*, trans. Jonathan Griffin (New York: Urizen, 1977) [*Notes sur le Cinématographe* (Paris: Gallimard, 1975)].

Breuer, Joseph, 'Theoretical Studies on Hysteria' (1893), in *The Standard Edition of the Complete Psychological Works of Sigmund Freud, Volume II (1893–1895): Studies on Hysteria*, trans. from the German under the general editorship of James Strachey (London: The Hogarth Press, 1955).

Broadbent, Geoffrey, 'A Plain Man's Guide to the Theory of Signs in Architecture', in Kate Nesbitt (ed.), *Theorizing a New Agenda for Architecture: An Anthology of Architectural Theory 1965–1995* (New York: Princeton Architectural Press, 1996).

Brough, John B., 'Translator's Introduction', in Edmund Husserl, *Phantasy, Image Consciousness, and Memory (1898–1925)* (Husserliana, vol. XXIII) (Dordrecht: Springer, 2005).

Burgoyne, Bernard, *Drawing the Soul: Schemas and Models in Psychoanalysis* (London: Rebus Press, 2000).

Butler, Frances, 'The Shadow Does Not Know: Disconnected Power', in David Murray (ed.), *VIA 11: Architecture and Shadow* (Philadelphia, PA: University of Pennsylvania, 1990), pp. 116–23.

Bykhovskii, Bernard, 'O metodologicheskikh osnovaniiakh psikhoanaliticheskogo uchenia Freida' ['On the methodological foundations of the psychoanalytical teaching of Freud'], in *Pod znamenem Marksizma* [*Under the Banner of Marxism*], 11–12 (Moscow, 1923), pp. 158–77.

Cabanne, Pierre, *Dialogues with Marcel Duchamp*, trans. Ron Padgett (New York: Viking Press, 1987 [1971]).

Carus, Carl Gustav, *Lectures on Psychology* [*Vorlesungen über Psychologie, gehalten im Winter 1829–30 zu Dresden*, 1831] (Leipzig: Verlag von Gerhard Fleischer).

———, *Psyche: On the Development of the Soul, Part One: The Unconscious*, trans. R. Welch (New York: Spring Publications, 1970 [1846]).

Cassirer, Ernst, *The Individual and the Cosmos in Renaissance Philosophy* (Chicago, IL: The University of Chicago Press, 2010).

Cheatle, Emma, 'To Look at the Maison de Verre (from the Other Side of the Glass) with One Eye, Close To, for Almost an Hour, Again', in Emanuel de Sousa and Kirk Wooller (eds), *Propositions: Ideology in Transparency* (London: AA PhD Publications, 2011).

———, 'Recording the Absent in the Maison de Verre', in *IDEA Journal* (Interior Design / Interior Architecture Educators Association, 2012).

———, 'Part-architecture: The *Maison de Verre* through the *Large Glass*' (unpublished doctoral thesis, University College London, 2013).

———, *Part-Architecture: The Maison de Verre, Duchamp, Domesticity and Desire in 1930s Paris* (Farnham: Ashgate, 2016).

Chipperfield, David, Kieran Long, and Shumi Bose (eds), *Common Ground: A Critical Reader* (Venice: Marsilio Editions, 2012).

Clarke, David, Marcus A. Doel, William Merrin, and Richard G. Smith (eds), *Jean Baudrillard: Fatal Theories* (Abingdon: Routledge, 2009).

Clément, Catherine, *The Lives and Legends of Jacques Lacan* (New York: Columbia University Press, 1983).

Coldwell, Paul, *Morandi's Legacy: Influences on British Art* (London: Philip Wilson, 2006).

Collins, Peter, *Changing Ideals in Modern Architecture* (Montreal and Kingston, London, Ithaca: McGill-Queen's University Press, 1965; 2nd edn, 1998).

Cook, E.T., and Alexander Wedderburn (eds), *The Works of John Ruskin* (London: George Allen, 1904–13).

Craig, Edward (ed.), *Routledge Encyclopedia of Philosophy* (London: Routledge, 1998).

Crary, Jonathan, *Techniques of the Observer: On Vision and Modernity in the Nineteenth Century* (Cambridge, MA: The MIT Press, 1992).

———, *Suspensions of Perception: Attention, Spectacle, and Modern Culture* (Cambridge, MA: The MIT Press, 2000).

Curtis, William, *L'achitecture moderne depuis 1900* (Paris: Phaidon, 2006).

Danze, Elizabeth, and Stephen Sonnenberg (eds), *Space and Psyche, Center 17* (Austin, TX: Center for American Architecture and Design, 2012).

Debray, Régis, *Vita E Morte Dell'Immagine: Una Storia Dello Sguardo in Occidente* (Milan: Il Castoro, 2004).

Deleuze, Gilles, *Kant's Critical Philosophy: The Doctrine of the Faculties* [*La Philosophie Critique de Kant*], trans. Hugh Tomlinson and Barbara Habberjam (Minneapolis, MN: University of Minnesota Press, 1984 [1963]).

Deleuze, Gilles, and Félix Guattari, *The Anti-Oedipus: Capitalism and Schizophrenia*, trans. Robert Hurley, Mark Seem, and Helen R. Lane (London: Athlone Press, 1972).

———, *A Thousand Plateaus: Capitalism and Schizophrenia, Volume 2*, trans. Brian Massumi (Minneapolis, MN: University of Minnesota Press, 1987) [*Mille Plateaux: Capitalisme et schizophrénie tôme 2* (Paris: Minuit, 1980)].

Derrida, Jacques, 'Freud and the Scene of Writing', in *Writing and Difference*, trans. Alan Bass (Chicago, IL: The University of Chicago Press, 1978).

———, *Margins of Philosophy*, trans. Alan Bass (Chicago, IL: The University of Chicago Press, 1982).

———, *Archive Fever: A Freudian Impression*, trans. Eric Prenowitz (London: University of Chicago Press, 1996).

Dixon, Lurinda S., *The Dark Side of Genius: The Melancholic Persona in Art, c. 1500–1700* (University Park, PA: The Pennsylvania State University Press, 2013).

Dokuchaev, Nikolai, 'Arkhitekturnyi fakul'tet VKhUTEMASa', in *Arkhitektura: raboty arkhitekturnogo fakul'teta VKhUTEMASa, 1920–1927* (Moscow: Izd-vo Vkhutemasa, 1927).

———, 'Poiasnitel'naia zapiska k kursu 'iskusstvo arkhitektury' dlia khudozhestvennykh tekhnikumov' ['Explanatory note to the course "The Art of Architecture" for art professional schools'], in *Sbornik materialov po khudozhestvennomy obrazovaniu* [*Collection of Materials on Artistic Education*] (Moscow: Gos. Izd., 1927), pp. 79–81.

———, 'Osnovy iskusstva arkhitektury (Kurs dlia khudozhestvennykh tekhnikumov)' ['Foundations of the art of architecture (A course for art professional schools)'], in *Sbornik materialov po khudozhestvennomy obrazovaniu* [*Collection of Materials on Artistic Education*] (Moscow: Gos. Izd, 1927), pp. 82–103.

Douglas, Charlotte, 'Mach and Malevich: Sensation, Suprematism, and the Objectless World', in *The Structuralist*, vol. 49/50 (Saskatoon: University of Saskatchewan, 2009), pp. 58–65.

Duchamp, Marcel, *From the Green Box*, trans. George Heard Hamilton (New Haven, CT: Readymade Press, 1957).

———, *Marcel Duchamp, Notes*, trans. Paul Matisse (Paris: Centre national d'art et de culture Georges Pompidou, 1980).

———, *Manual of Instructions for Étant donnés: 1° – la chute d'eau, 2° – le gaz d'éclairage* (Philadelphia, PA: Philadelphia Museum of Art, 1987).

Du Prel, Carl, *The Philosophy of Mysticism*, trans. C.C. Massey, 2 vols (London: George Redway, 1889).

Dürer, Albrecht, *Underweysung der Messung mit dem Zirckel und Richtscheyt* [*Instructions for Measuring with Compass and Ruler*] (Nuremberg: Albrecht Dürer, 1525).

———, *Vier Bücher von Menschlicher Proportion* [*Four Books on Human Proportion*] (Nuremberg: Hieronymus Formschneyder, 1528).

———, *The Writings of Albrecht Dürer*, trans. and ed. W.M. Conway (London: Peter Owen, 1958).

Dutton, Denis, 'Aesthetic Universals', in *The Routledge Companion to Aesthetics*, ed. Berys Gaut and Dominic McIver Lopes (London: Routledge, 2001), pp. 206–10.

Eisenman, Peter, 'Maison Dom-ino and the Self-referential Sign', in *Oppositions*, 15/16 (New York: Institute for Architecture and Urban Studies, Winter/Spring 1979), pp. 118–28.

———, 'The House of the Dead as the City of Survival', in *Aldo Rossi in America 1976 to 1979*, ed. Kenneth Frampton (New York: Institute for Architecture and Urban Studies, 1979), pp. 4–15.

Ellenberger, Henri, *The Discovery of the Unconscious: The History and Evolution of Dynamic Psychiatry* (New York: Basic Books, 1970).

Ellis, Eugenia Victoria, and Andrea G. Reithmayr (eds), *Claude Bragdon and The Beautiful Necessity* (Rochester, NY: RIT Cary Graphic Arts Press, 2010).

Etkind, Alexander, *The Eros of the Impossible: The History of Psychoanalysis in Russia* (Boulder, CO: Westview Press, 1997).

Evans, Dylan, *An Introductory Dictionary of Lacanian Psychoanalysis* (New York: Brunner-Routledge, 1996 / London: Routledge, 2006).

Evans, Mark, 'Dürer in Italy Revisited: The German Connections' (2003), paper delivered at the 2003 Albrecht Dürer and his Legacy Conference, organised by Giulia Bartrum, British Museum Online. Available at: https://www.britishmuseum.org/pdf/1%20Durer%20and%20Italy%20Revisited.pdf [accessed 24 August 2015].

Ewen, Stuart, *Pr!: A Social History of Spin* (New York: Basic Books, 1996).

Faflak, Joel, *Romantic Psychoanalysis: The Burden of the Mystery* (Albany, NY: State University of New York Press, 2008).

Fechner, Gustav Theodor (Dr Mises), 'Der Raum hat vier Dimensionen', in *Vier Paradoxa* (Leipzig: Leopold Voss, 1846), pp. 15–40.

———, *Elements of Psychophysics*, trans. Helmut E. Adler, ed. Davis H. Howes and Edwin G. Boring (New York: Holt, Rinehart and Winston, Inc., 1966).

———, 'Author's Preface', in *Elements of Psychophysics*, trans. Helmut E. Adler, ed. Davis H. Howes and Edwin G. Boring (New York: Holt, Rinehart and Winston, 1966).

Ffytche, Matt, *The Foundation of the Unconscious: Schelling, Freud and the Birth of the Modern Psyche* (Cambridge: Cambridge University Press, 2013).

Fink, Bruce, *The Lacanian Subject: Between Language and Jouissance* (Princeton, NJ: Princeton University Press, 1995).

———, *Lacan to the Letter: Reading Écrits Closely* (Minneapolis, MN: University of Minnesota Press, 2004).

———, 'Fantasies and the Fundamental Fantasy: An Introduction', in *Virtualia* 13, Revista digital de la Escuela de la Orientación Lacaniana (June/July 2005). Available at: http://virtualia.eol.org.ar/013/pdf/fink-en.pdf [accessed 27 September 2015].

Fletcher, John (ed.), *Essays on Otherness* (London: Routledge, 1999).

Fontana-Giusti, Gordana Korolija, 'Water, Cities and Signification', in *Book of Proceedings, 1st Symposium on Waterfronts in the Danube Region* (Novi Sad: University of Novi Sad, 2006).

Forrester, John, *Language and the Origins of Psychoanalysis* (London: Macmillan / New York: Columbia University Press, 1980).

Foster, Hal (ed.), *The Anti-Aesthetic: Essays in Postmodern Culture* (Washington, DC: Bay Press, 1983).

Forty, Adrian, *Words and Buildings: A Vocabulary of Modern Architecture* (London: Thames and Hudson, 2000).

Foucault, Michel, 'Nietzsche, Genealogy, History' in *Language, Counter-Memory, Practice: Selected Essays and Interviews*, ed. Donald F. Bouchard (Ithaca, NY: Cornell University Press, 1977).

———, *The Order of Things: An Archaeology of Human Sciences* (London: Routledge, 1991).

———, 'Of the Other Spaces: Utopias and Heterotopias', in *Architecture Culture 1943–1968*, ed. Joan Ockman (New York: Rizzoli, 1996), pp. 421–2.

Frampton, Kenneth, 'Maison de Verre', in *Arena, The Architectural Association Journal*, 81(901) (London: The Architectural Association, 1966), pp. 257–62.

———, 'Maison de Verre', in *Perspecta*, 12 (Cambridge, MA: The MIT Press, 1969), pp. 77–128.

———, 'Pierre Chareau: An Eclectic Architect', in Marc Vellay and Kenneth Frampton (eds), *Pierre Chareau: Architect and Craftsman 1883–1950* (London: Thames and Hudson, 1985), pp. 235–48.

———, *Modern Architecture: A Critical History* (London: Thames and Hudson, 1992).

———, 'Maison de Verre', in *Perspecta* 12 (1969), pp. 77–128, reprinted in Robert A.M. Stern, Alan Plattus and Peggy Deamer (eds), *[Re]Reading Perspecta: The First Fifty Years of the Yale Architectural Journal* (Cambridge, MA: The MIT Press, 2004), pp. 268–75.

Frampton, Kenneth (ed.), *Aldo Rossi in America 1976 to 1979* (New York: The Institute for Architecture and Urban Studies, 1979).

Frascari, Marco, Jonathan Hale, and Bradley Starkey (eds), *From Models to Drawings: Imagination and Representation in Architecture* (Abingdon: Routledge, 2007).

———, 'Introduction: Models and Drawings – The Invisible Nature of Architecture', in Marco Frascari, Jonathan Hale, and Bradley Starkey (eds), *From Models to Drawings: Imagination and Representation in Architecture* (Abingdon: Routledge, 2007).

Freud, Sigmund, *Group Psychology and the Analysis of the Ego*, trans. James Strachey (London and Vienna: The International Psycho-Analytical Press, 1922).

———, *An Outline of Psycho-Analysis, The Standard Edition*, trans. and ed. James Strachey (New York: W.W. Norton, 1949).

———, 'The Ego and the Id', in Sigmund Freud, *The Major Works of Sigmund Freud*, trans. Joan Riviere (Chicago, IL: William Benton / Encyclopaedia Britannica, 1952), pp. 697–717.

———, 'The Interpretation of Dreams', in *The Standard Edition of the Complete Psychological Works of Sigmund Freud, Volume V (1900–1901): The Interpretation of Dreams (Second Part) and On Dreams*, trans. from the German under the general editorship of James Strachey (London: The Hogarth Press, 1953 [1900]).

———, 'Zur Auffassung der Aphasien', in Sigmund Freud, *On Aphasia: A Critical Study*, trans. E. Stengel (New York: International Universities Press, 1953 [1891, Vienna]).

———, 'Paranoia', Draft H, 24.1.1895, in Sigmund Freud, *The Origins of Psycho-Analysis: Letters to Wilhelm Fliess, Drafts and Notes: 1887–1902*, ed. Marie Bonaparte, Anna Freud, and Ernst Kris, trans. Eric Mosbacher and James Strachey (London: Imago, 1954), pp. 109–15.

———, 'Beyond the Pleasure Principle', in *The Standard Edition of the Complete Psychological Works of Sigmund Freud, Volume XVIII (1920–1922): Beyond the Pleasure Principle, Group Psychology and Other Works*, trans. from the German under the general editorship of James Strachey (London: The Hogarth Press, 1955 [1920]).

———, 'Repression' and 'The Unconscious', in *The Standard Edition of the Complete Psychological Works of Sigmund Freud, Volume XIV (1914–1916): On the History of the Psycho-Analytic Movement, Papers on Metapsychology and Other Works*, trans. from the German under the general editorship of James Strachey (London: The Hogarth Press, 1957 [1915]).

———, *The Psychopathology of Everyday Life: Forgetting, Slips of the Tongue, Bungled Actions, Superstitions and Errors*, trans. Alan Tyson, ed. James Strachey (New York: W.W. Norton, 1960 [1901]).

———, *The Ego and the Id : The Standard Edition*, trans. Joan Riviere, ed. James Strachey (New York: W.W. Norton, 1960).

———, *Beyond the Pleasure Principle: The Standard Edition*, trans. and ed. James Strachey (New York: W.W. Norton, 1961).

———, 'Civilisation and Its Discontents', in *The Complete Psychological Works of Sigmund Freud – The Future of an Illusion, Civilization and its Discontents, and Other Works, The Standard Edition*, vol. XXI, trans. James Strachey (Hogarth Press: London, 1961).

———, 'The Ego and the Id' (1923), in *The Standard Edition of the Complete Psychological Works of Sigmund Freud, Volume XIX (1923–1925): The Ego and the Id and Other Works*, trans. from the German under the general editorship of James Strachey (London: The Hogarth Press, 1961 / Hogarth Press and the Institute of Psycho-analysis, 1962).

———, 'Introductory Lectures on Psycho-Analysis' (1917), in *The Standard Edition of the Complete Psychological Works of Sigmund Freud, Volume XVI (1916–1917): Introductory*

Lectures on Psycho-Analysis (Part III), trans. from the German under the general editorship of James Strachey (London: The Hogarth Press, 1963).

———, 'The Dissection of the Psychical Personality' (1933), in *The Standard Edition of the Complete Psychological Works of Sigmund Freud, Volume XXII (1932–1936): New Introductory Lectures on Psycho-Analysis and Other Works*, trans. from the German under the general editorship of James Strachey (London: The Hogarth Press, 1964).

———, *The Interpretation of Dreams, The Standard Edition*, trans. James Strachey (New York: Avon Books, 1965 [1900]).

———, 'Sketches for the 'Preliminary Communication' of 1893', in *The Standard Edition of the Complete Psychological Works of Sigmund Freud, Volume I (1886–1899): Pre-Psycho-Analytic Publications and Unpublished Drafts*, trans. from the German under the general editorship of James Strachey (London: The Hogarth Press and the Institute of Psychoanalysis, 1966).

———, 'On the Theory of Hysterical Attacks' (1893), 'Project for a Scientific Psychology' (1895), and 'Letter 52' (dated Vienna, 6 December 1896), in *The Standard Edition of the Complete Psychological Works of Sigmund Freud, Volume I (1886–1899): Pre-Psycho-Analytic Publications and Unpublished Drafts*, trans. from the German under the general editorship of James Strachey (London: The Hogarth Press and the Institute of Psychoanalysis, 1966).

———, *The Psychopathology of Everyday Life*, trans. Alan Tyson (Harmondsworth: Penguin, 1975 [1914]).

———, *Civilization and its Discontents, Standard Edition vol. 21*, trans. Joan Riviere, ed. James Strachey (London: Hogarth Press, 1975).

———, 'Three Essays on the Theory of Sexuality' (1905), 'Fetishism' (1927), and 'Female Sexuality' (1931), in Sigmund Freud, *On Sexuality: Three Essays on the Theory of Sexuality and other works*, trans. James Strachey (Harmondsworth: Penguin Books, 1977).

———, 'On Narcissism: An Introduction', in *On Metapsychology: The Theory of Psychoanalysis: 'Beyond the Pleasure Principle', 'The Ego and the Id', and Other Works*, trans. James Strachey (London: Penguin Books, 1984).

———, 'Draft G. Melancholia' (1894) and 'Draft M. The Architecture of Hysteria, 25 May 1897' (1897), in *The Complete Letters of Sigmund Freud to Wilhelm Fliess, 1887–1904*, trans. and ed. Jeffrey Moussaieff Masson (Cambridge, MA: Belknap Press of Harvard University Press, 1985).

———, *Art and Literature, The Penguin Freud Library Vol. 14*, ed. Albert Dickson (Harmondsworth: Penguin, 1985).

———, *Civilization and its Discontents, Standard Edition*, trans. James Strachey (New York: W.W. Norton, 1989).

———, *New Introductory Lectures on Psycho-Analysis, Standard Edition*, trans. James Strachey (New York: W.W. Norton, 1990).

———, 'The Libido Theory and Narcissism', in *Introductory Lectures on Psychoanalysis*, trans. James Srachey (London: Penguin Books, 1991).

———, *Johdatus narsismiin ja muita esseitä [Introduction to Narcissism and Other Essays]*, trans. Mirja Rutanen, ed. Ilpo Helén and Mirja Rutanen (Helsinki: Love Kirjat, 1993).

———, *Standard Edition, vol. XII: The Case of Schreber, Papers on Technique and Other Works*, trans. James Strachey (London: Vintage, 2001).

———, 'Three Essays on Sexuality', in *Standard Edition, vol. XVIII: Beyond the Pleasure Principle, Group Psychology, and Other Works*, trans. James Strachey (London: Vintage, 2001).

———, 'Fetishism', in *Standard Edition, vol. XXI: The Future of an Illusion, Civilization and Its Discontents and Other Works*, trans. James Strachey (London: Vintage, 2001).

———, *Civilisation and its Discontents*, trans. David McLintock (London: Penguin, 2002).

———, 'Melancholia' (1917), in *On Murder, Mourning and Melancholia*, trans. Shaun Whiteside (Harmondsworth: Penguin, 2005).

———, *The Unconscious*, trans. Graham Frankland, with an introduction by Mark Cousins (London: Penguin Books, 2005).

———, 'Contributions to the Psychology of Erotic Love' (1910–18), in *The Psychology of Love*, trans. Shaun Whiteside (Harmondsworth: Penguin, 2006).

Fried, Michael, *Why Photography Matters as Art as Never Before* (New Haven, CT: Yale University Press, 2008).

Fuller, Peter, *Art and Psychoanalysis* (London: Writers and Readers, 1980).

Furnari, Michele, *Formal Design in Renaissance Architecture from Brunelleschi to Palladio* (New York: Rizzoli International Publications, 1995).

Fuss, Diana, *The Sense of an Interior: Four Rooms and the Writers that Shaped Them* (London: Routledge, 2004).

Gallagher, Shaun, *How the Body Shapes the Mind* (Oxford: Oxford University Press, 2005).

Gamwell, Lynn, 'The Role of Scientific Drawings in 19th- and Early 20th-Century Research', in Lynn Gamwell and Mark Solms, *From Neurology to Psychoanalysis: Sigmund Freud's Neurological Drawings and Diagrams of the Mind* (New York: Binghampton University Art Museum and State University of New York Press, 2006).

Gamwell, Lynn and Mark Solms (eds), *From Neurology to Psychoanalysis: Sigmund Freud's Neurological Drawings and Diagrams of the Mind* (New York: Binghampton University Art Museum and State University of New York Press, 2006).

Gandelsonas, Mario, 'From Structure to Subject: The Formation of an Architectural Language', in *Oppositions* 17 (New York: Institute for Architecture and Urban Studies, 1979), pp. 6–29.

Gardner, Sebastion, 'Schopenhauer, Will, and the Unconscious', in *The Cambridge Companion to Schopenhauer*, ed. Christopher Janaway (Cambridge: Cambridge University Press, 1999).

Garin, Eugenio, *L'Uomo del Rinascimento* (Roma: Laterza, 1988).

———, *La Cultura del Rinascimento* (Roma: Laterza, 2010).

Gibson, James J., *The Ecological Approach to Visual Perception* (Hillsdale, NJ: Lawrence Erlbaum Associates, 1986).

Giedion, Sigfried, *The Eternal Present: A Contribution on Constancy and Change* (New York: Bollinger Foundation, Pantheon Books, 1962–4).

Glover, Nicky, *Psychoanalytic Aesthetics: An Introduction to the British School* (London: Karnac, 2009).

Gorelov, Aleksandr, *Kontseptsiia nauki kak simvolicheskogo opisaniia v filosofii P. A. Florenskogo* [*The Conception of Science as a Symbolic Description in the Philosophy of P.A. Florenskii*] (dissertation Russian Academy of Sciences, Institute of Philosophy, 2008).

Gough, Maria, *The Artist as Producer: Russian Constructivism in Revolution* (Berkeley, CA: University of California Press, 2005).

Gowing, Lawrence (ed.), *The Critical Writings of Adrian Stokes, 3 vols* (London: Thames and Hudson, 1978).

Goy, Richard J., *Venice: An Architectural Guide* (London and New Haven, CT: Yale University Press, 2010).

Green, André, 'Freud's Concept of Temporality: Differences with Current Ideas', in *International Journal of Psychoanalysis* 89(5) (London: Institute of Psychoanalysis, 2008), pp. 1029–39.

———, *Illusions and Disillusions of Psychoanalytic Work*, trans. Andrew Weller (London: Karnac, 2011).

Greenberg, Jay R., and Stephen A. Mitchell, *Object Relations in Psychoanalytic Theory* (London: Harvard University Press, 1983).

Güse, Ernst-Gerhard, and Franz Armin Morat (eds), *Giorgio Morandi: Paintings, Watercolours, Drawings, Etchings* (Munich: Prestel, 1999).

Halbwachs, Maurice, *The Collective Memory*, trans. Francis J. Ditter Jr. and Vida Yazdi Ditter (New York: Harper & Row, 1980 [1950]).

Hambourg, Maria Morris, and Douglas Eklund, 'The Space of History', in *Thomas Struth 1977–2002*, ed. Douglas Eklund, Ann Goldstein, Maria Morris Hambourg, and Charles Wylie (New Haven, CT: Yale University Press, 2002), pp. 156–65.

Haralambidou, Penelope, *Marcel Duchamp and the Architecture of Desire* (Farnham: Ashgate, 2013).

Hartmann, Eduard von, *Philosophy of the Unconscious*, trans. William Chatterton Coupland (London: Routledge & Kegan Paul, 1931 [1868, 1893]).

Hauser, Arnold, *The Social History of Art, Vol. 2*, trans. Stanley Godman (New York: Vintage Books, 1951).

Hays, K. Michael, *Architecture's Desire: Reading the Late Avant-garde* (Cambridge, MA: The MIT Press, 2010).

Heidelberger, Martin, 'Gustav Theodor Fechner and the Unconscious', in *Thinking the Unconscious*, trans. Simon Thomas, ed. Angus Nicholls and Martin Liebscher (Cambridge: Cambridge University Press, 2010).

Henderson, Linda Dalrymple, *The Fourth Dimension and Non-Euclidean Geometry in Modern Art* (Princeton, NJ: Princeton University Press, 1983).

Hendrix, John, *Platonic Architectonics: Platonic Philosophies and the Visual Arts* (New York: Peter Lang Publishing, 2004).

Hendrix, John Shannon, *Architecture and Psychoanalysis: Peter Eisenman and Jacques Lacan* (New York: Peter Lang Publishing, 2006).

———, *Unconscious Thought in Philosophy and Psychoanalysis* (Basingstoke: Palgrave Macmillan, 2015).

Hendrix, John Shannon and Charles H. Carman (eds), *Renaissance Theories of Vision* (Farnham: Ashgate, 2010).

Herman, Ellen, *The Romance of American Psychology: Political Culture in the Age of Experts* (Berkeley, CA: University of California Press, 1995).

Hersey, George, *Pythagorean Palaces: Magic and Architecture in the Italian Renaissance* (Ithaca, NY: Cornell University Press, 1976).

Hess, A.F., and L.J. Unger, 'The Cure of Infantile Rickets by Sunlight', in *The Journal of the American Medical Association*, 77(1) (Chicago, IL: The American Medical Association, 1921), pp. 39–41.

Hildebrand, Adolf von, 'The Problem of Form in the Fine Arts', in *Empathy, Form, and Space: Problems in German Aesthetics, 1873–1893*, trans. Harry Francis Mallgrave and Eleftherios Ikonomou (Santa Monica, CA: Getty Center for the History of Art and the Humanities, 1994), pp. 227–80.

Hinshelwood, R.D., *A Dictionary of Kleinian Thought* (London: Free Association Books, 1989).

Hinton, Charles Howard, *A New Era of Thought*, completed by Alicia Boole and H.J. Falk (London: Swan Sonnenschein & Co., 1900 [1888]).

———, *The Fourth Dimension* (London: Swan Sonnenschein & Co., 1906 [1904]).

Holm, Lorens, *Brunelleschi, Lacan, Le Corbusier: Architecture, Space and the Construction of Subjectivity* (London and New York: Routledge, 2010).

———, 'Psychosis and the Ineffable Space of Modernism', in *Journal of Architecture*, 18(3) (London: Routledge, Royal Institute of British Architects, 2013), pp. 402–24.

———, 'Space and its Assembled Subjects: The Neurotic, the Psychotic and the Pervert', in Louis Rice and David Littlefield (eds), *Transgression: Towards an Expanded Field of Architecture* (London: Routledge, 2014), pp. 40–56.

Hume, David, *Treatise on Human Nature*, ed. L.A. Selby-Bigge and P.H. Nidditch (Oxford: Clarendon Press, 1978 [London, 1739]).

Husserl, Edmund, *Phantasy, Image Consciousness, and Memory (1898–1925)* (Husserliana, vol. XXIII), trans. John B. Brough (Dordrecht: Springer, 2005).

Hustvedt, Siri, 'Not Just Bottles', in *Modern Painters*, 11(4) (New York: Louise Blouin Media, Winter 1998), pp. 20–25.

Hyldgaard, Kirsten, 'The Conformity of Perversion', in *The Symptom*, Issue 5 (online journal for lacan.com, Winter 2004).

Irigaray, Luce, 'Flesh Colors', in *Sexes and Genealogies*, trans. Gillian C. Gill (New York: Columbia University Press, 1993).

———, *The Forgetting of Air in Martin Heidegger*, trans. Mary Beth Mader (London: Athlone, 1999).

Jacquette, Dale (ed.), *Schopenhauer, Philosophy, and the Arts* (Cambridge: Cambridge University Press, 1996).

James, William, 'The Hidden Self', in *Scribner's Magazine*, 7(3) (New York: Charles Scribner's Sons, 1890), pp. 361–74.

Jameson, Fredric, *The Political Unconscious: Narrative as a Socially Symbolic Act* (Ithaca, NY: Cornell University Press, 1982).

———, 'Imaginary and Symbolic in Lacan', in *The Ideology of Theory, Essays 1971–1986, Volume I: Situations of Theory* (Minneapolis, MN: University of Minnesota Press, 1988).

Janaway, Christopher (ed.), *The Cambridge Companion to Schopenhauer* (Cambridge: Cambridge University Press, 1999).

———, 'The Real Essence of Human Beings: Schopenhauer on the Unconscious Will', in *Thinking the Unconscious: Nineteenth-Century German Thought*, ed. Angus Nicholls and Martin Liebscher (Cambridge: Cambridge University Press, 2010), pp. 140–43.

Jay, Martin, *Lacan, Althusser and the Specular Subject of Ideology* (London: University of California Press, 1994).

Jimenez, Carlos, 'Mystic Signs: A Conversation with Aldo Rossi', in *Cite: The Architecture + Design Review of Houston*, 24 (Houston: Rice Design Alliance, Spring 1990), pp. 16–17.

Johnson, Mary Vaughan, *L'Art de Vivre Moderne in the Toilet Rooms of the Maison de Verre* (Virginia Tech, unpublished PhD thesis, 2016).

Juranville, Alain, *Lacan et la philosophie* (Paris: Presses Universitaires de France, 1984).

Kant, Immanuel, *Critique of Pure Reason*, trans. Norman Kemp Smith (London: MacMillan & Co., 1968).

———, *Anthropology From a Pragmatic Point of View*, trans. Victor Lyle Dowdell (Carbondale, IL: Southern Illinois University Press, 1978).

———, *Theoretical Philosophy 1755–1770*, trans. and ed. David Walford (*The Cambridge Edition of the Works of Immanuel Kant*, Cambridge: Cambridge University Press, 1992).

Kemenov, V., 'Dovol'no metafiziki! (Protiv idealizma Novitskogo)' ['Enough metaphysics! (Against Novitskii's idealism)'], in *Za proletarskoe iskusstvo [For a Proletarian Art]* 11–12 (Moscow: Ogiz-Izogiz, 1931), pp. 8–12.

Khan-Magomedov, Selim, *Ratsionalizm (Ratsio-arkhitektura) 'Formalizm' [Rationalism (Ratio-architecture) 'Formalism']* (Moscow: Arkhitektura-S, 2007).

———, *Viktor Balikhin* (Moscow: Russkii Avangard, 2009).

———, *Mikhail Korzhev* (Moscow: Russkii Avangard, 2009).

———, *Nikolai Ladovskii* (Moscow: Sergey E. Gordeev, 2011).

Kite, Stephen, *Adrian Stokes: An Architectonic Eye* (Oxford: Legenda, 2009).

Klein, Melanie, 'Infantile Anxiety-Situations Reflected in a Work of Art and in the Creative Impulse', in *The International Journal of Psychoanalysis* 10 (1929), pp. 436–43.

———, 'Love, Guilt and Reparation', in Melanie Klein and Joan Rivière, *Love, Hate and Reparation* (London: Hogarth, 1953 [1937]).

———, 'Our Adult World and its Roots in Infancy', in M. Masud and R. Khan (eds), *Melanie Klein: Envy and Gratitude and Other Works* (London: Hogarth Press, 1975), pp. 247–63.

———, 'A Contribution to the Psychosis of Manic Depressive States', in *The Selected Melanie Klein*, ed. Juliet Mitchell (Harmondsworth: Penguin, 1986 [1935]).

———, 'Notes on Some Schizoid Mechanisms', in *The Selected Melanie Klein*, ed. Juliet Mitchell (New York: Macmillan, 1986 [1946]), pp. 176–200.

Klein, Melanie, Paula Heimann, Roger Money-Kyrle (eds), *New Directions in Psycho-Analysis: The Significance of Infant Conflict in the Pattern of Adult Behaviour* (London: Tavistock Publications, 1955).

Klibansky, Raymond, Erwin Panofsky, and Fritz Saxl, *Saturn and Melancholy: Studies in the History of Natural Philosophy, Religion and Art* (London: Nelson, 1964).

Köhler, Wolfgang, *Gestalt Psychology: An Introduction to New Concepts in Modern Psychology* (New York: Liveright, 1970).

Koolhaas, Rem, 'Whatever Happened to Urbanism?', in Rem Koolhaas and Bruce Mau, *S M L XL* (New York: The Monicelli Press, 1997).

———, 'Junkspace', in *October* 100, 'Obsolescence' (Cambridge, MA: The MIT Press, spring 2002), pp. 175–90.

Krauss, Rosalind E., *The Originality of the Avant-Garde and Other Modernist Myths* (London: The MIT Press, 1977).

———, 'Sculpture in the Expanded Field', in *The Anti-Aesthetic: Essays in Postmodern Culture*, ed. Hal Foster (Washington: Bay Press, 1983), pp. 31–42.

———, 'The Story of the Eye', in *New Literary History*, 21(2) (Baltimore, MD: Johns Hopkins University Press, Winter 1990), pp. 283–98.

———, *The Optical Unconscious* (Cambridge, MA: The MIT Press, 1993).

———, *Bachelors* (London: October Books, 1999).

Kurbanovsky, Alexei Alexeyevich, 'Freud, Tatlin, and the Tower: How Soviet Psychoanalysts Might Have Interpreted the Monument to the Third International', in *Slavic Review*, 67(4), (Pittsburgh, PA: Association for Slavic, East European, and Eurasian Studies, 2008), pp. 892–906.

Lacan, Jacques, 'Of Structure as an In-mixing of an Otherness Prerequisite to Any Subject Whatever (1966)', in Richard Macksey and Eugenio Donato (eds), *The Structuralist Controversy: The Languages of Criticism and the Sciences of Man* (London and Baltimore, MD: The Johns Hopkins University Press, 1972), pp. 186–95.

———, *Le Séminaire Livre I: Les Écrits Techniques de Freud* (Paris: Seuil, 1975).

———, *Écrits: A Selection*, trans. Alan Sheridan (New York: W.W. Norton / London: Tavistock, 1977).

———, *The Seminar, Book XI: The Four Fundamental Concepts of Psycho-Analysis*, trans. Alan Sheridan (London: Hogarth Press and Institute of Psycho-Analysis, 1977).

———, *Le Seminaire Livre III: Les Psychoses*, ed. Jacques-Alain Miller (Paris: Seuil, 1981).

———, *The Four Fundamental Concepts of Psycho-Analysis*, trans. Alan Sheridan, ed. Jacques-Alain Miller (New York: W.W. Norton, 1981).

———, *The Seminar of Jacques Lacan, Book I: Freud's Papers on Technique, 1953–54*, ed. Jacques-Alain Miller, trans. John Forrester (New York: W.W. Norton, 1988).

———, *Le Seminaire Livre VIII: Le transfert, 1960–61* (Paris: Seuil, 1991).

———, *The Four Fundamental Concepts of Psycho-Analysis*, trans. Alan Sheridan (Harmondsworth: Penguin, 1991).

———, *Écrits: A Selection*, trans. Alan Sheridan (London: Routledge, 1991).

———, *Le Séminaire Livre XI: Les quattre concepts fondamentaux de la psychoanalyse* (Paris: Seuil, 1992).

———, *The Seminar of Jacques Lacan, Book VII: The Ethics of Psychoanalysis 1959–1960*, trans. Dennis Porter, ed. Jacques-Alain Miller (New York: Routledge / W.W. Norton, 1992 [Paris: Seuil, 1986]).

———, *The Seminar of Jacques Lacan, Book III: The Psychoses 1955–56*, trans. Russell Grigg, ed. Jacques-Alain Miller (London: Routledge / New York: W.W. Norton, 1993).

———, *The Seminar of Jacques Lacan, Book XX, Encore 1972–1973: On Feminine Sexuality: The Limits of Love and Knowledge*, trans. Bruce Fink (New York: W.W. Norton, 1998).

———, 'The Function and Field of Speech and Language in Psychoanalysis' (paper delivered at the Rome Congress held at the Institute of Psychology at the University of Rome on 26 and 27 September 1953), in Jacques Lacan, *Écrits: A Selection*, trans. Bruce Fink (New York: W.W. Norton, 2002).

———, *Écrits: A Selection*, trans. Bruce Fink (New York: W.W. Norton, 2002).

———, 'The Instance of the Letter in the Unconscious or Reason Since Freud', in *Écrits: The First Complete Edition in English*, trans. Bruce Fink (New York: W.W. Norton, 2006 [1957]), pp. 412–41.

———, *On the Names-of-the-Father*, trans. Bruce Fink (Cambridge: Polity Press, 2013).

Ladovskii, Nikolai, 'Vyvody tov. Ladovskogo k analizu poniatii konstruktsiia i kompozitsia. Protokol No. 12 sektsiia otdela iskusstva INKhUKa' ['Analysis of the notions of construction and composition. Conclusions of Comrade Ladovskii. Proceedings No. 12 of the section of the INKhUK department of art', 1921] (Russian State Tretiakov Gallery, Manuscript Department, f. 148, op. 1, d. 87, l. 1).

———, 'Osnovy postroeniia teorii arkhitektury (pod znakom ratsionalisticheskoi estetiki)', in *Izvestia ASNOVA [ASNOVA Newsletter]*, no. 1 (Moscow, 1926), pp. 3–5.

Lahiji, Nadir (ed.), *The Political Unconscious of Architecture: Reopening Jameson's Narrative* (Farnham: Ashgate, 2011).

La Marche, Jean, *The Familiar and the Unfamiliar in Twentieth-Century Architecture* (Urbana, IL: University of Illinois Press, 2003).

Laplanche, Jean, 'Notes on Afterwardsness', in *Essays on Otherness*, ed. John Fletcher (London: Routledge, 1999 [1992]).

Laplanche, Jean, and Jean-Bertrand Pontalis, *The Language of Psycho-Analysis*, trans. Donald Nicholson-Smith (London: Hogarth and the Institute of Psychoanalysis, 1973 / New York: W.W. Norton, 1974).

Leader, Darian, 'The Schema L', in Bernard Burgoyne, *Drawing the Soul: Schemas and Models in Psychoanalysis* (London: Rebus Press, 2000).

Leiviskä, Juha, 'Rakennustaiteen keinot tänään' ['Contemporary means for the art of building'], in *Arkkitehti, Finnish Architectural Review*, 5 (1976).

Lippard, Lucy R., 'Lucy R. Lippard Talks about Eva Hesse with Nancy Holt and Robert Smithson', in *Artforum* (New York: Artforum International Magazine, February 2008), recorded on 5 June 1973.

Lipps, Theodor, *Psychological Studies*, trans. Herbert C. Sanborn (Baltimore, MD: The Williams & Wilkins Company, 1926).

Loukaki, Argyro, *The Geographical Unconscious* (Farnham: Ashgate, 2014).

Luber, Katherine Crawford, *Albrecht Dürer and the Venetian Renaissance* (Cambridge: Cambridge University Press, 2005).

Lunacharskii, Anatolii, 'Osnovy positivnoi estetiki' ('Foundations of positive aesthetics'), in *Ocherki realisticheskogo mirovozzrenia [Essays in a realist worldview]* (St. Peterburg: Izdatel'stvo S. Dorovatovskogo i A. Charushnikova, 1903), pp. 114–82.

Lynch, Kevin, *The Image of the City* (Cambridge, MA: The MIT Press, 1960).

Lyotard, Jean-François, *Duchamp's TRANS/formers [Les Transformateurs Duchamp]*, trans. Ian McLeod (Leuven: Leuven University Press, 2010 [1977]).

Mach, Ernst, *Beiträge Zur Analyse Der Empfindungen* (Jena: G. Fischer, 1886).

———, *Contributions to the Analysis of the Sensations* (Chicago, IL: The Open Court Publishing Company, 1897).

Machado, Rodolfo and Jorge Silvetti, 'Banfire', in George Baird and Mark Lewis (eds), *Queues Rendezvous Riots: Questioning the Public in Art and Architecture* (Banff: Walter Philips Gallery and Banff Centre for the Arts, 1994).

Magno, Alessandro Marzo, *Bound in Venice: The Serene Republic and the Dawn of the Book*, trans. G. Conti (Rome: Europa Editions, 2013).

Makkreel, Rudolf A., *Imagination and Interpretation in Kant: The Hermeneutical Import of the* Critique of Judgment (London and Chicago, IL: The University of Chicago Press, 1990).

Malathouni, Christina, '"Higher" Being and "Higher" Drawing: Claude Bragdon's "fourth dimension" and the use of computer technology in design', in Marco Frascari, Jonathan Hale, and Bradley Starkey (eds), *From Models to Drawings: Imagination and Representation in Architecture* (Abingdon: Routledge, 2007).

———, 'In Search of the Beauty of Conscious Life: Claude Bragdon's "Spatial" "Philosophy of Architecture" and the "Fourth Dimension" Tradition' (PhD dissertation, University College London, 2010).

———, 'Claude Bragdon Reads Arthur Schopenhauer: "Architecture is in Space Alone"', in *Claude Bragdon and The Beautiful Necessity*, ed. Eugenia Victoria Ellis and Andrea G. Reithmayr (Rochester, NY: RIT Cary Graphic Arts Press, 2010), pp. 3–8.

———, 'Architecture is the Pattern of Human Mind in Space: Claude F. Bragdon and the Spatial Concept of Architecture', in *The Journal of Architecture*, 18 (London: Routledge, 2013), pp. 553–69.

Mallen, Enrique, 'Pablo Picasso and the Truth of Greek Art', in *Athens Journal of Humanities and Arts*, 1(4) (Athens: Athens Institute for Education and Research, October 2014), pp. 283–98.

Mallgrave, Harry Francis, and Eleftherios Ikonomou (eds), *Empathy, Form, and Space: Problems in German Aesthetics, 1873–1893* (Santa Monica, CA: Getty Center for the History of Art and the Humanities; Chicago, IL: The University of Chicago Press, 1993).

Massey, Jonathan Rider, *Crystal and Arabesque: Claude Bragdon, Ornament, and Modern Architecture* (Pittsburgh, PA: University of Pittsburgh Press, 2009).

Melville, Herman, *Moby-Dick or The White Whale* (New York: Harper, 1851).

———, *Moby-Dick* (London: Everyman, 1991).

Merleau-Ponty, Maurice, *Phenomenology of Perception*, trans. Colin Smith (London: Routledge, 2002).

———, *The World of Perception*, trans. Oliver David (London: Routledge, 2004).

Mical, Thomas (ed.), *Surrealism and Architecture* (New York and London: Routledge, 2005).

Michaud, Yves, *L'Art à l'État Gazeux: Essai Sur le Triomphe de l'Esthétique* (Paris: Stock, 2003).

Mikhailov, Aleksey, *Gruppirovki Sovietskoi arkhitektury* [*Groups of Soviet Architecture*] (Moscow and Leningrad: OGIZ, 1932).

Miller, Martin A., *Freud and the Bolsheviks: Psychoanalysis in Imperial Russia and the Soviet Union* (New Haven, CT: Yale University Press, 1998).

Mitchell, Juliet, 'Introduction to Melanie Klein', in John Phillips and Lyndsey Stonebridge (eds), *Reading Melanie Klein* (London: Routledge, 1998), pp. 11–31.

Mumford, Lewis, *Technics and Civilization* (New York: Harcourt, Brace & World, 1963 [1934]).

Nesbitt, Kate (ed.), *Theorizing a New Agenda for Architecture: An Anthology of Architectural Theory 1965–1995* (New York: Princeton Architectural Press, 1996).

Nicholls, Angus, and Martin Liebscher (eds), *Thinking the Unconscious: Nineteenth-Century German Thought* (Cambridge: Cambridge University Press, 2010).

Nicholls, Angus, and Martin Liebscher, 'Introduction: Thinking the Unconscious', in Angus Nicholls and Martin Liebscher (eds), *Thinking the Unconscious: Nineteenth-Century German Thought* (Cambridge: Cambridge University Press, 2010).

Nietzsche, Friedrich, *Aurora e scelta di frammenti postumi* (1879–81), fragment from Spring 1880, in *Opere*, ed. Giorgio Colli and Mazzino Montinari, trans. F. Masini and Mazzino Montinari, vol. 5, tome 1 (Milan: Adelphi, 1964).

———, *Twilight of the Idols, or, How to Philosophize with a Hammer* [*Götzen-Dämmerung, oder, Wie man mit dem Hammer philosophirt*], trans. Walter Kaufmann and R.J. Hollingdale (Top 100 Classics Book series, Createspace, 2014 [1889]). Available at: http://www.handprint.com/SC/NIE/GotDamer.html#sect2 [accessed 21 April 2015].

O'Regan, John, and Aldo Rossi (eds), *Aldo Rossi: Selected Writings and Projects* (London: Architectural Design, 1983).

O'Riordana, Jeffrey L.H., and Olav L.M. Bijvoet, 'Rickets before the Discovery of Vitamin D', in *BoneKEy Reports, The Journal of the International Bone and Mineral Society* (Chicago, IL: International Bone and Mineral Society, published online 8 January 2014).

Othengrafen, Frank, *Uncovering the Unconscious Dimensions of Planning: Using Culture as a Tool to Analyse Spatial Planning Practices* (Farnham: Ashgate, 2012).

Ovsianiko-Kulikovskii, Dmitrii, *Voprosy psikhologii tvorchestva* (Saint Petersburg: D.E. Zhukovskii, 1902).

———, 'Vvedenie v nenapisannuiu knigu po psikhologii umstvennogo tvorchestva (nauchno-filosofskogo i khudozhestvennogo)' ['Introduction to an unwritten book on the psychology of intellectual creativity (scientific-philosophical and artistic)'], in N. V. Os'makov, *Psikhologicheskoe napravleneie v russkom literaturovedenii* [*Psychological Trends in Russian Literature Studies*] (Moscow: Prosveschenie, 1981), pp. 109–21.

Pacioli, Luca, *De divina proportione* (Venice: Paganini, 1509).

Pallasmaa, Juhani, 'Tangible Light: Integration of the Senses and Architecture', in *D&A* (07) (Hørsholm: Velux Group, 2008), pp. 8–13.

Panofsky, Erwin, *The Life and Art of Albrecht Dürer* (Princeton, NJ: Princeton University Press, 1971 [1943]).

———, *Studies in Iconology: Humanistic Themes in the Art of the Renaissance* (Oxford: Icon Editions, Perseus, 1972 [1939]).

———, *Perpective as Symbolic Form* (New York: Zone Books, 1997).

Panofsky, Erwin, and Fritz Saxl, *Durer's 'Melencolia I': Eine quellen-und typengeschichtliche Untersuchung* (Leipzig: B.G. Teubner, 1923).

Pellegrini, Marco, *Religione e Umanasimo nel Primo Rinascimento da Petrarca ad Alberti* (Firenze: Le Lettere, 2012).

Pérez-Gómez, Alberto, and Louise Pelletier, *Architectural Representation and the Perspective Hinge* (Cambridge, MA: The MIT Press, 2000).

Perls, Frederick S., *Gestalt Therapy Verbatim* (Lafayette, CA: Real People Press, 1969).

Perniola, Mario, '*La Società dei Simulacri*', in *Agalma: Rivista di Studi Culturali e di Estetica* 221 (Roma: Mimesis, October 2010–April 2011).

Phillips, John, and Lyndsey Stonebridge (eds), *Reading Melanie Klein* (London: Routledge, 1998).

Piaget, Jean, *The Origin of Intelligence in the Child* (1936), trans. M. Cook (London: Routledge, 1953).

Piaget, Jean, and Bärbel Inhelder, *The Child's Conception of Space*, trans. F.J. Langdon and J.L. Lunzer (London: Routledge and Kegan Paul, 1956).

Pile, Steve, 'The Un(known) City … or, an Urban Geography of what Lies Buried below the Surface', in Iain Borden, Jane Rendell, Joe Kerr and Alicia Pivaro (eds), *The Unknown City: Contesting Architecture and Social Space* (Cambridge, MA: The MIT Press, 2001).

Plant, Margaret, *Venice: Fragile City 1797–1997* (London and New Haven, CT: Yale University Press, 2002).

Potebnia, Aleksandr, *Iz zapisok po teorii slovesnosti* [*From Notes on the Theory of Philology*] (Khar'kov: Parovaiia tip. i litografiia M. Zil'berberg, 1905).

Ragland, Ellie, and Dragan Milovanovic, 'Introduction', in Ellie Ragland and Dragan Milovanovic (eds), *Lacan: Topologically Speaking* (New York: Other Press, 2004).

Ragland-Sullivan, Ellie, *Jacques Lacan and the Philosophy of Psychoanalysis* (Beckenham: Croom Helm, 1986).

Rancière, Jacques, *The Aesthetic Unconscious*, trans. Debra Keates and James Swenson (Cambridge: Polity, 2009 [2001]).

Rendell, Jane, 'Architecture-Writing', in 'Critical Architecture', in *Journal of Architecture*, 10(3) (London: Routledge, June 2005), pp. 255–64.

———, 'From Architectural History to Spatial Writing', in Elvan Altan Ergut, Dana Arnold, Belgin Turan Özkaya (eds), *Rethinking Architectural Historiography* (London: Routledge, 2006), pp. 135–50.

Rice, Charles, *The Emergence of the Interior: Architecture, Modernity, Domesticity* (London: Routledge, 2007).

Robinson, Daniel N., 'Fechner, Gustav Theodor', in *Routledge Encyclopedia of Philosophy*, ed. E. Craig (London: Routledge, 1998).

Rossi, Aldo, *L'Architettura della città* (Padova: Marsilio, 1966).

———, 'An Analogical Architecture', in *Architecture and Urbanism*, 56 (Tokyo: A+U Publishing, May 1976), trans. David Stewart, pp. 74–6.

———, 'My Designs and Analogous Architecture', in Kenneth Frampton (ed.), *Aldo Rossi in America 1976 to 1979* (New York: Institute for Architecture and Urban Studies, 1979), pp. 16–19.

———, *A Scientific Autobiography*, trans. Lawrence Venuti (Cambridge, MA: The MIT Press, 1981).

———, *The Architecture of the City*, trans. Diane Ghirardo and Joan Ockman (Cambridge, MA: The MIT Press, 1982).

———, *Teatro del Mondo*, ed. M. Brusatin and A. Prandi (Venice: Cluva Librería Editrice, 1982).

———, 'An Analogical Architecture', in John O'Regan and Aldo Rossi (eds), *Aldo Rossi: Selected Writings and Projects* (London: Architectural Design, 1983), pp. 58–64.

———, 'An Analogical Architecture', trans. David Stewart, in Kate Nesbitt (ed.), *Theorizing a New Agenda for Architecture: An Anthology of Architectural Theory 1965–1995* (New York: Princeton Architectural Press, 1996).

Sacks, Oliver, *A Leg to Stand On* (London: Picador, 2012).

Saint-Cyr, Viviana M., 'Créer un vide ou de la sublimation chez Lacan', in *Recherches en psychanalyse* 13 (Sorbonne Paris Cité: Psychoanalytic Studies Faculty of the University Denis Diderot, 2012), pp. 14–21.

Sanouillet, Michel, and Elmer Peterson (eds), *The Writings of Marcel Duchamp* (New York: De Capo, 1973).

Santucci, Andrea, *Il Mirabile Artificio, colonne, archi e capitelli dei portici di Bologna* (Bologna: Gli Inchiostri Associati Editore, 1997–8).

Sartre, Jean-Paul, *Being and Nothingness* (1943), trans. Hazel E. Barnes (London: Routledge, 1969).

———, *The Imaginary: A Phenomenological Psychology of the Imagination*, trans. Jonathan Webber (London: Routledge, 2004).

———, *The Imagination*, trans. Kenneth Williford and David Rudrauf (London: Routledge, 2012).

Saussure, Ferdinand de, *Couse in General Linguistics*, trans. W. Baskin (New York: McGraw Hill, 1966 [1915]).

Sayers, Janet, *Freud's Art: Psychoanalysis Retold* (London: Routledge, 2007).

Schjeldahl, Peter, 'Thomas Struth', in *Columns and Catalogues* (New York: The Figures, 1994).

Schopenhauer, Arthur, *The World as Will and Idea*, trans. R.B. Haldane and J. Kemp, 3 vols (London: Routledge & Kegan Paul, 1964 [1883]).

Schulz, Duane P. and Sydney Ellen Schulz, *History of Modern Psychology*, 7th edn (Orlando, FL: Harcourt College Publishers, 2000 [1969]).

Schwarzer, Mitchell, 'Schopenhauer's Philosophy of Architecture', in Dale Jacquette (ed.), *Schopenhauer, Philosophy, and the Arts* (Cambridge: Cambridge University Press, 1996).

Sciacchitano, Antonello, *Scienza Come Isteria: Il Soggetto Della Scienza da Cartesio a Freud e la Questione dell'Infinito* (Pasian di Prato: Campanotto, 2005).

Sebald, W.G., *Austerlitz*, trans. Anthea Bell (London: Penguin Books, 2002).

Segal, Hannah, 'A Psychoanalytic Approach to Aesthetics', in John Phillips and Lyndsey Stonebridge (eds), *Reading Melanie Klein* (London: Routledge, 1998), pp. 203–22.

Shore, Stephen, *Uncommon Places: Photographs* (New York: Aperture, 1982).

Sideris, Nikos, Η Εσωτερική Διγλωσσία [*Inner Bilingualism*] (Athens: Kastaniotis, 1995).

———, Ο ερωτισμός στην τέχνη – Εικαστικές φαντασιώσεις [*Eroticism in Art – Pictorial Fantasies*] (Athens: Metaixmio, 2010).

———, *Architecture and Psychoanalysis: Fantasy and Construction* (Athens: Futura, 2006 / Kindle edition, 2013).

Smith, Jeffrey Chipps, *Dürer* (London: Phaidon, 2012).

Solms, Mark, 'Sigmund Freud's Drawings', in Lynn Gamwell and Mark Solms (eds), *From Neurology to Psychoanalysis: Sigmund Freud's Neurological Drawings and Diagrams of the Mind* (New York: Binghampton University Art Museum and State University of New York Press, 2006).

Steck, Max, 'Dürer', in Charles Coulston Gillispie (ed.), *Dictionary of Scientific Biography* (New York: Scribner, 1970–90).

Steedman, Carolyn, *Dust: The Archive and Cultural History* (Manchester: Manchester University Press, 2001).

Stoichita, Victor I., *A Short History of the Shadow* (London: Reaktion, 1997).

Stokes, Adrian, 'Concerning Art and Metapsychology', in *The International Journal of Psychoanalysis*, 26 (London: Institute of Psychoanalysis, 1945), pp. 177–9.

———, 'Form in Art', in Melanie Klein, Paula Heimann, Roger Money-Kyrle (eds), *New Directions in Psycho-Analysis: The Significance of Infant Conflict in the Pattern of Adult Behaviour* (London: Tavistock Publications, 1955), pp. 406–20.

———, *The Critical Writings of Adrian Stokes, 3 Vols*, ed. Lawrence Gowing (London: Thames and Hudson, 1978).

Struth, Thomas, *Portraits* (New York: Marion Goodman Gallery, 1990).

———, *Strangers and Friends: Photographs, 1986–1992* (Cambridge, MA: The MIT Press, 1993).

———, *Unconscious Places* (Cologne: Schirmer Mosel, 2012).

Swales, Stephanie S., *Perversion: A Lacanian Psychoanalytic Approach to the Subject* (London: Routledge, 2012).

Szarkowski, John, *Atget* (New York: Museum of Modern Art, 2000).

Tafuri, Manfredo, *Venice and the Renaissance*, trans. Jessica Levine (Cambridge, MA and London: The MIT Press, 1989).

———, *The Sphere and the Labyrinth: Avant-Gardes and Architecture from Piranesi to the 1970s*, trans. Pellegrino d'Acierno and Robert Connolly (Cambridge, MA: The MIT Press, 1990).

Taylor, Brian Brace, *Pierre Chareau: Designer and Architect* (Koln: Taschen, 1992).

Taylor, Mark C., *Disfiguring: Art, Architecture, Religion* (Chicago, IL: University of Chicago Press, 1992).

Thiébaut, Philippe, *Gaudí: Builder of Visions* (New York: Thames and Hudson, 2001).

Troutman, Anne, 'The Modernist Boudoir and the Erotics of Space', in Hilde Heynen and Gülsüm Baydar (eds), *Negotiating Domesticity: Spatial Productions of Gender in Modern Architecture* (London: Routledge, 2005).

Tschumi, Bernard, *Architecture and Disjunction* (Cambridge, MA: The MIT Press, 1996).

Tucker, Paul, '"A Summing Up of All I Have Ever Thought": Adrian Stokes's "In Short" (1942) and his Other Writings of the Period', *Tate Papers* 20 (London: Tate, 19 November 2013), pp. 1–13.

Twitchell, James B., *Romantic Horizons: Aspects of the Sublime in English Poetry and Painting, 1770–1850* (Columbia, MO: University of Missouri Press, 1983).

Vanheule, Stijn, 'Lacan's Construction and Deconstruction of the Double-Mirror Device', in *Frontiers in Psychology*, 2 (Lausanne: Frontiers, September 2011), p. 2.

Van Praet, Douglas, *Unconscious Branding: How Neuroscience Can Empower (and Inspire) Marketing* (New York: Palgrave Macmillan, 2012).

Vasoli, Cesare, *Filosofia e Religione nella Cultura del Rinascimento* (Napoli: Guida, 1988).

Vellay, Marc, and Kenneth Frampton (eds), *Pierre Chareau: Architect and Craftsman 1883–1950* (London: Thames and Hudson, 1985).

Ven, Cornelis van de, *Space in Architecture: The Evolution of a New Idea in the Theory and History of the Modern Movements* (Assen/Maastricht and Wolfeboro, NH: Van Gorcum, 1977; 3rd revised edn, 1987).

Verhaeghe, Paul, *Beyond Gender: From Subject to Drive* (New York: Other Press, 2001).

Vesely, Dalibor, *Architecture in the Age of Divided Representation: The Question of Creativity in the Shadow of Production* (Cambridge, MA: The MIT Press, 2004).

Virno, Paolo, *A Grammar of the Multitude: An Analysis of Contemporary Forms of Life* (New York: Semiotext(e), 2004).

———, 'Three Remarks Regarding the Multitude's Subjectivity and its Aesthetic Component', in Daniel Birnbaum and Isabelle Graw (eds), *Under Pressure: Pictures, Subjects, and the New Spirit of Capitalism* (Frankfurt: Sternberg Press, 2008).

Vöhringer, Margarete, *Avantgarde Und Psychotechnik: Wissenschaft, Kunst Und Technik Der Wahrnehmungsexperimente in Der Frühen Sowjetunion* (Göttingen: Wallstein Verlag, 2007).

Voldman, Danièle, 'Le Parc De La Villette entre Thélème et Disneyland', in *Vingtième Siècle. Revue d'histoire*, 8(8) (Paris: Presses de la Fondation nationale des sciences politiques, 1985), pp. 19–30.

Wajcman, Gérard, 'Intimate Extorted, Intimate Exposed', in *Journal of the Jan van Eyck Circle for Lacanian Ideaology Critique*, 1 (2008), pp. 58–77. Available at: http://www.lineofbeauty.org/index.php/s/article/viewFile/6/54

Webber, Jonathan, 'Notes on Translation', in Jean-Paul Sartre, *The Imaginary: A Phenomenological Psychology of the Imagination* (London: Routledge, 2004).

Wertheimer, Michael, *A Brief History of Psychology* (New York: Holt, Rinehart and Winston, 3rd edn 1987 [1970]).

Whiting, Sarah, and Robert Somol, 'Notes around the Doppler Effect and Other Moods of Modernism', in *Perspecta* 33 (New Haven, CT: Yale University School of Architecture, 2002), pp. 72–7.

Wigglesworth, Sarah, 'Maison de Verre: Sections Through an In-vitro Conception', in *Journal of Architecture*, 3(3) (London: Routledge, The Royal Institute of British Architects, 1998), pp. 263–86.

Williford, Kenneth and David Rudrauf, 'Translators' Introduction', in Jean-Paul Sartre, *The Imagination* (London: Routledge, 2012).

Wilson, Colin St John, 'The Natural Imagination: An Essay on the Experience of Architecture', in *Architectural Review*, 185 (London: Emap Limited, 1989), pp. 64–70.

Wittkower, Rudolf, *Architectural Principles in the Age of Humanism* (London: Alec Tirani, 1962).

Wollheim, Richard, *The Image in Form: Selected Writings of Adrian Stokes* (Harmondsworth: Penguin Books, 1972).

Yates, Frances A., *The Art of Memory* (London: ARK Paperbacks, 1984 [1966]).

Young, Christopher and Andrew Brook, 'Schopenhauer and Freud', in *International Journal of Psychoanalysis*, 75(Part 1) (London: Institute of Psychoanalysis, February 1994), pp. 101–18.

Zerbst, Rainer, *Antoni Gaudí, Toute l'architecture* (Cologne: Taschen, 2002).

Žižek, Slavoj, *Looking Awry: An Introduction to Jacques Lacan through Popular Culture* (Cambridge, MA: The MIT Press, 1991).

———, *Leggere Lacan*, trans. Marta Nijhuis (Torino: Bollati Boringhieri, 2009).

Zweite, Armin, '... a certain sense of placelessness ..., Thomas Struth between Seoul, Cape Canaveral, Garching and Greifswald', in *Thomas Struth Photographs 1978–2010*, ed. Anette Kruszynski, Tobia Bezzola, and James Lingwood (Cologne: Schirmer/Mosel, 2010).

Index

Note: Page numbers in **bold** indicate Illustrations.

FSC
www.fsc.org
MIX
Papier | Fördert
gute Waldnutzung
FSC® C083411

Kolibri 360 GmbH
Ferdinand-Jühlke-Straße 7
99095 Erfurt, Deutschland
produktsicherheit@kolibri360.de